PUBLIC ISSUES
PRIVATE PAIN

For
FIONA and JESSICA,
CATE and JAMES

PUBLIC ISSUES PRIVATE PAIN

Poverty, Social Work and Social Policy

Edited by
Saul Becker, Senior Welfare Rights Officer, Nottingham
Social Services.

Stewart MacPherson, Lecturer in Social Administration,
University of Nottingham (Professor-Elect University of
Papua New Guinea).

Social Services Insight Books
An imprint of Care Matters Ltd
Pioneer House
44-48 Clerkenwell Road
London EC1M 5PX
[in conjunction with the Benefit Research Unit]
This edition first published 1988

British Library Cataloguing in Publication Data

Public Issues, Private Pain: poverty, social work and social policy.
   1. Great Britain. Welfare services for poor persons.
   I. Becker, Saul II MacPherson, Stewart
   362.5'0941
ISBN 1-871018-00-5 (paper)
      1-871018-05-6 (cased)

Phototypeset in 10pt Garamond by ECM2,
Clerkenwell Green, London.

Printed and bound in Great Britain by
Whitstable Litho, Kent

CONTENTS

Acknowledgements

The idea for this volume came two years ago. Drew Clode, Editor of *Insight,* agreed to publish a series of nine original articles on poverty and social work. The book developed fairly naturally from the series; twenty one further articles, exploring different issues and themes, were commisioned, while the original nine were developed in more detail. The result is this collection of essays. They share a common concern for the effect that poverty has upon social work, social services and social work users.

We are grateful to Drew Clode for his encouragement and enthusiasm. A journal editor has considerable power in bringing important, and often controversial issues to a wider audience. We are particulary pleased that *Insight* has shared our concerns and has promoted a discussion of these issues in its pages, and here. Ron McKay, *Insight* publisher and Stuart Christie have turned a series of manuscripts and ideas into a final product. We thank them for their expertise, efficiency and trust.

Our colleagues, particularly Richard Silburn of the Benefits Research Unit and John Hannam of Nottinghamshire Social Services, have given us encouragement and support. Marilyn Howard helped with the proof reading, Chris Isaacs and Nora Riley assisted with the typing.

We owe a debt of gratitude, and an apology, to our families, who have taken the brunt of our preoccupation and bad temper over the last year. As usual, without their support, very little could be achieved.

A major strength of a volume such as this is the breadth of perspectives around a common concern. We hope that the final version lives up to the expectations of our audience. Responsibility for the final version is, of course, our own.

Saul Becker and Stewart MacPherson
Nottingham, January 1988.

Introduction
Stewart MacPherson and Saul Becker

Managing Poverty

WHAT is the relationship between social work and poverty? Before the establishment and growth of organised social work practice, poverty and 'indigence' were distinguished. The former was the normal condition of most of those who laboured for wages, the latter was the condition of those dependent on the assistance of others, outside their families. The dominant explanations for such a condition drew sharp distinctions between the 'deserving' and the 'undeserving' – there were relatively few of the first. The second were undeserving not least because their condition was most often regarded as the consequence of moral weakness and degradation. The threat from the very poor was as much from contamination by the morally degenerate as it was from the risk of petty theft or public nuisance. But new knowledge brought new understanding. The problems of deep seated and long lasting poverty came to be seen much less in moral terms and much more in terms of the psychological and social adequacy of people to cope with the rigours of existence in industrial society. As the perspective shifted so did the response; social work is one part of the move from the primarily primitive weapon of the poor law to strategies of rehabilitation, re-education and re-socialisation.

An emphasis on individual and family 'functioning' has occasionally emerged very clearly, as in the emphasis on 'transmitted deprivation' sponsored by Sir Keith Joseph in the early 1970s. But when it has not been in high profile, it has had pervasive influence. There is a considerable body of literature, and more important for practice, of opinion, which focuses on poverty as the result of inadequacy. Despite the individual attitudes and opinions of social workers [see Becker, this volume] social work activity remains dominated by approaches which are intended to alter the poor themselves. Despite widespread acknowledgement of the structural nature of poverty, social work practice, and training [see Bailey, this volume] still emphasise social pathology in explaining poverty and in responding to it.

Sullivan [1987] puts a convincing case for the exercise of a 'social imagination' in social work, if those served by social workers are to really benefit rather than to be further victimised by the continual reinforcement of the false dominant ideas of poverty and its causes. He suggests the levels at which this sociological perspective might assist workers:

[1] It might help the practitioner to move behind taken for granted assumptions and in so doing to articulate the relationship between social structure on the one hand and the experience of poverty on the other.
[2] It may help to explain the persistence of social welfare ideology resistant to those understandings.
[3] It may point the way to appropriately critical and reflective practice with those who experience poverty [Sullivan, 1987, 158].

It is obviously the case that much of what social workers do is unrelated to financial and material poverty, although a great deal is very directly related to these problems. But poverty cannot be expressed in terms of weekly income or possessions alone. It is about the quality of life, and all that entails. The vicious emptiness of lives without hope, where subsistence needs are met but nothing else is possible, even in prospect, is of profound significance to social workers, who see the consequences. Poverty must be seen as a central concern of social workers, and of social services departments. In the chapters which follow this is made clear from many different perspectives. But poverty must be seen for what it is – a lived experience, which is the more pernicious the closer people are forced to live with evidence of the wealth of others. A society which exalts materialism and the pursuit of possessions manufactures needs on a never-ending upward spiral. To be poor in such a society is to be a victim, a scapegoat and an example to those who might otherwise question the nature of values which have come to dominate. We must see poverty in structural terms;

looking for the causes and attempting to enable people to fight them or avoid their worst effects. We must identify the effects of poverty and see them for what they are. Poverty is above all about power and the lack of power.

More poor clients

Two years ago we published our research report on the extent and nature of financial poverty among users of social work services [Becker and MacPherson, 1986]. In it we attempted to indicate the impact that poverty has upon referrals to social services and how the 'cash' and 'care' systems are inextricably entwined. Most users of social services are claimants. In particular we drew upon data from the largest social services department in Europe – Strathclyde Social Work Department. Strathclyde's analysis of data for 1982-83, and our own analysis of data for 1984-85 and 1986-87 suggest a pattern of referrals dominated by claimants.

Table 1.

Referrals to Strathclyde Social Work Department, 1982-1987, by claimant status.

Status	1982-83 [1]	1984-85 [2]	1986-87 [3]
In work	12%	12%	9%
On Supplementary Benefit	46%	52%	55%
On other social security benefits	42%	36%	36%
	100%	100%	100%
no. of referrals analysed	[72,000]	[73,000]	[62,000]

Source: [1] Strathclyde Regional Council, 1985, 21
        [2] Becker and MacPherson, 1986, 10-11
        [3] Data created 10/01/87 by Strathclyde Regional Council

Between 1982 and 1987 referrals have been increasingly dominated by claimants of supplementary benefit. In 1987, 55 per cent of referrals were from supplementary benefit claimants whilst referrals from people in employment had dropped from 12 per cent in 1985 to 9 per cent in 1987.

Our re-analysis of data referrals have been increasingly dominated by *Reform of Supplementary Benefit* [1984] suggests that 20 per cent of all supplementary benefit claimants are in contact with a social worker. Of these, 30 per cent had contacted the social worker for benefit advice only, 51 per cent were in 'occasional' and 19 per cent in 'regular' contact about something other than benefits [Becker and MacPherson, 1986, 2-4].

Poor people [and particularly the poorest] are the main users of social work services. Given the fundamental changes contained within the Social Security Act 1986 [and especially for the Social Fund] we are not hopeful that this pattern will change to any significant extent. Indeed our concern is that more poor people will turn to social services for help in the relief of poverty. Many others will become reluctant or hostile clients, their problems exacerbated by poverty and changes in income maintenance provisions.

How do social workers and social service departments respond to the life problems of poor people? How can or will they respond to the challenges forced upon them by changes in social security, and as Dillon and Parker [this volume] argue 'a central government onslaught on poor people and their opportunities to gain a reasonable standard of living'? As the contributors to this volume clearly show these issues have never been more timely.

The book is divided into four sections; the divisions reflect emphasis rather than distinct boundaries between topics. All contributors are concerned with the problems of poverty and the relevance of these for the policies and practice of social workers and the organisations in which they work. But poverty and its effects is a vast topic, with very many aspects. The different parts of the book examine many of these aspects from a range of perspectives. Part One has four chapters and is concerned with issues of definition, the monitoring and evaluation of social work services for poor people and the specific impact of the massive social security changes in 1988.

Part Two has three chapters dealing specifically with issues of the involvement of social workers in financial assistance to poor clients. The powers to make 'preventive' payments under child care legislation are discussed; the experience of social workers in other European countries is examined and the profound implications of the Social Fund for social workers and social service agencies are analysed.

Part Three has the largest group of chapters – seventeen – and provides a series of insights on the broad questions of poverty and social work, from a range of different perspectives. Several chapters are concerned with child care issues; others with dimensions of poverty and social work in relation to specific problems, such as mental illness, mental handicap, delinquency and disability. A number of the chapters in this group look at poverty and its relationships with social work in terms of the needs of certain population groups – elderly people, women, unemployed people and questions of poverty and race are among the topics explored here. But although all these chapters, and the remainder of those in this part of the book, have their own particular concerns and their own points of reference, they share some fundamental themes in common. As with the book as a whole, the essential issues are those to do with the inter-relationships between poverty, social work and social policy. In terms of both policy and practice, these chapters illuminate those inter-relationships and illustrate the immediacy and importance of poverty issues.

In Part Four there are six chapters which continue the themes established earlier but focus rather more on the action which might be taken by social services and social work departments, and by local authorities more generally, in the fight against the growing tide of poverty. The section includes an analysis of poverty, social work and the state, discussions of welfare rights and social work, community work, the view from one local area office and a review of local authority anti-poverty action.

Our intention from the outset was to bring together a diverse range of perspectives and concerns. We were also anxious to bring together contributions from a range of sources – from academics, from those engaged in social work practice and social work management and from researchers. In the chapters which follow there are many views and many interpretations of issues. But there is above all a common concern with poverty and its implications for social work; a concern that action must be taken, on very many fronts and in very many ways, to ensure that social work and social policy are committed to poverty and its consequences.

PART ONE

Defining, Monitoring and Evaluating Poverty

1

Definitions, meanings and experiences of poverty: a framework

Richard Silburn

T HE revival of widespread interest of a serious and sustained kind in poverty in post-war Britain is frequently linked with the publication in 1965 of Abel-Smith and Townsend's *The Poor and the Poorest*. This booklet certainly attracted a great deal of public attention, and it served to bring into being one of the most persistent and influential of British pressure groups, the Child Poverty Action Group, which is tireless in its efforts both to keep the problem of poverty high on the political agenda, and to foster and maintain a better-informed public opinion on poverty issues. Although *The Poor and the Poorest* attracted greater attention, it remains the case that much of Peter Townsend's earlier written work in the 1950s anticipated much of its central argument, and he consistently rejected the conventional view of the time that full employment and the Welfare State had between them effectively abolished poverty. But these earlier works, mainly articles in the learned journals, did not have the same impact that enables us to say that *The Poor and the Poorest* resurrected poverty as a major social issue. Certainly the intervening period of over twenty years has seen a considerable and ever-increasing volume of research into all aspects of poverty, deprivation and social disadvantage, and as the British economy in the 70s and 80s has slipped into deeper recession so, in some quarters at least, concern about poverty, and its many and diverse manifestations and effects has intensified.⌉

Relative poverty

Abel-Smith and Townsend's book reopened an important debate about the definition and meaning of the term 'Poverty', in the context of a relatively prosperous society. Its major theoretical contribution, which has since been greatly elaborated, is the assertion that any attempt to define poverty narrowly, in terms of basic survival, or by reference to some absolute subsistence standard, is inappropriate and sociologically naive. Rather, they argued, 'in any objective sense the word has no absolute meaning which can be applied in all societies at all times. Poverty is a relative concept' [Abel-Smith and Townsend, 1965, 63]. The device that they adopted, as a practical and justifiable measure of relative poverty was the rates of benefit being ·paid to claimants of National Assistance which 'has at least the advantage of being in a sense the 'official' operational definition of the minimum level of living at any particular time' [*op cit*, 17].

Townsend has since developed the idea of relative poverty at length and in detail in *Poverty in the United Kingdom*, published in 1979. The opening paragraph of this work states that:

> Individuals, families and groups in the population can be said to be in poverty when they lack the resources to obtain the kind of diet, participate in the activities and have the living conditions and amenities which are customary, or are at least widely encouraged or approved, in the societies to which they belong. Their resources are so seriously below those commanded by the average individual or family that they are, in effect, excluded from ordinary living patterns, customs and activities [Townsend, 1979, 31].

The first, and entirely practical, argument for accepting that poverty must be seen as a relative concept is that the alternative of an absolute level [of minimum needs below which people are regarded as being poor] turns out, in practice, to be difficult if not impossible to determine. For example, to calculate and quantify even something as basic as food needs involves making a host of value judgements based partly upon (constantly changing) views about dietary requirements, but inescapably involving assumptions of a socially determined kind about eating habits and styles. In short, Townsend concludes that 'definitions which are based upon some conception of "absolute deprivation disintegrate upon close and sustained examination and deserve to be abandoned' [*op cit*, 38]. A relative definition of poverty recognises that 'people's needs, even for food, are conditioned by the society in which they live and to which they belong' [*op cit*, 59].

It is not necessary to labour this point further; the case for a relative view of poverty is now very familiar, and for the most part so generally accepted, that it is tempting to say that this particular debate is over, and that we are all relativists now. Indeed a more diverting question to ask is, where were the absolutists anyway? Re-reading the major texts of the past 20 years one is struck by the lack of serious apologists for an absolute definition. A few [although no doubt influential] right-wing politicians and economists have fought some sort of a rear-guard action, urging that no-one in Modern Britain is forced to live at the level of bare subsistence. In most cases though, this assertion is not made in the context of a discussion of poverty as such, but is more concerned with the question of how best to maintain work-incentives, in the context of welfare and social security systems which enable even the poorest to survive at something more than starvation level.

A great deal of the rather laboured academic discussion about absolute and relative poverty seems to have been addressing two different, and essentially non-academic audiences. The first of these was typically represented by the DHSS and the social security bureaucracies, and was bound up with the campaigning activities of groups such as the CPAG who were endeavouring to demonstrate the inadequacy of the social security and supplementary benefit scale-rates to meet the needs of claimant families. The second and larger audience was that of a supposed public opinion; here the debate was an indirect response on the one hand to the tone of the discussion of poverty issues, and the nature of the evidence presented, in the more brutish sections of the popular press, which periodically panics about alleged welfare scroungers; and on the other hand was a reaction to an apparently very deeply-seated set of widespread public prejudices, fanned no doubt by the tabloids, but rooted much more deeply in British popular culture, in folk-memories of the stigma attached to the Workhouse and the Poor Law, and asserted either as a categorical denial of the possibility of there being poor people, or more equivocally expressed in such ambivalent and defensive cliches as 'poor but proud', 'poor but honest' etc.

Scouring the academic literature, most commentators, after exulting in Adam Smith's justly renowned definition of relative poverty from the *Wealth of Nations* have been forced to field the York poverty studies of Seebohm Rowntree as being, apparently, the best and most influential examples of an absolute poverty line. Now even this familiar confrontation is under attack. In a recent journal article, [which itself may come to have a watershed significance, as marking the conclusion of one set of arguments and the initiation of another and more interesting discussion] John Veit-Wilson has tried to rehabilitate Rowntree, and makes an elegant and eloquent case for Rowntree holding a relativist and not an absolutist view of poverty after all. The argument is a complex one, which requires a careful re-reading of Rowntree's own words. This is made more difficult by occasional confusions or inconsistencies in Rowntree's texts, as well as by his choice of terms which may be misleading. But Veit-Wilson demonstrates that an understandable but seriously wrong-headed misconstruction of Rowntree's views may have become taken as read. Properly understood, however, Veit-Wilson concludes that:

> Rowntree and his investigators were working with a relative definition of poverty which compared the living conditions of the people they surveyed with the living conditions which were conventionally recognized and approved. Apart from differences in measuring 'convention', they used a definition essentially comparable with Townsend's celebrated definition of relative poverty in the first paragraph of chapter one of Poverty in the United Kingdom [Veit-Wilson, 1986, 78].

It is perhaps over-optimistic to suppose that what has become a very stale and tedious dispute can now be taken as finally closed. But it is certainly the case that, accepting as a general proposition that both practice and intellect lead one to adopt a relative view of poverty, the real discussion, far from being over, has in fact only just begun, and a new critical set of problems and issues, both conceptual and practical, need to be confronted. Alas, it may well be that John Veit-Wilson was carried away by enthusiasm, euphoria and intellectual relief when he concluded his rehabilitation of Rowntree with the ringing declaration that:

> The effect is shattering. Decades of futile argument between middle-class experts, administrators and politicians about what goods or services should or should not be included in the list of necessaries for the poor are swept away, and the value of sociological expertise is revealed as the power to enable whole populations to speak for themselves systematically and incontrovertibly about what deprivation means' [op cit, 97].

Would that it were as easy as that! In fact, the important task of elaborating acceptable methods and measures for determining the extent and the nature of relative poverty in modern Britain has still to be tackled.

The 'deprivation standard' approach

In the last few years we have seen a number of interesting, important, and very different, versions of how a relative approach to poverty may best be pursued. The most well-known approach is that adopted by Townsend in

Poverty in the United Kingdom, first published in 1979. The 'deprivation standard' measure of poverty is based upon a list of indicators of 'styles of living', which reflect diet, household goods and amenities and participation in commonplace social activities, 'all the major areas of personal, household, and social life' [Townsend, 1979, 251]. Townsend's hypothesis is that 'in descending the income scale . . . a significantly large number of families reduce more than proportionately their participation in the community's style of living. They drop out or are excluded ' [Townsend, 1979, 249]. Moreover Townsend believed, and later analysts have confirmed (although this remains a contested issue) that as one goes down the income scale, there comes a point or 'threshold' at which non-participation [or relative deprivation] increases sharply.

There have been a number of criticisms of Townsend's approach; some have questioned the composition of the deprivation-index, suggesting that some at least of the items may indicate taste and preference rather than enforced hardship. Others have queried the statistical techniques and measures employed. But the indicator method remains, fundamentally, a very powerful one that is capable of considerable further refinement and elaboration, and indeed has been refined and elaborated in Townsend's more recent work.

The 'consensual' approach

A contrasting approach to defining and measuring relative poverty is that developed by Mack and Lansley for the London Weekend Television documentary series Breadline Britain. Mack and Lansley locate themselves firmly within what we can call the Townsend tradition, in that they attempt to 'measure the extent of poverty not in terms of some arbitrary income level but in terms of the extent to which the poor are excluded from the way of living that is customary in society today' [Mack and Lansley, 1985, 9]. But they reject Townsend's 'indicator method'; instead their study 'aims to identify a minimum acceptable way of life not by reference to the views of experts, nor by reference to observed patterns of expenditure or observed living standards, but by reference to the views of society as a whole' [Mack and Lansley, 1985, 42]. These views were canvassed in a survey of a sample of the general population, on the strength of which Mack and Lansley evolved a list of necessities identified as such by the great majority of their sample. These they described as 'socially perceived necessities. This means that the necessities of life are identified by public opinion and not by, on the one hand, the views of experts, or on the other hand, the norms of behaviour per se' [Mack and Lansley, 1985, 45]. This method they refer to as a 'consensual' approach.

There is considerable merit in this approach, not least because poverty is a political as well as a sociological and moral problem, and both politicians and policy-makers are quite properly sensitive to the views and reactions of the publics they serve. Similarly, a definition of poverty, no matter how theoretically refined, which took no account whatsoever of widely held views among the general public, where these are known, would lack persuasive power. But to claim that the consensual approach solves all theoretical or methodological problems won't do. Indeed, as Piachaud has argued:

> the social consensus approach still requires expert involvement in defining questions and interpreting answers, it fails to resolve the problem when the practices of the poor do not correspond with the priorities prescribed by the majority, and it does not necessarily produce a poverty level which taxpayers will pay for . . . finally, and perhaps most importantly, there may be no real social consensus – the opinions of those who are poor, of the majority, of taxpayers, and of those who are rich may be at odds; which opinions prevail depends on the distribution of power in society [Piachaud, 1987b, 151-2].

This last point can be developed further. Just as needs themselves are socially determined, so is public opinion, and the views of the public, and even a large majority of the public, although interesting and in their own way important, are not necessarily accurate, well-informed or acceptable as an objective measure. As Townsend put it, when reviewing Mack and Lansley's book:

> Certain needs of a community may not be perceived by any members of that community, or may not be perceived by more than a few, or may be underestimated universally by a population. These statements are hardly contentious. But they oblige us to look for criteria of need other than in social perceptions-whatever might be said about the valuable legitimating functions of mass endorsement of particular standards in a political democracy . . . For good reason, therefore, the social scientist cannot be satisfied with the 'consensual judgement of society at large' [Townsend, 1985, 44].

It is important not to put so much emphasis on the points of difference between these two perspectives that we obscure the very substantial points of similarity and agreement. Indeed, at this relatively early stage in what will be a prolonged debate, it is probably best to see the Townsend and Mack and Lansley studies as complementary to one another rather than as rivals or alternatives. Certainly there is a remarkable agreement and overlap as far as their conclusions are concerned, despite the methodological differences in approach. But at the theoretical level as well, there are many shared features. One such is their rejection of the more prescriptive approach that they criticise in Rowntree, and in many of the poverty studies modelled on Rowntree, and implicit in poverty measurements based on so-called budget standards.

The 'budget-standards' approach

The characteristic of this approach is for a list of necessities to be compiled, the cost of this list to be calculated, and a poverty line then to be established with reference to this set of calculations. Thus, Rowntree derived a poverty-line by drawing on the advice of nutritionists about the food needs of a family and arriving at a minimum weekly cost of a family diet, to which he added further sums to meet housing-costs, clothing and a short list of other necessary items of family expenditure. The major criticism of this approach is that it is based upon estimates arrived at after consulting so-called experts, and does not examine actual spending patterns, nor does it allow poor people any discretion to determine for themselves how their resources should be disbursed. In short, it is thought to be arrogantly elitist and prescriptive.

But is this always and necessarily the case? Are budget-standards the epitome of the absolute, minimalist approach to the measurement of poverty? As we have already seen, Veit-Wilson would defend even Rowntree against this criticism and would argue that Rowntree's budgets were not intended as a prescription, and that the very notion of secondary poverty was an acknowledgement that actual spending habits would not and should not be expected to conform to any one particular pattern. And indeed there is no reason in principle why a list of necessities and an associated budget should not be compiled and calculated that was sensitive to the complex pattern of evolving and socially determined needs, and to the wide variation to be found in the spending patterns of different individuals and social groups. Nor must budgets always be prescriptive. There are examples of important and useful social research which have used budget-standards to great effect and which are neither minimalist nor prescriptive. For example, David Piachaud has published a series of studies, [for example, see Piachaud, 1979] where he estimates in considerable and precise detail both the financial costs of raising a child, and the less tangible but no less real costs in terms of parental time and effort. These findings have not been presented in a prescriptive spirit; they are not telling parents what they should buy nor how they should behave. On the contrary, they were intended, and have generally been accepted, as a hard-edged demonstration that the social security scale-rate payments intended to meet the needs of children are manifestly inadequate. If they have any prescriptive purpose, it is aimed at politician and policy-maker rather than the poor.

In other words, although someone has to use their best judgement in drawing up budgets, there is no reason in principle why these should always be calculated at the minimal level, nor that they should be indifferent to what is known about people's actual spending patterns. So, it may be that budget-standards as an approach has some place in any set of measures of relative poverty.

This point has come to have an especial relevance today, as the major reforms of the 1986 Social Security Act come into effect, because, for the first time for two generations, the DHSS has started to refer explicitly, and as a matter of policy, to the budgeting habits of claimants. Ever since the introduction of National Assistance in 1948, the responsible department has been very coy about discussing the basis upon which the social security scale-rates are calculated. Although broad headings are indicated, there is no detail about the range, the quantity or the quality of the goods and services that they are supposed to cover, nor the assumptions that are being made about prevailing price-levels, probable price-inflation etc. It is widely, and probably correctly, believed that the original National Assistance scale-rates were based on calculations made during the war by Beveridge in the preparation of his report, and that he in turn drew on a number of exercises in calculating household budgets by Rowntree and others dating from the 1930s. But the DHSS has always resisted being drawn into a detailed discussion of these matters, and has never made plain their underlying budgetary assumptions. The official reason for this reticence has been that the Department has never wanted to give the impression that it was recommending, still less requiring, any particular spending pattern on the part of claimants. On the contrary, each claimant, as a free citizen, must be able to decide for himself [or more usually, for herself] how to spend the resources at their disposal. This attitude, admirable though it may be as a principle, does however enable the Department to avoid any detailed discussion of the adequacy of the social security scale-rates. It has also meant that research-exercises like Piachaud's, using the budget-standard approach to evaluate the adequacy or otherwise of the scale-rates, have some of the characteristics of shadow-boxing. The DHSS, so appropriately located at the Elephant and Castle, given its characteristically pachydermous and defensive posture, has been in this instance as gossamer as Will o' the Wisp.

New thinking at the DHSS?

It is consequently all the more significant that what amounts to the abolition in 1988 of most single payment grants to meet exceptional need, and their replacement by a system of so-called budgeting loans, has referred specifically to claimants' inability to manage their affairs properly and to their need for advice and counselling on domestic budgetting. This important change may of course be a simple manoeuvre intended to do no more than engineer a further cut in social security expenditure, but, as a public policy it has neither sense nor logic unless it is believed that the scale-rates, as from 1988 at least, are adequate, and demonstrably so. In this fresh context, the Piachaud exercise and others like it, have an immediate and very practical relevance. We must look forward to an ever more vigorous debate on this question in the coming months, not least because the staff of Social Work Departments are being dragged, reluctantly, into some sort of collaborative relationship with the DHSS in the administration of the Social Fund. Social Workers can make good partners, but poor accomplices, and so there is every reason to anticipate an unusually public but entirely healthy controversy over this question.

Poverty: qualitative approaches

So far the discussion has been confined to definitions and understandings of poverty that are esssentially academic in their approach and administrative in their application. These are both important considerations but they are not the whole story; indeed they have at least one serious shortcoming. Although they may help us to estimate the numbers of people in poverty, and they require us to form judgements about life-styles and living standards, the lack of which may constitute deprivation and disadvantage, they do not in themselves tell us anything, and may even distract us from finding out about poverty as an experience.

By any reckoning, several millions of men, women and children are living their lives in conditions of relative poverty. For them, poverty is not a matter for academic discussion, or administrative convention, but a daily reality, which impacts on every aspect of their daily lives. The careful documenting of this actual experience (in all its variety and complexity), the monitoring of the consequences for health, happiness and well-being, and the chronicling of the multifarious reactions, responses and coping strategies that the poor must evolve; this task of description and analysis is the necessary qualitative counterpart to the more technical work we have considered. Indeed documentary and descriptive accounts of poverty, whether they are written, or as is now so frequently the case, they are on film or video, probably do far more to inform and influence the wider public opinion. They help to create the context in which, for example, the opinions canvassed in Breadline Britain were fashioned, and they are instrumental in determining whatever level of public and political concern that poverty as a controversial issue arouses.

Consequently it is appropriate to conclude this review with a brief reference to another kind of literature altogether. There is, and there has been for at least 150 years, a tradition of research and explanation which draws on the skills, literary, observational and imaginative, of the social explorer and journalist who endeavours to grasp and to communicate the experience of poverty, to capture the feel of it, and document as vividly and as accurately as possible the ways in which the daily lives of ordinary people are affected by it. Drawing in some cases from first-hand experience of poverty, in others on exercises of participant observation, and in yet others on prolonged and detailed research of a more orthodox kind, there is now a library of graphic accounts of the lived experience of poverty.

This is an investigative tradition which goes back at least to Henry Mayhew's detailed investigations of social conditions in early Victorian England in *London Labour and the London Poor*. Later, at the turn of the century, the statistical investigations of Booth and Rowntree were complemented by such accounts as Jack London's *People of the Abyss*, which over 80 years later is still a rivetting description of London's impoverished East End. The effects of inter-war unemployment were explored by a number of investigators, of whom perhaps the best known is George Orwell, and *The Road to Wigan Pier*. In the same way, the period since the mid-1960s has yielded numerous descriptions of poverty in the context of the Welfare State. The Child Poverty Action Group has regularly published pamphlets based upon individual life-histories, or anthologies in which the poor have been given a platform to speak for themselves. Then there is the work of Jeremy Seabrook, who has drawn upon autobiography, and an acutely sensitive understanding of changing working class cultures, as well as the evidence of research interviews, to explore the nature and meaning of poverty, as both a national and an international phenonomen. Mention should be made of the work of Tony Parker, who developed the technique of the immensely detailed case-study interview, first to explore the world of the criminal, and more recently, in books such as *The People of Providence*, to unpack most painstakingly the nature and the dynamics of an impoverished community. Finally, there is the work of Paul Harrison, whose *Inside the Inner City* is an ambitious and largely successful attempt to expose the way in which the life conditions of the poor, and the most deprived of communities are at the mercy of powerful and impersonal economic, social and political forces over which the poor themselves have no leverage, but which interrelate to produce, in Harrison's powerful phrase, 'life under the cutting edge'.

Works such as these are of the utmost value and importance, not as an alternative to the more obviously 'academic' research but as an essential complement to it. The approach is different, the methods are different, but the underlying purpose is the same, to understand the nature of the world in which we live. We need sober, dispassionate, even God help us, bureaucratic analysis, but equally we need the more vivid, descriptive first-hand account. The first without the second can be formal and sterile, the second without the first can be sentimental, and lack theory. Together, the quantitative and the qualitative appeal to both our intellectual and our fraternal selves.

2

Poverty and Planning:
Developing an Information Base
Keith Moore, Isobel Freeman and Fraser McCluskey

I F social service managers are to take due account of poverty in planning services, it is necessary that they have access to information which will allow them to monitor the impact of poverty on social work and in turn to plan and monitor the effectiveness of social work responses. This chapter describes developments over the last 10 years of those elements of Strathclyde's information base which have direct relevance to poverty issues, including:

[a] the introduction of referral analysis

[b] the development of needs indicators for use in the department's annual *Social Needs and Social Work Resources* document

[c] the recent development of more direct poverty indicators.

Development has been incremental; regular refinements of approach have taken account both of the shortcomings in previous methods of analysis identified in the light of experience in applying the information, and of the availability of new data sets.

This chapter emphasises the value of an incremental approach by attempting to describe the context in which initial developments took place and the factors which lead to the recognition of the need of refinement in each of the three areas covered. A final section summarises current thinking on the value of the information base as it now is.

Referrals analysis

·Computer analysis of referral data in Strathclyde began in 1981 in response to pressure from area teams for a systematic means of reviewing, regularly and in some detail, the nature of the demands being made of them. There were clear advantages in a common system, not least in avoiding duplication of computer development effort. Equally, however, area teams were keen to retain maximum flexibility within the system in order to best meet their own needs. The end result was a single referral form, with agreed coding conventions. Within this framework, area teams were given complete freedom to use the forms as they wished; no attempt was made to impose a standard definition of a referral, for example, and the form included four local option boxes with no pre-determined coding conventions to allow individual teams to collect information on particular issues of concern to them if they so wished. No attempt was made to impose the use of the system on teams; very few who chose to use the system have subsequently opted out and by 1986 almost half the department's 56 area teams were involved. Since 1986 the restructuring of the department has resulted in a greater emphasis being placed on planning at area team and district level with the introduction of area team strategies and district plans intended to outline approaches to the development of services. This has resulted in a recognition by area teams of the need for data such as that provided through referral analysis, and by the end of 1987 it is expected the system will have covered all teams in the region. The system is now the subject of a major review which is seeking to build on the experience of the first six years.

Over the years, service units have adapted the basic form for use in their settings. The review group has been able to build on such developments to produce a basic form which in future will be capable of being used in any setting where direct contact with the public is made.

Input of data is via the council's computer services department: analysis and feedback is though the department's research staff. Included in the referral form are data, source and method of referral, up to three reasons for referral [including a range of poverty related reasons for referral], age, sex, receipt of welfare benefits, living group and unit post code of the client, details of whether the client is previously known to the department, the type of worker who dealt with the client and the immediate action taken.

The findings of Strathclyde's referral analysis in respect of the dependency of clients on welfare benefits are extensively presented in Becker and MacPherson's *Poor Clients* [1986]. Briefly:

* 88 per cent of all people referring to the social work department
  have a welfare benefit as the main source of income.
* 52 per cent of adults referring are in receipt of supplementary
  benefit [compared to 16 per cent of all adults in the region].
* 48 per cent of all people referring to the department gave 'financial
  reasons' [including rent arrears, DHSS problems and fuel bill
  problems] as the main reason for referral. Such referrals are largely
  dealt with by intake workers and do not proceed to become
  cases.

Referral analysis has prompted a wide range of initiatives in different
teams at different times; not all, of course are directly related to poverty. It
has been used, along with caseload and social economic and demographic
information, to argue the case for, and assist in the establishment of, patch
teams and caller stations. In this context, referral analysis can be useful in
two ways; it can help to identify areas with particularly high numbers of
clients which justify the creation of local teams. Conversely, it can help to
identify areas with much lower numbers of clients than expected given
social and economic conditions, where a more local, visible and accessible
social work presence is required to encourage the expression of need. Use
of referral analysis in this way is particularly important in relation to
poverty given the evidence, presented later in this chapter, that poor areas
tend to be areas of relatively low demand for social work.

Second, referral analysis has had an important role in the planning of
local campaigns. Take-up campaigns, both in relation to welfare benefits
and social work services, have been targetted at areas, and focussed on
issues, identified at least in part through analysis of referral data.
Community workers, working with community groups such as tenants
associations, have used referral analysis to support campaigns on issues
such as council house repairs and to assist in the development of voluntary
services.

Third, analysis of referral data has highlighted significant and time-
consuming patterns of demand which could appropriately be diverted to
more relevant agencies. Teams have been able to achieve significant
reductions in the number of inappropriate referrals by demonstrating to
local DHSS and housing offices the number of people referring themselves
to social work simply to be referred back, or on, to DHSS or housing
offices. Changes in DHSS and housing practice were then negotiated which
resulted in improved services to clients and considerable savings in social
work time.

Fourth, referral and other data has been used to monitor the effects on
communities and on social work of major industrial closures such as at the
Linwood car plant near Paisley. Such analysis has in turn been used to assist

in campaigns, involving local MPs, local authorities and the trades unions, to prevent closures by attempting to demonstrate the likely social and economic consequences; the campaign in 1983/84 to avert the closure of Scott-Lithgow shipyard in Greenock is a successful example.

The common feature of all these examples, and they are only examples, is that referral analysis and other data have allowed area teams to stand back from the day-to-day pressures of predominantly one-to-one working and identify patterns of demand which may be susceptible to other approaches involving organisational, procedural or policy change. Referral analysis has allowed assumptions and perceptions to be tested and has provided hard, quantifiable evidence which has greatly assisted in campaigning activity in negotiations with other agencies, and in practical improvements in local service delivery.

Many, if not most, of the area teams using the computerised referrral analysis system have used referral data very effectively to argue for additional resources. Indeed, it is clear that one of the major factors behind the steady increase in the number of teams using the system has been the growing recognition on the part of area managers that to compete for resources they have to be able to produce evidence to back up their bids. Two problems arise in using referral data in this way. The first stems from the fact that teams had been given a free hand to use referral analysis as best fits their own local needs; this means that data are not necessarily comparable between areas and provides a less than perfect basis for management at district or regional levels to assess competing demands for resources. A major finding of the review of the referral analysis systems was that teams wish to be able to draw comparisons with other areas and were willing to sacrifice flexibility to obtain comparative data. Even if the referral analysis forms are used in the same way comparison between teams will still be problematic because teams are organised in different ways. The referral pattern for a patch system for example will differ from that of a team operating an intake system; proper comparison must be based on a full analysis of a team's workload, including both referrals and caseloads, and taking account of groupwork and preventive and community development initiatives.

The second reason for not using referral data to assess competing demands for resources is much more fundamental. It is that referrals are a measure of demand, while the planning of social work services must take at least equal account of need. This distinction between need and demand is particularly important in the context of poverty and social work planning; there is extensive evidence in the literature to demonstrate that poor people, those in greatest need, are least aware of the existence of services and least able to articulate demands for services . Social work is not exempt from this phenomenon as is shown by a more detailed analysis of Strathclyde referral data. On the basis of a series of poverty indicators, including unemployment rates and proportions of single parent families and large families [four or more children], Strathclyde's 56 area teams have been classified into five groups of areas. Analysis of referral rates per thousand population show that the more prosperous the group of areas the higher the referral rate. In all five groups of areas, referrals are drawn disproportionately from people dependent on welfare benefits and supplementary benefit. However, reasons for referral vary substantially between the poorest and the most prosperous groups of areas; financial/material reasons account for 44.3 per cent of referrals in the poorest group of areas but only 13.6 per cent in the most prosperous group. A similar pattern is found in housing related referrals; 17.9 per cent of referrals in the poorest group of areas fall into this category compared with 7.3 per cent in the best-off areas.

Table 2.1
Referrals to Strathclyde social work department 1984/85

Area Teams	Referrals per 1,000 Population	% of Referrals with main reason Financial/ Material	Housing
Group 1: [poorest]	50.6	44.3	17.9
Group 2:	55.3	40.4	16.6
Group 3:	56.1	38.4	11.4
Group 4:	56.6	35.3	11.6
Group 5 [best off]	62.1	13.6	7.3

Note: Based on all referrals to the department. The analysis in *Poor Clients* [Becker and MacPherson, 1986] was only of those where benefit status known.

Needs indicators

This analysis suggests that, if social work planning is based on measures of demand alone, social work will compound the discrimination against the poor which is a feature of many other public services; referral analysis provides information on who gets a service not who needs it. Social work planning requires a means of assessing need which is independent of demands on service.

Towards this end, Strathclyde prepares an annual *Social Needs and Social Work Resources Report*. The first *Needs and Resources Report* was produced in 1978 in the former Glasgow division to provide a framework for the consideration of urban programme submissions. At that stage needs indicators were crude, consisting of referrals [now seen as a measure of demand], caseloads, number of free school meals and total population. In 1982 a major review of the form and content of *Needs and Resource Report* led to the production of needs indicators which for the first time allowed district level comparisons of sizes of caseloads and of service provision for client groups in relation to total and 'vulnerable' populations.

Crucial in the context of this chapter are the principles and methods underlying the quantification of 'vulnerable' populations. Strathclyde's *Social Strategy for the Eighties* specifically requires departments to discriminate in favour of the most disadvantaged:

> Services should not be provided on a uniform per head of population basis throughout the region. Standards of provision to be achieved should vary from area to area according to relative need [Strathclyde Regional Council, 1983, para 9.7].

The achievement of these political objectives puts the onus on central administrators within social work to allocate resources between areas in a way which takes account of the distribution of poverty and multiple deprivation. In turn, the onus is on managers responsible for service delivery at a local level to ensure that the most vulnerable individuals and families in their areas are encouraged and enabled to take advantage of services.

The selection of needs indicators is heavily constrained by availability of data which is comparable between areas and is capable of regular updating. Historically, DHSS and unemployment data, which provide the most direct measure of poverty have been problematical largely because there is invariably a mismatch between local DHSS, Department of Employment and social work areas. Population information from the census, and in at least some authorities from enhanced electoral rolls, has provided a more reliable base. Drawing heavily on Townsend's [1979] research into poverty in the UK, sub groups of children and elderly were identified which are particularly vulnerable to poverty. These sub groups were used to develop needs indicators for services to these two major client groups.

In the case of child care, for example, Townsend identifies children from single parent families, large families [four or more children], and families in social classes four and five as vulnerable to poverty. Significantly, children from families which fall into more than one of these categories are

particularly vulnerable. Thus, for example, while 56 per cent of families in
social class five live in or on the margins of poverty, and less than 50 per
cent of all families with three or more children live in these conditions, 89
per cent of all families falling into both categories live in or at the margins of
poverty. Based on this type of evidence children were defined as
'vulnerable' for the purpose of assessing needs for social work services
when they fell into two or three of three population groups.

Table 2.2

Need for services: share of children, vulnerable children and children in
care, by division 1985.

| Division | Divisional share | | Number of children in care [per 1000] | | |
	Total children aged 0–15 %	Vulnerable children aged 0-15 %	No. of children in care	Vulnerable children	Total children
Argyll/ Dumbarton	17.0	10.1	529	97	5.2
Ayr	15.9	11.4	764	122	7.9
Glasgow	28.9	45.4	2,094	84	11.8
Lanark	11.9	20.6	530	48	3.8
Renfrew	15.3	12.6	541	78	5.8
Strathclyde Region	100	100	4,458	81	7.3

Table 2.2 illustrates the dramatic effect of using the distribution of
vulnerable children between Strathclyde's five divisions as a measure of
need for social work services as opposed to the distribution of all children;
Glasgow division's share of need increases by more than 50 per
cent.

The table also illustrates the dramatically different impressions of relative
service and caseload levels which arise from using total and vulnerable
populations.

Important professional validation of these indicators comes from an
analysis of the family circumstances of children admitted to care in
Strathclyde in 1985 available from the department's child care information
system:

  * 55 per cent of children received into care came from single parent
    families

* 80 per cent are from households dependent on welfare benefits as their main source of income
* 39 per cent are from large families – that is families with four or more children. By comparison, only 13 per cent of all children in Strathclyde live in large families.
* 92 per cent of children received into care come from families with one of the three above characteristics.
* 67 per cent of children received into care come from families with two of the three above characteristics.

It is important to stress that these needs indicators simply provide an indicator of the likely level of relative need in one area as compared with another. They do not provide an absolute measure of need. For example, knowing that there are 1000 'vulnerable' children in Area A and 500 in Area B simply suggests that the fairest distribution of resources would be likely to occur if Area A had twice as many resources as Area B. It does not provide an estimate of the actual number of children who need a service in Area A or B; not all those defined as 'vulnerable' in terms of the indicators used will need a service and not all those who need a service will be 'vulnerable' in terms of the indicators used.

A significant problem has arisen in the use of social class four and five as one component of this composite needs indicator. Within an individual labour market it is reasonable to assume that people in social classes four and five will be most vulnerable to unemployment, low incomes, and uncertain incomes arising from lower job security. However, as actual unemployment levels vary greatly between local labour market areas, it is misleading to compare the number of people in social classes four and five in different labour market areas. A more direct measure of low income or poverty is required. It is difficult, in any case, to update social class statistics between census years.

Poverty indicators

Recognition of this problem has coincided with an improved availability of small area unemployment statistics, now available by district council wards or post code sectors, which can be better matched with social work areas, and a regular availability of supplementary benefits statistics, broken down by claimant group, at local DHSS office level. The opportunity now exists to exploit this improved data to provide a direct measure of the number of people living in poverty within social work area teams. These estimates, first calculated in 1987, are used in their own right in the planning of welfare rights activity and the use of direct financial assistance under section 12 of the Social Work [Scotland] Act. It is intended that they will also be used as an alternative measure to social class four and five in the more general composite needs indicators. The final summary section of this chapter further discusses the relationship between the general needs indicators and the new poverty indicators.

There are a number of problems in using numbers dependent on supplementary benefit as a measure of poverty. The first surrounds the ability of government to vary the value of the annual uprating of benefit levels relative to inflation, which means that the number of people defined as poor can be altered upwards or downwards independently of real changes in family incomes. This problem is not a serious limitation where a measure of relative levels of poverty between areas is all that is sought.

Second, there are a series of technical problems involving continuing problems of mismatch of DHSS and social work areas, improved availability of supplementary benefit statistics notwithstanding, problems of estimation of the numbers of people dependent on supplementary benefit claimants, and problems arising from non take-up of benefit. The formula designed to overcome these problems is simple. The numbers of unemployed, pensioner, single parent and disabled claimants in each DHSS office area which serves more than one social work area were split pro rata between the social work areas on the basis of the total numbers of unemployed, pensioners, single parents and disabled people in each of the social work areas involved.

The number of dependants then has to be calculated. Each year the DHSS produce by their regions the average numbers of dependants of the different types of supplementary benefit claimants. The numbers for Scotland for 1984 show pensioners on average have less than 14 per cent dependency ratio while the unemployed have an 82 per cent dependency ratio and single parents a ratio in excess of 100 per cent.

Finally some account has also to be taken of the numbers who are eligible for supplementary benefit, but who for various reasons do not claim. Every few years the DHSS produces estimates of non take-up by claimant type. Again the dependants of those eligible but not claiming have to be taken into account.

Other means-tested benefits such as housing benefits and free school meals have been used to test the validity of this method. It is hoped that the methods used by the department to establish the numbers of people living at or below supplementary benefit level will only be a short term requirement and the DHSS will develop a system enabling the numbers and types of claimants to be broken down by age, post code and length of time claiming.

In Strathclyde applying this formula highlighted that some 676,190 [29 per cent] of people in the region were living at or below supplementary benefit level. At a local level the figures varied from 62 per cent in areas like Castlemilk and Easterhouse, both large peripheral housing estates in Glasgow, and inner city Dalmarnock to 19 per cent in areas like the well-to-do Glasgow suburbs of Bearsden and Eastwood.

These numbers at or below supplementary benefit level underestimate rather than overestimate poverty as they exclude all those in full time employment who according to the EEC 'decency threshold' are earning low wages defined as less than £123 per week full time. The *Breadline Scotland* report published by the Low Pay Units [Smail, 1986] estimated that 24 per cent of working males in Strathclyde and 60 per cent of working females were earning low wages.

Summary

Social services managers are obliged to plan on the basis of the best available information, taking account of limitations in data in the way the information is applied. In these circumstances, incremental development and refinement of the information basis is both inevitable and essential as experience of using information exposes weaknesses which require to be addressed.

In the context of a constantly evolving poverty information base in Strathclyde the role of both of the older components described in this chapter has changed. In conclusion, it is worth setting out the interpretation currently placed on each of the three information sets and the ways in which they can be used together to ensure that poverty is fully taken into account in service planning.

Referral analysis provides a measure of demand for services. It can be used to monitor trends in the relative demands being placed on social work services by those dependent on welfare benefits, and those who are not. It can be used to monitor trends in the extent to which poverty is a reason for initial referral to the department. It can be used to review the demands being made on social work from areas in the region which have concentrations of poor people; empirically, such areas have been shown to be areas of low demand for service. In all these ways, referral analysis provides essential information to service managers and assists in the introduction of appropriate responses.

The recently developed poverty indicators provide the most direct measure of the numbers of people living in poverty in each social work area team. Capable of being broken down into the different types of supplementary benefit and other claimant, the poverty indicators are used in the planning of welfare benefits activity and in the deployment of the section 12 budget [direct financial assistance] within the region.

The more general needs indicators, currently being refined to introduce a more direct measure of poverty based on the poverty indicators work in place of the former social class four and five indicator, continue to be important in service planning. Initially developed as the best available proxy measure of poverty, the needs indicators are now seen as having a more general value and applicability; their use recognises that, for many services, poverty is one of a range of factors which requires to be considered in planning. Conversely, too, the inclusion of a poverty component within the general needs indicators means that poverty is taken into account in the planning of all services.

3

Evaluating Social Services for the Poor:
An Agenda for Research
Mike Titterton

THERE is a great paradox in social policy in Britain today. Austerity in the social services has heralded a deepening pessimism about what the latter can achieve in the face of massive and relatively invariant structures of inequality. At the same time there is growing willingness to question traditional assumptions concerning approaches to need and intervention, and to search for new modes of delivery and organisation and new ways of working with clients. The profound disillusionment of those working in the social services with their ability to bring about a fundamental realignment of relative disadvantage was made increasingly evident by the experiences of the 1960s and 1970s, through such sobering examples as the outcomes of the various CDP experiments [Loney, 1983]. Reviewing the evidence on intervention in the case of poor families with young children for the SSRC programme on deprivation, Fuller and Stevenson painted what they admitted was a 'bleak picture, conspicuously lacking in success stories' [1983, 194]. This seemingly harsh verdict was one that found many echoes in other areas of the social services [Brown and Madge, 1983].

Since these books were written, the interlocking and mutually determining structures of disadvantage and deprivation which the authors and others such as Rutter and Madge [1976] have described have changed in

some ways, but the underlying reality of a society where the distribution of
lifechances and social well-being remains profoundly unequal has not. The
prospects for intervention remain on the face of it as bleak as ever. Indeed
evidence is rapidly accumulating that fundamental social and economic
disparities are deepening further [Halsey, 1987; Walker and Walker, 1987].
New constituencies of need – of the long term unemployed, the frail
elderly, families dependent on state benefits – have been created over the
past decade. These result from the impact of major demographic changes
and through the complex interplay of such factors as economic recession,
the changing structures of the labour market, changing formal and informal
sectors of the economy, the intense restructuring of capital – changes which
are in turn overlaid by the intensification of social and geographical
divisions.

Of the developments in social policy in the late 1980s, two in particular
may be singled out in view of their importance and their political visibility.
Firstly, there has been the significant growth of the population dependent
on supplementary benefits, doubling in total from 1979 to 1984, and the
worrying rise in those judged to be living in or around poverty levels
[CPAG/LPU, 1986; Piachaud, 1987a]. The growth of poverty has however
been a spatially uneven process, with certain regions and localities being
especially hard hit. Fully one-third of Strathclyde Region, for example, are
now claimed to be living at or below the supplementary benefit level, with
the numbers claiming supplementary benefit rising from 158,000 in
November 1979 to over 316,000 in February 1986 [*Scotsman*, 17/9/87].
Very large proportions of households in certain urban areas are now
entirely dependent on some form of state benefit. A recent report for the
city of Edinburgh has claimed that one in three of the city's population are
living in some form of poverty, with large sections of the population in the
more deprived districts dependent on supplementary benefit, housing
benefit, free school meals, school clothing grants and the like [Edinburgh
District Council, 1987]. Though the present Government may contest it,
poverty is increasingly appearing on the social policy agenda.

The second development is altogether a much more insidious one and
appears to be curiously opaque to the inquiring eye. Throughout the 1980s
the redistributive capacities and functions of the Welfare State have been
and are being restructured in ways whose implications are not immediately
apparent. The opinion of academic commentators differs. Le Grand [1982]
in his provocative survey of social services spending claimed that the more
advantaged sections of society were deriving greater benefit. In contrast
O'Higgins [1985] has claimed that the pressures towards greater

inequalities have been significantly modified by social spending. The latest release of figures from Central Statistical Office give little comfort to those looking for more progressive signs in redistribution trends – the distribution of incomes in the period from 1975 to 1985 has become more unequal [Central Statistical Office, 1987b]. Though the growth in cash benefits helped to offset this trend, the distribution of *final* income has actually shifted in favour of the more advantaged. The redistributive function of the personal social services and the impact of these services on the distribution of inequality, disadvantage and poverty in the population has yet to be properly assessed. It may be the case that the personal social services are not particularly well designed to meeting redistributive goals. If the personal social services are to have a crucial role to play in the 1980s and 1990s in tackling inequality and poverty, then many quiestions about the the distributive impacts of these services, the targeting of resources, and the appropriateness of current strategies and forms of intervention must now be addressed.

Recent developments in government social policies make such evaluative assessments all the more urgent.

While the prospects for social services intervention to alleviate poverty have perhaps worsened, there have over the past decade been signs that certain trends started in the late 1970s, such as the questioning about the means and ends of social work, a reappraisal of old assumptions, a concern with effectiveness of social policy and the desire to examine more rigorously the outcomes of the personal social services, have continued apace. The paradox is that it has been the shift to the austere era of 'scarcity and social obligation' [Webb and Wistow, 1986] which has produced this search for innovation and greater efficiency in the social services. Occasionally this quest has been associated with critiques of centralism and bureaucracy within the welfare state and led to a re-examination of the assumptions underlying the delivery and organisation of social work services. This has been reflected in the growth of interest in decentralised and community-orientated initiatives, such as the development of 'patch' based services [Hadley and McGrath, 1980; Beresford and Croft, 1986] and neighbourhood based projects such as that at Dinnington [see the Dinnington Project papers such as Bayley *et al*, 1985]. The continuing interest in 'community social work' following the appearance of the Barclay Report [1982] and the search for 'preventive' strategies [Hadley and Dale, 1987; Hadley *et al*, 1987] have received much impetus from this re-examination. More recently there have been pleas for those responsible for developing personal social services to acknowledge the reality of the 'mixed economy of welfare' [Webb and Wistow, 1987] which is seen to characterise the welfare state in the late 1980s.

The implications of this mood of criticism and questioning and search for new models of welfare for developing services for the poor are as yet unclear and attention should now be turned towards the careful scrutiny of these implications. There are of course new initiatives and approaches to tackling deprivation and poverty which may be pointed to, such as the Strathclyde 'Social Strategy' [Strathclyde Regional Council, 1984; Hume, 1984]. There have been 'proactive' campaigns by some local authority workers to increase the take-up of welfare benefits, with recent attempts to target these campaigns on deprived areas, such as the South Tyneside initiative [Alcock, 1987]. Certainly there is a growing interest in developing localised and preventive strategies for deprived communities. One example is provided by Nottinghamshire Social Services Department, where in one disadvantaged area a social work team has sought to develop a more localised and flexible response to poverty, although with mixed success [Parker and Dillon, 1987, and this volume]. Many of these initiatives await systematic monitoring and evaluation. The irony is that the interesting initiatives, having arisen under the pressures of the new austerity, are now threatened by the severe resources squeeze being placed upon local authorities and by the fact that the room for manoeuvre by these authorities has been sharply circumscribed by the policies of past and present governments.

Evaluation

Evaluation within the context of the social services refers to what is in practice a wide ranging and extremely diverse set of activities. Generally speaking, these activities have in common a concern with the systematic examination of the resources, processes and outcomes of social care agencies in relation to the meeting of 'social needs', broadly defined. Evaluation studies in the British social services are beginning to grow apace. There are as yet many methodological and theoretical difficulties which await resolution if 'evaluation research' is to stake its claim in the field of social scientific knowledge [Titterton, 1986a]. Whatever vaunted claims are made about its objectivity, evaluation is arguably as much a process of making value judgements about the means and ends of social care as of anything else. 'Effectiveness' in social care is similarly a value judgement – it represents about whether the aims of a particular intervention or project have been met. Thus when we are called upon to evaluate the effectiveness of services for the poor, we are in effect being called upon to make judgements about the appropriateness of intervention into the lives of the most disadvantaged and politically powerless groups in our society. Evaluation then in the context of services for the poor has the potential to raise some fairly fundamental issues about the distribution of dependency and inequality in society at large and about the accountability of the bureaucracy of welfare to the impoverished.

There has as yet been disappointing progress in the systematic and rigorous evaluation of the distribution of poverty among social work clients and of the services for the poor. If poverty is indeed to be placed firmly back on the social policy agenda, then this evaluation must be placed at the centre of this renewed concern. The rest of this chapter suggests that there is now a pressing need for two types of evaluative activity; firstly, the evaluation of the distribution of disadvantage and poverty among those who receive social work and those who do not, and secondly, the evaluation of the specific outcomes of intervention into the lives of poor clients. It is suggested that the two types of evaluation may be usefully combined in order to throw light on some of the outstanding issues now facing those charged with developing social services for the poor. Some provisional guidelines for the conduct of an evaluation for managers, practitioners and others are appended to the chapter.

Evaluating the distribution of disadvantage and poverty among recipients and non-recipients of social work

According to Adrian Webb, in an argument originally framed at the start of this decade, theres is a widespread assumption that the "benefits" of the personal social services do in practice reach the poor and the working classes' [Webb and Wistow, 1986, 13]. He rightly complains that there has in fact been little effort to gather data on who actually benefits from these services and 'whether they reinforce or modify patterns of inequality' [*ibid*]. In other words, the distributional impact of the personal social services upon different social groups is difficult to assess. Le Grand felt unable to comment upon the personal social services, on the grounds that the statistical evidence was not available [1982]. Large questions about the overarching aims and objectives and overall impact of the personal social services remain to be answered. Who, for example, is actually receiving social work? What are their socioeconomic characteristics? What are the differences between those receiving social work and those not? What proportion of the poor are receiving social work? What is the distribution of poverty among social work clients? What associations may be identified between the use of social work services and forms of disadvantage and poverty?

We urgently require answers to these questions so that we can address a number of outstanding issues in the appraisal of the outcomes of social policy in respect of the poor. These are issues to do with the distributional and redistributional effects of a given strategy for the personal social services. They further touch upon questions of equity, on whether such services should be 'targeted' upon particular areas or upon particular groups in society and whether there is a 'target efficiency' in the allocation of such resources [Bebbington and Davies, 1983]. We need, moreover, to systematically investigate the associations between the use of services and poverty, for as Becker and MacPherson have contended, more detailed information on the links between poverty and the use of social services is essential, because without this 'the evaluation of social work action to ameliorate some of the harsher consequences of poverty is impossible' [1986, 54-5]. Unless more is known, it is difficult to evolve a meaningful proactive or preventive strategy for the social services as the authors suggest. Some fundamental questions have to be answered before we can begin to make judgements about the overall efficacy of social service interventions in the case of the poor and the deprived.

The author is currently reviewing the evidence which is available to throw light on some of these questions. It is obvious in this field that, compared to the study of the use of health services, for example, there is little robust data from which to draw meaningful inferences. There are in addition major methodological difficulties in much of the data that does exist however. Social work information systems are not notable for their ability to reveal data relating to the socioeconomic characteristics of clients, so that associations between use and disadvantage may be properly explored. Referrals data give a general idea of 'problems presented' to the agency but great care is required and inferences drawn from such data must be subject to strict qualifications. If we wish for example to compare referral rates from differing socioeconomic areas, there may be several factors which account for variations. Referrals analyses can be most usefully explored in conjunction with other information. However sources of client information such as case return data are often not readily available. The unique Scottish case return system was unfortunately discontinued in 1981 as a result of cuts in the government statistical service, although Lothian Region Social Work Department still maintains its case return system.

Two useful examples of information systems which can throw some light on the above questions deserve to be mentioned. One is the Strathclyde Region Social Work Department information systems built up by the research team at SWD, which has much valuable information [Moore and Freeman, 1987, and this volume]. Apart from their useful regular report on 'social work needs and resources' in Strathclyde [Strathclyde Region Social Work Department, 1987], the research team have built up a referrals analysis system and child care statistics which contain data relating to such items as employment status and benefit status of clients. The other is the collection of statistics based on cases notified to child abuse registers maintained by NSPCC special units for the period 1977 onwards [NSPCC briefing notes – various years]. The register form includes a request for information on social factors such as the occupation of both parents and their employment characteristics, and the NSPCC undertakes occasional extended analyses of this dataset [eg Creighton, 1984]. The inclusion of occupational class on the register form is especially interesting and statements about 'social class' and presenting problem may, with due caution, be inferred.

Evidence is accumulating which points to the growing proportion of persons referred to social work departments with financial and related problems, with a subsequent increase in the welfare rights work of the department [see Becker and MacPherson, 1986]. More research into the precise nature of the links between money problems, poverty and use of social work services is essential however. Ashley [1983] found that money problems were of a variable nature, some of which could produce crises leading to distress and hardship and others of a more chronic nature which could lead to a deprived lifestyle.

Finally, the growing evidence about the impact of unemployment on referrals to departments and on the work of the department should be noted [Balloch *et al*, 1985; Popay and Dhooge, 1985; Dhooge and Popay, 1987; Fife Regional Council, 1986]. The intricate links between employment characteristics, poverty and use of social services represent an important dimension for further exploration.

To support these and other findings, and to start exploring the associations between the use of social services and poverty, we need to consider ways of gathering the sort of 'epidemiological' data which is analogous to the sort used in health studies [see eg Struening, 1974] and now featuring in the analyses undertaken by health authorities and health boards [eg Greater Glasgow Health Board, 1984; Sheffield Health Authority, 1986; Liverpool Health Authority, 1987] particularly at the level of small area analysis. Patterns of need and the distribution of disadvantages and poverty can then be compared with patterns of service use. Controlled comparisons of receipt and non-receipt of the personal social services, perhaps with different mixes of forms of provision, could then be undertaken in selected deprived areas to shed more light on the effects of intervention.

One recent proposal for evaluation which is much in keeping with the discussion here comes from Goldberg and Sinclair [1986]. The authors undertook to examine the effectiveness of the 'family support exercise', with a broad look at the support being offered to families under stress by different agencies. In their review of the effectiveness of small scale interventions in supporting families the authors proposed that epidemiological area studies of those who get support and those who do not should be undertaken in conjunction with studies of specific services. They suggest that these area or community studies could explore the supposed prevalence of family problems in a particular community, identify families currently served by agencies, and include an interview survey of a random sample and a community survey of a sample designed to identify the number experiencing particular problems etc which would show whether those with the most severe problems were in touch with services and if so, which services they were using. Such an evaluative strategy could well be adapted to look at the effectiveness of services for the poor.

In discussing epidemiological and area approaches to evaluation and the implications for social services strategies in combatting poverty, it is important to remember the distinction between 'deprived areas' and 'deprived people' [Cullingforth and Openshaw, 1979]. It may well be that not all deprived persons live in deprived areas and may in fact reside outside such areas. There are implications for upholding this distinction in the targeting of resources, for example in whether a local authority was to choose an 'area strategy' or a 'client group based strategy' instead. It could be that a 'household strategy' where resources are targeted not on the area or client group but on specific *households* which have judged to have one or more disadvantages [and perhaps with a focus on *women* in the household in view of their greater vulnerability to poverty] might be a more effective use of scarce resources. These different strategies could be monitored and evaluated in the one exercise an' their effectiveness compared and contrasted.

Finally, the issue of accountability and involvement of local people in area and community approaches which is a strong element in the writings of advocates of decentralised services [eg Beresford and Croft, 1986] is one which evaluative studies need to be sensitive to. For example, one aspect of the 'effectiveness' of the Nottingham area team approach to poverty might be its success in working with local people, where an attempt was made to set up a forum of residents and workers for the identification of needs, the development of services and which could act as a pressure group [Parker and Dillon, 1987, and this volume]. Further, members of the local community might well want to be involved in or even undertake their own 'social audit' of the needs and resources of their community. Short of this, the results of evaluative studies can in turn be used by the local community, particularly where they have in some way been involved in the research. A nice example of this can be found in the field of health and housing. In a relatively deprived area of North Edinburgh there has been a project underway on health promotion and community development, where local people have helped identify targets for action, such as their housing conditions and particularly dampness. The links between ill-health and damp housing are being investigated by Sonja Hunt of the Health and Behavioural Change Research Unit and others. The research team used public meetings and leaflets to explain the study to tenants, and used local people to assist in the interviews which were undertaken in the study [Martin *et al*, 1987; Hunt, forthcoming]. Using a specially constructed questionnaire and a standardised measure of perceived ill-health, the team found strong associations between poor housing conditions and ill-health among children. The results of the study have been taken up by the district and regional councils and they have assisted the tenants in their campaign for better housing conditions.

Evaluation of social work intervention

Despite the fact that the traditional focus of social work has tended to encompass the areas of disadvantage and poverty, there are surprisingly few rigorous evaluations of the outcomes of intervention and deprivation. Writing about the transmitted deprivation debate, Fuller and Stevenson [1983] found that no intervention studies had been undertaken and were forced to rely on drawing inferences from other studies, for example Sainsbury's [1975] study of 27 deprived families. There are in fact overall far fewer controlled or semi-controlled British studies of social work intervention with outcome measures, compared to say studies of health intervention, though such studies have begun to grow in number and have improved in methodological sophistication [see the collections by Goldberg and Connelly, 1981; and Lishman, 1984]. To some extent there has been a swing of interest away from evaluating single interventions to evaluating models of the organisation and delivery of social services, such as the

Neighbourhood Services Project evaluation [see eg Bayley *et al*, 1985]. Perhaps the traditional type of evaluation of intervention has had its day [but see Sheldon, 1986 or the quasi-experimental approach of Davies and Challis, 1986]. The lack of explanatory research strategies has limited the usefulness of much of this work [Titterton, 1986a]. What we now require, particularly in examining the relationship between the personal social services and poverty, are evaluative studies which can combine the epidemiological or 'area' approach suggested above with studies of specific forms of intervention. For example, the outcomes of different styles and modes of organising social work in deprived localities could be compared in the light of the findings suggested by the epidemiological study.

Generally speaking, we may single out two problems which have tended to haunt attempts to evaluate the effects of social work intervention. The first concerns the role and functions of social work itself which came under some scrutiny in the Barçlay Report [1982]; the report favoured the idea of the 'community social worker' in contrast to the more traditional idea of the 'caseworker'. There is genuine disagreement on the nature of the social work task in respect of approaches to poverty eg of traditional casework versus community work. If we were to summarise the range of functions available to social workers, it might look something like this:

Possible functions of social work with respect to the poor
1. Assessor of needs and problems of clients
2. Mobiliser of resources
3. Welfare rights worker
4. Direct caseworker
5. Coordinator and monitor of different support services
6. Resource person to other helpers
7. Community worker
8. Advocacy

Six of the functions listed above have been derived from Goldberg and Connelly [1982] in respect of the care of the elderly, but these functions are now arguably to be found elsewhere. Two others have been added: welfare rights work and benefits work is of growing importance, though not everyone would accept that the social worker is best placed to undertake this function. Some writers [eg Fimister, 1986; and Hannam, 1987, both also in this volume] identify welfare rights work as essential to the work of social work and social service departments. Yet Michael Hill and his colleagues found in a study of 14 social services departments that social workers were 'deeply ambivalent' about welfare rights work [Hill *et al*, 1985, 26]. The social workers faced a key dilemma, in that while recognising that financial problems among their clients were pervasive and financial-related referrals were growing, they were reluctant to become 'experts' in welfare rights, suggesting a role for regular information and support from experts for teams.

'Advocacy' is suggested here as one area which may well be developed, not only advocacy on behalf of debtors and so on but also perhaps along the lines of a campaigning role with the intention of giving the poor a greater say in the identification of needs and in the sort of services which are developed. These diverse functions have still to be systematically developed and evaluated however. While direct casework has received a lot of attention in the evaluation literature, the effectiveness of the other functions has still yet to be examined.

Another problem in intervention studies involving poverty is the need to examine the complex problem of causality and the specification of the determining relationships of deprivation and the designation of the 'points of intervention' for effective social work action. The complex links in the causal chain and the etiology of personal and social problems have been discussed elsewhere [see eg Brown and Harris, 1978; Titterton 1986b; Irvine *et al*, 1987; and Irvine, this volume]. Figure 3.1 provides an analytical model of the hypothetical effects of poverty at different levels. Note the presence of 'mediating factors' in the model which, we may suppose, both filter and mould the effects of recession and poverty and which mean that the relationship between poverty, unemployment and its impact upon social services is a complex one. The exploration of the link between what C Wright Mills called 'the personal troubles of milieu' and the 'public issues of social structure' [1959, 14] is one of the great challenges facing social science today. Figure 3.2 provides a description of the different levels of social work intervention, according to the causal sequence of events. The development of primary intervention or preventive strategies is of central importance to social service approaches to poverty. 'Prevention' has proved something of a slippery concept for social workers [Fuller, 1987] and the concept has to be unpacked into meaningful goals for specific areas such as child care [Holman, forthcoming]. Evaluative studies of 'proactive' or preventive interventions will have to be alert to the need for greater specificity and clarity in social strategies intended to tackle the 'causes' or 'preconditions' of social problems.

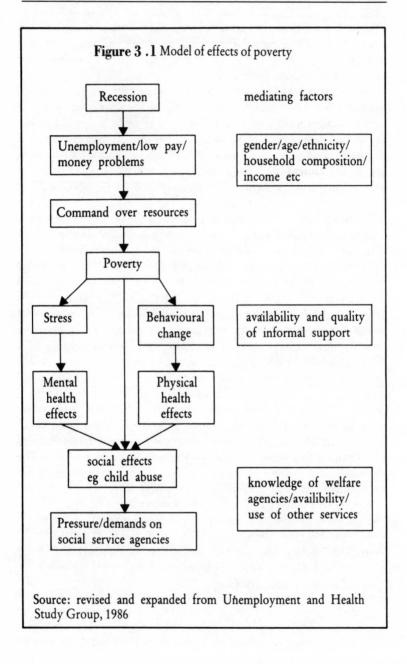

Figure 3 .1 Model of effects of poverty

Recession

mediating factors

Unemployment/low pay/
money problems

gender/age/ethnicity/
household composition/
income etc

Command over resources

Poverty

Stress

Behavioural
change

availability and quality
of informal support

Mental
health
effects

Physical
health
effects

social effects
eg child abuse

knowledge of welfare
agencies/availibility/
use of other services

Pressure/demands on
social service agencies

Source: revised and expanded from Unemployment and Health
Study Group, 1986

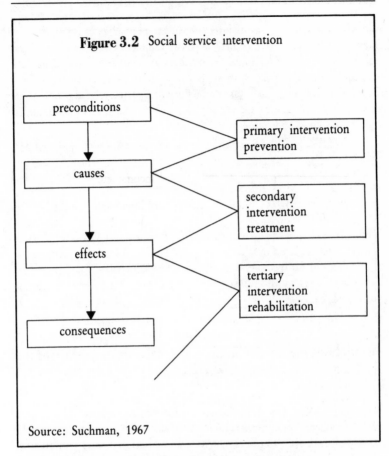

Figure 3.2 Social service intervention

Source: Suchman, 1967

Conclusions

This chapter has contended that the evaluation of social services for the poor and disadvantaged is urgently required, particularly in view of recent developments in social policy. Greater attention must be paid to the distributive and redistributive impacts of the social services upon patterns of inequality and poverty. Many fundamental questions about the personal social services remain to be answered, such as those concerning the socioeconomic characteristics of recipients and non-recipients and the association between poverty and the use of services. Specifically, it is suggested that two types of evaluation are called for, namely studies of an 'epidemiological' nature, to look at the distribution of poverty and disadvantage among those who do receive social work and those who do not, and studies of forms of intervention for poor clients. It was further suggested that such studies may be most usefully combined to produce valuable information for those responsible for the development of services for the poor. The aim of these studies would be as follows:

1. to describe the distribution and nature of poverty-related problems in selected populations and the social characteristics of those in receipt of social work and those who do not
2. to identify etiological factors in the genesis of personal and social problems
3. to provide data essential for the management, evaluation and planning of social services for the poor
4. to appraise different strategies and types of intervention in the light of this information

Evaluative research then has much to offer for the development of services for the poor. Only on the firmly grounded basis of this sort of research can the aspirations for more relevant models of social work and social services delivery and for more localised and preventive forms of intervention be fully realised.

Appendix
Guidelines for the evaluation of social service initiatives for the poor

What follows are some guidelines in the form of a checklist and questions which managers, practitioners and others who wish to evaluate a specific service or even set of services or who are involved in setting up initiatives for the poor might find helpful. To use the whole checklist would be an ambitious undertaking and it may be more appropriate simply to use parts of the checklist.

Checklist
1. Objectives
2. Needs
3. Resources
4. Implementation
5. Outcomes
6. Costs
7. Monitoring
8. Quality assurance

1. Objectives

Have the aims and objectives of the initiative been clearly identified?

Do they represent properly specified goals? ie have the primary objectives of the initiative been translated as achievable goals according to the appropriate level of provision?

How do they correspond to overall policy objectives set out by local and national policy statements?

2. Needs

Has an appropriate target group been identified? enumerated if possible?

Have the needs of the target group been properly identified? What data sources are available for this task? If no local survey data is available, can national or *ad hoc* studies be used to estimate the approximate size of the target group? Should the views of the local pressure groups be canvassed?

Are the needs of the target group likely to change and how can they be reviewed?

3. Resources

Have all the available resources – staff, volunteers, informal sources, availability of sources of finance, welfare and financial benefits, joint finances and bridging monies, etc – been properly identified and described? Are they adequate for the specified task in hand?

4. Implementation

How are resources to be deployed in respect of identified needs?

How are staff and resources being deployed in relation to objectives?

Are tasks being implemented in accordance with specified objectives?

Have the specific contributions which staff, volunteers, users have to make in the delivery of help been identified?

Have training needs been taken into account?

Can the 'inputs' of care be moved around to obtain a more effective use of resources?

5. Outcomes

Are there clear and unambiguous criteria for the success or failure of the initiative?

Can the effects of the intervention upon the financial or material circumstances of the client (and perhaps his or her well-being) be ascertained and measured?

Are there other possible impacts upon the wider circle of poverty or deprivation which might in some way be demonstrated? eg effect on the use of other services, effects on health, etc?

6. Costs

Is it appropriate to gather cost information? what information is readily available and what might have to be specially collected? Just financial costs, or real resource costs? Which costs are relevant – those that fall upon the agency or project or those that fall on other agencies eg health agencies? Can meaningful comparisons be made with the cost of alternative forms of help?

7. Monitoring

Has a monitoring and review system been established?

What sort of information should be regularly recorded and how often?

What sources should be used and who should gather the information?

Are there mechanisms for monitoring referrals and reviewing cases?

8. Quality assurance

What attention has been given to the problem of assuring the quality of services and help being provided?

What mechanisms can be established to check on quality eg could consumer and user views be fed back in some way?

Can the effects of shortfalls/cutbacks in provision on the quality of service be demonstrated in some way?

Could the service be made more accountable to the poor and their views?

Final checklist

What is the evaluation for?

Who is it for?

Who will carry it out?

How will it be carried out?

What difference will it make to poor clients?

4

Real Losses and Unreal Figures:
The Impact of the 1986 Social Security Act
Mark Svenson and Stewart MacPherson

P OVERTY has always been at the heart of social work and social services. From the beginning of organised services, the problems of financial poverty have cast a grim shadow over the lives of the vast majority of those seeking help from social workers. This chapter has a straightforward and narrow purpose; to document the recent trends in financial poverty and to indicate the specific impact of the current social security changes on particular groups of claimants. The data presented here have been produced using methods developed in a major programme of work to establish the impact of the 1986 Social Security Act in a number of local authority areas.

The poor

In recent years the financial position of the poorest has worsened; there are many more poor people now than ten years ago and when the Act comes into force in April 1988 poverty will be harsher still for very many.

In 1983, 16.4 m people lived at income levels less than 140 per cent of supplementary benefit rates. Over one in four people in Great Britain suffered severe financial hardship. As later tables show the number of people living at these low income levels has continued to increase since

1983.

The government has argued that 40 per cent of the increase in poverty is due to the raising of supplementary benefit levels over this period, so that people not previously counted are now included. But this, as Piachaud points out, does not explain the remaining 60 per cent of the increase [1987a, 24].

Table 4.1
Increase in poverty 1979 – 1983

	No.	1979 % of pop	No.	1983 % of pop	pop increase
Below SB	2.1 million	4	2.8m	5	33%
On SB	4.0 million	8	6.1m	12	52%
On or below SB	6.1 million	12	8.9m	17	47%
On, below or up to 140% above SB	11.6 million	22	16.4	31	42%

Source: DHSS, (1986 c).

Notes: 1 These figures represent all those in 'assesment units' receiving Supplementary Benefits *at some point* in the relevant year. Figures for the number of people claiming, or dependent on, SB are more usually given in terms of the number at *a particular date* in a year. The latter method is essentially a 'snapshot' and as such seriously understates the significance of SB for the population affected by this part of the social security system. The method adopted in this table is a somewhat better indication of the 'flow' of claimants.

2. The bases on which Table 4.1 and Table 4.3 are derived are different and so are not directly comparable.

Setting a poverty line at 140 per cent of supplementary benefit levels incorporates the notions that historically these levels have proved to be inadequate, and that poverty must have a relative aspect. The government's argument suggests it prefers the use of an absolute poverty level, not directly linked to supplementary benefit rates, so that increases in supplementary benefit reduce the number of those in poverty. The linking of supplementary benefit rates with the Retail Price Index rather than the incomes of those in work is further evidence of reluctance to accept the validity of the relative conception of poverty. The effect of this approach in widening the inequalities of income is seen clearly in Table 4.2 which compares benefit rates and earnings.

Table 4.2

Supplementary benefit scale rates
as a percentage of earnings (i)

Uprating date	Single non-householder	Single householder	Couple
November 1982	24.3	30.4	46.5
November 1983	23.6	29.5	45.0
November 1984	22.7	28.4	43.1
November 1985	22.3	27.9	42.4
July 1986 (ii)	21.2	26.5	40.3

Source: House of Commons Parliamentary Debates, [*Hansard* (1987 Vol. 119 No. 17 Col. 460 Written answers]

Notes i)Net average earnings of all males (gross average earnings less tax and national insurance contributions at the non-contracted out rate)

ii) Benefit rates uprated in July 1986

The rise in the number of claimants

Major changes within the social security system are taking place. Whatever view is taken as to what is an adequate level of income, people now dependent upon supplementary benefit will be the first to feel the full impact of these changes.

Table 4.3 shows the huge increase in the numbers reliant on supplementary benefit between November 1979 and February 1986. This period saw a 2 million increase in the number of claimants and a 4 million increase in the total of people dependent upon supplementary benefit. Each claim supports approximately 1.6 people.

The 1981 census of Great Britain gave the population as 54.3 m. The latest available estimates suggest a 0.9 per cent increase in the population of England and Wales from mid-1981 to mid-1986 [OPCS Monitor PP1 87/1

p. iii]. On the assumption of a similar trend in Scotland it appears that the GB population is presently very close to stable. The increased number of supplementary benefit claimants and dependants therefore represents a very much larger proportion of a stable population rather than a constant proportion of a growing population. The February 1986 total of over 8 m people dependent on supplementary benefit represents more than one in seven of the population. If this figure were not stark enough it must be remembered that the supplementary benefit population is not static. The data in Table 4.3 are derived from a sample survey conducted on a particular day and is thus a 'snapshot' which cannot reflect the movement of people into and out of the SB system; very many more people will live on supplementary benefit incomes at some point in the year.

Table 4.3
Dependency on Supplementary Benefit

	No. of SB claimants	Thousands No. dependent on SB[i]
November 1979	2855	4370
December 1980	3118	4863
December 1981	3723	6121
December 1982	4267	7068
December 1983	4349	7238
December 1984	4609	7729
December 1986	4937	8291

Note: [i] claimants and 'dependants'.
Source: DHSS, [1980 d];DHHS, [1981 b]; DHSS, [1982]; DHSS, [1984 b]; DHSS, [1985 g]; DHSS, [1987 e].

Has this huge increase in the numbers on supplementary benefit been consistent over the various claimant groups, or have certain groups been more adversely affected than others?

Table 4.4 gives details by claimant group, and shows that the number of supplementary pensioners has remained comparatively stable with an overall increase of only 4 per cent between 1983 and 1986. The main increase has been in the number of single pensioners, notably those '80 and over'. This reflects the ageing of the population; although supplementary pensioners '80 and over' form a small proportion of all supplementary pensioners [26.9 per cent in 1983, 29.0 per cent in 1986] the proportion will increase further in coming years.

The increase in the number of single parents over this period has been marked. Over 100,000 more female single parents were on supplementary benefit in February 1986 than in December 1983. There was an increase of 28 per cent in the number of single parents in little over 2 years. While it is difficult to get an an accurate estimate of the number of single parents in the population as a whole it is clear that at least half of all female single parents are on supplementary benefit and that this proportion is rising [see Slipman, this volume]

The number of unemployed claimants has risen overall by 16 per cent. The greatest increases have been in single men 25 and over [a 39 per cent increase] and single women 25 and over [a 35 per cent increase]. This same period has seen an extra 80,000 claimant couples of whom 50,000 have children.

The Social Security Act 1986

The Fowler review and the 1986 Act made a number of claims as to how the new legislation would help those in the greatest need and how extra resources would be directed to those with children. The Technical Annexe accompanying the White Paper detailed the likely financial consequences of the changes, based upon a series of illustrative benefit rates [DHSS, 1985d]. In October 1987 the government announced the rates to operate from April 1988 for the new system of income related benefits. Accompanying the new rates the government presented revised tables giving their estimates of the gainers and losers as a result of the social security reform.

The remainder of this chapter is concerned with the effects on claimants of supplementary benefit, who, under the new scheme, will receive income support. It shows how their future benefit position will be a great deal worse than the government intends us to believe.

The Act is not fully implemented until April 1988, but changes have *already* been introduced which adversely affect claimants. Worsening the position of claimants prior to the 'changeover date' means that the reforms, when presented, appear to be more beneficial than they are.

The vast majority of *additional* requirements [extra weekly payments for special needs] are for heating. Apart from a 10 pence rise in the higher rate heating addition these payments have been frozen since November 1985. This means the *real* value of heating additions has been shrinking throughout this period. If their value had been maintained the position for many claimants would be worsened at the point of changeover. Many of those *seeming* to gain in April 1988 would gain less [or lose]; those appearing to be subject to no change would lose, and those losing would lose more.

Table 4.4
Supplementary benefit recipients by claimant group

Thousands

	Population Totals	Dec 1983	Dec 1984	Feb 1986
			On supplementary benefit	
Pensioners [i]	[9167]	1651	1683	1717
Single women ‹80		861	859	878
Single women 80+		357	381	401
Single men ‹80		119	129	129
Single men 80+		46	52	52
Couples ‹80		227	220	212
Couples 80+		41	42	45
Single parents [ii]	[1000]	449	492	575
Men		17	21	22
Women		432	472	553
Unemployed[iii]	[3235]	1826	1953	2121
Single men ‹25		456	470	479
Single men 25+		350	395	487
Single women ‹25		275	277	282
Single women 25+		136	156	184
Couples with children		453	484	504
Childless couples		155	172	185
Total		3927	4128	4413

Source: DHSS, 1984d, 1986d, 1987e.

Notes: [i] Pensioner population in mid-1986 from *Population Trends 48*, Table 7 p.62, HMSO, 1987.

[ii] Estimated given by One Parent Family organisation of number of lone parent families in 1987 [personal communication].

[iii] Department of Employment count; unadjusted Unemployment total in April 1986, [*Unemployment Unit Briefing*, 1986, Statistical Supplement: June 1986, London, Trojan Press].

A further example of this 'attrition effect' is the cut in mortgage interest assistance to owner-occupying claimants. This change introduced in January 1987 meant that anyone becoming unemployed after that date only had half the interest on their mortgage paid for the first four months on supplementary benefit. The change produced a saving of £23 million [*Guardian*, 1987a] but obviously resulted in increased hardship for many claimants.

The reduction in *single payments* [lump sum grants for exceptional needs] provides the best example of these pre-April 1988 cuts. Prior to August 1986, annual expenditure on single payments had risen to over £300 million a year and was likely to rise to over £400 million. The changes implemented in August 1986 reduced expenditure considerably and enabled this comment when the benefit rates for the reformed social security system were introduced:

> The gross amount of £203 million for the Social Fund looks reasonable alongside the reality of the expected level of expenditure on single payments this year, which is running at around £190 million. John Moore, Secretary of State, House of Commons, [*Hansard*, 1987, Vol.121 No.30 Col. 190]

Put this way the social fund provision appears generous. But even if the £200 million was for grants it would in fact constitute a severe cutback in comparison to single payments expenditure before the effects of the Act. As it is, 70 per cent of this £200 million fund will be in the form of *recoverable loans*.

Each of these changes has resulted in a saving to the government on present expenditure within the supplementary benefit system. A further saving has been established for the new system prior to its introduction, which establishes an even more subtle and devious employment of these 'shifting the goalposts' tactics. The 'illustrative' *personal allowances* figures in the Technical Annexe to the White Paper did not include any compensation for claimants having to find the 20 per cent of their rates bill the proposals required them to pay. Under pressure the government conceded that the actual personal allowance levels for the new system would include compensation for this additional outgoing. When announcing the actual new rates it was claimed that the illustrative personal allowance levels had been 'fully uprated' in line with the movement in the Rossi index [Retail Price minus housing costs index] and compensation for the 20 per cent rates contribution had been included. It then became clear that this was not the case. Either the allowances had been uprated and the

£1 or £1.30 allowance for rates not been fully included *or* the full rates
allowance had been added in *without* personal allowances being fully
inflation proofed. The government failed to acknowledge that the setting of
the personal allowance levels constituted a further cut.

Gainers and losers: two views

Tables 4.5, 4.6, 4.7 and 4.8 show the marked differences between DHSS
estimates and our own. Tables 4.5 and 4.7 show the figures from the DHSS
of gainers and losers from the reform; no explanation has been offered by
the DHSS of the exact basis on which these figures are reached. We do
know however that no attempt was made to include loss of single payments
in the DHSS estimates of gain and loss. For that reason alone those
estimates present a false picture of the effects on the resources of
supplementary benefit claimants.

Table 4.5

People on income support – **DHSS estimates** of changes in
disposable income after meeting housing costs [i]

	Gainers	Thousands No Change	Losers
Pensioners			
Singles	470	450	530
Couples	100	40	180
Non-pensioners with children			
Lone parents	330	80	200
Couples	450	20	70
Non-pensioners without children			
Single age 25+	360	110	380
Single under 25	450	200	160
Couples	20	10	150
Total	2190	920	1660

Source: DHSS, [1987d, Table 2b]
Note: [i] 'Effect of Structural Reform':

The omission of single payment loss is especially significant for lone parents
and couples with children. Our calculations suggest that these two groups
had the greatest reliance upon single payments and will consequently suffer
the greatest losses as a result of their removal.

Table 4.6

People on income support – **Benefits Research Unit** estimates of changes in disposable income by family status

[Effect of Structural reform]

	Gainers	Thousands No Change	Losers
Pensioners			
Singles	397	402	557
Couples	20	9	224
Non-pensioners with children			
Lone parents	137	3	402
Couples	4	94	407
Non-pensioners without children			
Single age 25+	190	–	416
Single under 25	–	428	282
Couples	–	1	184
Total	1008	1006	2125

Source: Benefits Research Unit

Note: Changes in the housing benefit system have not been accounted for in this table. The changes are likely to worsen the benefit position of many claimants, especially pensioners.

Our analysis of the impact of the Social Security Act provides markedly different conclusions from those of the DHSS. Tables 4.6 and 4.8 give a summary of this analysis and are based upon a detailed examination of the current benefit levels of each claimant group. This involved determining for each group how many claimants were householders, how many were non-householders, how many were on short-term or long-term rate supplementary benefit and how many received additional requirements. For those receiving additional requirements we constructed a range of levels of additional requirements. In order to make a fair comparison we uprated the 1987 supplementary benefit scale rate by 3.2 per cent (the September 1987 inflation rate as measured on the Rossi index) to find what the supplementary benefit rates *would have been* in April 1988, if the social security system had not been changed. The levels of additional requirements were not uprated.

Our intention here is to compare the position of supplementary benefit claimants in April 1986 with the position facing income support claimants in April 1988. We decided upon this because, as we saw earlier, many changes have been introduced *prior* to the full implementation of the 1986 Act in April 1988. There will be 'transitional protection,' for existing claimants after April 1988, but this will gradually 'wither away' for all claimants. We are concerned here with real loss of entitlement when comparing one scheme with another.

This intention is most clearly seen in our treatment of single payments, where the weekly loss for each claimant group is based upon the level of expenditure existing in April 1986. Having established the single payment expenditure for each claimant group this was then expressed as a weekly loss for *every* claimant in the group. As is the case with any average this presentation overstates the loss for some claimants while understating it for others. The average, however, is based upon the *real* level of expenditure so it does reflect the amount of money leaving the system.

The introduction of the Social Fund in place of single payments means that legal rules are abandoned in favour of individualised discretion in response to needs not covered by basic rates and premiums. This change means that all claimants suffer a loss of entitlement to single payments *whether they were receiving such payments or not*. We note this loss of entitlement but have not given it a monetary value in our calculations of losses. Similarly we note the changes in the system of mortgage interest assistance but have not built into our model the loss of £23 million these changes entailed. The loss of assistance with the payment of water rates *has* been included where appropriate. The loss for those receiving assistance is based upon the average amount of assistance for each particular group in February 1986.

These are the principal issues in the methods and assumptions employed in our analysis. We have at all times erred on the side of caution in order to present what we believe is the *minimum* impact of the Act on supplementary benefit claimants.

The DHSS estimate that only 35 per cent of claimants will lose (Table 4.7). We estimate that nearly 60 per cent of claimants will lose as a result of the social security changes. Slightly under a quarter of claimants will be no better off and less than one in five claimants will gain (Table 4.8). For those losing weekly loss may be in some instances as high as £12. Gains for some may be up to £9. But one person's gain does not offset or soften another's loss.

One of the declared intentions of the reforms was to provide extra help to

Table 4.7
DHSS estimates

Gainers and Losers [by Claimant Group]

Family Status		Gainers	No Change	Losers	Effect of structural reform Base= [100%]
Pensioners					000s
singles	%	32	31	37	1450
couples	%	31	13	56	320
Non-pensioners with children					
lone parents	%	54	13	33	610
couples	%	83	4	13	540
Non-pensioners without children					
single age 25+	%	42	13	45	750
single under 25	%	56	25	20	710
couples	%	11	6	83	180
Total	%	46	19	35	4770

Note: based on Table 5
Source: DHSS [1987d, Table 2b]

families with children via the family premium. Observers have expressed concern that if this premium was not set sufficiently high it would be largely ineffective. Berthoud (1986) suggested that the premium should be a minimum of £6.60 (at a time when the illustrative figure was £5.75) before it could be claimed that the new scheme would help families with children. We estimate that 80 per cent of couples with children and 67 per cent of lone parents will lose as a result of the reformed structure. These figures confirm the view that the family premium is set too low to improve the benefit position of families with children. When one considers that the changes have been implemented as a nil-cost reform it is hardly surprising that the premiums levels are low.

Two groups particularly badly hit by the reforms are unemployed single people under 25 and unemployed childless couples. Almost without exception childless couples will lose from the changes. We estimate that almost 40 per cent of this group will lose approximately £5 per week, 25 per cent will lose £7, and slightly under 20 per cent will lose £3. In the under 25 group non-householders aged between 18-24 will be largely unaffected by the reforms; 60 per cent of unemployed single people under 25 are non-householders. The remaining 40 per cent is comprised of 16-17 year old non-householders and 18-24 year old householders, all these will lose in excess of £5 per week. The position of 16-17 year olds is especially precarious. The government intends to provide training places for all 16-17 year olds. Refusal to take part in such schemes will result in disqualification from benefit. In the absence of training places benefit will be payable but at a much lower level than under supplementary benefit.

Table 4.8
Benefits Research Unit estimates
Gainers and Losers [by Claimant Group]

Family Status		Gainers	No Change	Losers	Base=[100%]
Pensioners					000s
Singles	%	27	30	43	1356
Couples	%	8	4	89	253
Non-pensioners with children					
Lone parents	%	25	1	74	541
Couples	%	1	19	81	504
Non-pensioners without children					
Single age 25+	%	31	–	69	607
Single under 25	%		60	40	710
Couples	%	–	1	99	185
Total	%	17	23	60	4155

Source: Benefits Research Unit
Note: based on Table 6

The pensioners who stand to lose most from the reforms are those with high levels of additional requirements at present, that is the neediest. It seems anomalous that those claimants whose needs have been defined as the least severe under the supplementary benefit system will gain the most. This ignores any questions of non-take-up and needs not being fully met under the present system. The position of pensioners as shown in Table 6 will be ameliorated for those claimants who successfully claim the disability premium. It is impossible to predict what proportion of pensioners will be successful, but the proportion is unlikely to be large.

Overview

The official case – that the Social Security Act benefits more people than it makes worse off – cannot be supported from the evidence. The basis upon which government figures are produced is deficient, in a number of ways.

The tables produced by the DHSS do not include the loss of single payments and therefore cannot reflect the full extent of the changes. The proposed Social Fund payments are in the form of *loans* and cannot negate the loss of single payments *grants*, even if the level of financial provision *seems* comparable. Many changes have already been implemented; this masks the *real* levels of loss. The amounts of payment for many additional requirements have been frozen and single payment expenditure has been halved. Personal allowances under the Income Support scheme will include an element towards payment of 20 per cent of domestic rates bills. But the allowances, have not been fully uprated so the claimed level of assistance will not in fact be provided. The Act increases poverty; to argue otherwise is either to 'economise with the truth,' or to fail to comprehend the arithmetic. The latter is very unlikely.

PART TWO

Money Matters

5

Section One Expenditure; Insider Views

Jaqi Nixon

Section 1 (1) of the Child Care Act 1980 provides:

It shall be the duty of every local authority to make available such advice, guidance and assistance as may promote the welfare of the children by diminishing the need to receive children into or keep them in care under this Act or to bring children before a juvenile court; and any provision made by a local authority under this subsection may, if the local authority think fit, include provisions for giving assistance in kind, or, in exceptional circumstances, in cash.

Para. 18 of the White Paper, The Law on Child Care and Family Services, January 1987 proposes:

To give local authorities a broad 'umbrella' power to provide services to promote the care and upbringing of children, and to help prevent the breakdown of family relationships which might eventually lead to a court order committing the child to the local authority's care. Within this power . . . The local authority will also be able to offer financial assistance in exceptional circumstances.

NEITHER professional nor academic interest in Section One payments is new. [See, for example, Lister and Emmet, 1976; Rees, 1978; Valencia and Jackson, 1979; Hill and Laing, 1979; Stewart and Stewart, 1986; Becker and Macpherson, 1986]. The proportion of a Social Services Department's total expenditure on Section One is actually very small. In the social services department [SSD] featured in this chapter, for example, Section One expenditure accounts for only about 2.4 per cent of the total departmental budget and about 26 per cent of its preventative budget for child care. And yet Section One payments have attracted the attention of social services commentators for over ten years. A number of conventional reasons for this interest may be noted. First, it permits social workers to pay cash to clients and thereby raises fundamental questions about boundaries of responsibility for income maintenance and about relationships between SSD and DHSS social security staff. Secondly, the payment of cash to clients renders Section One an area of discretion and, as such, expenditure has tended to be demand led. Thirdly, it has given rise to professional concerns about whether the payment of grants and loans adversely affects social workers' relationships with their clients.

Further reasons for continuing interest in Section One payments are now apparent. First, reported increases in Section One payments to individual families suggest increasing financial hardship for low income social services clients with children. The ADSS, for example, has stated that an increase in Section One expenditure is largely the result of greater financial pressures on families [1985]. Secondly, recent changes in Supplementary Benefit single payments, together with the proposed introduction of the Social Fund in April 1988, are likely to have implications for Section One payments. Much of the well documented opposition of social services personnel to the Social Fund claims that this will indeed be the case with SSD budgets being put under even greater strain than they are at present. Thirdly, the reintroduction of more discretion in the administration of the Social Fund has led to renewed and, now, very politically charged debates about relationships between SSDs and the DHSS and the most appropriate locus of responsibility for meeting the special financial needs of low income families: the local authority or central government. More specifically, the payment of community care grants from the Social Fund, which is to include payment to 'families under stress' [DHSS, 1987c], will require the collaboration of SSD field staff and DHSS local office staff if families most in need of this additional financial support are to be identified.

In view of these additional factors which are likely to affect Section One expenditure, it would seem to be important to have regard to current trends in Section One before the introduction of the Social Fund. In this way a more accurate assessment of the impact of the Social Fund may emerge. It would also seem necessary to examine the views and perspectives of professional social services staff, especially as these help to shape both current policy and practice concerning Section One expenditure, and, hence, are likely to affect future responses to the interrelated cash and care problems of families on low incomes.

This chapter attempts to throw some light on these issues. While the main focus of the discussion is Section One expenditure, a number of points relate to aspects of the Social Fund which are commented on in more detail elsewhere. The material is based on quantitative and qualitative data obtained from one local authority SSD. The analysis of the quantitative data should, therefore, be treated with caution and the commentary and conclusions should be regarded as tentative. With these necessary caveats in mind, it is hoped that the following discussion will provoke further debate on the overlapping cash and care needs of 'families under stress' concerning which 'there is serious doubt whether a clear-cut policy can be identified; it is a minefield which should be entered with great caution' [Berthoud, 1987].

Analysis of Section One computerised data

The data presented here are confined to two urban based area teams within an otherwise rural locality. Together, the two areas comprise eleven patch teams which serve more readily identifiable local communities. The data are limited to the extent that methods of classifying Section One payments tend to vary depending on how much care is taken by fieldworkers and administrative staff in completing the necessary forms. It should be noted, too, that a variety of factors may influence the number of claims and the decisions taken concerning Section One payments. These may not be directly associated with either DHSS social security or SSD policy and practice. One obvious factor is the client profile of each patch team. Another may be the level of unemployment which will vary between areas. As regards the possible impact of the 'patch' organisation itself on Section One expenditure, some staff who had moved further away from the central DHSS office argued that dissatisfied supplementary benefit claimants could no longer 'take advantage' of the proximity of a SSD office to request further help. In contrast, others argued that a patch system encourages Section One payments, because staff are more sympathetic to clients who do not have such easy access to the the DHSS office – especially critical when giros are lost or when payments are delayed.

Table 5.1
Section One Expenditure March 1986 – February 1987

Team	Total S1 Expenditure £	Number of Families Receiving S1	Average Payment to Family £	Project Expenditure as % of Total S1
1	473	8	58	2
2	382	13	29	0
3	2025	26	78	0
4	2334	25	44	53
5	3313	27	98	20
6	3728	42	38	38
7	5726	44	37	37
8	6120	42	45	69
9	8765	17	50	90
10	9198	66	107	23
11	32138	80	73	82

Table 5.1 shows the extent to which both amounts and number of Section One payments varies very considerably between patch teams. Team 1, for example, is at one extreme, with a total annual expenditure of £473 which provided assistance to only eight families. This compares with Team 11 which serves an area with a high proportion of families likely to be in need of assistance and had a total annual Section One expenditure of £32138. Even when comparisons are made between teams serving similar communities, Teams 4 and 10, for example, considerable differences are discernible in respect of both numbers of payments made and amounts awarded. One further important difference to be noted is the proportion of the total budget spent on preventative projects or services, eg family support groups, rather than on payments to individual families. Team 10, for instance, spent a similar overall amount as Team 9 and yet devoted only 23 per cent, as compared to Team 9's 90 per cent, of its total annual budget on projects.

The proportion of expenditure devoted to projects rather than to families appears to be directly related to neither a high nor a low total annual Section One budget. Team 4, for example, with a very modest total expenditure, spent over one half of it budget on preventative projects. Team 3, with a similar total expenditure, spent nothing. Team 11, with the highest overall expenditure, used 82 per cent of its budget for projects, whereas Team 10, with the next largest total budget, spent only 23 per cent for this purpose. Similarly, both high and low spending teams had, in some cases, made similar average payments to individual families. Since no clear pattern emerges in respect of Section One expenditure, it would seem, therefore, that considerable discretion had been used by teams in allocating Section One money and in determining what level of payments should be made. However, staff members themselves argued that the situation was otherwise [see below].

In view of the concern expressed about the possible implications of the Social Fund for local authority expenditure [see Stewart and Stewart, this volume], it is important to note certain changes in respect of Section One expenditure, at least in this particular SSD, during a twelve month period which *predates* the introduction of the Social Fund.

Table 5.2

Changes in S1 Expenditure (Monthly) May 1986 – May 1987

Patch Teams	Total S1 Expenditure	% on indiv payments	Total S1 Expenditure	% on indiv payments
1	10	100	10	100
2	77	100	74	100
3	307	100	173	100
4	657	70	85	100
5	1356	78	153	100
6	215	12	70	100
7	884	49	605	9
8	580	37	166	100
9	841	16	1102	0
10	1131	95	1197	77
11	2393	27	4302	22

The most noteworthy point to emerge from Table 5.2 is a very dramatic reduction in some teams in the monthly Section One expenditure. Figures for Section One spending between May 1986 and May 1987 [not shown] suggest that this downward spiral for Teams 3 to 8 is part of a trend and that the May 1987 figures are not simply an aberration. It seems highly unlikely that there would have been a corresponding drop in client need for Section One payments during the same period, to account for the reduction [indeed all available evidence suggests the contrary]. We may assume, therefore, that some team managers, either in concert or individually, have deliberately decided to reduce Section One spending. Factors which may have influenced such a decision are examined below.

A second point worth noting in Table 5.2 is that in teams where Section One total expenditure actually increased in May 1987, a smaller proportion was now spent on individual payments to families. At the very least, therefore, any future assessment of the impact of the Social Fund on Section One will have to take account of changes which took place prior to, and independently of, the implementation of the Fund. It could be argued that, in some localities, social services teams have already developed effective strategies for ensuring that Section One expenditure will not be available to help more families under stress, even after the Fund has been introduced. Either they have reduced total Section One spending to a minimum, or they have transferred most of the Section One budget to preventative projects.

The data so far presented suggest that developments are under way within this particular SSD which affect Section One expenditure and which are independent of changes in social security policy. However, it is also necessary to examine those aspects of Section One spending which account for a good deal of the controversy concerning overlapping responsibilities between the DHSS and SSDs. As the Stewarts make clear in this volume, Supplementary Benefits should not be paid to meet needs which another statutory authority is responsible for, and yet it is recognised that, on occasion, Supplementary Benefit has to be used to do just that. Similarly, while local authorities may not accept that they should have to shore up an inadequate and inefficient basic income support system, nevertheless they do. Unlike other studies on the subject, this inquiry did not reveal overwhelming evidence that a large proportion of Section One payments were made because of administrative inefficiency on the part of DHSS. It did show, however, that too many payments were being made to cover basic needs.

The first issue to be raised in respect of Table 5.3 is that it highlights the familiar problem of inadequately recorded data on Section One payments. This makes it difficult to provide any reliable quantitative assessment of what Section One payments are actually used for. Table 5.3 does show, however, that, at *a minimum*, [the 'other' and 'not stated' categories are likely to include payments for similar items], about a quarter of payments during the year were for items such as food, fuel, and clothing which are supposed to be covered by either the basic weekly benefit or an additional single payment [or, from April 1988, by a Social Fund Loan]. Thus, the level of basic benefit to be paid under the new Income Support system,

Table 5.3
Payments to families
March 1986 — February 1987
Total no. of payments [1] 572

Item	%[2]
Food/subsistence	15
Fuel/meter	2
Baby items/clothes	2
Clothing/shoes	4
Household item/	3
Rent/temp.accom.including B & B	5
Fares/petrol	10
Childminding	16
DHSS payment not made	1
Other/where more than one item included	15
Not stated	26[3]

[1] These are actual payments. The number of weeks for which one payments was intended to cover, varied.

[2] Total does not equal 100 per cent due to rounding.

[3] There was partial evidence to suggest that a number of these payments were made for childminding.

together with the amount payable as a family premium, could crucially affect the number of Section One payments made for these items. And, as Berthoud [1987] has argued, 'it would be better if most of the money now spent on making up claimants' basic needs were transferred into a significant increase in the regular income of families with children'. [p14]. As it is, high priority needs such as clothing and shoes for families with children are excluded from the 'complex list of priority needs' outlined in the DHSS guidelines on the Social Fund. Yet such needs are manifestly the responsibility of the income maintenance system.

In contrast, the payment of fares or other travel costs is, under certain circumstances, the responsibility of both the DHSS and the SSD. Indeed, it could be argued that, since meeting the cost of fares is an essential part of social work support for some families under stress, this should be borne by the SSD. Alternatively, had it been possible to isolate discussion of the Social Fund from its political context, there might have been scope here for fruitful collaboration between both DHSS and local authorities, with the Social Fund providing a discretionary grant and the SSD identifying families in need of such assistance.

A final point to note in respect of Table 5.3 is the sizeable proportion of Section One payments made to meet childminding costs [paid directly to the childminders] of individual families. This use of Section One funds may be contrasted with the alternative approach noted above, namely paying for preventative projects within the community from which a number of parents and their children may benefit.

Staff perceptions of policy on Section One

The following information on staff views was obtained from group discussions with both team managers responsible for teams in the two areas and field staff from three patch teams. These discussions were held during mid-1986, before details of the Social Fund had become available and before the White Paper on child care law and family services had been published [DHSS, 1987a].

A number of team managers and their field staff identified their own departmental policy as one which was guided by the general principle that Section One should not become a substitute for income maintenance. There were others, however, who felt that there was no one coherent policy, but rather a number of policies from which both team managers and field workers could choose, depending upon their own professional preferences. This diversity was attributed, in part, to the administration of the Section One budget by the finance section of the department, whose response to requests for payment and whose coding of payments varied, some argued, from one day to the next. It was also the case, as the data in Table 5.3 indicate, that social workers themselves were able to use Section One to meet a variety of individual client needs, including basic needs, but also for family outings, respite care, holidays and the purchase of childrens' sportswear.

Among the wide range of views expressed on Section One, there was at least a common view in respect of income maintenance. Predictably, team managers and field staff were at one in castigating the DHSS either for not providing an adequate basic income for families in need, or for failing to pay entitled benefit on time. Informants agreed that, in principle, Section One money should not be used to remedy the deficiencies and gaps created by the social security system.

There was also general support for the development of preventative strategies and projects to relieve family stress. Opinion was divided, however, as to whether such a development represented proper use of Section One money. A number of staff, primarily at field level, felt that projects should be financed from a separate budget, as is the case in some local authorities. Others – mainly team managers – wanted to see Section One itself renamed in order to reflect more appropriately a broader approach to family support.

Views about whether social workers should make direct payments to families differed widely. At one end of a spectrum of opinion, some team managers wanted a continuing reduction in one-off payments to families, arguing that these were not cost-effective. At the other end, some staff expressed concern about the trend away from individual payments. They contrasted the relative ease with which Section One funds could be secured for projects with the considerable difficulties encountered in trying to obtain larger amounts of money to support individual families in the context of a longer term planning strategy. [Requests for individual payments in excess of £400 have to be submitted to the social services committee].

In summary, although there was a consensus concerning the need to use Section One powers in a 'more imaginative approach to preventative work in general', [DHSS 1985e], there was a divergence of opinion as to how this should be interpreted. Some staff maintained that the imaginative approach should still be addressed to the needs of individual families, for example the payment to childminding costs or provision of a family aide; others argued that it meant giving priority to preventative projects. The Government White Paper could be seen as supporting both approaches:

'The local authority will be able to provide services to a child at home. . . at a day centre. . . or residential facilities' [DHSS, 1987a, 4-5]. Nowhere is it suggested that Government expects to see a diminution in financial assistance to families.

Area and patch team practice concerning Section One

Team managers' perception of departmental policy and their own views about appropriate use of the Section One budget will, in turn, influence patch team policy. But the extent to which their general directives are upheld or undermined depends not only on principles, but also on practices and procedures adopted at each level of the department.

Each area management team [consisting of all patch team managers within the area] received a fixed budget for Section One, based largely on past expenditure. Similarly, the area management teams' decisions concerning distribution of the budget to individual patch teams were influenced as much by past trends and experiences as by current or future demands. A more rational approach, as one area management team was prepared to concede, would be to include an assessment of each patch team's past Section One spending, plus estimates of preventative projects and some assessment of possible future individual demands. There was disagreement among team managers as to whether such an approach should also include a notional amount for each team to hold in reserve. As it was, some team managers were putting in a bid for a small amount to cover contingencies, others were not. Moreover, at the time these discussions were held, no use was being made of the patch client data base, eg number of families with children 'at risk', in order to provide, albeit a limited, indicator of possible future demand.

To date, both area management teams included in this study have been able to balance their Section One budgets, compensating for overspending in some teams by underspending on others. Team managers have been prepared to co-operate in this process of adjustment, and thus had helped to ensure some flexibility in Section One expenditure. However, given the greater demands likely to be made upon this budget, whether for projects or for individual payments, managers will want, in future, to be satisfied that overspending by any team is 'justifiable'. Insofar as this question of legitimate Section One expenditure had been addressed at all by team managers, it would seem to require the following:

1. evidence of attempts to contain expenditure within the set budget
2. evidence to show an overall reduction in direct payments to families
3. checking that expenditure could not have been made from another budget head

From the May 1987 data presented in Table 5.2, there would appear to be some evidence that concern about justifiable expenditure has now taken a hold within the department. However, the possible adverse consequences of this are underspending on the budget and greater standardisation in the use of Section One. These outcomes would seem to be contrary to team managers' own views about the need for imaginative approaches as well as greater discretion for themselves in how they spend Section One money.

Grants versus loans

The issue of whether grants are to be preferred to loans has been hotly debated in respect of the Social Fund. Rather less attention has been given to the matter in respect of Section One payments to individual families. [An important exception is Hill and Laing (1979, 34-38)]. While the practice of giving loans appeared to be common in the department studied here, views at both manager and field worker levels were divided as to the efficacy of Section One loans. In the context of casework, some social workers argued that awarding a loan damages relationships with clients who, knowing they cannot pay it back, would be fearful of making further contact. Others thought a loan was regarded by clients as more of a 'right' and, therefore, was less of a stigma than receiving a grant. [Is it possible that recipients of a Social Fund loan could hold such a view?] The idea that loans could be used as a means of controlling or rationing Section One payments gained some support, especially in cases where it was felt that a client may try to take advantage of the system. Both managers and field staff had to acknowledge, however, that most loans were written off. This does raise the question of whether loans are really worthwhile, even from a casework perspective. From an administrative point of view there would seem even less to commend them since two transactions, not just one, are involved – both the payment and the receipt of cash. Team managers were especially conscious of the additional burden which loans create for the administration and so thought that steps taken to discourage the use of loans might be worth considering. Somewhat incongruously, fieldworkers believed that they *should* be awarding loans, rather than paying grants, because these were easier to justify to their team managers!

Cash versus services in kind

This is another time-honoured theme for debate in social policy generally, though rarely has it been discussed in relation to Section One expenditure. Staff views and preferences will depend, in part, upon what alternatives to cash are actually made available. Already, we have noted the predilection of most team managers for projects rather than for payments to individual families. But even where the Section One budget was used for cash payments to families, other 'in kind' provision was also made. Five of the eleven patch teams included in the study made use of a food cupboard and three had some form of voucher scheme for the purchase of basic items.

The food cupboard was regarded as especially useful where access to shops was difficult and in cases where staff had to ensure that the immediate needs of the children were given priority over, say, a parent's need for tobacco or alcohol. Some staff supported the use of a cupboard because they felt it helped to dispel the notion that the SSD would always make good any DHSS shortfall. [Will more social services teams install food cupboards before the Social Fund is introduced?] Other team members, more certain that the food would go to the children, acknowledged that it helped to reduce their own anxieties about judging whether or not a family deserved material support. Where teams had not had recourse to a food cupboard, however, the prevailing view was that it would only help to perpetuate the stigma associated with the poor law treatment of needy families.

The use of vouchers was more widely supported, particularly in areas where access to the shops was not a problem. It was acknowledged, however, that all client needs could be met by these means. One team manager explained that some clients justifiably argued 'you can't put a tin of soup into the electricity meter'. Thus, neither food cupboard nor voucher removes altogether the need for social workers to make cash payments to some clients 'in exceptional circumstances'. The dilemma remains.

Does Section One meet its objective?

It was clear that most staff still thought of Section One largely in terms of a direct payment to families to remove the need to receive a child into local authority care. Following on from this, the majority acknowledged that most Section One payments had nothing to do with this likely occurrence. Non-payment of Section One would very rarely have led to a child being taken into care. Some staff even argued that Section One actually encouraged parents to put their children at risk in order to qualify for assistance.

What seems to be preferred, then, is a broader interpretation of the purpose of Section One, one which enables help to be given to reduce family pressures and thereby to maintain certain standards of family care in the longer term. This is to be contrasted with the current crisis-orientated approach which aims to prevent children going into local authority care. By removing the obligation for local authorities to diminish the need to receive children into care and by stressing, instead, the need for positive measures to reduce the risk of long term family breakdown, the White Paper [DHSS, 1987a] is clearly providing support for the grassroots view. More traditional opinions about the use of Section One were also expressed. For example, it was seen by some as providing one tool in a social worker's kit with which to negotiate terms with a client. [Indeed, it should be evident from what has been said about food cupboards that the wish to control the client can be achieved just as well by payment in kind as by payment in cash. And, as Hill and Laing argue in their response to Jordan, effective control of the social worker/client relationship may be achieved in a variety of ways –

handing out money being only one of these]. Some field staff were also prepared to accept that, whatever they may wish to the contrary, Section One did provide the safety net beneath Supplementary Benefit. It was *the* bottom line and, as such, it was appropriate for staff to use it to respond to individual financial need.

Whatever the perceived aim of Section One, it is important that the type of payment made is the most appropriate to meet the desired end. As the DHSS points out in its *Review of Child Care Law*, for example, it is possible to distinguish between a family which is exceptional, as compared to other families, and an ordinary family which experiences an exceptional circumstance [1985e, para 5.19]. A small one-off payment may assist in the latter case but would do nothing in the former. Similarly, one small Section One payment would hardly be much use in striking up bargains with clients who need longer-term support, but it could help someone who, for one reason or another, has temporarily fallen through the social security net.

Views on the Social Fund

Of staff members who had any knowledge of the Social Fund most agree, predictably perhaps, with their professional organisations, most notably BASW, ADSS and the ACC. 'Back to the poor law' and 'the thin end of the wedge' were common responses. The better informed, however, recognised that the actual impact of the Social Fund on their work would depend upon a host of factors, not least the number and level of loans to be paid out, the conditions set for repayment and, most importantly, the level of basic income for families. Others admitted that if good relations obtained locally between DHSS staff and social workers, then, as at present, procedures for allocating loans to families under stress may not necessarily have adverse consequences for their clients. Exceptionally, one or two members of staff were prepared to consider a possible advantage of the Social Fund: if the Social Fund officers were prepared to become more involved with some families, they could, over a period of time, help to improve the financial circumstances of families under stress.

Social workers are already involved in income maintenance work, not only in their role as advisors and advocates, but also inasmuch as they currently write reports to support a client's claim for an urgent payment. So in some areas the DHSS may only make a single payment when it is underwritten by a social worker. In such circumstances social workers are already key 'gatekeepers' in the process of obtaining income support for clients. Even in the more recently constructed system of social security this is not as some commentators have suggested, a new role for social workers [eg: BASW 1985, reported in *Community Care* 4 June 1987].

For the foreseeable future, at least, there will continue to be an inescapable interconnection between SSD responsibilities and income maintenance. Although staff views differ concerning the desirability of this overlap, it is nevertheless the case that social work involves the payment of cash to clients and Section One payments continue to represent an important, even if diminished, part of this work. It is to be regretted that the overwhelming weaknesses of the Social Fund have discouraged local authority Social Service Departments from working in collaboration with the DHSS, with a view to providing an assessment and support service for families under stress. A collaborative approach might have produced a more effective and efficient package of care and cash which would have been to the greater benefit of some vulnerable families.

6

Shifting the Safety Net:
Social Services Financial Powers and Social Security Policy
Gill Stewart and John Stewart

ONE-OFF payments of extra benefit to meet claimants' 'exceptional needs' have been abolished under the income support scheme starting in April 1988. Former entitlement to 'single payments' is replaced by loans for most claimants or discretionary 'community care' grants for a few priority groups from the pre-set, cash-limited budget of the Social Fund. 'Exceptional needs' will no longer be met as they arise but only as and when the budget and the rules allow. We examine the origins of this change and suggest that it can be understood in the wider context of government thinking on the role of the social services.

Asking for more

Income support – like supplementary benefit, national assistance and unemployment assistance before it – provides a basic subsistence for people without the means to support themselves and who are not entitled to a comparable level of benefit from another source. A structural problem is presented to any subsistence benefit scheme by claimants who ask for more, because they call into question the adequacy of the basic scale rate. So while allowance was always made within the supplementary benefit scheme and its predecessors for extra payments to meet 'exceptional needs' it was an uneasy arrangement. Prosser [1981] has illustrated how concern about payments to meet 'special circumstances' and 'exceptional needs' in the 1930s anticipated the debates on discretion which raged during the late sixties and the seventies. In the post-war period, in between, Rowntree and Lavers [1951] concluded that primary poverty had been all but eradicated and that families with children would fall below the 'poverty line' only through mismanagement of their benefit income. More recent empirical studies [reviewed by Cooke and Baldwin, 1984, and Walker and Dant, 1984, on the post-1980 scheme] have shown how families with children in particular need extra benefit to pay for quite basic household items and avoid debt.

Before they were abolished, single payments accounted for only four per cent of supplementary benefit spending which itself made up 19 per cent of the total social security budget [House of Commons Debates, 1986a; Treasury, 1987]. On this basis, extra payments to claimants who ask for more are statistically insignificant yet in the government's recent review of social security, they were said to have made the whole supplementary benefit scheme unworkable. [DHSS, 1985c, paras. 2.30-1] The same had been said about 'exceptional needs payments' during the review of *Social Assistance* which was conducted by the last Labour government [DHSS, 1978, para 1.9, ch. 9]. Announcing cuts to single payments in advance of the Social Fund, the minister said, 'we believe that the present torrent of claims could cause the breakdown of the entire social security system' [House of Commons Debates, 1986b, col 444]. The government's Social Security Advisory Committee [SSAC, 1987, para. 45] have expressed the true significance of single payments and the Social Fund which replaces them as 'an important symbol of the way in which we operate the safety net for the poorest members of society'.

Needing extra benefit has been rationalised by DHSS under successive governments as the claimant's fault. They have been characterised as bad managers, 'cases needing special attention' – not more money, but casework provided by Special Case Officers [SCOs] who were the predecessors of Social Fund Officers [SFOs]. The work of SCOs was mainly concerned with 'serious and persistent mismanagement [or] misuse of resources as evidenced by failure to manage essential living expenses'; and the criteria for referral to SFOs remain similar. Latterly, in practice, SCOs' response with three quarters of their clients was to 'award a single payment or an unclaimed additional requirement [both of which are now abolished], which suggests that the problem had really been inadequate benefit income and DHSS failure to meet claimants' entitlement [SSPI, 1984; DHSS, 1987c, paras. 1004-7; DHSS, 1987b; the presentation of claimants as 'bad managers' is elaborated in Stewart and Stewart, 1986, 52-4]

When the minister announced restrictive regulations in the Commons during the week of a royal wedding in July 1986, he blamed escalating expenditure on single payments on social workers and welfare rights take-up campaigns which he described as 'manipulation of the poor... manipulation and exploitation on a scale beyond what Parliament ever intended' [House of Commons Debates, 1986b and 1986c, cols 23-4, 28]. The government maintained that the single payment regulations were not meeting 'real' needs and that the only way to distinguish the deserving from the undeserving was to remove all entitlement and rely on local office discretion guided by unchallengeable rules.

A cut in the level of single payments by about 50 per cent was achieved in advance of abolition by 'redrawing the rules of entitlement' to exclude large groups of claimants [Cmnd. 9836, 1986, para. 49; the impact of the single payment changes is described in Stewart and Stewart, 1988]. The cash limit and abolition of appeal rights which accompany deregulation under the Social Fund are intended to prevent loss of control over expenditure in the future. But SFOs have also been given a new weapon to use in their management of discretion: under s33[9] [b] of the Social Security Act 1986 they 'shall have regard ... to ... the possibility that some other person or body may wholly or partly meet [the need]' before making an 'award'.

A matter of principle

The *Social Fund Manual* explains that in the context of 'community care' grants, this means:

> ... if the LA has a duty to provide assistance ... The purpose of CCGs is to help people live as independent a life as possible in the community. Local authorities have the major responsibility for community care as they are able to assist people in many different ways ... a community care grant may not be awarded in respect of ... any expenses which the local authority has a statutory duty to meet' [DHSS, 1987f, paras. 6001-4].

In the draft manual, SFOs were referred to an annex which:

> summarises the main statutory responsibilities placed upon local authorities to provide personal social services. . . [It] does not set out to be an exhaustive account but to illustrate the wide range of these responsibilities'.

This annex was subsequently withdrawn, presumably following pressure from the local government lobby.

The ensuing list of fourteen enactments applying to England and Wales

[Scottish legislation was to follow], did not bear very close examination. For example, the Health Services and Public Health Act 1968 which was described as 'giving local authorities some responsibility for promoting the welfare of old people' specifically excludes the payment of money to individuals, in s45 [4] [a], which is all that is likely to interest Social Fund applicants. But the general message is clear enough, and repeated throughout the manual, that social services financial powers should be called upon whenever there is any possibility of relevance. Only social services are mentioned, not the general 'power of local authorities to incur expenditure for certain purposes not otherwise authorised' including to individuals, under s137 of the Local Government Act 1972. Nor is there mention of probation officers powers to give financial help to clients under rules 41-43 of the *Probation Rules 1984* [SI no. 647], although 'ex-offenders requiring resettlement' are listed as a priority for community care grants.

Charities, however, are regarded as a resource for claimants and grant-making charities have already reported a huge increase in applications as a result of the changes in single payment regulations immediately before the Social Fund came into operation. SFOs are directed to consider 'charities and benevolent funds as 'possible sources of help' before they make a 'crisis loan' [DHSS, 1987f, para. 4058]. We can foresee a new welfare safety net patched together by SFOs out of social services' financial powers, grant-making trusts and charitable furniture and clothing stores, quite outside the state social security system. This accords well with Victorian tradition which the present government avowedly admires and which emphasises the role of charity in a minimal state, with local authorities as residual providers of poor relief. It is no romantic anachronism but what many Tories would like to see happen. An academic writing for the party's think tank has already proposed that the Social Fund, along with all means tested benefits, should be handed over to voluntary sector management [Davies, 1986].

The role for social services' financial powers which seems to be envisaged in the Social Fund is consistent with the way in which DHSS social security policy has developed during the eighties. It has become a matter of principle that benefit should not be paid to claimants for anything which another agency may be regarded as primarily responsible for, a position which SSAC [1985a, paras. 7, 15] has stated and endorsed. Over the years, the DHSS has developed a policy of not allowing claimants benefit for anything when another agency can be persuaded to pay. The government's Social Security Advisory Committee stated and approved this policy in a report to the Secretary of State about 'single payments' in 1985:

> We would certainly not agree with any suggestion that supplement-
> ary benefit should take on by default responsibilities arising from the
> failure of other agencies to provide services. Nor do we think it
> would be sensible to allow a situation where both supplementary
> benefit and another agency had an undefined power to provide the
> same things. . . A general principle of the supplementary benefit
> scheme has been that benefit is not payable to meet a need for which
> another statutory authority has a power or a duty to provide.

Despite the *Draft Social Fund Manual*'s long list of enactments under which local authorities allegedly have financial duties it would probably be agreed that the only ones of use on any scale are Section One of the Child Care Act, 1980 and the Scottish equivalent s12, and s2 of the chronically Sick and Disabled Persons Act, 1970. In both cases, significant changes are likely to occur towards the end of the decade which will influence the nature and level of demand for assistance from the social services department. Where disabled people are concerned, the change will come obliquely in the form of housing legislation to means test home improvement grants, which was promised in the 1987 Tory election manifesto and in the subsequent Queen's speech. In the absence of any more specific indicators, we can only conjecture about what may happen on the basis of the existing green paper on the subject [Department of the Environment, 1985]. Restricting eligibility for improvement grants to claimants of income support or another 'passport' benefit; turning many grants into loans and giving the housing authority an accumulating equity share in the property; redefining 'unfitness' to include only the most dilapidated housing: the effect of these proposals would be to reduce the numbers and willingness of homeowners who could obtain financial help to adapt a house for the needs of a disabled family member. An increase in applications to the social services department under s2 of the 1970 Act would be an obvious consequence [we discuss this further in Stewart and Stewart, forthcoming, ch.2].

One of the potentially more attractive types of 'community care' Social Fund grant is for 'improving living conditions' of 'vulnerable groups' including adults who are elderly, mentally handicapped, mentally ill, physically disabled or chronically sick; the objective is to:

> help an applicant or partner to remain in their home in the
> community rather than enter institutional or residential care. . . The
> likelihood of care does not have to be immediate [DHSS, 1987f,
> paras. 6371,3].

Of course only some homeowners who are refused improvement grants will be eligible to apply to the Social Fund because of the income and capital resource barriers. But if they are, they will be excluded from this particular provision for 'improving living conditions' if the social services department is thought to have duty towards the disabled person under s2 of the 1970 Act [para. 6377]. Whether or not social services accept and act upon this duty seems not to be a consideration for the DHSS. What matters is that the local authority has a duty, not that an alternative source of help is actually available to the claimant.

It was exclusion from entitlement to single payments arising from a claimant's 'medical need', including disability, that occasioned the SSAC's statement of principle, which we quoted above. They recognised then what the consequences for claimants could be:

> The thought lying behind this principle is that public money spent on the provision on welfare services should be channelled through the services themselves and allocated by those responsible for administering them. . . The way in which local authorities exercise [their s2] powers does however vary considerably, reflecting different interpretations of 'need', the authority's priorities and, inevitably, the availability of resources. It is certainly true that the nature of the local authority's legal obligation to supply these services, coupled with financial constraints, can mean that some kinds of help which are in theory available are in practice very difficult to obtain. . . However logical the principle that supplementary benefit should not provide what other agencies have a power or a duty to provide, the variations in services actually available must inevitably lead to pressure in individual hard cases for supplementary benefit to come to the rescue [SSAC, 1985a, paras. 7, 12, 14].

SSAC said that this 'determined the boundary of supplementary benefit's responsibilities'. In their directives for operating the Social Fund, the DHSS have changed the boundaries between social security and the social services.

Changing Section One

As for social services' financial powers under Section One, change is expected in the primary legislation. It was outlined in the Child Care White Paper [DHSS, 1987a] which concluded a two-and-a-half year review process, although no bill was timetabled for the 1987-8 parliamentary session.

The existing duty and accompanying financial power under Section One of the Child Care Act 1980 is to prevent reception into care or continuation in care. Scottish and Northern Irish equivalents to Section One are less used and will not be affected by the proposed changes to English legislation. Research on Section One has shown that cash help is mainly given for parents to buy food and fuel when they have no money at all. This use of Section One prevents reception into care, under the terms of the Act, only in a very general sense. Really it is compensating for breakdown in benefit delivery – missing giros – and substituting for 'urgent needs payments' which are particularly difficult to obtain. This has been demonstrated recently by a local study in the Finsbury area of Islington [Rainbow, 1985]. So it is possible to see how DHSS could have got the idea that SSDs might be willing to contribute to a new safety-net.

Recent patterns of Section One expenditure have shown wide and unpredictable variation between, and within, individual authorities around the country. Actual amounts spent during 1984-85 ranged from £2,000 to over £1 million with the average at £92,000 per authority [Chartered Institute of Public Finance and Accountancy, 1987]. At the higher end, these sums obviously include expenditure on preventive services like day centres with probably only a small proportion going on cash help to families. The Association of Directors of Social Services [1983] has described Section One payments as 'no more than pittances which tide families over a crisis'. Overall, Section One expenditure accounts for only 2.0 per cent of the total child care budget. Just as single payments were an insignificant part of the S.B. scheme, so Section One is insignificant in relation to child care expenditure within social services. And in 1985-86, Section One expenditure accounted for only 3.9 per cent of the value of single payments. In these circumstances, local authorities' financial powers are simply not capable of compensating for the loss of single payments to poor families. Although statistically insignificant at a national level, single payments were still worth a lot of money at £263 million in England and Wales in 1985-86, and families were the main recipients [House of Commons Debates, 1986a].

Section One powers as presently constituted would allow social workers to refuse a Social Fund Officer's request for a cash payment to a family as long as there was no immediate risk of the children's reception into care. Any social security official would find it hard to challenge a social worker's judgement on such a child care matter. Of course, a lot of social work time could still be taken up saying 'no' to routine Social Fund approaches and this in itself could constitute a drain on resources which SSDs should monitor. However, the proposals in the Child Care White Paper would significantly change the terms of social services' financial powers. A restricted duty to prevent compulsory reception into care would continue but expenditure under it would be confined to funding services, precluding cash help for individual parents. A new "umbrella" power is proposed:

> to promote the care and upbringing of children, and to help prevent
> the breakdown of family relationships which might eventually lead to
> a court order committing the child to the local authority's
> care.

This would include a power to 'offer financial assistance in exceptional circumstances' [DHSS, 1987a, paras. 18, 21, 22a].

The proposed new provision is much more general in scope than the present Section One. This is welcome if it results in more cash help for families from social workers who will no longer have to justify their actions in strictly preventative terms. But on the other hand, it could be much more difficult under a non-specific power for social workers to refuse requests from Social Fund Officers for grants to claimant families, including even non-clients. Who could deny, for example, that a new pair of shoes would 'promote the care and upbringing' of a child? Or that cooking facilities enabling a family to eat at home together would 'help prevent the breakdown of family relationships which might eventually. . . etc'?

If they are in tune with current DHSS thinking, Social Fund Officers will be trying to get SSDs to provide money for claimants who cannot afford children's shoes or a new cooker out of their benefit income. And if the only alternative on offer is a DHSS loan which would make matters worse, many social workers will want to agree. Giving financial assistance to promote the care and upbringing of children or to prevent family breakdown sounds like just the sort of power which DHSS would expect social services departments to exercise. Such an expectation would draw local authorities further towards an income maintenance role.

It seems that financial powers which are presumably intended [by one part of DHSS] to be specific to child care social work, will be taken for granted [by another part of DHSS] as making local authority money available as a safety-net for poor families. This would not just be an overdue exercise of proper SSD responsibilities, which is the assumption behind the DHSS principle. To make Section One or its successor part of a new safety-net for claimant families would involve a significant change in role for social workers and a potentially major drain on resources for local authorities.

It is unlikely that civil servants on the social services side of DHSS have knowingly gone along with this. They have their own agendas. From a policy point of view, they want to move away from a negative image of reception into care which is implied by the present preventative duty. Child care lawyers, on the other hand, wish to override what they regard as a misinterpretation of Section One responsibilities expressed in an appeal court case in 1981, about a homeless family in Wandsworth [DHSS, 1985e, para. 5.4; DHSS, 1985f, 16; DHSS, 1987a, para. 21; we discuss the background further in Stewart and Stewart, forthcoming, ch.4]. The social security side of DHSS have probably played only a minor part in drafting the Child Care White Paper. It has fallen into their laps like a gift from the Treasury.

Now that entitlement to extra benefit payments for essential furniture and basic household equipment has been abolished, only Social Fund loans will be available to families with children in most circumstances. Yet as the SSAC has pointed out, the benefit scale rates are not set at levels which allow for the purchase of 'major capital items', so loan repayments 'will be deducted from rates intended to cover only normal weekly living expenses' [SSAC, 1987 and accompanying press release 87/2315]. Under this scenario, we can predict a recurring dilemma for social workers whether to take children into care rather than let them sleep on bare floorboards in a cold house that is empty of furniture. The alternative is that social services departments will have to be prepared to furnish claimant client's homes out of massively increased Section One budgets. Our research for the Welfare Rights Officers Group into the pre-Social Fund restriction on single payments has shown that such choices are already being made [Stewart and Stewart, 1988].

In response to these pressures, local authorities are starting to formulate and publicise policy guidelines for the use of financial powers under Section One. Islington, for example, did this in 1986 and Newcastle-upon-Tyne in 1987. This development in open local government is a sound stratagem in several respects. First, having a public policy should help to protect claimants from inappropriate referral by DHSS to social services for things like washing machines, which local authorities do not stock [despite what the manual suggests in para. 6491]. Secondly, it might avoid the kind of situation which arose after the coal dispute in Fife and Strathclyde whose directors of social work faced a personal surcharge for section 12 payments made to childless striking miners which the controller of audit said were outside the terms of the Social Work [Scotland] Act 1968 [*Community Care*, 26 June 1986, p. 3 and 28 August 1986, p. 2]. Thirdly, open policies and accompanying publicity about local needs could provide a powerful weapon for local government in the continuing propaganda struggle with the DHSS.

Blaming local authorities

At a meeting about the Social Fund organised by the Association of Metropolitan Authorities [AMA] in July 1987, concern was already being expressed that central government would blame social services authorities for what was regarded as the scheme's inevitable failure. Not only the Labour controlled AMA considers the Social Fund to be 'both unfair and unworkable': these were SSAC's words [1987 accompanying press release].

It would not be the first time that DHSS ministers have put the blame for problems with social security policies onto local government. We have already referred to the parliamentary exchanges wherein social workers were accused of whipping up unjustified demand for single payments. Other allegations were made in connection with the board and lodging regulations. Escalating benefit payments to elderly people in private residential homes were said to be caused by SSDs withdrawing financial sponsorship from residents and thereby reneging on their duties under the National Assistance Act [discussed more fully in Stewart *et al*, 1986]. Young boarders were subject to a move-on rule under the 1985 regulations and their main prospect of exemption from benefit cuts and imminent homelessness lay in verification of client status. The *S Manual* directed that time-limited claimants should be referred to social services for advice about exemption [S13/85 amndt. 4 para. 13]. Suicides followed and it was a short logical step for Edwina Currie as health minister to argue that these were the fault of welfare agencies, not the DHSS:

> much of the blame for the current anguish lies with certain voluntary and political organisations which, for a variety of motives, have not read the exemptions and have not therefore attempted to apply them. . . .They did not [commit suicide] because of the DHSS. In all the cases that have been put to us, they did it because they were suffering from mental illness; and all those people who are busy writing reports about them . . . would have been better advised to look after these people rather sooner, before they reached that state. . . I say that particularly to social workers and probation officers who should have been looking after them much better [House of Commons Debates, 1985a and 1985b].

This was despite other ministerial denials that the board and lodging changes would have any 'significant effect on the work of social services departments, whose statutory duties and responsibilities remain unchanged' [House of Commons Debates, 1985c and 1985d; we pursue the argument in Stewart and Stewart, 1987].

The Secretary of State's long-standing responsibility for the welfare of claimants has been repealed under the Social Security Act 1986. This will make it easier for the DHSS to abdicate responsibility for the arbitrary effects of Social Fund cash limits and to argue that a welfare safety net should be provided by social services departments. It rationalises what has been happening for some time in practice. In some parts of the country, DHSS administration for the delivery of benefits has virtually broken down and helping agencies of all types have had to cope with the consequences. A survey by the Greater London Citizen's Advice Bureaux [1986] described the situation in local offices around London. The National Association of Citizen's Advice Bureaux together with the Child Poverty Action Group and the London boroughs of Hackney and Islington have sought judical review of DHSS's failure to make benefit payments within the statutory 14 days.

Islington social services' initiative to draw up a Section One policy was largely prompted by the demands which were being made on their Section One budget to compensate for non-delivery of benefit, as demonstrated by Rainbow [1985]. Reports from social services area teams in neighbouring Camden illustrated the effects on practitioner grade social workers during 1986. The Regents Park team wrote about:

> the deterioration in service provided by the local DHSS office, increasingly plagued by overwork and poor labour relations. Not only has this put increased burden on families when benefits fail to arrive, it has also meant increased work for social workers who are increasingly stepping in with emergency advice and Section One payments.

In SomersTown:

> The team spends much of its time plugging holes in a disintegrating welfare service, eg, non-arrival of benefit, fuel disconnection of vulnerable people . . . It is a matter of considerable concern that our local DHSS office . . . currently has 4,000 unopened letters.

The Camden Town team reported to committee that:

> The increase in work brought about by the growing inability of . . . DHSS to administer the welfare benefits system in an effective way, is a constant source of concern. Social Work staff feel they are becoming, by default, an arm of the Social Security system. There is considerable cost to Camden Council in carrying out this shoring-up operation.

The pressure on DHSS local office staff caused by over work, low pay and bad working conditions, [Mandla, 1987] led to a series of strikes in areas including London, parts of Scotland and the north of England. The government's response was to give local authorities general powers – which they had not sought and for a while were unaware of – to make interim payments of benefit 'on account' to claimants who were affected by the strikes. There was no mention of this in the relevant regulations [SI 1987 no. 491] and an *S Manual* entry under 'Emergency payments by local authority' [para. 12821] was missing, listed as 'not yet available'. The instructions for local authorities were contained in a special letter to DHSS local office managers, amending *J Code* 600-8. These instructions were not available to the public, including most local authority staff.

Claimants who could not get into picketed local offices were redirected to the social services department and the minister said in the House of Commons that, 'If claimants cannot manage to tide themselves over the few days until their girocheque arrives, they may be able to obtain help from their local authority' [House of Commons Debates, 1987]. This was a much more systematic attempt by the government to involve local authorities than had happened during a previous DHSS strike in Birmingham [Coetze, 1983]. Great pressure was brought to bear on Labour controlled authorities which were reluctant to engage in organised strike-breaking and some complied, although the DHSS's instructions proved to be virtually unworkable. Others bypassed the government's special arrangements and increased their use of existing Section One powers, although money spent in this way was not reclaimable from the DHSS. A report to the Association of London Authorities described the situation in inner London, based on a survey by local authority welfare rights officers. Much trouble and some violence was caused to social workers by the desperate situation of many claimants whose benefit income had been cut-off. Haringey's director of social services presented the dilemmas from a management point of view [Townsend, 1987] while an intake team leader from the north west gave a vivid account of what it was like for practitioners [Robinson, 1987].

The experience during the civil servants' strike was the nearest social services departments have come so far to adopting a general income maintenance role. Twenty years ago, the Seebohm Committee [1968, paras. 602-3] pondered:

> whether the social services department should have a general power to give direct financial help to those members of the public with whom it comes into contact. It is clear that the power to do this may be a most valuable instrument for good in the hands of social workers.

They rejected the idea because it would constitute a breach of the DHSS's [the SBC's] responsibility for income maintenance. Since then, successive governments have publicly reasserted the correctness of preserving separation between social work and social security services. But behind the public statements there has developed a hidden agenda for change.

Ten years ago, a DHSS report on *Relations with Social Services* discussed options for dealing with 'cases where a joint approach is needed. . . [to]. . the most problematic cases of both agencies'. They suggested:

> It could be envisaged that SSDs should develop a discretionary financial function and take full responsibility, alternatively that the SB organisation embodies some social work expertise to provide an integrated service within the SB organisation [DHSS, 1979, paras. 2.33-4].

There are elements of both of these options in the Social Fund, as we have argued elsewhere [Stewart and Stewart, 1986]. Some British commentators have welcomed closer integration of 'cash' and 'care' services and drawn attention to the existence of 'financial social workers' in other countries as a a favourable precedent [eg Leaper, 1986 and this volume]. But reports by practitioners and researchers from these other countries suggest that the involvement of social workers in benefit administration has not worked well, at least as far as the social workers and their clients are concerned [eg Hooper, 1987; Piven and Cloward, 1972].

Making social services departments take financial responsibility for claimant clients is an objective on DHSS civil servants' long-term agenda.

The combination of this officers' agenda with Thatcherism's political vendetta against local authorities has given the Social Fund, at least in government circles, the strength of an idea whose time has come; both ministers and senior civil servants are evidently committed to it. This government has already been prepared to use social security policy as a political instrument against the trades union movement by depriving dependents of benefits during an industrial dispute, on the argument that they should be receiving non-existent strike pay which is treated as a 'notional resource' [Sutcliffe and Hill, 1985; Boothe and Smith, 1985]. The DHSS are redrawing boundaries between social services' financial powers and social security entitlement so as to disqualify from certain payments, claimants who are also clients. The onus will then be on the social services department to meet their financial needs, or take the blame for not doing so. The DHSS is using claimant clients to force local authorities down a road which they do not wish to take.

7

Cash and Care in a European Perspective

R.A.B. Leaper

T HIS chapter will be concerned with cash and care, comparing
British practice with that of three neighbouring countries. We shall
compare the way in which public authorities deal with those who
claim help in cash form because of low income and those who seek help
with family and personal problems. We are not concerned here with the
large majority of people receiving cash benefits, namely from a social
insurance entitlement, but only with the minority whose entitlement to
benefit is related to a low income. In European institutional terms we are
concerned with social assistance, not social security.

Similarly we shall be concerned not with the large majority of people
with personal or family problems which are dealt with by their own
extended family or by a network of friends and neighbours, but with a
minority who are helped by social workers and other professional helpers
[Abrams, 1980; Yoder and Leaper, 1985]. Recent research suggests that
often the same people have a combination of cash and care
problems:

Tentatively:

on average about 52 per cent of social work referrals [in areas of
Britain surveyed] are from people on supplementary benefit. This
mean does not reflect the wide variation among different client

groups. Some [for example single parents] are much more likely be in receipt of supplementary benefit, whilst others [for example pensioners] are less likely to be in receipt of this benefit . . . There is evidence to suggest that about a fifth of all supplementary benefit claimants are also in contact with a social worker . . . with dependent partners and children, there are likely to be over 2 million people currently dependent on supplementary benefit who are also in contact with a social worker [Becker and MacPherson, 1986, 14 and 19].

A quick reaction to evidence of a common clientele for workers in supplementary benefits and in social services, both of which involve some enquiry into the personal situation and needs of the person concerned, is that all people in need ought to be dealt with by the same workers. This would be too simplistic a conclusion. Many other professional workers – doctors, nurses, housing officials, income tax assessers, for example – are likely to delve into the situation of the same people and help to meet needs. But it is not generally agreed that each of these specialist workers should be abolished in favour of a generic social helper who would deal with all the health, housing and cash needs of the same people. The case for considering income-related cash help and social work care together is rather the claim that these two are closely inter-woven in the clients' lives and also that the workers charged by society with meeting these needs have to consider simultaneously in practice both the cash and the care needs of their clients. As we shall see, different societies have found different solutions to this question, and they have evolved practices hallowed now by tradition, defended by practitioners, and hardened in pattern by political stances. It may help us to question the logic of attitudes in Britain if we examine practice elsewhere – 'to argue that the home country cannot properly be understood save by reference to other countries may seem paradoxical to some at least, yet a moment's reflection should convince most observers otherwise' [Jones, 1985,4]. Yet in each case the solutions to the needs of people have to be seen in their political, organisational and professional setting, which is a daunting task for the average student of social provision.

The relationship between cash help and social care must be seen also in the context of the levels of income considered by society to be the minimum entitlement for citizens. The extent and complexity of the systems of aid available will range along a continuum from a society which has a legal minimum wage, a defined minimum income related to it, with simple and clearly defined additions for the recipients' dependents, to – at the other extreme – a complicated system allowing for variations in entitlement to cash assistance according to age, dependents, housing situation, state of health, heating provisions, weather, long-term disabilities physical or mental, and occasional crisis needs. The Supplementary Benefit system in Britain is – or was until 1987 – of the latter type. Hence the attempts to reform the system in 1980, of which some of us [Leaper, 1980] had high hopes, and the decision to alter the system made under the 1986 Social Security Act.

The government's plans for the Social Fund's implementation in 1988 under the Social Security Act 1986 ran into strong opposition. One after another the local authority associations, the British Associations of Social Workers, Age Concern, local authority Welfare Rights officers [predictably perhaps] and even Peter Barclay, the Social Security Advisory Committee chairman, either condemned outright the Social Fund or voiced grave misgivings about its implementation as described in the Social Fund manual of draft guidance and direction for DHSS officers [*Social Services Insight*, 1987; *Community Care* 1987a, 1987b; DHSS, 1987c]. This chorus of disapproval may well have drowned out the possibility of a calmer examination of the close connection in practice between cash and care. Worse still it diverted attention away from the really basic issue of policy: the establishment of a sufficiently high level of basic income for all. This in turn would imply the abolition of complex additions for special needs and the reduction of single payments to really exceptional and unforeseeable circumstances: both these would be greatly to the advantage of people in need.

The central issue is the amount to be laid down as a national minimum for all. Bill Jordan has argued cogently and persistently for a Basic Income scheme which 'would give an individual enough income for subsistence before he or she enters the labour market or the family' [Jordan, 1987a, 160]. Jordan's proposals have been regarded with scepticism by some, but they have the great merit of a radical proposal to re-think our whole income-maintenance provisions, not simply to patch and add scraps. Eric Midwinter takes a radical approach to the question of income in retirement, pressing that 'the older person be regarded as a citizen-pensioner, not as a welfare beneficiary.' He proposes 'a social income – *a wage of retirement* – by reference to normal household spending patterns, which by 1985 valuations, would be £80 each per week' [Midwinter, 1985, 1] up-dated to £90 per week in 1986 [Midwinter, 1987, 2]. This is, as he admits, contrary to the general trend of government policy as made explicit in successive White Papers, and he admits that his scheme would have to be phased in over a period of time. However, he argues that since retirement is certain, unless death intervenes, this clearly foreseeable contingency should be planned for and paid for through the taxation system to produce a pension per head which allows for full participation in normal social activities on costings which he works out carefully and explicitly.

A similar approach to those in employment is taken by Sheffield Social Security Campaign which advocates a scheme, not dissimilar to the Basic Income proposals advocated by Jordan and others [1986]. This is not the place to examine in detail the costings and operational details of these proposals. What is important here is to see that the link between cash and care to be effective must be based on some commonly accepted minimum of income for all, subject to clear and simple conditions of entitlement. If agreement could be reached on this, the question of single payments or of loans would fade into comparative insignificance – but it would have in its place in really exceptional circumstances and for a minority of people who have a whole complex of problems including lack of enough cash. In 1986-7 in Britain there was so much tension and mistrust between central government responsible for almost all income maintenance and local government responsible for social work that each tended to take up a political stance and indulge in polemic. This particularly applied to issues of cash and caring. Richard Berthoud of the Policy Studies Institute seemed one of the few committed to a critical but objective examination of the potential good and bad of the Social Fund [Berthoud, 1987].

Cash and care in Belgium

I now review briefly the systems of cash and care prevailing elsewhere – first in Belgium. Social assistance in cash is a major function of the commune through the *Centre Public d'Aide Sociale/Openbaar Centruum voor Maatschappelijk Welzijn*, established under the 1976 Act [Berger and Bataille, 1985]. However, the concept of 'social assistance' under the Belgian Act is wider and more generic than that of income-related cash payments. The Centres provide the local social work service, supplemented by that of a number of independent agencies. The Centres are also responsible for the management of local public hospitals. The function of financial assistance has to be seen in this wider context. In any case insurance-based social security aims to provide for a larger proportion of the population in need than in Britain – assigning a comparatively residual role to income-related cash help. By law qualified social workers *must* be attached to all CPAS/OCMW [in proportion to total population of the relevant communes] and all first applications for help are customarily dealt with by a social worker interview. I have studied at first hand over some ten years the work of two Centres – in Brugge [Vlanderen] and Charleroi [Wallonie]. There is much local variation. Brugge and Charleroi are typical of two very different areas – linguistically, occupationally, politically and demographically. All Belgian citizens have a right to a 'minimex' provided that proof can be given of no other resources; this is a minimum level of income laid down by Parliament [related to cost of living indicators]. Centres have the right to pay discretionary additions above the minimum, including allowances for special needs. The number of people in Belgium entitled to minimex payments has gone up from 9,436 in 1976 to 43,774 in 1986. The average age of beneficiary has gone down; ten years ago the majority were people over the age of 65, whereas in 1986 56 per cent of them were under 40 years, and in Wallonie 25 per cent were under 25 years old. While precise figures are not provided nationally there seems likely to have been a rise in discretionary additions [*Revue Belge de la Sécurité Sociale*, 1986; *Mouvement Communal*, 1987]. Under Article 60 par 7 of the 1976 Act, local Centres are empowered to find work for beneficiaries sometimes by establishing work schemes themselves. Assistance beneficiaries become social insurance contributors and are entitled to insurance benefits when unemployed, thus reducing the number of people dependent on assistance. The fact that social workers are always employed by the Centres means that social workers are involved in seeing the *whole* situation of a claimant, in assessing the need for an entitlement to help and of what kind, and in advice and assistance on budgetting for cash beneficiaries and their families. The decision on entitlement to financial assistance is taken by the Commisision of the Centre, appointed from the local elected commune council[s], which consider the recommendations of the social work section of each Centre. In both Brugge and Charleroi their recommendations are generally accepted by the Commission, but it has the power of decision. There is no provision within the relevant Act [and amendments to date] concerning loans to cash help applicants to Centres. Some Centres have agreed with an applicant to become the guarantor for debt repayments to fuel suppliers, landlords, and other creditors, and to recoup in graduated payments from the assisted person the money which is owed. This is not widespread as a practice and it is always seen as a part of budgetting advice and guidance from the Centre's social work staff [personal communication, Madame Piérard, CPAS, Charleroi, 1987]. Far more common is the practice of giving an 'advance' on cash benefits awaited or expected from social security agencies who sometimes delay in making payments. The management and social workers at both Centres have often complained about acting as banker for social security agencies slow in paying benefits. They have also expressed strong reservations about making loans in any regular way, preferring other solutions whenever possible.

Under Belgian law family relatives are responsible for assistance beneficiaries. This responsibility is much wider than in Britain, covering in Belgium two generations in either ascendancy or descendancy. There are limits to the amount recoverable from relatives and the cash must have covered specified eventualities [the cost of medical treatment, for example]. A recent modification in April 1987 to Article 100b of the 1976 Act somewhat eases the position of relatives over the 'obligation to maintain' [*Moniteur Belge*, 1987; *Arrêté Royal*, 1987] In a sense money paid out by a Centre to a beneficiary is a *loan*, if it is repayable from a liable relative. Brugge has recently been more strict than hitherto in this regard, and the social work director claims that this has enabled the Centre to have more funds for discretionary additions to the minimex [personal communication, W. Vanderleen, OCMW, Brugge, 1987]. The political differences between the two communes involved do not seem to have been decisive in determining attitudes towards discretionary additions nor in following up family obligations as determined under Belgian law. Brugge has had a coalition in local government over the past ten years, while Charleroi has retained a solid Socialist majority. The councils of the CPAS/OCMW tend to reflect the political forces in local politics, but their policies are not markedly different in the two cases quoted. Both have supported the general complaints about delays in central government paying its share of their social assistance expenditure. What is different is the nature of the clientele with whom they have to deal, which reflects the economic and social situation of a Flemish town with a balanced demography, comparatively low unemployment [*Sociale Dienst*, 1986] and a high level of new forms of economic enterprises contrasted with a large Walloon agglomeration with declining steel and disappearing coal industries struggling to transform its economy and its living environment, and to cope with a high proportion of elderly in the population.

Cash assistance in France

In France, responsibility for income-related cash assistance is spread over a number of different agencies – the State *Direction Départmentale de l'Action Sanitaire et Sociale* [especially for child care and maintenance], the commune *Centre Communal d'Action Sociale, the Caisse d'Allocations Familiales* [family allowances fund – CAF which makes income-related additions to allowances in specified situations]. Generally speaking

Sociale, social assistance, is the reponsibility of the CCAS, whose name until 1986 was *Bureau d'Aide Sociale*. Social workers are employed to help the clients of all the agencies mentioned including household budgetting. The latter is a specific function of the CAF and also of social workers appointed by the courts to supervise certain families [Dupeyroux, 1985; Thévenet, 1986; Bertrand, 1987].

The CAF do have a system of *prêts d'honneur* which are short-term loans to help needy families meet periodic heavy expenses which their basic family allowance does not completely cover. These are discretionary on the advice of the social worker and do not represent a high proportion of the expenditure of the average CAF.

Before 1986 the CCAS were not authorised by law to give loans to cash beneficiaries. In practice, however, several were in fact giving 're-imbursable cash help' at the direction of the local committee and on the recommendation of the Centre staff. They had no right of recovery if the beneficiary defautlted on the repayment of a short-term loan. the Act of January 1986 however, has allowed loans to be made under certain conditions, by stating that the CCAS may intervene by means of repayable or non-repayable cash allowances. Centres seem only just now in 1987 to be experimenting with loans under the new dispensation and it is too early to say how far this provision will go [UNCCASF, 1987].

At the Rennes CCAS, studied at first hand over several years, the pattern of social assistance follows the usual division in France between *Aide Légale* whose conditions are laid down nationally for all Centres and *Aide Facultative* whose operation is discretionary according to the policy of the local management committee and the professional judgement of the Centre staff. *Aide Légale* deals with such eventualities as the cost of medical care for those without the normal insurance cover and without sufficient other resources, help with the costs of mental health care, the preparation of case papers for old peoples' housing benefits [actually payable through the CAF].

The *Aide Facultative* section deals with situations in which 'according to cash limits set and criteria decided by the administrative council and the management of the CCAS, help is given to persons temporarily in difficulty who for various reasons cannot claim – or cannot claim sufficiently – what they need by applying to the other forms of social protection established by law" [CCAS Rennes, *Annual Report*, 1986]. The situations referred are in fact many and various, including special attention to rent arrears. 'Exceptional grants' were given in 11 per cent of cases, but repayable loans in less than one per cent. Of the beneficiaries 58 per cent were aged under

30. Only three per cent were over 60; this is almost certainly because retired people have a guaranteed minimum income, eliminating the need for special grants. 'Exceptional grants' are given only on the advice of a social worker in a report to the commission responsible for decisions in these matters.

Since 1980 several Centres in France have experimented with the provision of a guaranteed minimum income to all applicants furnishing proof of lack of resources. Rennes followed the pioneering example of Bescançon [Huet, 1975]. In 1985 a research group at Rennes University co-operated with the many agencies in the city which supplied cash help on an 'assistance' basis in drawing up a report on the prevalence and effects of discretionary cash help. The report drew attention to the somewhat haphazard nature of cash help arrangements outside the insurance or family allowance fund. The assistance agencies agreed to co-operate in an experiment which provided for a unified guaranteed minimum income for a sample of families [Savina and Gruel, 1985]. A second report gave the results of the experiment, and it included a critical analysis of the attitudes and activities of the social workers employed in the various agencies involved in the experiment [Savina and Gaultier, 1987]. Their role and involvement in assessment for assistance was – and still is – crucial. The report also concluded that the needs of clients were very diverse – 'insufficient resources, poor training for work, difficulties over child care, marital tension' – not all of them could be solely ascribed to lack of money and social workers had to respond flexibly according to the cluster of different needs in their clients [Savina and Gaultier, 1987, 205/6]. The grant of a regular minimum income did generally improve the situation, but in many cases it did not eliminate budgeting problems nor the call for exceptional grants or loans.

In both these countries we see a close integration of cash and social care, contrary to the stance adopted in Britain of keeping the two quite separate. But the framework of the French and Belgian operations are markedly different from Britain: higher social security contributions, higher replacement income generally speaking, a national minimum for all who can prove lack of income from other sources, greater family responsibility for maintenance, greater local discretion over income-related benefits, and the employment of social workers by a wide variety of agencies instead of having only two agencies as in Britain with the virtual monopoly of social work and related services [Thévenet and Désigaux, 1985].

Social assistance in the Irish Republic

In the Irish Republic we are fortunate in having the voluminous evidence assembled by the recent *Report of the Commission on Social Welfare* [1986]. In the Irish context 'social welfare' means income maintenance of all kinds outside the wage system. The central government Department of Social Welfare has the major responsibility for income maintenance functions, though some responsibility is carried by the Department of Health. Moreover, it is the latter Department which has been most active over recent years in promoting the development of social work in Ireland.

There are a variety of social assistance schemes provided by the Department of Social Welfare, eligibility for which is based either on category qualification or on test of needs and means. The original 'home assistance scheme', a hang-over from old Poor Law provisions, was replaced in the 1975 Act by the supplementary welfare allowance scheme which eventually came into effect in 1977. An influential study by O'Cinneide [1970] led to a general acceptance of the need to remove the stigma attached to the old scheme and to replace it by standard basic minimum income, payable as of right, on test of means. It is administered by the Health Boards and is the responsibility of Supplementary Welfare Officers employed by them.

Dick Doyle, the doyen of home assistance in Ireland, reported in 1984 on growth in expenditure over ten years from two million pounds a year on Home Assistance in 1975 to forty million pounds on supplementary welfare in 1984. He extends the analysis of the Eastern Health Board [covering Dublin and its environs] to the generality of other areas to the effect that 'at least 50 per cent of all basic payments are substitute payments to persons awaiting social welfare payments,' a situation satisfactory to nobody involved. Doyle reviews possible options for the reform of the scheme, concluding:

> The Community Care needs which arise from working with other disciplines such as the Social Work service and Public Health nursing could be catered for on a consultative basis at area and regional level.'
> On the other hand the advantage of relocating the service in the Social Welfare Department would be 'to create a *caring and real welfare* element in the Department of Social Welfare . . . if staffs were free of paying functions and available for close work with clients' [Federated Workers Union of Ireland, 1984].

[There is an interesting comparison here, not made by Doyle, with the DHSS special case officer in Britain.]

Irish social workers and social assistance officers remain between two systems with their professional role defined from the ethics of their profession drawn from social work literature and in their training, with their answerability structure separately designated and the pattern of any co-ordination between the two undefined and dependent on the vagaries of good will and personal connection.

The problem is not only one of better administrative organisation [though that is obviously important], it is also one of an unresolved ideological debate in Ireland between on one hand a belief in family, local and small group responsibility and, on the other, an assertion of universality of rights and provisions which has grown in recent years [Leaper, 1975; Higgins, 1981].

One element of potential tension and of professional answerability is, however, not present in the Irish system – that of central – local dichotomy in the provision of social services. All the services organised by statutory bodies in Ireland are central government responsibility and both social workers and social assistance officers are attached to central government departments – to Health and to Social Welfare. There is no equivalent in Ireland of the British local authority social services committee or the Belgian commission of the *Centre Public d'Aide Sociale*. Of course the Health Boards have each a separate identity and within the limits of general government policy have discretion within their own area which reflects on the extent and type of social work engagement. Only the voluntary bodies remain separately organised as employers of social workers or as residual charity donors, and even they have now accepted a relationship with government departments which *should* make for better co-ordination of effort to help with the cash and caring needs of people. Some social workers are employed by local authority housing departments, or for specialist work with itinerant families, and their work has also to be co-ordinated with that of health and social welfare, but they are small in number [Commision on Social Welfare, 1986].

The services in Ireland providing for health and income maintenance may fairly be described as a compromise between continuity and change. Elements of continuity can variously be seen in maintaining some of the structure inherited from the British connection and from the close and continuing exchange of people with Britain. Elements of continuity can be discerned [very differently] from the desire to maintain the Republican tradition inherent in the early declaration of the first Dail Eireann that 'It shall be the first duty of the Republic to make provision for the physical, mental and spiritual well-being of the children, to secure that no child shall suffer hunger or cold from lack of food, clothing or shelter, but that all shall be provided with the means and facilities requisite for their proper education and training as citizens of a free and Gaelic Ireland' [quoted in Chubb, 1983]. This was carried over into and expanded upon in the Constitution *Bunreacht na h Eireann* [Republic of Ireland, 1937]. Changes – demographic, economic and social – have demanded alterations and adaptations of the services. Changes have, however, been incremental and piecemeal. It is hardly surprising that in 1985 the Social Welfare Commission was charged with preparing proposals for the wholesale overhaul of the income maintenance system. If there is no similar alterations to the social and financial aspect of the health services, only half a reform will have been accomplished. A large independent social help agency like the St Vincent de Paul Society has progressively re-defined its role and its membership over the past twenty years. Introduced into Ireland in 1844 and for many years a male preserve it has been an important auxiliary source of financial help to poor families – and still is, especially at Christmas. It now has voluntary workers of both sexes, engages far more in family counselling and relates its own financial help to rehabilitation and to referral to social workers in case of family breakdown [St Vincent de Paul Society, 1984 and 1986; personal communication, M. Dowling, St Vincent de Paul Society, Dublin, 1986]. It appears to work quite closely with the Supplementary Welfare Officers, though the extent of overlap or of co-ordination did not appear to be systematically documented.

The continued vigour of independent voluntary bodies in Ireland is consistent with the doctrine of *subsidiarity* which lays stress on the importance of mutual aid at the smallest level of organisation and of growth from the bottom upwards [Leaper, 1975].

Consistent with this same general philosophy was the growth of Social Services Councils, starting with the well-documented Kilkenny Social Services Council [Kennedy, 1981]. Closely linked to the church and providing an umbrella organisation for many different social service bodies of volunteers the Councils spread rapidly and now appear to employ about 30 workers. Since 1971 the National Social Services Council [now re-formed and re-named National Social Service Board] has acted as a resource centre to help voluntary social services development. The Department of Health has encouraged, and financially aided, this development in addition to funding a limited number of posts as 'community workers', notable in Cork, to liaise with local community associations and to ensure better co-ordination between the Department's Community Care section and self-help and mutual aid bodies [Smith, 1980]. The general attitude behind this development is reminiscent of the Gulbenkian studies on community work in the 1970s in Britain and the later patch methods of community social work in Britain advocated by Hadley and others [Hadley and Hatch, 1980]. Though the concepts of accountability and group determination define differently the role of the social case-worker, the connections with income maintenance agencies remain much the same. The Social Welfare Department and the Supplementary Welfare section of the Health Boards were seen by Irish community organisations as sources for obtaining more material help for people in need; social workers and community organisations should act as advocates and supporters of people in need, while the agencies should supply the cash to the needy-with-rights.

'Only recently have social workers been employed on any extensive scale in Ireland. The main impetus to the development of social work has been the establishment of the Community Care Programme by Health Boards' wrote John Curry in his standard text on Irish social services [Curry, 1980; Department of Social Welfare, 1987]. Irish social workers do not have powers of financial assistance as in Britain under the 1963 Act or in France under *Aide Sociale à l'Enfance*; such support does not therefore feature in accounts of child care work – which is the major pre-occupation of Health Board social workers. Nevertheless it is striking that a recent very thorough account of social workers and children in care in the Dublin area makes no significant mention in over 300 pages to contacts or liaison with income maintenance services of any kind. Psychiatric social workers do have limited powers to help emergency cases, such as temporary lodgings on discharge from hospital. Such payments have to be authorised by programme managers.

It was argued by the promotors of 'The Campaign for the Development of the Social Services' in 1985 that a separate identity for social services workers within the Health Boards would ensure greater flexibility of service and better co-ordination of the social assistance staff with the social workers. The 500-page report of the Commission on Social Welfare in a wide-ranging series of recommendations advocated an expansion and improvement of social welfare benefits and greater co-ordination of the tax and benefit systems. While accepting 'a differential of 10 per cent between insurance and assistance payments', it advocated a common basic assistance payment rather than variable ones based on different assistance schemes [*Commission on Social Welfare*, 1986, 15]. There should be a transfer of income maintenance functions from Health Boards to the social welfare department, and an integration of the supplementary welfare allowance scheme into general social assistance. It recommends the continuation of exceptional needs payments with a review of their working every two years, and the Community Welfare Officers [the nearest Irish equivalent to British Supplementary Benefit Officers] having responsibility for assessment and award. An appeal system would operate as part of the general social assistance appeals. The report considers that the best hope for effective liaison between cash and care in the case of recipients of supplementary assistance lies in having the responsible officers integrated into the social welfare department and liaising with Health Board social workers from that position. Whatever formulae may emerge after the public discussion of the report of the Commission on Social Welfare – and the 1987 government seemed hesitant about it – Irish services for public financial assistance have been described in the report as confusingly, organised in at least two government departments with the relationship between social assistance officers and social workers either very weak or only spasmodically organised. It seems unlikely that they will be seen as essentially complementary in service to the total needs of their clients until there is some form of internal re-organisation within each of the services. This is a surprising conclusion in a small country which has recently given intense public consideration to the need for combined efforts to reduce poverty and inequality – a general aspiration enthusiastically supported by all political parties, the Church's Council for Social Welfare, voluntary bodies and the social work profession. The case of Ireland shows a high degree of fragmentation of services for cash and caring. This is partly due to a series of disjointed reactions to social problems without an agreed overall policy of social provision despite the far greater degree of basic ideological unanimity than in other countries.

What light do these references to other countries throw on the British cash and caring situation? First, it is clear that social work attitudes and practice can be integrated into the provisions of social assistance. In principle there is no real reason why DHSS special case officers should not be trained and qualified social workers. Indeed if one were planning a really effective operation of a properly organised Social Fund for people with acute difficulties it would make good sense for Social Fund officers to have social worker training. Two essential provisos are: that decisions about entitlement are subject to review by some other body and that the basic income level for all in a clear and strictly enforced system makes discretionary grants [or loans] really exceptional. The British system of total nominal separation of cash and caring is an oddity, not a norm. We are the prisoners of our present system of administration which we disguise as a matter of principle. British social workers in any case make decisions about cash awards to their client families under the 1963 Act. It has become clear that payments under this Act were only marginally concerned with the limited and specific purposes of the Act – to prevent family break-up [ADSS, 1985]. Logically one would have expected social services departments and their social workers to refuse to operate under this Act since it certainly involved them in making judgements about the eligibility of their clients for cash help. Yet on the contrary they hold tenaciously to their powers under the Act. They are also repeatedly involved in decisions concerning the liberty, liability, and culpability of citizens in a way which demands diagnosis and judgement. Why are judgements about cash entitlements so different in principle?

In not allowing appeals against officers' decisions, however, the Social Security Act 1986 was wrong. In other European countries there is some form of appeal against decisions made on discretionary social assistance. If the Social Fund provisions of the 1986 Act were to continue without some independent appeal system, Britain would be out of step with almost everyone else. There is a case, however, for a different kind of appeal procedure about discretionary benefits. Any decision about cash or care to a citizen should be subject to appeal and review. But a combined residual service for people in need requires a different appeal system concerned with the *reasonableness* of decisions rather than the amount of the entitlement.

The terms of reference of the Ombudsman are more relevant to a new kind of appeal body over cash and caring decisions than the tribunal systems for social security questions. However, some system of appeal and review must be available in all cases of intervention in clients' lives. It should not be resisted by social services departments with regard to the activities of their own staff any more than for those of social security workers.

From my own reviews of relationships between social security offices and social services departments in Exeter, Lancashire and Cambridgeshire, as from Sue Tester's general study in 1985 [Tester, 1985], it seems that the recommendations in the booklet *Liaison in Practice* [DHSS, 1980c] have filtered down to the operational level. Social workers and supplementary benefit officers had – at least until the 1986 Act – worked out some methods of mutual contact and co-operation in the interest of their clients. The development has however, been very patchy and has depended a great deal on local goodwill and personal contacts. Both 'sides' keep, for example, meticulous records, but in neither case is there any systematic recording of the need for referral. In the case of the DHSS this is partly motivated by care not to appear to record any 'judgemental' entries – in part a sensitivity to welfare rights organisations which are suspicious about judgements on the deserving and the undeserving. In the case of social services departments a handbook on records is instructive. The intention of records is primarily, it claims, to help the client; help is likely to be more effective if a reasonably uniform system of recording is adopted by social workers, to share where appropriate, data with other social worker colleagues. No mention is made of the DHSS or of any referrals there. Of the 26 social services departments which responded with the forms used by social workers, only 8 per cent had any mention of the financial matters of the client. More authorities in fact recorded data on the religion or creed of client than on their financial situation. There is one paragraph referring to material aid which states:

'Some clients classified as "cases" under children's legislation might benefit from material aid and domiciliary services, while clients not classified as 'cases' in this sense might benefit from "casework" as well as material aid' [Kinnibrugh, 1984].

It follows that there must be a co-ordination of income maintenance with other legislation on family and civic responsibilities – which makes nonsense of, for example, the variation of benefits at age 25 rather than the legal age of adulthood at 18, or the assumption of total independence under 18. It is within this context – and only on these conditions – that a reformed and residual provision for income maintenance and social care legitimises and encourages the joint involvement of carers and cash awarders.

The White Paper proposed – [DHSS, 1985d] – and the subsequent 1986 Social Security Act endorsed it – that there should be a separation of regular income support for those with inadequate income from short-term emergency help or lump-sum replacement help to those who

  – face greatest difficulty in managing on their normal income
  – need a more varied response to inescapable individual need
  – can be dealt with without upsetting the general income support scheme

Here the Green Paper [DHSS, 1985c] gave an interesting gloss and was more explicit than the later White Paper:

The type of approach needed in dealing with cla: iants who will often be experiencing stress has marked similarities with that expected of professionals, such as social workers or health care staff. A large part of the social and health needs which the community provisions now meet are the financial counterpart of other services. However, there have been long-standing tensions and difficulties over where the boundaries of the respective responsibilities lie. We do not believe that a wholly satisfactory balance has been established. There can be problems in ensuring both that social services and financial provision do not take on each other's roles and, more particularly, that an individual receiving help from a variety of sources receives a well balanced mix of cash and care. The Government see attractions in moving over a longer period towards a more flexible system, which might be extended to those not receiving income support. Such an approach would need to be developed in joint working with other professionals [DHSS, 1985c].

There is only one comparative reference in the White Paper – namely to New Zealand. However, the proposed separation of Income Support from the Social Fund is very similar to *Aide Légale* and *Aide Facultative* in the present French system. The proposed help with family management is a commonplace to the French Family Allowances social workers, and the decision to abandon designated suppliers is paralleled by the phasing out of food tickets in France.

So-called means-tests are not 'reserved for the poor' [despite Deacon and Bradshaw, 1983] but are the commonplace of any modern personal tax system. What *is* deplorable is to have a whole range of variable assessment tests which confuse and distress both citizens and social workers. To that extent at any rate, moves towards uniformity in assessment in the Social Security Act 1986, are to be welcomed. Supplementary Benefit officers are overwhelmed with increasing hordes of claimants for whom there is inadequate staff. Whole categories of people – elderly, sick, certified unemployed, those with dependent children, could be made eligible for cash benefits without recourse to proof of means and needs. This would involve an almost certain increase in tax and insurance contributions as evidence of social solidarity. This, then, would leave Beveridge's safety net for *emergencies* [not for 4 million people] and social workers to deal with those who have personal problems [often linked with cash] in a better co-ordinated way.

British institutions have installed a separation of the two functions, but the examples from France and Belgium show that other models are possible. They are worth study and experimentation. The definition of the role and tasks of social workers in social service or in probation departments is partly determined by the profession and partly by the institution which they serve. It should be possible to try out the effects of giving training as social workers to staff in the residual part of a reformed social security service and to define their role as all-purpose social workers within the framework of income maintenance. We need also to study the integration of cash grants with preventive family care. Underlying the

whole matter of services varied according to individual needs, is the more
radical question of a minimum guaranteed basic income derived from work
or from a combination of work and social benefits. Without a firm basis of
cash, the most skilful caring rests on an insecure foundation.

Reference was made to the advantage of the Belgian and French systems
in having an established minimum wage and in the case of Belgium a
national subsistence income. This should not be taken to mean, however,
that such established standards are universally accepted nor permanently
established. The national minimum is subject to periodic review and
revision in both countries. It is moreover frequently criticised as
insufficient and the amount is subject to on-going political debate
[Wresinski, 1987]. The *Union Nationale des Centres Communaux* in
France carries critical articles in its monthly journal on the subject,
indicating that the agency management also feels free to express opinions on
the adequacy of minimum income level, the support for families and other
aspects of income-related cash assistance. The need for local
supplementation of the national scale, for example, was recently
commented on:

> Most CCAS are obliged to pay out local social assistance supple-
> ments over too long a period, often several months or even several
> years; they resent the precarious nature of this kind of help just as
> they reluctantly concur with the term 'supplementary' which is
> applied to local supplementation, when very often it is a life-belt
> which cannot be withdrawn from the individual, or the family, which
> would sink entirely without it ... without doubt the assistance
> given by the CCAS remains insufficient. Many crises, many
> controversies would have been undoubtedly avoided if, as we often
> suggested, the legislation has provided the required ear-marked
> resources to enable communes and their CCAS to fulfil their mission
> of 'solidarity' as emphasised in the Act of January, 1986 [Lejeune,
> 1987, 5, author's translation]..

The Belgian social workers employed by the Social Assistance Offices
[CPAS/OCMW] do not feel unduly inhibited from expressing opinions on
the level of minimum income laid down for beneficiaries. There is a ready
acceptance that any worker performing family case work and cash
assistance assessment often faces difficulties in judgements and in
recommendation over complex family situation [UCVB, 1987]. However,
in my meetings with the social work team at the Brugge OCMW, for
example, discussion of the dilemmas facing social workers in the assistance
office has led to the generally supported view that every agency employing
social workers lays down certain terms of reference for the work to be

done, and that workers who find the agency's conditions unacceptable ought not to seek employment there. This is a very different perspective from that prevalent in Britain, where the virtual monopoly of social work employment by social services departments or the probation service, coupled with the separation of the cash assistance function, pre-disposes social workers to an adversarial stance towards cash assistance officers – and vice-versa. One has to question seriously whether this is really in the long-term interest of needy clients.

PART THREE

Poverty, Social Work Practice and Policy

8

A Window on Child Care, Poverty and Social Work

Pauline Hardiker and Mary Barker

T HIS book bears testimony to the nature and dimensions of institutionalised poverty in advanced, industrialised societies. Social workers cannot evade the structural parameters of the private troubles and social problems which they face daily, and nowhere is this more true than in child care. McIntosh [1973, 211] aids our understanding of the structural processes which underly some social problems by her observation that:

There is crime because there is law;
there is theft because there is property;
there is fraud because there is trust'.
We might add:
There is poverty because there is wealth.

From this perspective, social problems are structurally located and reinforced by majority social interests. The structural links between child care and poverty are thus forged through social inequalities plus ideologies about familialism, parental autonomy and the boundaries of society's duties towards its children [Barrett and McIntosh, 1982; Fox, 1982; DHSS, 1985e]. These distribute resources unequally and limit those services [income, housing, day-care and family support] which potentially reduce the impact of poverty on children and parents.

Nevertheless, any social worker who views poverty and child care *solely* in structural terms is presumably more or less incapacitated from trying interventions that might remediate the difficulties of raising children [Hardiker and Barker, 1981]. Accordingly, we shall attempt to make our task in this brief chapter manageable by outlining three levels of analysis in social theory and practice and presenting selected case illustrations from our larger project [Hardiker and Barker, 1986].

It is necessary to disaggregate different levels of analysis to avoid reductionist explanations and misdirected interventions. Poverty can be explained structurally in terms of social inequalities in the distribution of incomes and resources [Townsend, 1979]. These inequalities are reinforced through social class, gender, age, disabilities, ethnic and regional divisions [Westergaad and Resler, 1975; Walker and Townsend, 1981; Newnham , 1986; Phillipson and Walker, 1986; Glendenning and Millar, 1987; Walker and Walker, 1987; Disability Alliance, 1987b]. At least thirty per cent of children in Britain live in poverty, their mothers typically bearing the brunt, and those experiencing disabilities, racial discrimination and the north/south divide being further disadvantaged. Neither social workers, social services nor local authorities can overcome such poverty *directly*, though they can ensure that their policies and practices do not reinforce the associated inequalities [House of Commons, 1984; Townsend, *et al*, 1987]. If social workers understand the structural dimensions of poverty, this will enable them to identify the boundaries of feasible interventions with children and families [Bailey, 1980].

Poverty can be explained at an **organisational** level in terms of needs and resources [Davies and Challis, 1986]. There is an inverse relationship between the needs for child care resources and the availability of such services as income support, housing, day-care, community and family assistance [*Equality for Children*, 1983]. Still, the links between needs and resources are extremely complex and mediated by decision-making processes [DHSS, 1985f; Packman, *et al*, 1986]. Direct social work interventions in these circumstances must be targetted at maximising parental access to benefits and scarce facilities. Indirect service delivery activities should monitor needs and shortfall in provisions [especially for the most vulnerable groups of children] and collate evidence on the links between poverty and admission to care, and the financial impediments to maintaining links between parents and their children in care, or to rehabilitating children home [Portsmouth, 1975; Thoburn, 1980; Holman, 1980; Strathclyde, 1982; Farmer and Parker, 1985; Family Rights Group, 1985; Millham, *et al*, 1986; Beresford, *et al*, 1987.

Poverty may also be viewed from an *interactionist* or *psychosocial* perspective, which focuses upon the ways public issues may have a bearing on private troubles [Mills, 1959]. Even if some of the sources of a family's difficulties [eg parenting] are external to individuals [eg social deprivations], there is no reason why social workers should not provide a *personal* social service to them [Jacoby, 1975; Philp, 1979; Pinker, 1982]. Our research report [*op cit*] outlines the nature of psychosocial approaches in child care; suffice it to note here that there is a structural space in British society for social workers to intervene at the level of the person-in-the-environment [Hollis, 1972; Webb, 1981; Hudson, 1985].

We shall now present four examples to illustrate the feasibility and boundaries of **direct**, interactionist interventions in relation to child care, poverty and social work.

Dimensions of poverty in child care
The B family

Mr and Mrs B were in their late twenties and had met in their youth, when both of them were attending a 'subnormality hospital' as day patients. The couple had led a nomadic existence for some years and during this period had a baby who was placed for adoption. The current social worker became involved when they were living with Mr B's sister, and then in lodgings, where there were many strains, stresses and crisis situations. At this time they married, started attending an Adult Training Centre and applied for a local authority tenancy. The social worker supported their application, and when they were allocated a flat he recruited a group of four volunteers to support them in their aim of living 'ordinarily'in the community. The volunteers were accepted by Mr and Mrs B and became 'more like friends'. The Adult Training Centre and Mencap also gave practical help and encouragement. This time was described as 'the longest period of stability and happiness the couple have ever known'.

It had been anticipated that Mrs B might become pregnant and that a decision would have to be made about the parents' ability to care for their baby in the community. After Mrs B conceived, the social worker and his supervisors decided to support the parents in their wish to keep their baby, though several factors had to be considered:

1. **Previous history**: the mental handicaps of the parents could not be ignored and there appeared to be some carry-over of feelings and attitudes from the adoption of their first baby.

2. **Housing**: the B's stable accommodation arrangements brightened their prospects; their flat was on a housing estate, on a 'bus route and near a telephone kiosk'.

3. **Economic circumstances**: various housing and welfare benefits were mobilised at each stage; though these still left Mr and Mrs B in relataive poverty, this was not considered to be a contra-indication, especially since many families are expected to manage on similar low incomes.

4. **Policy of the social services department**: the statutory obligation to prevent the reception of children into care was actively practised in the agency. This policy was buttressed by a range of resources, including the allocation of the social worker over a long period, a subsidised day nursery place, and small amounts of financial and material aid.

Issues

1. The inter-relationship between a variety of factors which can bring a family to the door of a social services department: in this case, poverty was one; mental handicap, lack of housing and estrangement from relatives were others. The B family's situation when their first baby was born, compared with their second, was not only a matter of poverty. The social worker needed to pay attention to the family's resources, and also to their housing arrangements, their ability to manage the practicalities of daily living, their networks of social support and their access to various welfare provisions.

2. The complexity of the links between poverty and reception into care: statistical evidence demonstrates the correlation between the two, but it is not a simple cause and effect. The social worker had to work out an equation of risks, needs and resources, in an uncertain situation [Curnock and Hardiker, 1979]. The greatest unknowns were how Mr and Mrs B would relate to their baby, and whether they had enough knowledge of his needs and requirements to ensure his survival and development. On this occasion, proper housing, sufficient material resources and a variety of social supports probably tipped the balance in enabling them to care for this child. The social worker was conscious of the dangers of 'labelling' them, and also considered that their situation was no worse than that of other families who had not come to the attention of the social services, [Schorr, 1975].

3. The social control functions of the social services: there was some tension between the parents' wish 'just to stay at home with their baby' and the informal pressure that was put on them to use the day nursery and [in the case of Mr B] to attend the ATC. The day nursery was used as a means of monitoring the baby's care and, if necessary, to supplement that care. The social worker was also looking ahead to the time when Mrs B might need different kinds of support and guidance with a lively toddler, when the child might need more active stimulation than he received at home. In an attempt to counter Mrs B's isolation, an informal group of mothers whose

children attended the nursery was started, but Mrs B was the one mother who did not attend! Mr B's partial withdrawal from the ATC [which he regarded as 'not a proper job'] was also seen as limiting his social networks and access to welfare benefits. It could endanger the family's level of income, if he reverted to the status of being unemployed. Social control was evident in both these aspects, but was humanely administered with an eye to improving the parents' opportunities, as well as the baby's development. As Mr and Mrs B demonstrated their love and care of the child, their wishes to reduce attendance at the nursery and the number of volunteers who visited them were respected.

The social work interventions based upon the psychosocial assessment outlined were successful, at least in the short term, but were now without their dilemmas and difficulties. Mr and Mrs B's baby, Tom, was described as 'healthy and happy as the day is long'.

The C family

Mr and Mrs C lived in a council flat with their two children, Dana aged 5 and Mark aged 3. They married in their late thirties and were socially isolated, as Mrs C had few contacts with her own family and Mr C had been brought up by a distant relative who [it was said] showed him no affection. Mr C had been a miner, but was dismissed because of frequent absences and poor time-keeping.

The family had some previous contact with the social services when Dana was received into care briefly during her mother's absence in hospital. She was later allocated a place in the day nursery at her parents' request because her speech was severely retarded. Mark too, was admitted to the day nursery on account of speech difficulties and because he was too active for his parents. Both children did well there.

The social worker became involved after Mark was reported to have abrasions and bruises to his head and back. The parents told her that Mark had disturbed them repeatedly during the night. Mr C had picked him up from his cot, shaken him and thrown him roughly back across the sides of the cot, in order 'to teach him a lesson'. In her assessment, she noted a number of personal, interpersonal and environmental stresses:

1. The family lived in a tiny, two bedroomed flat with no play space. One bedroom was not in use because it was filled with 'clutter', and the children slept in their parents' bedroom.

2. The family had the problem of managing on a much-reduced income and received supplementary benefits. There were considerable rent arrears but no other debts, though Mrs C sometimes kept the children from the

nursery because she could not afford the fares and the [reduced] fees.

3. There were constant arguments between the parents, in which each accused and blamed the other. Mr C led an active social life and Mrs C was often very short of money for household needs complaining that Mr C would take money out of her purse.

4. Mr and Mrs C had few social supports and little self-esteem. They seemed to have limited knowledge of children's needs and management. Mr C showed affection for Dana but seemed harsh with Mark, who was a bright, lively and very active little boy.

Intervention

A case conference was held and it was decided that the children should be put on the 'At Risk' register, and that the social worker as 'key worker' would undertake preventive work while the children remained at home. The social worker was anxious about what she was undertaking but found the parents very willing to work with her in the following ways:

1. She helped the parents to clear the second bedroom, into which the children moved. A contract was made with the parents that her department would match their contributions towards the rent arrears and arranged a meeting with the housing manager and local district councillors which led to the allocation of a three bedroomed house with a garden.

2. With the Cs consent, the DHSS agreed to pay 'rent direct' to the housing department. The day nursery fees were remitted, and transport for the children was arranged.

3. In joint discussions with Mr and Mrs C, the social worker insisted that they spoke one at a time, listened to each other and made their own suggestions about how to improve their own relationship. Financial problems and the distribution of resources were among the bones of contention between them. She was careful not to take sides with either partner but encouraged them to follow up their own suggestions. In time, she thought they paid more attention to each other, achieved some agreements, and there was less tension in the household.

4. She helped the parents to improve their handling of the children by demonstration and by devising a simple programme for a consistent response to Mark's behaviour. She also arranged for Mrs C to spend a day a week at the nursery where she might learn something of their methods. She thought Mrs C enjoyed the company.

5. She also recognised and praised the parents' efforts and achievements, and as their situation improved there was a gradual increase in their self-esteem.

These interventions took place over two years, after which the situation was evaluated as 'much inproved'. There were no further injuries, the children made a good start at infant school and their names were removed from the 'At Risk' register. There were still some rent arrears and the social worker planned to work with the family to try to clear these before closing the case.

Issues

1. 'At Risk' registers are often discussed in terms of loss of rights, invasion of privacy and risk of labelling. As measures of social control, designed to protect children from parents, they include all these elements. They can also function as a 'privilege list', releasing resources which reduce the disadvantages experienced by some children and parents [Scott, 1975].

2. There are many question marks over preventive social work, whose failures sometimes reach the headlines and whose successes are less well documented. This example illustrates effective social work, between a social worker [who described her approach as 'practical down-to-earth, task-centred'] and parents who in the event also wanted changes.

3. Improving families' financial and material circumstances seems to be part of most preventive social work. Assistance given from social services departments 'Section 1' budgets is however, temporary and small-scale [Heywood and Allen, 1971; Jackson and Valencia, 1979]. Skilled welfare rights advisers can sometimes negotiate longer-term increases in income [eg in cases of disabilty], but research has demonstrated that social workers' clients often do not receive their full entitlements. In this case, improvements were achieved, but we have no means of knowing whether the C's income was fully maximised. The case illustrates, however, some of the ways in which material need is inter-related with interpersonal and environmental factors. Financial and material aid and advice were given, but simultaneous efforts were made to improve the use and distribution of resources with the family [not easy, because of the many meanings attached to the possesion and spending of money in our society]. Probably, social workers do their best work on money matters in such cases, which receive high priority in departments. But, whatever is done to improve families' material circumstances, the end result can only help them to survive better in the poverty which they share with a large minority of the population.

The D family

Although the great majority of clients of social services departments are living in poverty, there are exceptions. In the D family, other forms of deprivation were the cause of concern and money had symbolic importance.

Mr D had a white-collar job, as had Mrs D until her marriage. In fact, their employment sometimes led them into conflict with other residents of the working-class estate where they lived, and they were socially ostracised. The family were referred to the department for the first time when Andy was three because of his 'failure to thrive'. Problems had come to light when a student health visitor recognised that he was grossly underweight. The paediatrician assessed him as physically retarded, severely emotionally deprived and without speech, and recommended his immediate removal.

The social worker arranged a day nursery place for Andy while he made his own assessment. Mrs D told him that she had not wanted another child. She thought perhaps the maternity hospital had given her the 'wrong baby', and she was unable to tolerate him. At times she thought he was 'plotting against her'. She had a history of 'nervous breakdowns' but was not receiving any psychiatric treatment. Mr D was attached to Andy and took over his care as much as possible but, according to his wife, he denied her feelings and this led to conflict between them. Andy was kept in a playpen in the hall and learned to stay in the background. The social worker records:

'The fewer demands he made on mother, the less he was criticised, so he kept very quiet; it came full circle when she complained that he was very quiet and that there must be something wrong with him because he did not do anything'.

There were difficulties about attendance at the day nursery because, despite remissions, the parents refused to pay the fees. In contrast to the other two children, very little money was spent on Andy; for instance his birthday was not acknowledged by cards, presents or parties. It was while Mr D was getting Andy ready for the day nursery that he slapped him hard enough to cause bruising. This, on top of other forms of deprivation, led the department to seek a Place of Safety Order and later a Care Order. Once a compulsory order was made, it was experienced as a great release by the parents, and they requested in court that he should be adopted. Although this was followed by feelings of guilt and ambivalence, they did not deviate from their decision that he should be adopted.

Issues

This was said to be a classic textbook case of 'failure to thrive' [Iwaniec, *et al*, 1985]. Only selected themes from the complex events surrounding the D family have been outlined here.

1. The D family was not in financial poverty; in fact their relative prosperity and status heightened their social isolation in the community where they lived. They had great difficulty, however, in spending money on this particular child. Refusal to spend money on a child may be interpreted in various ways. From a psychodynamic perspective, it is a symptom of the withdrawal of love; such emotional abuse affects not only a child's physical development, but also its sense of well-being and self-esteem. From a social learning perspective, money may be seen in the context of exchange. It is withheld as a punishment, becomes a bargaining technique and produces asymmetrical relationships. Parents involved in such exchanges deny themselves any altruism.

2. The social worker in this case was under pressure to remove the child immediately, but resisted this until he had gained an understanding of the family situation and assessed the possibility of preventive work. Practical support and counselling would have been the measures of first choice, but it seemed that the severity of the child's condition, and the partners' lack of any wish for help over him, precluded rehabilitation. The social worker's honesty in facing the parents with the reality of what was happening, and the alternatives and consequences, seemed to enable them to reach a decision they could stand by. Other forms of help were offered to and accepted by them subsequently.

Although preventive work can be very effective, there is the risk that, without adequate psychosocial assessments, social workers may become caught up in protracted and ultimately fruitless helping activities.

The E family

Sylvie E was brought up in a repressive home, by parents of Afro-Caribbean origin who belonged to a religious sect. When she was 15, she ran away from home and was received into care when her parents refused to have her back. She was pregnant and went to live in a purpose-built hostel, which included small flats where residents could look after their own children if they wished. Before and after the birth of her baby, Gemma, she was adamant she wanted her adopted and made no preparations for her care. However, after a visit from the maternal grandmother, she asked for time to make up her mind and at her request Gemma was received into care and placed with a local short-term foster-mother. The social worker and hostel staff supported her in her wish to build an independent life for herself and, meanwhile, to reach her own decision about Gemma's future. During the next two and a half years, the following resources were mobilised:

1. Income support.

2. Facilities for her to have Gemma with her at the hostel, full-time or part-time, with staff back-up.

3. Continuation of short-term foster-care for Gemma with full access.

4. Payment of registration fees and fares for Sylvie to take a CSV course, to train for community service.

5. Negotiations with the housing department leading to an offer of a council flat for Sylvie and Gemma, backed up by a rent guarantee from the social services department as she was under 18.

6. Offer of day-nursery and part-time care facilities if mother chose to have Gemma with her.

Sylvie did well in care, finding and keeping a job against the odds, and eventually moving into her own accommodation. She was encouraged to visit Gemma, to have her for weekends, and to make plans which gave her the option of having Gemma, but there were long periods when she dropped out of contact with her completely. In practice, she avoided contact, while not being willing to consent to long-term plans for her. Much work was undertaken with Sylvie, her mother and the foster-mother to try to reach an agreed plan, but to no avail, and eventually the social worker recommended that Gemma should be 'freed for adoption', by application to the County Court, under new legislation. Sylvie visited the prospective adoptors several times, got on well with them and did not appear in court to oppose the application. The social worker concluded:

> All necessary resources were made available to facilitate Gemma's rehabilitation to her mother. It was a very painful piece of work – any social worker would feel absolutely ridden with guilt about taking a big step like freeing for adoption. It has not been easy, but I am very satisfied with the outcome. I feel in my heart of hearts that I did everything to the best of my ability to try to rehabilitate the child with her mother and then to find suitable prospective adopters.

Issues

This account is included as an example of one aspect of social work: the provision of needed and wanted resources in order to create space for families to decide what they want for their children, even if, as in this case, the decision proves elusive. Other examples came up in our research. For instance, parents who were beginning to reject their new baby [born with Down's Syndrome] were offered short-term foster-care while they started to come to terms with the situation and made some decisions about the future.

In the E family, we see again a situation of divergent interests between parents and children. Sylvie [possibly due to the influence of the maternal grandmother] wanted indefinite postponement of long-term plans though Gemma needed a home, either with her mother or another long-term carer. It is difficult to determine whether 'everything' was done to achieve rehabilitation with her mother, but certainly considerable efforts were made and resources offered. At the same time, Sylvie was helped in her own right to achieve her potential. She may have felt she was being 'put through hoops' in the pressure that was put on her to keep in touch with the baby and to come to a decision [DHSS, 1985f; Fisher, *et al*, 1986], but here again, the social control function of social service departments is apparent; difficult, coercive decisions sometimes have to be taken [Handler, 1973].

Conclusion

Four cases were presented to illustrate different dimensions of child care and poverty. We believe that case material is important to demonstrate the range of social and personal difficulties experienced by some families, and the variety of methods which social workers may use to assist them. We have chosen cases in which some good work was done and relatively positive outcomes were achieved, in the belief that such work is under-reported and that much can be learned from studying constructive ways in which resources can be used. Recording them so briefly, when the outcome is known, does not do full justice to the dilemmas which the social workers faced, the risks they took and the interactional skills they used. From a policy point of view, there is the possibility of distortion when material is presented in this way, since generalisations or structural variables cannot be derived from individual cases. Still, since we need not be blinkered by the case, we shall explore briefly some of those larger issues raised by this material.

1. The structural axes of disability, gender, social class and ethnicity permeated the lives of the families described:

- The B family might have been further helped through positive discrimination [eg additional benefits] to counteract some of the deprivations associated with disabilities [*Disability Alliance*, 1987b].

- Mrs C might have been a classic example of the feminisation of poverty, given the expectations of her budgeting, household management, child care and conjugal roles, [Glendenning and Millar, 1987]. Section I monies might have shored up inadequate income maintenance services.

- the parenting difficulties in the D family might have been structural and personal, requiring social care planning in relation to their isolated social networks [Garbarino, 1981; Barclay, 1982].

- the E family points to the potential dangers of permanency planning becoming a contemporary child rescue movement in relation to class, ethnicity and marital status [*Equality for Children*, 1983; Tunstill, 1985; Ahmed, *et al*, 1986; Thoburn, 1986; Peters, 1987]. The importance of income support, housing day-care and social networks was evident in all four cases.

We are obliged to note that some families are caught up in complex cycles of disadvantage upon which interventions have little purchase, save social protection [Jordan, 1974; Rutter and Madge, 1976; Fuller and Stevenson, 1983; Hardiker and Barker, 1986].

2. The poverty dimension. It is no longer open to debate that most clients of social services [specifically and increasingly families with children] are in poverty, though the dimensions and relevance of poverty to policies are reviewed here only summarily. Social workers and social services departments cannot begin to address the needs of everyone in poverty in our society. Why specific children in poverty become cases and what services are provided are intricate consequences of need-definitions and legal/administrative policies, as well as individual and interpersonal factors. The priority afforded NAI is a good example of such selectivity, and it is no accident that risk registers figured in our examples [Dingwall, *et al*, 1983; Parton, 1985].

It is also the objectives of agencies which shape responses to poverty. We have explored some links between social work practices and agency objectives in relation to mental handicap elsewhere [School of Social Work, 1981; Hardiker and Barker, 1981] and the same concepts are relevant to child care and poverty. For example, if agencies do not give priority to the poverty in their client loads, many families may not receive their full benefit entitlements and preference may be given to 'rescuing' children at the expense of preventive services [*Equality for Children*, 1983; House of Commons, 1984]. Ultimately, though, the objectives of agencies are bounded by economic and social policies, and this is nicely illustrated in the proportion of the GNP [2.6 per cent 1985/6] allocated to personal social services.

3. The multirole practitioner. We suggested earlier that social workers

have different roles to play according to the level of intervention chosen. As Stevenson states [Becker and MacPherson, 1986, iv]:

> Social workers . . . have to engage with poverty in two ways. One involves a general response to its impact on their clients, with an obligation to describe and discuss for a wider audience whose concerns can be mobilised. The other . . . requires the social worker to consider the most effective ways of helping the individual in poverty who is a unique person in unique difficulty.

✱ Accordingly, social workers have a variety of roles to play in relation to child care and poverty, from counsellor, protector, enabler, and broker, advocate, coordinator, to consultant, researcher, educator [Rein, 1970; Baker, 1976]. Work is also undertaken with, and for, families and children who may never figure on caseloads, through community projects, family support initiatives and interagency collaboration [eg Goldberg and Sinclair, 1987; Goldberg, *et al*, 1987].

Ultimately, we need to remind ouselves of the modesty of social work's complex endeavours. Even when interventions in relation to child care and poverty are relatively successful, those aided are restored to the imperfect and difficult life which we all share. Moreover, we still marvel at:

> . . . what so many people, especially women, manage. Why is there not . . . more physical injury in lives reduced to survival on the dole, or supplementary benefits, or as a homeless family in bed and breakfast? [Peters, 1987].

Perhaps it is the personal and social *costs* of managing to rear children in poverty that we should be exploring.

Acknowledgments
We should like to express our thanks to colleagues in the School of Social Work and Professor Martin Herbert, University of Leicester, for their help and advice in the preparation of this chapter.

9

Child Abuse and Poverty

Rob Irvine

THE latest Department of Health and Social Security low income families   tables highlight the rise in the number of children living around or below   supplementary benefit levels; from 2,370,000 in 1979 to 3,880,000 in 1983, a rise of 64 per cent. [See MacPherson and Svenson, this volume]. As many as 30 per cent of children in Britain are living around or below the supplementary benefit level. At the same time statutory authorities, and some voluntary agencies, have detected an increase in the number of referrals in reported episodes of child abuse. It is timely to examine the association between poverty and referrals to social services of child abuse.

Models of child abuse causation

Consideration of child abuse by the professional and lay communities is a relatively recent development. Child abuse became fixed in the public consciousness and placed on professional agendas as a result of the publication in 1962 of an article by Kempe and his associates in which they laid out, for the first time, the pattern of symptoms associated with the emotive concept, 'the battered baby syndrome'.

Since the publication of this seminal account of the physical abuse of very young children the question 'what causes child abuse' and its corollary what should we do about it' have been the subject of hotly contested debates. The principal point of contention in this dispute is identified by the extent to which commentators and practitioners associate child abuse with a set of causes located either in parental failure or the social context in which incidents of child abuse take place.

The distinction in these two approaches is shown clearly by two reports, both published in 1986. The first states that:

> living in poverty can lead to depression, apathy or anger; being depressed can lead to it becoming impossible to make use of the limited resources at one's disposal. Children, many hundreds of thousands of them, are suffering as a result . . . debts, marital discord and unemployment are most commonly cited by parents as triggers which preceded the abuse of children [*National Children's Homes*, 1986,

In contrast to this situational perspective, Lestor [1986] asserts 'child abuse is not necessarily or exclusively a problem of poverty and should not be treated as such' [p.8].

These two positions are not necessarily contradictory. The authors of these particular reports seem likely to support the possibility of a link between the two stances, an interaction between the personal and social. When we turn to the mainstream research literature, however, the two positions appear to be more clear-cut and polarized. Indeed much of the research into child abuse resembles a conceptual battlefield of competing ideologies and assumptions. For example, Steele and Pollock [1974] argue:

> Unquestionably social and economic difficulties and disasters put added stress into people's lives and contribute to behaviour which otherwise remain dormant. *But such factors must be considered as incidental enhancers rather than necessary and sufficient cause [of child abuse]*. [My emphasis, p.108].

Authors like Steele and Pollock adopt an individualistic perspective of the problem which presupposes that the abusive behaviour of the adult carer, usually the parent, is a sign or product of some personal traits, constitutional defect or experiences which differentiates or isolates them from the rest of the normal population.

Since the early 1960s numerous researchers have engaged in studies which Matza [1964] has described as the 'search for differentiation': attempts have been made to answer such questions as; 'What kinds of people abuse their children?', 'What is wrong with them?' and 'How did they get this way?' Researchers have therefore presented data which implicate the individual characteristics of the parent who is portrayed as suffering from the full gamut of individual and social pathologies. Abusive parents have at one time or another been labelled as: exhibiting emotional disequilibrium; lacking in adequate parenting; alcoholic; drug dependent; promiscuous; mentally ill; immature; self-centred; lacking self control; low in self-esteem. [See Francis, 1963; Donovan and Wong, 1965; Isades, 1972; Bishop, 1975; *International Journal of Child Abuse and Neglect, passim*]. Such defects in personality and experience are said to predispose some parents to violent outbursts.

The pathologizing of child abuse into categories derived from psychology and psychiatry has held sway among researchers and practitioners working in the child welfare field. At the same time, the media has been instrumental in popularizing this model of child abuse among the lay community [Nelson, 1984]. Yet a growing number of writers have been critical of the pathological model; doubts have been expressed about its explanatory and diagnostic power [Freeman, 1983; Parton, 1985]. Shepard [1982] offers a critical discussion of the relationships between individual pathological models of child abuse and social work practice.

While those who adopt the pathological model are united in their belief that individual characteristics are causally associated with the occurrence of child abuse, they disagree over what constitutes the definitive characteristics or attributes of the abusive parent. Gelles, in a review of the child abuse research literature, found that of the nineteen traits referred to by authors which describe the psychopathology of the abuser, only four figure in the accounts of two or more authors. Each remaining trait was mentioned by only a single author [Gelles, 1973]. Similar findings have been reported elsewhere in the literature [Spinetta and Pegler, 1972; Parke and Colmer, 1975].

The lack of consistency between research findings has lead some authors to question whether or not it is possible to identify abusers. Bourne [1979], for example, argues that 'a clear-cut psychological distinction between abusers and non-abusers does not exist'. Not all abusers have the psychological characteristics generally attributed to them.

While the psychological model of child abuse may not necessarily be incorrect, it is incomplete, inadequate and too narrow. It fails to give sufficient emphasis to the material and structural context within which abusive episodes take place. By attributing the symptoms of violence to psychologically damaged or defective individuals, the model ignores socio-economic variables such as unemployment, poverty and structural inequality which may make adequate parenting problematical. Even when social factors and socio-economic factors are taken into account these are conceptualized in terms of the personality characteristics of the parent, the child or the family, and to personal health. This reductionist approach to the problem has a number of implications for the way child abuse is perceived and explained. Firstly, we are unable to decipher the meaning and complexity of the problem of child abuse. Secondly, the function of social inequality and class is obscured. Lastly, the pathological model de-politicizes the issue of child abuse by ignoring the question 'What is wrong with society?' which may predispose some people to violence [Gil, 1970; Gelles, 1973; Steinmetz and Spears, 1974; Strauss *et al*, 1979; Freeman, 1983; Parton, 1985].

Such doubts about the heuristic value of more orthodox accounts of child abuse have given rise to competing sociological explanations which focus on social or 'environmental' factors such as unemployment, poverty and structural inequality. Individual psychology is accounted for in terms of people experiencing a particular class, and more recently gender, position within the social structure.

The fact that attention is drawn to a putative relationship between socio-economic variables and child abuse is, perhaps, not surprising. Research carried out in the UK suggests that inadequate income undermines the ability and capacity of families to provide contexts for positive child development. Wilson and Herbert [1978] in their study of the development of school-age children in 56 Birmingham households argued that poverty in the home environment was linked, in some unspecified way, to certain child rearing practices which the parents themselves regarded as undesirable.

Holman [1980] reaches a similar conclusion in his analysis of inequalities in child care. He argues that for some poor families, socially depressing conditions create a barrier to the achievement of certain accepted child care objectives. Environmental factors, especially economic deprivation and its correlates, large families, low socio-economic status and substandard housing are, therefore, thought to have a determinate effect on the overall quality of parent-child relations. Those who adopt this situational perspective of parental behaviour argue that people respond to their environment. It follows that if opportunities were available to parents, they would change their behaviour toward their children in a positive direction.

There is a growing body of evidence which draws a more positive link between socio-economic variables and class position and certain forms of child abuse. In a national survey of child abuse in the United States, Gil [1970] concluded that child abuse is directly linked to structurally produced stresses of poverty, poorly paid and alienating work, overcrowding and a competitive work ethic which labels some groups as losers.

Unemployment and child abuse

In a recent survey of cases seen by the Child Protection Team [CPT] at the University of Colorado Hospital over a fifteen year period, the authors report a significant positive correlation between local rates of unemployment and the number of cases of physical abuse seen by the CPT [Krugman *et al*, 1986]. These initial findings were substantiated by the authors when they undertook a secondary analysis of 30 randomly selected cases from CPT records: 49 per cent of the 120 families who were reviewed were found to be unemployed at the time the case was reported. These data support the findings of earlier studies which indicate a relationship between child abuse and unemployment [Gil, 1971; Light, 1973; Steinberg *et al*, 1981; Segal, 1984].

In this country, the NSPCC has produced figures on the employment status of parents of children placed on child abuse registers held by the NSPCC from 1977 to 1982 [Creighton, 1984].

Table 9.1

	Employment characteristics of parents of abused children by year				
Year	Mothers Employed*	Unemployed	Fathers Employed*	Unemployed	Supplementary Benefit Recipients
1977	123 (17.6)	494 (70.7)	331 (58.4)	217 (35.0)	337 (46.6)
1978	111 (15.0)	592 (80.2)	350 (56.4)	219 (35.3)	301 (40.2)
1979	104 (15.5)	555 (82.7)	330 (57.2)	230 (39.9)	303 (42.6)
1980	122 (15.6)	601 (76.7)	313 (47.1)	257 (38.7)	367 (45.0)
1981	109 (12.6)	704 (81.2)	277 (38.7)	257 (38.7)	514 (57.2)
1982	98 (12.9)	662 (81.8)	226 (36.0)	365 (58.2)	483 (61.7)

* Percentages relate to the different numbers of mothers and fathers in the sample when parental situation is adjusted for.
Source: Creighton, 1984. Table 13. p12

Table 9.1 shows that the percentage of mothers in paid employment in any one year is relatively small - only 12.6 per cent were employed in 1981 compared with a national figure of 51 per cent for married women and 48 per cent for lone mothers with dependent children. Moreover, the proportion of mothers in paid employment remained relatively stable over this period. When we turn to the employment of fathers, however, a more striking picture begins to emerge. In 1977, 35 per cent of the male care takers with children on the abuse register were unemployed. This figure increased to 58 per cent of fathers in 1982. It can be argued that this upward trend will have further increased since these reports were published, as the level of unemployment has grown.

Similar evidence is reported by Strathclyde Social Work Department. A survey of children on the 'At Risk' register in June 1980 reports that almost two-thirds of male carers of children thought to be at risk of non-accidental injury were unemployed [Strathclyde, 1982]. More recently, of approximately 2,500 children received into the care of that department in 1985, the primary reason for reception in 10 per cent of the cases was suspected child abuse or schedule offences. Less than 20 per cent of these families had incomes from employment. The results of these surveys remind us, if such reminders are necessary, that unemployment is not a problem experienced by individuals; rather it affects entire families, including families with children.

There is a danger in generalising too far from these data. While unemployment appears to be a significant factor, one cannot deduce that unemployment necessarily causes child abuse. Nor can we state with any degree of certainty why this relationship may occur.

Child abuse and poverty

A number of writers have argued that poverty is associated in some complex way with child abuse. The links between unemployment and poverty are widely acknowledged but poverty is much wider than unemployment alone: 4.1 million of those currently living in or on the margin of poverty; nearly 40 per cent of the total living in non-pensioner households were dependent on a full-time wage. We have virtually no data on the association between working poverty and child abuse; most research relating to poverty and abuse focuses on those dependent on benefits, and on supplementary benefit in particular.

Over 46 per cent of the families on the NSPCC's register in 1977 were recipients of supplementary benefit [Creighton, 1984]. The proportion of families in receipt of supplementary benefit in 1982 had increased to 61.7 per cent of the sample [see Table 9.1]. In an earlier survey, the NSPCC [1976] reports that one-third of the parents had expressed financial worries and half had a history of debt, mostly rent arrears.

Similar results were obtained from a survey of referrals for child abuse and neglect to a sample of social work offices in Strathclyde.

Table 9.2

	Strathclyde referrals 1984-85 child related, by income			
	Referrals not on state benefits	Referrals on supplement-ary benefit	Referrals on other benefit	Total
Child related	404	900	129	1433
	28%	63%	9%	100%
Child abuse	18	87	10	115
	16%	76%	9%	101%
Child neglect	28	147	16	191
	15%	77%	8%	100%
Child offence	25	39	9	73
	34%	53%	12%	99%
Child/parent relationship	127	255	43	425
	30%	60%	10%	100%
Truancy	35	74	8	117
	30%	63%	7%	100%
Child handicap	2	0	0	2
	100%	0%	0%	100%
Other	0	2	1	3
	0%	75%	25%	100%
All child related referrals	639	1504	216	2359
	27%	64%	9%	100%
All referrals	8651	38521	26614	73686
	12%	52%	36%	100%

Source: Becker and MacPherson, 1986, Table 3.5, p33

Table 9.2 shows that approximately 76 per cent of the child abuse referrals to the selected offices [and 77 per cent of child neglect referrals] were from supplementary benefit claimants. If we were to add households who were in receipt of some other form of benefit, eg Family Income Supplement, these figures increase to 85 per cent both for child abuse and child neglect referrals. This compares on average with about 15 per cent of such referrals from non-claimants. These results confirm the findings of the earlier study of 719 cases placed on the At Risk Register in June 1980: supplementary benefit was reported to be the main source of income in half of the cases.

District rates of non-accidental injury were also compared with a range of poverty indicators, eg percentage of children receiving free school meals; neonatal mortality rates; family size. The multiple correlation co-efficient between non-accidental injury rate and the deprivation mark was 9.8 representing a strong positive association between non-accidental injury and poverty. And, like the NSPCC findings, in half of the cases the social workers reported that the families were experiencing financial difficulties, mostly rent arrears and financial debt. In the majority of the cases it was the social worker's judgement that the client's financial problems were due to low income rather than poor management [Strathclyde, 1982; Creighton, 1976].

Child abuse and social class

Much of the research reported so far seems to indicate a positive link between child abuse and social factors: unemployment, poverty or other social deprivations. Poverty is also associated with class. Parents with low socio-economic status are certainly over-represented in samples of children who have been abused, or are thought to be 'at risk' of abuse. The NSPCC reported that only 5 per cent of the parents of children registered on 'At Risk' registers in 1976 were classified as having non-manual occupations; the majority of parents were classified as being in semi-skilled or un-skilled occupations. Consequently some writers have argued that child abuse, in terms of both its prevalence and severity, is strongly related to the socio-economic status of the parent. Indeed there are those who argue that child abuse is essentially a working-class phenomenon or an element of a culture of poverty. Put crudely, only the working class physically abuse their children [Skinner and Castle, 1969; Smith *et al*, 1973; Creighton, 1976; Creighton and Outram, 1980; Nixon *et al*, 1981; Creighton, 1984].

The notion that socio-economic status is a powerful determinant of child abuse, particularly non-accidental injury, is subject to much debate and should be treated with caution. The need for such caution is demonstrated by the figures provided by Strathclyde Social Work Department [Table 9.2] which show that *proportionately equal* amounts of referrals for child abuse come from supplementary benefit recipients as from those not in receipt of benefits, approximately 2 per cent in each case. There is also the danger of manufacturing broad generalisations about the etiology of child abuse which rest upon data which are essentially flawed.

Studies of child abuse are based for the most part on the retrospective analysis of referrals to social welfare agencies. These data tend to be subject to systematic bias. For example, data derived from the records of social work agencies will tend to be skewed in the direction of those who make most use of the services – the poor. Since most studies of child abuse are based on case reports which come from public authorities, there is a bias of detection in the direction of the poor and families of low socio-economic status.

There are other sources of bias. The detection of children who are labelled as being 'at risk' is more likely to occur in families whose circumstances are better known to the public officials. By going into the homes of poor clients and getting to know the families, considerably more abuse and neglect is discovered than typically comes to the attention of public authorities. More affluent families are better equipped to maintain their privacy and isolation: concealing their private lives and personal difficulties from the gaze of public officials [Parke and Collmer, 1975; Egeland, 1979].

A number of studies which have investigated the process of case identification suggest that the unfavourably high incidence of reported cases of child abuse among families with low socio-economic status might also be a function of the social distance between the professional worker and the service user. It is postulated that if the parent and professional share similar characteristics, especially socio-economic status and income, they will be less likely to be labelled 'abusive'; any injuries sustained by the child will be diagnosed as 'accidental'. Consequently, when the social distance between the provider and recipient is great, there will be a positive association bias; poor families and families with low socio-economic status will be prone to being typed 'abusive' and their children's injuries diagnosed as 'non-accidental' [O'Toole *et al*, 1983].

The impact of socially induced bias, personal judgement and prejudice in the diagnosis of child abuse highlights another, more fundamental problem: child abuse is neither theoretically nor clinically well defined. As a result, families risk being typified as abusive and the child misclassified as 'at risk' as a consequence of misdiagnosis [Light, 1973; Daniel *et al*, 1978; Altenmeir *et al*, 1984]. Additionally much of the data on abuse is not comparable because of the varying definitions adopted by researchers.

Perhaps it is not surprising that a certain type of child abuse is more prominent among the propertyless and powerless in our society; that it is a product, at least in part, of the contradictions and inequalities associated with our economic arrangements. Poor parents on supplementary benefit or on a low weekly income require great ability to bring up children to middle class standards. Many simply cannot do it. Conversely there are many in more affluent households who run little or no risk of neglecting their children through financial poverty. Parents living in these more affluent environments have available to them a number of choices which are unavailable to the poor. Some are able to spend part of their income on other methods of child care such as babysitters, nannies, au pairs, and, if so desired, boarding schools, so reducing the stresses associated with bringing up children. But even so evidence is growing which suggests that this group, while more hidden from the gaze of social workers, nonetheless abuse their children. It is evident that while physical abuse and cruelty is more prominent in poorer households, other forms of abuse cut across all income and class backgrounds. Incest, for example, is prevalent in wealthy, educated families as well as in poor and socially isolated familes who enter the courtroom and hospital statistics. The link between child abuse and social class is not, therefore, unambiguously supported by the evidence. Certainly the majority of poor or working class parents do not abuse their children, nor is the phenomenon absent from more affluent families [Maisch, 1973; Armstrong, 1978].

Within the limits of the existing data, perhaps all we can say with any degree of confidence about the relationship between class and child abuse is that a characteristic of those who are referred to social welfare agencies for child abuse is that they will be poor and/or of low socio-economic status.

Conclusion

It is not possible to prove that poverty and its correlates cause child abuse, but sufficient circumstantial evidence has been amassed to indicate that for many poor people it is an important factor, perhaps precipitating a form of abuse. Many of the existing studies on child abuse and on poverty are emotive and, in some cases, value laden. In addition, both subjects represent highly charged political issues. Both subjects should be areas of intense sociological investigation. Further research is needed for two reasons. First, the existing data are fragmentary and based on a wide variety of sources. We therefore require more systematic information on the subject in order to confirm the association between child abuse, particularly non-accidental injury and poverty. Second, to learn how poverty affects the care and security of children within the family. It is unlikely that definite causal relationships will ever be established. Nevertheless, more detailed and accurate information is required if we are to enhance the quality and depth of understanding of this complex subject.

If the association between child abuse and poverty holds, it will point to new directions and goals in terms of policy and practice; shifting the emphasis away from the individual case and the selective application of individualised treatment methods, toward areas of broad political significance which are not directly child-related: unemployment, low income, substandard housing. This is not to say that individual therapy, counselling and intense social casework is unimportant: individual treatment is essential to the protection of children and the facilitation of change within the family, particularly among parents who wish to be assisted to provide care for their children. Nor for that matter is subjective awareness of the political dimension of child abuse sufficient enough in itself to change the inequalities associated with the economic system. On a social work level we are forced to ask questions about the adequacy of specific resources such as day and child care facilities, the effectiveness of government policies, and the range of non-criminal agencies associated with the child protection field.

Research into the origins of child abuse is, like the phenomenon itself, a political issue. Given that the state allocates funds for research, it has a strategic role to play in encouraging or suppressing the debate about the etiology of child abuse. At a time when the numbers – and particularly the number of children – living in poverty or on its margins are increasing dramatically, one can only speculate whether such research, despite being central to the debate, will be commissioned or encouraged.

10

Family Poverty, Social Work and The Care System

Jo Tunnard

GOVERNMENT statistics make no provision for recording children as being admitted to public care on account of family poverty and, of course, some children are separated from their parents for reasons in no way connected with poverty. But local research studies during the past decade point to a clear relationship between social deprivation and child separation. A study in Newcastle revealed that 80 per cent of children admitted to care over a six-year period came from families at or below supplementary benefit levels. Birmingham social services found that, at the time children entered care, more than half the parents were dependent on supplementary, unemployment, invalidity or other benefits. A study in Portsmouth showed that over two thirds of the children in public care came from the city's five wards with the highest proportion of low wage earners, lone parents and poor housing conditions. In Strathclyde 70 per cent of all children received into care were from families whose head of household was unemployed [see Becker and MacPherson, 1986]. Mostly recently, the 1984 DHSS report [DHSS, 1984a] to the Secretary of State for Social Services about the 79,000 children then in care, shows that the local authorities with the highest proportion of children in care – up to three times the national average – are still those inner London boroughs and depressed urban areas with extensive poverty, high unemployment and inadequate housing.

The many problems that beset families before children have to leave home can, and all too often do, turn the struggle to make ends meet and to keep family links alive into a nightmare for parents and other family members already devastated by the loss of their children to public care. Few central government benefits are paid for children away in care and, at local government level, families have little hope of squeezing cash out of departments when so many payments are not only discretionary but carry no right of appeal to elected members or an independent body. Some families do not qualify for any financial support even when they are making regular contributions towards their child's maintenance while others are asked to pay a contribution that far exceeds their ability to pay. Many fail to claim the benefits that are legally theirs and some lose contact with their children simply because they cannot afford to keep in touch [Becker and MacPherson, 1986].

This chapter takes a look behind the statistics to highlight the experiences of hard-pressed families who turn, or are turned, to social services for help with the exacting task of raising their children. We look at problems involved in trying to organise alternatives to family separation, at access arrangements between children and their relatives, and at the problems that stem from punitive rules about parental contributions and state benefits. We include proposals for some of the changes in law and professional practice that we believe are needed to enable and encourage families and social workers to provide well for children.

The experiences we draw on are those of a few of the many hundreds of families who contact FRG for help and advice each year because their children or young relatives are in public care or involved in child abuse procedures. The families who approach us may be unrepresentative of the child care sector at large in that they are of course but a minority of families in society and they are, inevitably, the ones who are not happy with some aspects of the service on offer. Nevertheless, when we compare their worries and their satisfactions with the recent research findings [DHSS, 1985a] about the circumstances of 2000 children in care in 49 English and Welsh local authorities, we find a striking similarity between the two groups.

Alternatives to family separation

There are many problems about cash payments that strike us in our work with families and local authority social workers. One is ignorance of the provisions of Section One of the Child Care Act 1980 [Section 12 in Scotland]. While workers generally know that payments can be made to avoid admission to care many do not realise that cash can also be paid to reduce the length of time children stay in care. Those who are keen to use their powers are at times frustrated by the bureaucratic hurdles that face them when trying to get tiny amounts for families. Others face opposition from managers who have adopted rigid policies which we believe to be unlawful: one local authority forbids the use of Section One for children in compulsory care, another forbids it for children home on trial, and a third has a policy of not using it for fuel bills. Problems arise for families because of the reluctance of some social workers to give cash, the discretionary nature of payments made, and the lack of information available about what can be provided.

The relationship between Section One payments and social security benefits causes particular problems for local authorities who want to use Section One money to counter family separation. A problem arises if, for instance, a local authority with a child in care and living with relatives on supplementary benefit who have been receiving boarding-out allowances for the child, decides that it is right for the care order to be discharged believes that the discharge should not automatically lead to a reduction in family income. A similar problem arises if the local authority considers that admission to care could be avoided by regular cash payments to parents on SB. It arises, too, if the local authority agrees that family members other than parents should be enabled to care for a child, without the need for formal reception into care, and if the local authority decides that such payments constitute a proper use of their discretionary power under Section One. In all such cases the problem is that regular Section One payments are taken into account in full for SB purposes, apart from a £4 disregard.

* Two teenage children were being fostered by their grandparents. There were no social work reasons for the children remaining in care and the children and their carers were in agreement with the local authority's plans to apply for a discharged of the care orders. The local authority wished to replaced the boarding-out allowance with an equivalent amount of Section One money but, as the grandparents were in receipt of SB, they were unable to do so without a reduction in family income occuring.

* An aunt applied for a boarding-out allowance for her young niece and nephew. The fostering panel of the local authority rejected her application on the grounds that they were unwilling to accept relatives as foster parents. The social worker who was supporting the aunt's application argued for the payment of Section One

money to help the aunt care for the children. The Section One money awarded was much less than the boarding-out allowance normally paid by the local authority and would have affected the aunt's SB had she had to leave her low-paid job.

Another difficulty stems from the enormous unmet demand for daycare places. Families who cannot afford to pay for daycare themselves and so turn to the local authority for help may find that there is no provision available or no choice about the sort of service that suits them best. In order to gain access to those services that they cannot afford, some families have to demonstrate that they have already failed their children: in many areas a daycare place is now granted only after it is thought that the child has suffered non-accidental injury. In other areas parents who do not have paid work are not considered to be in need of daycare provision. It is policy in some local authorities to use sponsored child minders rather than offering the choice of nursery, playgroup, minder or family centre. One mother who contacted us recently had been refused a daycare place for her toddler because her social worker considered that the mother did not have a good-enough relationship with her son to merit her having a place.

Access between children and their families

The financial worries of parents that arise from maintaining links with their children in care are often underestimated or deliberately avoided by social workers. In our experience most families have no extra resources to enable them to meet the cost of going to see their children or of having the children come to visit them at home. Few know that help is available from the local authority. Those who might think of asking for help may well be deterred from doing so in case their inability to pay their way is seen as more evidence of their failure as parents. Sadly, if they do ask for help they may be met with a social worker who does not know what powers are available to him or her. We still come across parents who have been told to ask the DHSS for a grant for visiting expenses. The DHSS office has no power to make such payments, but the local authority does, under Section 26 of the Child Care Act 1980. This provides for help to anyone – not just relatives – for any expenses involved in visiting a child in public care. Apart from direct travel costs, it can include other essential expenses such as childminding fees for other children, food and entertainment for the child being visited, and the cost of overnight stays. The only criteria are that the expenses are reasonable and the person is in need of help to make the visit.

  * FRG's solicitor asked for help with fares for an access visit and was

told that the mother needed to pay only 60p for the bus ride. The social worker) had not calculated that for both parents to visit the cost would be £1.20, and double that if they were to return home. Add on the cost of a small present for their teenage daughter and the total was nearer £5 – a sizeable chunk from weekly benefit which is all but spent by the time weekend visits come round.

* A mother's social worker said that she had unrestricted access to her five year old daughter in care. In order to use the 'unrestricted access' the mother, who lived 100 miles from the office and the same distance from her daughter, had to phone the social worker from a public call box and find her in, and not in a team meeting, in supervision, seeing a client in the office, or out on a visit. Having had the request for a visit, the social worker then spoke to the foster family to find out when a visit would be convenient. The mother then had to call back, and again usually several times, before getting to speak to the social worker and hearing the arrangements that had been made. The mother made the journey on public transport, financed out of her supplementary benefit, and waited for the money to be repaid to her later. After the visit she had to start the whole process again to set up her next 'unrestricted' access visit. All these manoeuvres meant that the mother and her daughter saw each other only once every three months. The social worker's view was that the arrangements should be made through her; she had no concept of the hoops and hurdles that this involved for her client.

There are various reasons why money is not paid out as regularly and as generously as families need. Small budgets can limit a social worker's willingness to help with cash payments. Unfortunately, some workers and teams have an unwritten practice of withholding help with finance as a way of testing parental motivation. In addition, social workers sometimes compare those who ask for help with those who do not. They seem to take the view that because many people do not ask, and then appear to manage without financial assistance, those that do ask are remiss in some way. This view is faulty for two reasons. First, it assumes that all the other people could ask and did not feel inhibited from doing so. Second, it assumes that their assessment that this group can manage is correct. Yet we know that the majority of children who have no contact with their families find themselves in that position because contact has withered away, not because the local authority has deliberately restricted it. Recent research into access arrangements found that of 170 children still in public care after 2 years, 81 had no access to their natural parents. For 67 of those children no social work decision had been taken to stop access. It seems reasonable to assume that for many of these families contact had withered away and that financial difficulties may have played some part in that. Social workers need to recognise that where they do not offer financial help they cannot say that there is no restriction on access. Lack of money is a most severe restriction.

Parental contributions

Local authorities have the right, in many cases, to require the parents of a child in care to contribute towards the costs of care. They also have the power to decide not to charge in any individual case. A relaxation of the rules in 1984 to exempt parents from payment if they are in receipt of supplementary benefit or family income supplement has done much to free many parents from worry and hardship and many local authorities from some of the costly time involved in assessing and collecting contributions from some parents and from taking legal action against those who cannot or will not pay.

But the experience of the numerous families that FRG has advised and represented in connection with contributions continues to present a distressing picture of parents struggling to keep in contact with their children and had to cope with the council's demands for cash.

* A mother wrote 'I pay over £18 a week to social services for my 13 year old child in foster care. After tax I earn £50 per week and I have my widow's pension. I visit my daughter weekly and every few weeks she and her foster sister eat with me. I buy gifts etc for her two foster brothers also and pay half of any joint family outings. Obviously this expenditure is optional but I feel I would not be allowed to visit as frequently if I did not pay as the foster mother appears materialistic. I understand I shall have to pay for her care until she is 16. It is very expensive. On most other grounds I have to be satisfied with the fostering arrangement as my physical and mental health are not reliable.'

* We acted for a couple who were taken to court for an increase of weekly contributions from £18 to £22. The court ordered weekly payments of £25, including arrears. Cases of three other parents were being dealt with at the court that morning. One mother, on FIS and so now exempt from current payments, was being pressed for arrears for two children in care whom she was not allowed to visit. Another

mother was being pressed for arrears of over £600 for her teenage daughter who was refusing to visit her mother. The mother said that she had been assured by the local authority at a High Court hearing earlier in the year that she would not be asked for contributions. Three days later she had received a demand for contributions of £46 per week. The third mother had had her child returned to her a year earlier and was being pressed for a debt of £100 from that care period. Her income at the time of the court hearing was weekly child benefit and urgent needs payments from DHSS to supplement erratic maintenance payments from her husband. Two months later the local authority changed from a means test to a standard maximum charge of £7.50 per week. But the couple we had represented continued paying £25 per week for seven months before the local authority took action to reduce the amount of the court order.

Our work convinces us that contributions are a death-knell to any sort of good practice between families and professionals. They cause resentment in parents and tension between parents and social workers, between practitioners and managers, between social work sections and finance departments, and sometimes between parents and their older children. The burdens they impose can destroy the prospect of rehabilitation and can sour the relationship between parents and the local authority once children have returned home.

Furthermore, the rules treat different groups of parents in different ways. If a young offender is sent to a detention centre, there is no charge on charge on parents but if the offender is committed to care the parents are assessed to pay. If a handicapped child is in hospital there is no charge but if in care there is. A child in need of boarding school education in a special school is often committed to care because of the shortage of boarding school places. There is no charge for the boarding school but there is a charge if the child is in care and goes to a day special school. If a mentally-handicapped child is cared for by the social services department under mental health legislation the service is free but if a child is in care under children's legislation there is a charge.

In our view the fairest, most sensible and least costly option is to abolish charges and free those local authority resources which are locked up in imposing and enforcing charges for the more socially-desirable tasks of preventing family breakdown and reuniting separated families. We welcomed the recommendation of the House of Commons report on children in care [House of Commons, 1984] which advocated the end of charges on parents, save in exceptional cases, and we very much regret that the government has not yet accepted this proposal.

State benefits

There are also anomalous and punitive rules in the social security which adversely affect families with children in care. Child benefit, for instance, raises many problems, not least because of the restricted circumstances in which the benefit is paid. While many children in care spend occasional holidays and weekend visits with their parents, relatively few are at home long enough or regularly enough to satisfy the test of entitlement. The rules hamper contact between the child and the family, take no account of social work plans for returning a child home gradually over a period of weeks or months, and discriminate against families separated by admission to care. Families with children at boarding either through parental choice or because of a child's educational needs, receive child benefit continuously provided the children return home at holiday periods. Parents with children in hospital continue to receive child benefit as long as they have regular expenses in connection with the child; it is accepted that parents will want to maintain contact and that expense will be incurred. The position of many parents with children in care is no different, yet they are treated differently, and with harsh consequences.

> The parents of two children we advised wrote to say:
> when increased contact was started by social services with the view of our children returning home, they started coming home first for a few hours during the week, then for a whole day at weekends, and finally the weekends, which did cause financial stress. We couldn't claim child benefit for either of them at that time, and had many problems anyway with money. It seemed there was no help available for this agreement and we just plodded on until they returned home for good. Then it was another 10 weeks until the child benefit came through.

A mother wrote:
> My daughter was taken into care five years ago from her father from whom I have been divorced for the past ten years. As I am working and he is not it is up to me to maintain her. I was taken to court by the local authority to pay £3 per week. Up until now I have managed to scrape through but now the local authority say they want £8.40 per week and they want this backdated for four months. I work in a biscuit factory on the night shift. If I had to pay any extra I would find it extremely difficult to manage.

In making a nil assessment, the chair of the juvenile bench said she doubted the wisdom of bringing proceedings against the mother for such a small amount of money, bearing in mind that in less than a month the daughter would be 16 and that the mother was doing well to support herself and her other child at home.

Comment

Social workers cannot be expected to make good the inadequacies of the welfare system. But as the job of social work is to cope with the casualties of poverty, the financial worries of clients cannot be ignored. At the very least social workers must ensure that clients receive their legal entitlement to benefits and are treated favourably under schemes for cash help from the local authority.

There are issues for local authorities also, about the way they allocate resources as between different services and about the attitudes that underpin their financial decisions. We regret the growing interest in departmental child care policy documents that see no place for a partnership between the state and families in caring for children who are not able or are not allowed to be cared for within their own family. Local authorities are making drastic reductions in the residential resources that enable them to respond to the individual needs of children and their families. The enthusiasm for fostering and adoption is fuelled by audit reports on child care which argue that fostering and adoption give local authorities good value for money but include no discussion of the value judgements that lie behind such choices. We are concerned that the upsurge in the interest in placing children in new families has been accompanied by the investment of time, skills and money into specialist teams and schemes that has not been matched by a similar specialism and commitment to promoting the well-being of children within their own families.

This was something that the House of Commons select committee addressed when it commented 'the truth is that money is being spent at the wrong end, paying residential homes or foster parents to look after other people's children'. They challenged local authorities to use imagination and money to redress the imbalance that they detected and that is now widely acknowledged.

The challenge for central government is as urgent and as great. Given the high proportion of children in care with parents dependent on supplementary benefit for their income, we are convinced that an improvement in benefit rates would have some effect on the number of children entering and remaining in care unnecessarily. We recommend too that child benefit be paid continuously for children in care and in contact with their families; that the system of charging parents be abolished; that the supplementary benefit regulations be relaxed so that Section One payments are disregarded; and that legislation should underpin the general principle that daycare facilities should be available to any family who needs them. But any increased payment to families who risk losing their child should not be made at the expense of the living standards of other low-income families. The much-needed reforms could, and in our view should, be taken from the system of tax relief and concessions that have in recent years been channelled disproportionately to those least in need in our society. As government proposals for tax and benefit reforms unfold in the months to come, the treatment of families in the care system will perhaps provide a useful measure against which to judge the amount of care and cash that those with power are willing to invest in those without.

11

Delinquency, Poverty and Social Work

David Thorpe

'The causes of crime must be initimately bound up with the form assumed by the social arrangements of the time. Crime is ever and always that behaviour seen to be problematic within the framework of those social arrangements' [Taylor, Walton and Young, 1973, 281-282].

THIS chapter takes as its broad heading three social phenomena, those of delinquency, poverty and social work. Each represents what Taylor, Walton and Young have described as a 'social arrangement' and the purpose of this chapter is to explore actual and potential relationships between these phenomena. The word 'relationship' is used quite deliberately as an alternative to the word 'links', since it will become clear during the discussion that the most accurate way of describing the arrangements is one which denotes complex association rather than simple, direct causality. The fact is that very probably, in most instances, there is absolutely no immediate causal link between crime and poverty. Sadly, many popular lay and professional assumptions suggest that this link exists, yet the truth is that as the social worker and probation officers go about their day-to-day business of 'explaining' delinquency, they will not be paying attention to the routine criminal activities of themselves, their colleagues and virtually everyone with whom they have contact. The chances are high moreover that this lack of attention is primarily a product of the human tendencies of forgetfulness, misconception and ignorance. An extra ten minutes for lunch, an agency-supplied ballpoint pen left at home, a mistake in calculating expenses, a misrepresentation of character to another official. Middle-class crime can be seen in this context as part of a 'social arrangement' which we can define as routine bureaucratic behaviour – in other words the very behaviours which the agency expects and demands of its employees will automatically place them at risk of committing offences. If there were no free supply of ballpoint pens, writing paper or an expectation of professional character judgement, then crimes of this nature would be prevented. Even having access to a telephone creates a risk of crime since it is inevitable that private and personal communication will take place.

It is clear however that we do not see these work places as targets for crime prevention programmes [other than office security] and newly employed social workers and probation officers are not accorded client status in the preventive intermediate treatment programmes which they run. All this despite evidence that they are 'at risk' of offending by virtue of the way in which their agencies conduct their day-to-day business. The reasons for this are two-fold. First, white collar and corporate crime is very difficult to detect in that it takes place well away from public view and, secondly, the victims of these offences are very rarely aware that they are victims since one would have to classify the broad mass of tax-payers and rate-payers as victims.

In the recent past, much media attention has been paid to corporate crime although the focus of attention has been primarily on individual senior executives who authorised the expenditure of relatively large sums of money [millions of pounds] in order to achieve *organisational* as opposed to *personal* goals. This individual focus very closely matches the media's interest in individual working class delinquents. Crime is presented and explained as personal decision rather than a consequence of a complex 'social arrangement'. Senior executives who offend are seen to be motivated by greed, while delinquents are variously described as economically and emotionally deprived [by the liberal press] or predatious and calculating [by the right-wing press]. No attention is paid to the behavioural demands of particular social settings – whether it is that of the multinational corporation or the street corner. The fact that the street corner is seen as a setting where crime is more likely to occur, is a consequence of other 'social arrangements' – those of social structure and the inequalities inherent in social structure. Social work agencies operate always within the constraints of structure so it is perhaps inevitable that probation officers will supervise unemployed adults rather than senior executives.

In order to situate the argument this chapter will deal briefly first of all with two other settings for crime, before going on to look in detail at the third setting which is the primary focus of social work activity. The first setting is that of the large corporation, the second that of the working routine of the low-ranking entrepreneur [the bread salesman] and the third that of what I have referred to as 'the street corner' but which could now perhaps best be described as 'the shopping centre'. Crime, it will be shown, is a significant feature of all these situations. In the first two examples it is largely hidden from view, but its cash value, particularly as far as corporate crime is concerned, is infinitely greater than anything which the most committed and persistent delinquent could ever contemplate. What all three settings have in common, however, is that crime is more likely to arise out of the constraints of specific social expectations which stand largely outside the individual. The social processes at work in these very different societies all produce crime as a direct consequence of the need to make a profit [for the company], sell bread [for the bakery], or prepare youths for unskilled, low-paid work [for the state, commerce and industry]. To believe that it is individuals in these settings who make deliberate, personal, deviant decisions to offend is to completely misunderstand the scale and nature of crime. The boardroom and the pedestrian areas of the shopping centre may be very different places but a significant by-product of the interactions which take place in these settings will break the law.

In accounting for the lack of public awareness of corporate crime, Box [1983] suggests that:

> The root causes[s] of this collective ignorance is not too difficult to uncover. Corporate crime is rendered invisible by its complex and sophisticated planning and execution, by non-existent or weak law enforcement and prosecution, and by lenient legal and social sanctions which fail to reaffirm or reinforce collective sentiments on moral boundaries [Box, 1983, 16].

Large corporations are organisations which have very clear and specific goals – those of profit. Indeed they exist for absolutely no other reason and the larger and more complex the organisation, the less interested it is likely to be in the production of goals and services unless they can be seen to have a direct effect on the balance sheet. For it is this balance sheet which at the end of the day determines success or failure. If organisations produce desirable goods and services but show a bad balance sheet, then they will cease to exist. Box maintains that:

> This defining characteristic – it is a goal-seeking entity – makes a

corporation inherently criminogenic, for it necessarily operates in an uncertain and unpredictable environment such that its purely legitimate opportunities for goal achievement are sometimes limited and constrained. Consequently, executives investigate alternative means, including law avoidance, evasion and violation and pursue them if they are evaluated as superior to other available strictly legitimate alternatives [Box, 1983, 35].

Routine organisational responses to uncertainty and the pressure for profits include stealing ideas from, or taking over competitors in ways which break the law; avoiding tax and attempting to illegally influence politicians or local and national government officers; ignoring or short-cutting safety procedures and dishonestly misleading customers and consumers. Virtually all organisations will undertake one or perhaps even all of these activities at some time or other. According to the Low Pay Unit, up to 40 per cent of employers in shops, hotels, restaurants and clothing workshops illegally paid their workers less than the minimum wage in 1986. The cumulative value of illegal low pay for that year was estimated at about £2.5 million [Byrne, 1987a].

One of the more interesting crime studies of recent times [Ditton, 1977] contains accounts of the ways in which bread salesmen become 'part-time' criminals. The particular criminal acts committed by bread salesmen consist of systematically over-charging customers for bread and cakes. This activity – 'fiddling' – is effectively taught by supervisors and is supported by management. Management encourages salesmen to overcharge simply by denying them the exact knowledge of their personal sales performance and then formally telling salesmen that their balance sheet is 'short'. Supervisors support this by dropping broad hints as to how 'fiddles' can be worked. As with corporation executives, crime is not necessarily a consequence of greed, but a result of organisational demands. In that sense, probably all employees in many profit-making organisations are encouraged to commit criminal acts.

The juvenile delinquent differs from other offenders in three significant ways. The first is that unlike employees and employers, delinquents do not have opportunities to offend as part of a working routine. The second is that many of their offences are visible and take place in public places rather than the relative privacy of office, shop floor or home. The third significant difference is in part a consequence of the first two – that because delinquency is visible and therefore easily reportable, detectable and processable, delinquents are assumed to be more criminal than most other sectors of the population. As has been shown, this is most certainly not the case, but it has permitted the media, politicians and the police to create and sustain beliefs about the scale and importance of delinquency which are completely at odds with the true picture.

Young people, especially those from working class backgrounds are as much at risk of becoming offenders as older people. They are, however, much more likely to be caught, and given much working class youthful misbehaviour is public, the chances of working class youths being caught are greater than is the case for middle and upper class youths. In his study of 1,425 London boys Belson [1975] said that:

> Whereas there is a tendency for the incidence of stealing to fall off in going from the sons of the unskilled to the sons of the professionally occupied, that fall-off is not especially sharp . . . it is clear that stealing is widely spread through the different occupational strata, with the sons of the professionally occupied sector being quite substantially involved [Belson, 1975, xii].

Belson's conclusions were based on a self-report survey as opposed to official police reports. What, however, is illuminating about the slight association between social class and delinquency, is the nature of the offences committed by boys who had fathers who were unskilled, skilled or professionally employed.

> Some types of theft behaviour tended to occur more among the sons of the less skilled, for example: stealing food, sweets; taking things from a bike or motor bike; stealing from work; from a stall or barrow, from a goods yard; getting into a place and stealing from a meter. For others, however, the theft level is much the same across the 'social gradient', for example: cheating someone out of money; fare evasion; taking something for a dare; pinching from one's own family or relations; stealing from a changing room; stealing from a telephone box [Belson, 1975, xii].

Belson also discovered that:

> The likelihood of a boy being caught by the police for the stealing he commits varies with his background, being lower for those boys whose fathers are in the upper professional bracket; who are Jewish; who attend Grammar or Public School; who are younger [Belson, 1975, xiii].

Poverty as such did not feature in Belson's findings although there was a clear bias in terms of social class.

However, equally revealing in Belson's research was the association between high self-reported delinquency scores and a strong 'desire for a lot of fun and excitement'. These desires were not necessarily associated with social class, but fun and excitement for middle class youths can usually be provided in the context which is far removed from the street corner or shopping centre. The very architecture of middle class communities, but even more importantly the structure, expectations and routines of middle class youth sub-cultures will create crime which is relatively invisible and opportunities for fun and excitement which do not necessarily enter the public domain. In contrast, lower class youths live and interact under somewhat different conditions. Only very rarely do agents of the state take the trouble to explore or comprehend the social world of the youths whom they teach, supervise or process. Instead, their social activities are discused by means of phrases such as 'easily led' or 'mixes with delinquent peers'. Such expressions expose an utter naivety and ignorance of the ways in which young people use their time and the social and geographical spaces open to them. As Blagg [1987] has recently commented:

> Young people do not live their lives conveniently parcelled up into discrete institutions created for them by society . . . it is the rest of us who tend to interact with them as they journey through only one of the daily 'stations', of a statutory or informal variety, who fail to see the complex modes of interstructuring of environments that together constitute the daily 'life paths' of young people [Blagg, 1987, 3].

Blagg, in his study of youth culture in an East Midlands new town discovered that to a certain extent the 'street corner' of classical subcultural criminological theory had become considerably augmented and extended by shopping centres. Willis [1984] identified newly created shopping centres as a 'mecca of images' in which working class youths could 'express the longings of a frustrated consumerism'. In these settings, youths pursue a range of activities, only some of which may be officially classified as illegal. Blagg's ethnographic description of a youth-conducted tour of the town bears eloquent testimony to the complexity of working class youth subculture:

> The older group's activities utilised school, the locality, the street, youth clubs and the city centre and as such they had a high public profile. Moreover, they moved from one scene to another with great speed; they literally hurled themselves through time and space, propelled by an inflammable, volatile fuel of adolescent frenzy, the key element of which was profound frustration . . . The majority of the offences committed by this group reflected behaviour that was spontaneously driven, unplanned, opportunistic. Assaults that were a sudden response to loss of status in which it was difficult to separate out victim from offender, acts of criminal damage that were considered to be just 'having a laugh' or 'mucking about'. Along with these were many cases of shop-lifting and theft – burglaries were rare and there were no genuinely violent crimes. 'Nicking' itself though had little rationality beyond immediate gratification. Objects in the 'mecca of images' were seen and seized in a spontaneous fashion [Blagg, 1987, 18].

In this description we see routine adolescent street corner behaviour translated into a completely different and new geographical and social space. Moreover, the shopping centre is usually heavily policed, both by the state and private security firms and it is of course very much more public than the housing estate street corner. The shopping centre is a focus of consumer activity from people of all social classes, which Blagg suggests enables middle class people to indulge in consumerism 'without the problems of the street' – it is a 'privatised realm in which youths with little money have no business at all' [Blagg, 1987, 15]. It is hardly surprising that the youthful, usually petty offending which takes place in such a public and heavily policed environment reinforces the belief that this is an area where crime is a major problem. The boardroom, the office and the breadround simply do not compare since there is no one to detect crime and no obvious victim.

Some youths make a conscious decision to engage in public anti-social activity as an end in itself. These are the youths for whom fun and excitement do not merely represent a way of controlling time and space, but who come to adopt public unruliness as a badge, as a symbol of opposition to accepted convention especially in public arenas such as shopping centres. The offending patterns of such youths can become connected with drink, drugs, violence and other forms of *public* challenge. Thorpe undertook a qualitative study of offenders and victims in another new town in the Midlands. In conversation with these youths it transpired that 'having a laugh' in public represented an overt rejection of convention. One youth was asked 'What sort of things does society want you to do that you don't want to do?' He replied:

> Well, you know, go out, get a job, get married, you know, all the normal things. Not go out and have a really good laugh, and go and get out of your head, and like this Stonehenge thing, that's the latest thing isn't it? You can't go down there, you can't go to no festival no more. You know, soon, fact's fact, soon they're just going to walk all over your head ain't they? You can't even smile without being nicked these days. You know, if people don't do something about it, I dunno what's going to happen.

To conventional people, this type of motivation makes no sense, superficially it appears to be completely irrational. Offending is unpredictable, impulsive and without apparent desire for material goods. Another youth described his offending behaviour thus:

> Stealing milk bottles. When I was drunk I stole two pints of milk on the way home from the pub. I didn't know. I did 't even know I did it, you know and this thing which was when I went up Old Town and had a fight with some gang of mods – just two different gang fights, that's all, you know, that's all of that. And I got done for theft

of a hat, you know. I took this geezer's hat off him, off his head.
Really, just stupid things, that's what all my charges are, just stupid,
like disturbing the peace.

These understandings of delinquency do not appear to provide any space
whatsoever for poverty as a *causal* factor. Rather, they rely much more on
the unique social situations in which working class youths find themselves,
where offending is easily detectable and often reacted to. Nevertheless,
there is some evidence to suggest that in both the Blagg and Thorpe studies
as well as the West and Farrington longitudinal Cambridge study, that
employment – or lack of it – can affect future criminal activity. Empirically,
it is well established that delinquents 'grow out' of crime. Qualitative
studies reinforce that view. Blagg returned to the East Midlands new town
two years after his earlier ethnographic research, to discover the same boys
and girls now in employment. He began by re-acquainting himself with
these youths in a bar where he was 'treated to rounds of fizzy lager' by
'stylish and socially skilled' teenagers. The lives of these young people had
clearly changed dramatically, particularly their self-perceptions. This was as
true of those on very low wages as it was for those who earned enough to
conduct a relatively affluent life-style. Similarly, Thorpe's new town
offenders linked the cessation of overt delinquent activity with
employment. One youth commented on why he had stopped
offending:

> I think it's because I've now got a job, and I've now got money
> coming in, so, and in my mind, my conscience says you've not to do
> it again, you've been a naughty boy twice now, you've been let off
> fairly easy both times, and that's pushing your luck a third, fourth
> time is going a bit too far. So er, I passed my driving test just
> afterwards, actually just after I'd been caught so I needed that. Once I
> had got that I got the job which helped.

Another offender gave a similar reason for the cessation of a friend's
offending activities:

> Yeah, he came out [of Detention Centre] and you always give it a few
> months when you come out, sort of calm down see if you want to
> stay straight, and he got a job down Coca Cola – £150 a week. He has
> got his car now and everything . . . yeah he has definitely stopped, I
> know he has for a fact.

Even the more committed subcultural offenders eventually succumb to the
pressures of adult life, the rewards of employment and adult relationships.
As one youth put it: 'Because you can't keep doing it can you, can't keep
going like that for years . . . It's pointless innit? You have got to grow out
of it some time haven't you? And that's what's happening now, I'm doing
that now aren't I?' This youth had acquired a girlfriend and a job.

It is worth noting in this context that maturational forces do not simply consist of economic factors, they also include other adult-status items such as a driving licence, and adult relationships both within and outside work. For young, unemployed adults some of these factors do not operate. The adult right to claim benefit, to possess a driving licence and to have adult relationships exists, but the bonds to convention created by being in employment are absent. In some circumstances a significant relationship can override the experience of poverty and reduce the likelihood of offending, In Thorpe's study a persistent offender, living in poverty relates his refusal to participate in criminal activities:

> Well, I'll tell you now. I've already been offered a burglary, by the same feller I was partnered up with before, 'coz we got, we both went to prison the same day sort of thing, both went to the same prison to do a course, but er he had a burglary he wanted doing in a local town. I looked at my girlfriend, I said, well I'll have to think about it sort of thing. He said he'd come round the next day sort of thing, and I thought, and the money was very attractive, yeah. I could have used the money. But I, as it was, I went out before he came round because I was scared, I'd die, I haven't got the bottle, right, any more.

Within the context of this conversation, it was clear that this offender, despite his poverty, was deterred by fears of upsetting his girlfriend by continuing to offend.

On the whole, however, recent evidence would suggest that under certain circumstances, poverty does influence delinquency rates. In 1986, Farrington *et al* re-analysed their data on the 411 8-to-9 year old boys which they began to study in the early 1960s [Farrington *et al*, 1986]. By the early 1970s these boys had reached the age of 18 years and several years on from that, a limited study was undertaken on the relationship between unemployment and crime in the years immediately following school-leaving. A series of very elaborate statistical tests were used to explore the possibility of direct links between offending and unemployment and the effects of other factors in this equation such as a 'predisposition towards offending' and a 'low status job history'. Farrington and his colleagues concluded that there *was* a link between unemployment and crime for those **particular youths** at that **particular time** and that 'one link in the chain between unemployment and crime may be financial need' [Farrington *et al*, 1986, 351]. This conclusion was derived from the fact that the association related to a higher rate of crimes committed for material gain as opposed to other types of crime. However, the link was strongest for those youths who were already deemed to be 'delinquent-prone' and who had 'lower-status' employment histories. This suggests once more that it is not possible to make crude, general statements about poverty and crime. As the Thorpe study suggests, a range of factors can affect behaviour under conditions of material stress, including strong relationships with significant others as well as past histories of delinquency. The Farrington research confirms this empirically.

The reactions of social workers and probation officers to delinquent youths from unconventional family backgrounds is already well recorded. One of the most negative effects of social work in juvenile justice was the assumption that children from disorderly working class families were more likely to be delinquent than children from conventional homes. During the 1970's this naive assumption led to a vast proliferation of 'preventive' intermediate treatment for non-delinquents from social work services. Additionally when children from disorderly homes became delinquent, they were frequently committed to care under Section 7 [7] of the 1968 CYPA as a consequence of either a specific recommendation from a probation officer or social worker. Often, even though there was no overt recommendation, a description of family circumstances was sufficient to persuade juvenile courts that removal to care would compensate for the miseries and uncertainties of a turbulent home life, thus reducing the likelihood of further delinquency. There were two unfortunate and unintended consequences as a result of the assumption that direct links existed between delinquency and family instability. One was that when non-delinquent youths who had received 'preventive' intermediate treatment actually became delinquent, they were placed at risk of excessive penal intervention [Thomas and Millichamp, 1982; Bilson, 1986]. The second was that the use of residential care in the 1968 CYPA Section 7 [7] Care Order, actually served to increase the chances of further delinquency [Thorpe *et al*, 1980]. During the past few years, especially after the passing of the 1982 Criminal Justice Act, many juvenile courts adopted a 'justice' model which has had equally deleterious effects. This time, the assumption was that juvenile offenders had made rational calculations to offend and therefore they might best respond to a rational punishment – in this case, the new Youth Custody Sentence [Burney, 1986]. Youth Custody, preventive intermediate treatment and Section 7 [7] Care Orders are all a result of excessive reactions to juvenile crime whether they be described as 'welfare' or 'justice'. These excessive reactions are in part a result of simplistic notions of causation, which ignore the complexity of delinquency but reduce it to a 'sad' or 'bad' formula.

There is some limited evidence to show that similar simplistic thinking exists within juvenile criminal justice systems, in respect of the links between poverty and delinquency. Moreover, these simplistic assumptions are ones which in *welfare* systems, appear to lead to an excessive reaction by the system.

Given that the tendency of the 'justice' ideology of delinquency is one reaction to the offence, the tendency of the 'welfare' ideology is to react to the youth and his or her circumstances. While 'justice' reactions usually take the form of arbitrary punishments – they rarely consist of a 50 pence fine for a first offence, a 51 pence fine for a second offence and a 52 pence fine for a third offence – 'welfare' reactions will more often than not entail further contact with juvenile criminal justice system officials. Two recent empirical examples of this exist in respect of the Scottish Children's Hearing system and the South Australian juvenile criminal justice system. Both systems have been heralded as 'progressive' in comparison with what are commonly believed to be reactionary 'justice' systems.

In December 1986, the Reporter's Department of Fife Regional Council produced a Report on the relationship between unemployment and juvenile crime in Fife. The Report shows that during 1985, a total of 1,187 children were referred to that Department by the police for offending, and that of these, 363 [30.6 per cent] were from families where both parents were unemployed – more than twice the average per household for that Region. The police clearly discriminated at this level against children from poorer families, perhaps in the belief that they would receive help. However, at the next stage of the juvenile justice process, the Reporter's Department compounded that discrimination by selecting these children for attendance before a Children's Hearing. Of the 1,187 children originally referred by the police, 252 were then brought before Children's Panels. Of these 252, a total of 166 [65.9 per cent] came from households where both parents were unemployed. Again, it may have been that the Reporter's Department believed that Children's Hearings can only have beneficial effects, but it also suggests that both police officers and Reporters believe that children from poor families are more likely to be in 'need' of compulsory measures of care than other children who get into trouble. The net effect of these beliefs is that poor children become singled out for further official action.

In South Australia, while researching juvenile criminal justice system reactions to aboriginal youths, Gale [1985] came to a similar conclusion. The gross over-representation of aboriginals in criminal justice systems in Australia is legend, but using a series of elaborate statistical tests on police arrest decisions in respect of a number of factors, Gale discovered that in South Australia, unemployment was a much more powerful factor than race. 'No matter what kind of test was used on what kind of grouping applied, unemployment came out well at the head of the list of predictions of police arrest decisions. In fact unemployment was found to have a predictive value ten times that of aboriginality alone'[Gale, 1985, 8].

Gale specifically mentions the 'welfare-oriented system of juvenile justice' as creating a process which, in adhering to 'middle class welfare principles' does not hesitate to arrest, refer to court and detain. Such procedures are perceived as being to the advantage of impoverished youths, who, unlike middle class children, have little to lose.

To claim that poverty is an immediate and direct cause of delinquency is to ignore the widespread nature and extent of adult corporate, business and working class crime. Affluent executives and workers offend less for reasons of greed, than they do as a consequence of routine occupational pressures and expectations. Similarly, working class youths appear to offend not so much as a *direct* result of their poverty as much as a result of the traditional youthful pursuit of fun, excitement and the overt rejection of convention. Nevertheless, poverty appears to be a factor in late adolescent/young adult offending, but it would appear that other factors including previous work experience, relationships and delinquent histories are equally important. Unfortunately, when juvenile criminal justice systems have a 'welfare' orientation, the evidence from Fife and South Australia suggests that these systems actually even further disadvantage poorer youths. While this data relates only to police and Reporter decision-making, on past evidence, social workers and probation officers have always tended to single out such disadvantaged youths for further and more intensive formal actions. It would not be surprising if that proved to be the case. The only antidote to crude and naive assumptions about the links between poverty and delinquency is an awareness of the scale of adult, corporate crime and a willingness to listen carefully to the explanations which youths give for their behaviours.

Unquestionably, poverty will feature in some of these explanations and as such, it deserves serious attention from welfare agents. It is however unlikely to be the sole reason for delinquency and it certainly does not merit the use of measures which will even further stigmatise and disadvantage those youngsters who are rendered most vulnerable by virtue of class, race and low income.

12

Poverty and Mental Health

Joe Pidgeon and Gill Shepperson

I N this chapter we do not intend to concentrate on the long standing debate about the cause and meaning of mental illness, but rather on our concerns as social workers about the real life consequences for people who become seriously mentally distressed. One of the first major impacts that many people experience is an initial dependency on social security benefits as a major, if not sole source of income. In our particular work settings this dependency will, in most cases, be for the foreseeable future.

We want, therefore, to look at the implications of this claimant status on the lives of people who have serious mental health problems. As a way into this discussion we have drawn up four profiles of people whose experiences and circumstances are illustrative of this inter-relationship. The first profile is concerned with a young man who is living independently; the second with a family with children; the third with a man who is living in a private registered home; and the last profile is of a middle-aged woman who has for most of her life been dependent on her parents. Their stories are taken, in part, from our own work experience over the last four years. We have tried to be as representative as possible in terms of the age range, situational circumstances, and the kind of difficulties that social workers and others are working with.

Mark

Mark, a young man of 25, became unwell mid-way through a polytechnic course and finally had to give up altogether following two successive acute admissions to psychiatric hospital. The psychosis that he experienced was treated with major tranquilisers with the result that some of his more disturbing symptoms were quelled. Mark, however, was left feeling bereft of confidence, isolated and unable to cope with the many every-day demands of life.

He was to spend nearly a year in a hospital psychiatric unit. Latterly Mark began to take tentative steps to explore and regain a life outside of the hospital. By the end of his first year in hospital his invalidity benefit had dropped to £7.90p per week. This benefit, designed to provide for 'personal expenditures', was manifestly insufficient to meet his needs. Frugality was then to become a way of life for Mark with horizons more limited than he had ever before experienced.

After 3 years on a City Council waiting list Mark was made the offer of an unfurnished flat. As is so often the case for people claiming the various sickness benefits, Mark was not eligible for single payments to furnish the flat. Any invalidity resettlement benefit due would be late in coming and, anyway, far too little to help Mark.

He himself had no household possessions of his own except some bedding, a kettle and a record player. His mother wanted to help but was herself dependent on supplementary benefit. Mark's social worker estimated that a minimum of £500 would be required to very basically furnish the flat.

The social worker then spent the equivalent of five full working days with Mark just on the tasks that this move necessitated. These involved applying for and handling grant help from the Social Services Department [£150] from an already limited budget; visiting and selecting furniture from a second-hand charitable furniture store and organising transport; sorting out invalidity benefit and standard housing benefit; laying carpets and cleaning the flat up; and, most importantly, spending time with Mark offering encouragement, support and explanation at this time of major transition.

Mark successfully moved into his tenancy and began the process of learning to live on invalidity benefit income. For the year 1987/88 Mark's benefit is set at £47.80 per week, a relatively high level of benefit. Out of this he has to pay a balance of £11 in weekly rent and he is also faced with paying for his prescription at £2.40 a time. He is not eligible for any public transport concessions.

Mark in reality now faces an indefinite future on an income on the margin of the state's standard of poverty. In the employment market he is triply disadvantaged with the high unemployment rate in the city, the discrimination that the stigma of his psychiatric illness causes, and the inflexible regulations of social security vis-a-vis working while claiming benefit.

Michelle

Very soon after Michelle gave birth to her second child her own mother became very ill and, within days, died in hospital. Michelle was understandably devastated. To make matters worse her husband, Steve, was made redundant a month after this bereavement. Michelle, optimistic by temperament, believed that he would fairly easily find another job.

The couple owned their home, something that had never posed any financial problem, given that Steve's average monthly take home pay was £400 [plus a free company car]. However, after being out of work for three months, his redundancy pay hardly made up for their diminished financial circumstances. Their weekly benefit comprising unemployment benefit, child benefit and supplementary benefit amounted to £70.15.

Steve managed to get another job as a sales representative, but was working a larger more distant territory. Along with more reps' chasing fewer orders, his basic monthly pay was a mere £200 plus an average sales bonus of £150. They did have a company car again.

Michelle spent an average of two nights each week on her own as Steve had to stay away regularly, which was an extra blow to her as he had been a constant support to her for three months. She found that her sleep patterns became disturbed and her GP gave her sleeping tablets to help. After several weeks with little sleep and a growing sense of despair and isolation she went back and was put on a course of anti-depressants.

One evening when Steve returned home, he found Michelle slumped in the chair. Having taken the children to bed she had then taken a large overdose of tablets; she survived and after 8 weeks on the psychiatric in-patient unit, returned home.

Michelle's confidence had, however, collapsed. Her ability to manage the home and children was thus diminished, and her sense of isolation was compounded by the loneliness and loss of support her mother's death and Steve's absences had created. After another three admissions in 6 months to the psychiatric unit, she finally refused to return home, knowing she could not cope alone.

Steve had used most of the redundancy money to pay child minders to enable him to retain his job. He moved to employment closer to home which was lower paid, but finally gave in and left his job to stay at home with Michelle and the children. The family now live on supplementary benefit, unemployment benefit and child benefit, have no savings and no car and are unsure whether they will be able to remain in their home in the future. Living on the good will of the Building Society is no substitute for hard cash.

Paul

Paul is a 48 year old man living in a private registered home for those people that fall into the DHSS category of having suffered from a mental disorder. He claims supplementary benefit which pays for his board and lodging charge which is set at the prescribed maximum of £130 per week. In this benefit Paul has a set personal allowance of £9.25 per week.

Paul was brought up in Nottingham where he and his family are still resident. It was at the age of 22 that he first began to experience major mental distress. He became afflicted with hallucinatory thought, almost stopped eating, and was spending longer and longer periods in bed. He became more distanced from his friends and, with his parents, a wary and often conflictual atmosphere developed.

Paul left home. There then followed some four years of living in various lodgings and rented rooms. Contact with psychiatric services was fitful and invariably associated with a readmission to hospital due to Paul's antipathy to major tranquiliser medication and his consequent breakdown. His fifth and final admission to hospital was in 1978. This time Paul accepted the suggestion put to him to live in a hostel as a way of preventing repeated readmissions. He was not thought able to live independently.

In his registered home Paul receives a complete board and lodging package for his £130 – three meals a day, laundering and staffing cover night and day. He shares a bedroom with another resident. Paul's personal allowance of £9.25 is meant to provide for his clothing requirements, personal toiletries, and all social activities. Cigarettes alone cost Paul about £6 a week. The proprietors provide Paul with second-hand clothing and also operate a savings fund for most of their 15 residents. Paul thus has for him £2 per week for clothing and for 'pocket money' for an annual holiday paid for by the proprietor. After his cigarettes Paul is now down to £1.25.

His financial penury is slightly relieved by the £4 that he earns from the five days work he does at the psychiatric hospital's industrial therapy workshops. Paul and his fellow residents' lifestyle is one largely oriented around walking the streets, teas at various drop-in centres, and much T.V. watching. If Paul chooses to eat out or go away for a weekend, he will not usually be reimbursed by the home.

For the social worker attempting to enhance Paul's choices this personal poverty is an inescapable reality. Unless he wishes to be helped with a move on to more independent accommodation [and thus control over a high level of benefit] Paul's options remain limited. Discretionary bus passes or reduced charges to sports centres do not apply to Paul. Going away for the day or weekend other than 'with the home' or 'with the day centre' is rarely possible. An occasional drink at the local does not extend to contemplating other more expensive social activities such as film-going, visiting a restaurant, joining a club or going on holiday.

Catherine

Catherine is preparing to leave hospital after two years on a rehabilitation ward – this will be the first time as an adult that she has been able to consider an independent lifestyle. After being diagnosed as having a schizophrenic illness in her early 20's her parents have provided continuous care and support for Catherine in their home.

Catherine had been employed as a textile worker on and off after she left school in the 1960's, did not get married, and by her early twenties was beginning to spend much of her spare time in her room alone. When Catherine unexpectedly tore up a batch of work, the works supervisor sent her home and suggested she needed to see her doctor – she never worked again.

During the last twenty years, very little has changed for the family. Catherine now receives invalidity benefit, rather than sickness benefit. On the occasions she has needed hospitalisation, her parents were re-assured and encouraged to continue supporting her on discharge.

Catherine's mother used to clean for three families, but was forced to give up her job – which always paid for a holiday or outings. She felt that when Catherine was 'ill' she shouldn't be leftalone as she might 'wreck' the house. No one ever suggested that Catherine might be eligible for other benefits and she herself knew little or nothing of the welfare benefit system.

Catherine's father was a storekeeper in a local factory and had always been poorly paid, but rarely missed a day, even when Catherine was unwell. His wife willingly accepted the 'family burden' at these times. On the occasions when Catherine could not be cared for at home, usually as a result of a disagreement with her mother over something 'trivial', she would go into hospital for a few weeks, uncomplainingly. These were the only times her parents had any respite from their responsibility to care for her.

Catherine's long stay on this occasion arose when her parents had made a desperate attempt to liberate their daughter by finding a flat nearby, furnishing it and visiting her everyday. As the family were unfamiliar with claiming benefits, a four month delay in housing benefit led them to give up the tenancy for Catherine in exasperation and move her back home with them. The disturbance was such that Catherine's mental state deteriorated dramatically, her stay in hospital was much longer than usual and an early discharge was unlikely.

During the twenty years Catherine's parents have cared for her, their health has deteriorated considerably. Although the couple are now of retirement age, they still find money they can ill afford to subsidise Catherine who receives only a small payment of £7.90 a week as her IVB is now downrated.

Catherine and her parents have both at times felt entrapped by their mutual situation. Their relationships are based on the responsibilities of parenthood extended indefinitely – and never free to grow as they might have done as equals with needs, hopes and ambitions for themselves.

These four individuals have all had traumatic experiences. The immediate outcome for them has been one of devastating loss – of confidence, role and personal identity, and also the loss of many essential life skills. Social stigma, vulnerability, and unemployment may well be the result of such an experience.

All of the four individuals or their relatives in our profiles had to give up work. This in itself can be an extremely painful process [whether it be for the person involved or indeed a carer] and will involve for most people a radical transformation of their everyday lives. Social status, self esteem, social contact and financial independence are all likely to be negatively affected [Birch, 1983].

The loss of financial independence is something that has afflicted all four individuals. This would not be unusual, for all studies of long-term sickness and low income living have found a correlation between the two. One of the latest sets of figures that were available for 1983 showed that 60 per cent of the disabled population were living in or on the margin of poverty [Disability Alliance, 1987a].

Low income living has a particularly disadvantageous effect on people who already have a disability to contend with:

For disabled people whose income often barely covers the basic essentials of living, there is nothing left over to pay for a fuller and more satisfying existence. It is the lack of money as much as the illness and its effects which prevents them from pursuing and attaining the good things of life. It is for these reasons that disabled people need more rather than less in the way of financial support [Locker, 1983, 120].

One other feature of the four profiles is the great variety of benefit levels of income support that individuals receive. It is also evident that there is great unevenness of health and social services provision to meet their needs. The whys and wherefores of benefit disparity are questions frequently put to social workers by clients, both in and out of hospital, whose situations and conditions may well be similar. The answer, as we know, lies in the separation of the contributory and non-contributory benefit system. To disabled people, and indeed to us, it seems inequitable that a person who is afflicted with, for example, a severe schizophrenic condition will receive variable benefit levels and other entitlements according to whether or not they have worked for a year or so earlier in their lives. The effects of the condition may be similar, so too may be their material living conditions and needs, yet there may be considerable disparity in weekly income.

These benefits have their own diverse regulations and passporting effects which in turn have a major impact on people depending on them. Mark, for example, could not get a single payment grant to help furnish his flat after 14 months in psychiatric hospital, while Paul on the other hand, would be eligible. Mark, with the permission of his doctor and DHSS could attempt to get a job while remaining on invalidity benefit and earn up to £26 per week. Paul, however, could only earn up to £4. While Paul is subject to capital savings limits Mark is free of them. Mark has to pay the full prescription charge for his medication while Paul is exempted. The list of disparities is lengthy.

The four profiles also demonstrate that in order to ameliorate the condition of low income dependency, it is essential that all those planning the development of new resources and organising individual hospital programmes must have a good working knowledge of present and future social security regulations. Social workers need to occasionally think and plan in wider terms than individual 'cases'.

We have been involved in a number of projects which illustrate the importance of this. Where, for instance, residential rehabilitation schemes or hostels are 'funded' wholly by Health Authorities with no charges being asked of the residents, the DHSS status of the claimant will be crucially affected. S/he will then only receive a weekly personal allowance which can be as low as £7.90; this in turn imposes severe restraints on the potential of the resident to meaningfully participate in community life. Another example would be in group homes and shared living arrangements where it is important that the implications for tenants of inclusive rent and coverage of voids is fully explored in order not to unnecessarily reduce already low benefit levels.

On a broader front the 1986 Audit Commission report, *Making a Reality of Community Care*, has highlighted some of the 'perverse effects of Social Security policies' [p.43] in terms of mismatch between state financial support and individual need:

> At best there has been a shift in services from old remote long-stay hospitals to long-stay residential homes, missing out a wider range of more flexible, more cost-effective forms of community care on the way. At worst, and particularly for the mentally ill, there is an inadequate service [p.27].

One alternative approach, and one which is increasingly being explored by both Health Authorities and Social Services Departments, is the provision of intensive support services for individuals living in ordinary housing. This has the double benefit of being what most people want for themselves while ensuring householder status in terms of social security and housing benefits, thus in most case maximising benefit.

The complexity of the welfare system, both in its financial maintenance and its services provision components, is one that can prove daunting and unhelpful to people suffering from mental health problems. This has already been highlighted in the profile of Catherine. The following examples are from families quoted by the National Schizophrenia Fellowship. They illustrate well the sort of problems encountered:

> The greatest difficulty is that it is at the time when she needs help – medical or financial – that she is usually unable to cope with the normal procedures for seeking it. One result is that when, as on this last occasion, she gives up her job [because, perhaps she is beginning to have delusions about her colleagues] she is unable to get unemployment assistance and is also in difficulty about sickness benefit because she has not put herself in the hands of doctors! [National Schizophrenia Fellowship, 1974, 22].
> In another case a claimant's situation was:
> complicated by frequent changes of address and consequent changes of DHSS branch plus difficulties of revealing her exact condition in the face of her opposition to having it revealed and variability of

medical certificate descriptions from 'schizophrenia' to 'nervous disability'! [p.23].

The circumstances described above will be recognisable to social workers as immensely time-consuming and requiring a good understanding of the relationship between DHSS regulations and medical certification, as well as a sensitivity to the feelings involved.

For people who have been admitted to psychiatric hospital, a frequent source of anxiety is the low level of in-patient benefit which is not designed to take any account of the responsibilities of people's lives outside hospital. Standing charges on fuel, H.P. agreements and debts are not things that just go away. This benefit level is impoverishing enough without compounding the financial difficulties that patients may have had before admission. Such difficulties may be worse if hospitals do not have adequate welfare benefit advisory services for in-patients, and studies have shown a serious shortfall in these services [Bradshaw and Davis, 1986].

The second quotation from the National Schizophrenia Fellowship is a particularly apt one as it raises a dilemma frequently found by workers. While it can be argued that disability and its resulting low income requires positive discrimination in terms of service provision and benefits, the kind of labelling that that may require can result in such a feeling of stigma, that benefits or services are simply not taken up. This, in our experience, can lead to further isolation, stressful dependency on relatives or even breakdown and admission to psychiatric hospital.

Increasingly in the modern welfare state, medical certification of disability has become the major passport to non-medical financial benefits [Stone, 1984]. What seems to be lacking is a more flexible, sensitive and sophisticated method of determining disability and consequent eligibility for benefits. The Disability Alliance has proposed the creation of a regional Disablement Assessment Board that would be involved in a more sophisticated and participatory assessment procedure that would hopefully reduce the stigma and resultant 'identity spread' that current sickness certification can produce.

What is clear from our four profiles and the resulting discussion is that living on the margins of the state's poverty line is often one of the inevitable consequences of suffering major mental health problems. That there is an inter-relationship between ill-health and low income has been re-emphasised by the recent *Health Divide Report*. One of the report's conclusions is that:

the unemployed and their families have considerably worse physical and mental health than those in work. Until recently, however, direct evidence that unemployment caused this poorer health was not available. Now there is evidence of unemployment causing a deterioration in mental health, with improvements observed on re-employment [Whitehead, 1987,2].

The editor of the *British Medical Journal*, in commenting on the report,

also refers to its evidence that for poorer people 'their material deprivation limits their ability to choose healthier lifestyles' [Hock, 1987, 858]. Our earlier descriptions of four peoples' lives endorses that statement.

For many people the prospect of long-term dependence on benefits is made worse by the double jeopardy of the stigmatizing effect of mental illness on employability and, as the Disability Alliance put it, 'the absurd distinction in the present system where people are assumed to be capable of permanent full-time work or totally incapable of work' [Disability Alliance, 1987a, 3]. Mental ill-health fluctuates in its duration and severity and we have found in our work that the social security regulations surrounding therapeutic earnings, earnings disregards and medical fitness for work do not make sufficient allowance for this and, consequently, can reinforce a feeling of entrapment, frustration and insecurity.

Our experience of the inadequacy and variability of benefits leads us to support the case for a comprehensive disability income scheme, designed to lift people off the poverty line and make allowance for the disadvantages that are associated with particular disabilities.

In this respect, the outcome of the social security reviews has not been a helpful one. One particular area does merit further mention here and that is the'community care grant' component of the Social Fund. That it is circumscribed by eligibility for income support is problem enough, but there must be doubt about how effective it can be in helping individuals to 'remain in the community' and in avoiding 'exceptional pressure on that person or family' [DHSS, 1987c]. There will need to be a more radical switch of resources to home support than the community care grant represents if these laudable aims are to be met. The fact of the matter is that many people who are dependent on invalidity benefit are living at home supported by family members and on an income not greatly above income support level. The vast majority of help received comes from another person inside the household – a spouse or a younger relative and usually a woman, but rarely will the claimant or carer meet the criteria for receiving either attendance allowance or invalid care allowance. They may also receive few services from the state in terms of day care, domiciliary services or relief care. The new community care grants will not, of course, apply to them:

In such circumstances, the state is not operating a community care policy which complements informal networks. Rather it is penalising these families willing to retain the primary caring functions, and by doing so may force many to give up the task prematurely [Hudson, 1987, 5].

We would like to conclude by emphasising the perspective of Stanley Cohen [1975] when he urges social workers to 'refuse the ideology of casework' but nonetheless to think of cases. The key to undoing the reality of powerlessness and poverty of income and services our clients often feel, is to translate their experiences wherever we can into a broader analysis for our managers to promote effective change through influencing policy makers, politicians and the public. We have used this chapter as our way of presenting an analysis of the experience of poor people with mental health problems.

13

Poverty, Mental Handicap and Social Work

Roger C Sumpton

THIS chapter is about the financial position of mentally handicapped people. It is based on two main assertions: Firstly, that few mentally handicapped people are in paid employment. As a consequence, the majority of mentally handicapped people in this country are dependent on the social security system. Secondly, that many people with mental handicap are social services clients. They may be clients by virtue of their attendance at day centres [Adult Training Centres or Social Education Centres]; living in residential establishments provided by social services departments or by ones run by voluntary or private bodies and registered by social services departments; or by their need for support as people living 'in the community', and not in some form of residential care. It is this latter category which is bringing more and more mentally handicapped people under the aegis of social services departments and their social workers. In 1977, social services spending on mental handicap services accounted for just 26 per cent of all money spent on these services. By 1985, this figure had risen to 35 per cent.

Before the advent of 'community care', most people with a mental handicap were residing in large institutions run by the NHS. Their poverty tended to be overshadowed by the poverty of their residential environments [King *et al*, 1971; Raynes, Sumpton and Flynn, 1987]. A 1971 White Paper on mental handicap services set targets for the run down and closure of these institutions [DHSS, 1971]. These targets are clearly not being met [DHSS, 1980b; Sumpton *et al*, 1987]. Consequently, over 40,000 mentally handicapped people still live in mental handicap 'hospitals'. However, some people have moved out of hospitals and admission rates have slowed down. There has been a growth in the number of local authority residential places for mentally handicapped people and some people, who would otherwise be in residential care, have found their way to living in the community alongside the rest of us. The poverty of this latter group of people cannot so easily be ignored.

All of this faces social workers with a dilemma: Is community care for mentally handicapped people to be equated with poverty? Are we going to exchange the poverty of institutional environments with the poverty of inadequate housing, employment, recreational and social opportunities and · call it 'community care'? Can social workers promote community care for their mentally handicappped clients and help to keep them out of poverty? These are the basic questions with which this chapter is concerned. There are no adequate answers, given the resources available to both social workers and their clients. However, in the absence of improvements in such resource levels, discussion of the questions can show some ways forward.

What I intend to do in the rest of the chapter is to consider several aspects of social work with mentally handicapped poor clients. Firstly, we shall continue the above discussion and ask whether mentally handicapped people share the same needs and problems of other groups of poor clients. Does their poverty and their mental handicap mean that they have different needs from, say, poor children or elderly people?

Secondly, we shall look at mentally handicapped people as claimants of welfare benefits. Here, the concern will be with take-up problems and we shall ask whether the handicap exacerbates such problems.

Thirdly, I want to think about a much-discussed idea – normalisation – in the context of social work and mentally handicapped people's poverty. The social worker's desire to encourage autonomy is relevant here. Does the client's position as a claimant conflict with that desire?

Fourthly, I want to discuss mentally handicapped people's need for budgetary advice. Again, what are the implications for the social worker's role?

Finally, I shall raise a few points on the implications for social workers and their mentally handicapped clients of the introduction of the new Social

Security Act.

In all of the following, it should be noted that I am referring to 'social work' in its broadest sense. I am therefore including fieldwork, residential and day-care work in the discussion. The points to be raised do have different implications for workers in each of these settings.

Mentally handicapped people as poor clients

It could be argued that the poverty of mentally handicapped people gives social workers no different a task as does the poverty of, for instance, an unemployed single parent. Each will need advice in claiming their entitlement to benefits, in managing their resources, in 'making do' and in coping with the depression and loss of dignity consequent upon their poverty. The mentally handicapped client is, however, likely to need more from the social worker to help gain some understanding of his or her position. The single parent may well be able to deal with the DHSS and the Council, armed with the necessary information about benefits. Most mentally handicapped clients, however, are going to have to call upon the social worker as advocate and ask for his or her direct involvement in such matters.

Another way in which social work with mentally handicapped people is different from that with other groups of clients is that the mentally handicapped person, although the client, may not be in a direct relationship with the social worker. In other words, members of the mentally handicapped person's family may 'intervene' between the social worker and client. Of course, in many instances this will be part of 'good practice' – to enlist the involvement of carers in 'a case'. While being a part of good casework as far as, for example, implementing a behaviour modification programme may be concerned, a relative's involvement may be obstructive in tackling the client's financial affairs. Some parents may be worried by the stigma of their dependant being a 'claimant'. Many more parents and carers will not be aware of the benefits to which the mentally handicapped person will be entitled. And of course, if no one ever asks them, 'do you know about supplementary benefit', they are likely to remain in ignorance. This does not only apply to those mentally handicapped people living in the community with their families. It can also apply to people who live in residential care. Although families may say, 'Oh yes, we give our Joan what she wants', residential care staff can be heard to say the same thing. In my experience, we too infrequently hear carers saying 'Oh yes, we see Joan gets what she's entitled to'.

A case in point here concerns claims for mobility allowance by people living in residential care. I have often heard staff remark that a claim has not been made because 'we [the staff] wouldn't be able to spend it anyway'.

Wray and Wistow [1987] point to a similar problem. They raise the possibility that some families who have a mentally handicapped dependant living with them may – as a unit – become dependent on the mentally handicapped person's social security benefits. This can then act as a disincentive to families to allow their dependant to leave home and live elsewhere, more suitable for his or her own needs and desires.

The above reinforces the need to remember *who* is the client [or claimant, or recipient, or customer]. Mentally handicapped people are claimants in their own right. They may have agents – paid or unpaid – who claim benefits for them, but at the end of the day, the benefit is theirs.

A solution to this problem can be to ensure that welfare rights work is integrated within the services provided to mentally handicapped people [Sumpton, 1985; Wray and Wistow, 1987]. Social services departments can aim to ensure that their mentally handicapped clients' status as claimants is given a high priority. Wray and Wistow describe the advantages of multi-disciplinary community mental handicap teams which include welfare rights workers alongside the more traditional team members.

Mentally handicapped people as claimants

As mentioned earlier, in this section I want to consider mainly the problem of take-up of benefits by mentally handicapped people. Low take-up is a problem which affects all social services clients, not only mentally handicapped people. There are, however, some factors which are unique to the position of mentally handicapped people as claimants.

As suggested earlier, stigma of claiming benefits may be one reason for low take-up. It has been argued that there is less stigma associated with the non-means tested benefits, such as mobility allowance, attendance allowance and severe disablement allowance. Less stigma may be associated with these benefits because they can be regarded as arising out of 'unavoidable need' [Blaxter, 1974]. The argument goes that it is more difficult for people to see claims for means-tested supplementary benefit, for instance, to arise from unavoidable need. However, it is important to realise that for mentally handicapped people the non-means tested benefits *do* require a means test – one of a psychological and physiological nature. The stigma, or whatever one may wish to call it, associated with the application procedure is not conducive to encouraging take-up. The task for a social worker is therefore clear, particularly, as discussed in the preceding section, when the mentally handicapped person's carer[s] are involved in making a claim for the benefit.

A number of studies have demonstrated the rewards that follow from social workers giving attention to low take-up of benefits by mentally handicapped people. My own work in Nottinghamshire showed that among a small sample of mentally handicapped people, benefits were under-claimed by 11 per cent. In other words, claiming full entitlement would have given each claimant in the study an 11 per cent increase in income [Sumpton, 1985]. A take-up campaign in the same county subsequently generated over half a million pounds in increased annual benefit and arrears for 445 mentally handicapped people [Wray and Wistow, 1987]. In Wandsworth, a similar campaign resulted in 34 mentally handicapped people receiving over £100,000 in supplementary benefit weekly additions [Laurence, 1987]. Welfare rights work can have a valuable role as part of the service offered to mentally handicapped people by social services departments. It needs to be stressed, however, that increasing take-up does nothing to stem the poverty resulting from the inadequate benefit levels themselves.

Poverty and normalisation

Normalisation refers to the use of culturally normative means to facilitate behaviour which itself is as culturally normative as possible. It is not about making mentally handicapped people 'normal'. It is about helping mentally handicapped people to achieve 'patterns and conditions of everyday life which are as close as possible to the norms and patterns of mainstream society' [Nirje, 1970, 181]. The *Jay Report* [DHSS, 1979b] used normalisation in its statement of the principles of mental handicap services. This stimulated the use of the concept in this country, although the concept's simplicity has generated much confusion. More recent policy statements, which relate to the Care in the Community initiative [DHSS, 1981a;1985h] have used the *Jay Report* principles, with their focus on normalisation. Therefore, we have a definition of care in the community as:

> an integrated service network to support mentally handicapped people according to their individual needs in a setting – own home, sharing someone else's home, group home, etc. – which provides maximum opportunities for ordinary living among ordinary people [DHSS, 1985h, 42].

Now, one of the important 'opportunities for ordinary living', I would argue, is financial security and an income above poverty level. The majority of mentally handicapped people in this country do not have income sufficient to give them 'ordinary living'. Flynn [1986] interviewed a sample of mentally handicapped people who were living in their own tenancies. She found that their average weekly income [when interviewed in 1985] was £39, with a range of incomes from £13 to £76. Ordinary living and community care must surely be extremely difficult to sustain with such low incomes. What can be done? As pointed out earlier, receipt of full benefit entitlement will still not give mentally handicapped people a reasonable income. The position of those people who attend Adult Training Centres [or Social Education Centres] is no better. For their 'therapeutic' work, they receive an extremely small sum. Some would argue therefore that social services departments, far from raising mentally handicapped people's standards of living, actually contribute to their poverty.

One other aspect of normalisation is that of autonomy. As the *Jay Report* [DHSS 1979b] stated, 'Mentally handicapped people have a right to be treated as individuals' [p.35] and that they have 'the right to make or be involved in decisions that affect them' [p.36]. So, autonomy is to be encouraged. This poses a problem when we examine our social security system. Over the past few years there has been a growing emphasis upon direct payment of a claimant's needs, such as housing and fuel costs. This removes the need for the claimant to get involved in payment of bills for routine, everyday services. Some people would welcome these arrangements for mentally handicapped people, since they seem to simplify some of the complexities of claiming benefits. They do nothing, however, to encourage autonomy or to offer the opportunites to learn about money.

For those mentally handicapped people living in residential care, there is a similar problem. These people receive an 'allowance', often referred to as pocket money. In a recent study of social services hostels, hospitals and voluntary homes for mentally handicapped people, it was found that only in the hostels were any of the residents able to have some control over their income [Raynes, Sumpton and Flynn, 1987]. However, having this control only applied to 6 per cent of the sample of people living in hostels. For the remaining 94 per cent of hostel residents and for all the hospital and voluntary home residents, income was usually 'pooled' and spent by staff for the group of residents in their care. Consequently, very little autonomy was given to the residents in spending what little money they did have.

Two points emerge therefore on the relationship between normalisation and mentally handicapped people's poverty. The first highlights a contradiction between policy statements on community care and the limits to achieving community care set by our social security benefit levels.

Secondly, benefit levels aside, there is the question of how social services personnel handle money matters so as to encourage autonomy and thereby work toward one aspect of normalisation.

Budgetary advice for mentally handicapped people

In this section I want to point to a potential set of conflicting roles for social workers working with mentally handicapped people. On the one hand, social workers are needed to encourage mentally handicapped people to develop skills in handling money and budgetting within the strict limits of their incomes. On the other hand, social workers ought, as Townsend [1982] has said, to be involved in 'improving the wretchedly inadequate system of benefits' [p.106]. So, while working within the system and therefore tacitly accepting it, social workers need to be critically reviewing that same system. This applies to work with all clients – not only the mentally handicapped. The conflict is perhaps more pronounced when the clients are mentally handicapped. It is then that the social worker will be involved in claiming benefits in the first place, and in trying to help the clients manage on a low income once the full entitlement has been claimed. Many mentally handicapped people, particularly those new to community care, need a lot of help in managing money [Flynn, 1986]. Other clients may not get this sort of intervention from social workers until they are in a position where debt counselling is offered. Accordingly, working for people with a mental handicap is more likely to generate a conflict for social workers. This conflict is set to grow under the new Social Security Act, to which we now turn.

The future

Thus far, I have raised several points which demonstrate the inability of the present social security system to support policies of community care and to support social workers' efforts to implement these policies for mentally handicapped people. This failure was one of the features highlighted by the Audit Commission's [1986] report on community care. The report referred to the 'perverse incentives' of the social security system which encouraged people to go into residential care. Changes to the social security system have posed and, under the new Act, will continue to pose an even greater threat to community care policies.

To illustrate this point, one only needs to review the August 1986 cut in supplementary benefit grants for furniture and household equipment for people leaving institutional care. A flat rate payment of less than one hundred pounds has replaced single payments for essential equipment. This sum cannot go very far to meet the cost of setting up a new home.

Under the new Social Security Act, the 'social fund' will provide for community care grants or loans. At the time of writing, what constitutes community care needs as opposed to other needs which would attract social fund payments remains unclear. The distinction, however, is important. A mentally handicapped person may seem to have a need for a community care grant. However, if the need is interpreted by social fund officers as not being related to community care, then the social fund payment will be a loan – to be deducted from the claimant's benefit.

Other considerations portray an even more depressing picture for mentally handicapped people and their social workers. Social fund payments will be cash limited, with reference to a fixed annual budget. In other words, a group of mentally handicapped people leaving the same institution will be competing with each other for community care grants. Social fund payments will be discretionary. The right of appeal under supplementary benefit regulations becomes a right to a 'review' by the officers who make the decision under social fund regulations. Furthermore, social fund payments may be restricted if some other person or body – such as a relative or the local authority – can meet the need.

No wonder then that there are predictions that implementation of the new Act will encourage dependent groups of claimants to seek residential care, as relatives become less able to cope financially with dependants living in the community. The Audit Commission's 'perverse incentives' seem set to reign into the future.

What of the future for social workers striving to achieve community care for mentally handicapped people? I have already explained that mentally handicapped people need their social workers to act as advocates in claiming benefits. The Government is suggesting that there should be closer liaison between Social Services Departments and the DHSS in assessing the need for social fund payments, especially those relating to community care needs. This, of course, would give social workers the dual and conflicting roles of providers and advocates. Such conflict already exists, as we have seen in discussing the need for budgetary advice in work with mentally handicapped people. The demand for social workers to be involved in making decisions about social security payments can only further compromise their advocacy role. If we return again to the example of a group of mentally handicapped people leaving long-term institutional care, we can see that distinguishing 'deserving' from 'undeserving' cases among such a group will be impossible for the social worker. Such distinction will, however, be made.

Conclusions and summary

This chapter has covered a wide range of issues. The need for a focus on welfare rights in social work with mentally handicapped people was emphasised. The contradictions between, on the one hand, policy statements about work with mentally handicapped people and, on the other, the social security system have been discussed. It has been argued that social workers are left 'somewhere in the middle' between these conflicting sets of demands.

I have been able to point to only a few resolutions open to social workers and their departmental policy-makers. In general, however I can only conclude by saying that social workers are not in a position to themselves resolve the problems I have identified. Perhaps the most optimistic conclusion to be drawn is that policy statements in the field are continuing to be made. The problems I have raised are not static ones. They do at least seem to be influenced fairly readily by statments of policy. Whether we can hope for future policy statements which will ameliorate the problems is questionable and does not leave as much room for optimism.

14

Poverty, Disability and Social Services
Dulcie Groves

POVERTY₁ is disability's close companion. Disabled adults of working   age commonly find that their earning powers are inhibited or   extinguished. Such disadvantaged occupational status puts them severely at risk to long-term poverty extending into old age. Furthermore, disability in child or adult tends to generate extra costs and can have a very serious financial impact on the household and family of a disabled person, especially where a 'front-line carer' is obliged to remain outside paid employment or limit his or her hours of paid work so as to look after an incapacitated person. And even where all welfare entitlements have successfully been claimed, some of the poorest households in the UK incorporate disabled members and carers struggling to live on the inadequate cash benefits provided via a highly complicated statutory income maintenance system. Some of the poorest individuals, however, are people with disabilities who live in residential care.

This brief discussion of selected issues on the theme of poverty, disability and social services will focus initially on the position of disabled people in relation to the labour market. The next section addresses the inadequacy of income support for disabled people whose earning capacities are interrupted or impaired, with subsequent comment on the financial position of 'carers', the majority of whom are middle-aged or elderly women. A concluding review of the links between poverty and disability will open up some wider issues of social service provision. This chapter mainly concentrates on issues relating to physically disabled people of working age, since other chapters deal with allied material on old age, mental handicap and mental illness.

In examining the situation of disabled people in the context of their risk to poverty, it has to be borne in mind that each person is an individual with his or her own particular disability and circumstances. Writing on social work with disabled people, Michael Oliver [1983, I] is at pains to emphasise the inadequacy of the models and theories of disability adopted by social workers and other professionals. These 'individual' explanations emphasise that the difficulties experienced by disabled people arise from the nature of their disability, so that the job of the 'professionals' is to make the person as 'normal' as possible and help him or her to come to terms with a disabling condition. Oliver argues that an alternative 'social' explanation of disability is more helpful than the individual model since it focuses 'on the way physical and social environments impose limitations upon certain groups and categories of people' [1983, 15]. As illustration he points out that paid employment and work places are geared to the needs of 'able-bodied' people, thus excluding disabled individuals who are, in consequence, at risk of being perceived as 'dependent' [Oliver, 1983, 26].

Topliss [1982, 2-3] has observed that there is 'no clear, objective and unambiguous distinction between the point at which normality ends and disability begins . . . '. She notes the difficulty which this has caused in estimating the actual number of disabled children and adults in the UK. The statistics and information contained in the most recent government survey [Harris, 1971; Buckle, 1971] date from the 1960s, as does the material in Townsend's [1979] sample survey of poverty. It will be 1988 before the full results are available on a new [1985] government survey of the numbers of disabled people, their income levels and their needs [Disability Alliance, 1987b, 7].

Harris draws a distinction between impairment, disability and handicap in which impairment is defined as the loss of part or all of a limb, or any defect of organ or mechanism or the body . . . 'while disability was the lack of function which resulted directly from the impairment' [1971]. Handicap is defined as 'the limitation on normal activities of self-care and mobility consequent upon the loss of function caused by impairment' [Topliss, 1983, 3]. This distinction between impairment, disability and handicap, including the extent to which such conditions are socially created, is discussed at length by Townsend [1979, 686-695] and Stone [1984]. Relevant issues are also addressed by the Disability Alliance [1987b, 35-50] in the context of properly recognising the degree of a claimant's incapacity within an adequate state cash benefits system; also by Lonsdale and Walker [1984, 9-11] in relation to paid employment.

Poverty, disability and paid work

A major cause of poverty among disabled people is their restricted access to the labour market and their typically disadvantaged position as paid employees. For women, members of ethnic minority groups, older workers and young people attempting to get a first job, disability compounds existing disadvantage. It is perhaps indicative of the lack of official priority given to issues concerning disabled people that it is impossible to state, with confidence, how many disabled people are in paid work, searching for work or are non-employed, though the 1985 survey when published, should throw light on the economic activity of people with disabling physical and/or mental conditions [*Hansard*, 9/12/1986, col. 124].

Townsend's massive study of poverty in the UK, based on a 1969 sample, identified disabled people and those with long-term illnesses as accounting for 'a substantial proportion of poverty' [Townsend, 1979, 685]. A substantial proportion of individuals in these categories were of 'working age' [Table A71 1048], their risk of disability increasing with age. Equal numbers of men and women under fifty were found among the more severely disabled individuals: among the over-fifties, the number of very incapacitated women exceeded men. However, a greater number of younger women than men had an incapacity of some kind.

The most striking correlation found by Townsend was between disability and occupational class, with 'a significantly higher proportion of manual than non-manual classes' having 'minor, some, appreciable or severe incapacity' [1979, 709]. Much evidence has been assembled in the 1980s on the link between poor health and low socio-economic status [Townsend, 1987a, 82-87]. In 1969, the link between disability and poverty was particularly strong among adults of 'working age' [then 15-65 for men and 15-60 for women]. At a time of low unemployment by comparison with the 1980s, there were nearly three times as many appreciably or severely disabled people under forty identified as living in very low income households as non-disabled people in the same age group [Townsend, 1979, 711]. Disabled people suffered not only from low incomes but also lacked financial assets and personal possessions, experiencing, in addition, wider material deprivations such as poor housing and lack of adequate heating [714-717].

Townsend argued that 'major controlling factors' in bringing about the typically low resources of disabled people were 'the economic and social expectations and obligations governing access to employment and, once in employment, access to types of jobs and levels of earnings'. Four specific disadvantages were demonstrated – fewer disabled than non-disabled people were in the labour market, higher earnings were under-represented, disabled people tended to work longer hours in order to achieve the same level of earnings as their non-disabled peers, while slightly fewer incapacitated people had good conditions of work [Townsend, 1979, 727].

Such findings echoed a 1965 survey of persons registered as disabled with local authorities in the Greater London area. Sainsbury [1970, 89] concluded that 'most handicapped people faced serious employment difficulties. Even skilled persons in open employment usually experienced a drop in earnings and status after the onset of disability.' Similarly, Buckle concluded that 'persons who, even by our definition, have a 'minor' impairment, may have difficulty in getting a job, or working in open employment, or they may have difficulties in getting to work or while at work' [1971, 59].

In a later commentary on employment and disability, Townsend argues that an optimistic view was taken of the employment prospects of disabled people following the Disabled Persons [Employment] Act 1944 and the setting up of a voluntary disablement register from which employers of more than twenty persons were required to draw a 3 per cent 'quota' of their workforce [Townsend, 1981, 52-4]. Certain occupations [lift operator and car park attendant] were reserved for people who had registered as disabled for the 'quota' and a range of sheltered workshops were set up under statutory and voluntary auspices, along with special state employment services for disabled people who at that time included many veterans of the Second World War.

Recent commentaries on public policies regarding disabled people and employment are critical of the way in which the above provisions have been operating in the 1970s and 80s, still governed by the earlier legislation, with minor amendments [Townsend, 1981; Lonsdale and Walker, 1984; Gladstone, 1985]. Much criticism and debate has centred on the 'quota' system, reviewed in the early 1970s by a Conservative administration with a recommendation for abolition on the grounds that fewer disabled people were registering and that there was no evidence that the scheme was effective in enhancing their employment prospects [Townsend, 1981, 62-3]. The quota scheme was reprieved by a subsequent Labour government but once more put under scrutiny by the Manpower Services Commssion in 1979 with a later recommendation that, despite opposition from interested parties, the scheme should be abolished. Employers would be given a code of practice and required to 'take reasonable steps to promote equality of opportunity in employment for disabled people' [Townsend, 1981, 63].

In point of fact, since its inception, the quota never seems to have been enforced, despite relatively high unemployment among disabled people over four decades. Nor have disabled people been encouraged to register or otherwise supported adequately by public policies designed to enhance their chances of finding and keeping paid work [64-65]. There was a steep fall in the number of people registering as disabled in the 1980s, a time of growing unemployment during which the Conservative government was cutting employment services for disabled people [Lonsdale and Walker, 12-14; 38]. As Gladstone [1985, 103-4] comments, by this time disabled people were being viewed increasingly as 'surplus labour' and had become disproportionately represented among the long-term unemployed. In its Review of Assistance for Disabled People [1982], the Manpower Services Commission acknowledge that unemployed disabled people had 'much greater problems in regaining work than unemployed people generally' [Gladstone, 1985, 104]. Yet, as Gladstone points out, recent government policies have continued to favour persuasion rather than the compulsion favoured by organisations representing disabled people themselves, who would like to see employers being compelled to keep disabled workers on their payroll, via a strengthened quota system [1985, 106].

Lonsdale and Walker are similarly critical of recent government policies relating to disabled people and unemployment. They consider that the position of disabled people in the labour market has weakened considerably in the face of high unemployment, public expenditure cuts and renewed prejudice against incapacitated workers [Lonsdale and Walker, 1984, 7]. A recent article explaining current government policies and provisions headlines the information that 'More than any other sector of the workforce, people with disabilities face barriers in finding and keeping employment' [Leese, 1987]. The Conservative government has, in fact, retained the quota system and introduced a Code of Good Practice on the Employment of Disabled People [1984] with which employers are invited to comply voluntarily.

Meanwhile, available evidence suggests that disabled people are heavily over-represented among those looking for and holding manual semi-skilled and unskilled jobs [Lonsdale and Walker, 17-18]. These are the very categories of jobs which have been disappearing in recent years [Hawkins, 1987, 99-102]. Disabled people are at risk to low pay. Under the Wages Council Regulations, 1979, it is legal for some employers to pay disabled workers at even lower rates than permitted for non-disabled.

Very low pay is permitted in sheltered workshops [Lonsdale and Walker, 1984, 20-22]. In addition, disabled workers, by virtue of their typically low occupational status and interrupted earnings are liable to be excluded from the 'fringe benefits', such as occupational retirement and widows' pensions, not to mention disability pensions, enjoyed by established, higher grade workers [see Small, Green and Hadjimatheou, ʻ1984].

Finally it must be remarked that disabled women are a group whose employment problems have been taken far less seriously than those of men [Townsend, 1981, 61]. Among the women sampled for the 1980 survey of life-time employment, which has no section specifically devoted to issues of disability, 19 per cent of 'working-age' women who were non-employed and not looking for work gave illness or injury as the reason [Martin and Roberts, 1984, Table 7.3, 87]. The importance of paid work to women will be discussed later in this chapter. One final point of particular relevance in the context of disability is that employers and potential employers tend to put far more emphasis on the physical appearance of women employees than men, especially in some of the 'service' occupations in which women are heavily concentrated. A visibly 'impaired' woman seeking a typical 'women's job' as a secretary or waitress, for instance, is likely to be especially disadvantaged by this manifestation of sexism at work.

Disability, poverty and income maintenance provision

Disabled people, given their difficulties in the labour market, are in many cases obliged to rely on state income maintenance. A glance through the current edition of the *Disability Rights Handbook* [Disability Alliance, 1987a] well illustrates the multiplicity of benefits and complicated rules of eligibility, many of which relate to the nature of the disability and the way in which it was acquired. While it is true that income support provision for disabled people did improve in the 1970s, more recently there have been cutbacks and it appears likely that the Social Security Act 1986 will worsen rather than improve the financial lot of disabled claimants.

The Disability Alliance and its member organisations have long campaigned for a comprehensive disability income for all disabled people so as to combat poverty and bring the incomes of disabled people more in line with 'average' incomes, bearing in mind the extra costs of disability. Some medical charges can arise under National Health Service treatment and not all appliances and aids come free from the NHS or local authority. There may be additions to the ordinary household budget for items such as special diets, extra heating, paid domestic assistance, special household gadgets, etc. [see *Disability Alliance*, 1987b, 8-10].

With such a multiplicity of benefits, a few points only will be made to illustrate both their low level and complicated nature, together with some allied issues of sex discrimination. The major long-term contributory national insurance benefit claimed by disabled people is the invalidity pension. There is also a non-means tested attendance allowance payable to severely disabled people at a higher rate for attendance by day *and* night with a lower rate for day *or* night. Eligibility for this benefit is based on a medical judgement as to degree of disability and consequent need for attendance. Disabled people without a sufficient National Insurance record who can prove long-term incapacity for work can apply for a severe disablement allowance. There is a mobility allowance for those with walking difficulties, paid only to people under 65.

Some disabled people also claim war pensions or industrial injuries benefits, have occupational disability pensions or have received forms of lump sum disability compensation as a result of accidents or injuries sustained as victims of a crime. Disabled people may 'top up' low benefits by claiming [if able to prove 'main breadwinner' status] means-tested supplementary benefit. The plight of supplementary benefit claimants living in poverty will be clear from other chapters in this book. Supplementary benefit will be replaced in April 1988 by an even more stringent form of social assistance to be known as income support.

The low level of cash benefits for disabled people can be illustrated by the invalidity pension payable since 1971 to those claimants with a National Insurance entitlement which may represent contributions made over many years. The claimant must previously have spent six months on statutory employer's and National Insurance short-term sick pay, at which point £35.90 per week [1987 rates] will be paid to the claimant plus an adult dependant's allowance of £23.75 provided that the 'dependant' earns no more than £31.43 weekly after deduction of permitted expenses. There are dependent child allowances of £8.05 but these are progressively lost if a spouse or partner earns or has an occupational pension greater than £85 per week, a 'cut' introduced in 1984.

The invalidity pension may be supplemented in the case of claimants of 'working age' [who are more than five years off pensionable age] by a small invalidity allowance ranging from £8.30 per week for people under 40 to £2.65 for people over fifty. Under permitted sex discrimination relating to

the differential ages at which women [60] and men [65] can, if eligible, claim
a state basic retirement pension, a women loses her invalidity allowance at
55, five years earlier than a man. Another example of recent cuts in
disability benefits is that, since 1985, any disability payments due as a result
of contribution to the State Earnings Related Pension Scheme are deducted
up to an amount equal to any invalidity allowance received. It is usually
lower earners and, especially, women, who are in SERPS and not an
occupational pension scheme. [For detailed information on the above
benefits see *Disability Alliance*, 1987a; Lakhani and Read, 1987; Luba and
Rowland, 1987].

In 1975 a non-contributory invalidity pension was introduced payable at
60 per cent of the National Insurance invalidity pension to those disabled
people of 'working age' who had either never worked or had insufficient
National Insurance contributions due to a non-existent or insufficient
employment record. When NCIP was introduced, it did nothing to relieve
the poverty of low-income married or cohabiting women, since they were
deemed ineligible since, as housewives, they might be 'at home in any
event'. After strenuous lobbying inside and outside of Parliament,
'housewives' were eventually [1977] granted their own particular version of
the benefit [HNCIP] with an extra eligibility requirement that they be
'incapable of performing normal household duties' [the unpaid work of the
home] as well as incapable of paid employment [Glendinning, 1980]. It
took several years of protest against the discriminatory nature of HNCIP
before both non-contributory benefits were replaced by a most
complicated benefit, the severe disability allowance [see *Disability Alliance*,
1987a, 62-8], still payable at only 60 per cent of a contributory invalidity
pension and with similar dependants' rates.

SDA is available to former H/NCIP claimants, those incapable of paid
work up to their 20th birthday and those of 'working age' who can prove an
80 per cent disability which precludes paid employment. The substitution
of SDA for HNCIP abolished a blatant example of sex discrimination
within the social security system which might otherwise have been
challenged under EEC sex discrimination regulations. However, as
Luckhaus [1986a] makes clear, SDA was devised as a nil-cost replacement,
with eligibility conditions which, while they included very severely
disabled married and cohabiting women, excluded some less disabled men
and women who would previously have qualified. Luckhaus argues that the
benefit may still discriminate indirectly against women since a stringent
disability test is applied to all claimants over 20 and it is married and
cohabiting women who are less likely than men to have made sufficient

contributions for the larger, though hardly generous, National Insurance invalidity pension.

A further aspect of the impoverishment which can arise from disability relates to the position of 'carers', most of whom are women. Yet, until recently, married and cohabiting women were denied entitlement to the one benefit designed for carers – the invalid care allowance [see Groves and Finch, 1983]. While married women had, increasingly, been doing paid work since World War II, by the mid 1970s, a time of high inflation, it was clear that many households would be in poverty but for wives' and female partners' earnings [Rimmer and Popay, 1982]. Yet the HNCIP and ICA had been introduced in the mid 1970s following publication of a White Paper [House of Commons, 1974] riddled with assumptions about married women being 'at home' with full responsibility for unpaid domestic labour.

In reality, the presence of a disabled child or adult in a household was a likely cause of poverty. Not only might an incapacitated woman find herself unable to earn and contribute to household finances to the extent that otherwise would have been the case and not necessarily be eligible for any cash benefit in her own right. A non-disabled married or co-habiting female carer might have to give up paid work, or restrict her hours of employment, but again could claim no ICA nor supplementary benefit. Glendinning [1983, 64-75] has catalogued the extra costs of caring for a disabled child and the restrictions placed on a caring mother's paid employment opportunities. The 1980 survey of women's employment found that 19 per cent of all women felt that their work opportunities had been affected by having to care for a sick or elderly dependant [Martin and Roberts, Table 8.35; 112-114]. In 1986, after the UK had been taken to the European Court as being in breach of Community law on sex discrimination, eligibility to ICA was extended to married and co-habiting women. Despite the fact that the pool of applicants is limited to women of 'working age' whose dependant is so severely disabled as to qualify for attendance allowance, this writer heard the BBC Radio Four *You and Yours* programme announce [24/8/1987] that no fewer than 118,500 carers had applied for ICA, backdated to 1984, where appropriate.

Conclusion

Indubitably, many disabled people are at a disadvantage in the labour market and at risk to poverty. A key policy issue is the extent to which employers should be required by law, rather than persuaded, to exercise positive discrimination in favour of disabled workers. The Manpower

Services Commission has maintained that disabled workers typically have middle age and/or poor skills in common with other disadvantaged workers and has emphasised the desirability of 'normalisation' as a guiding principle in training and employment services for disabled people [Gladstone, 1985, 108]. This position emphasises personal 'deficiencies' and fails to recognise long-standing social disadvantages commonly experienced by disabled people such as lack of access to adequate education, training or rehabilitation of a type which capitalises on potential, hostile working environments and a state income maintenance system which fails to recognise partial incapacity for paid work. The 'segregation versus integration' debate discussed at length by Lonsdale and Walker [1984, 39-53] is highly relevant in the context of poverty and disability since it raises the major issue as to whether public policies on the employment of disabled people should be governed by principles of economic efficiency or social welfare, if, indeed, these are polar principles.

Attention has been drawn to the complicated and inadequate cash benefit system on which many disabled people and their dependants have to rely. The Disability Alliance have long argued the case for a comprehensive state disability income scheme and have recently produced detailed proposals for disablement pension provision which would address poverty by recognising partial capacity for paid work [*Disability Alliance*, 1987b, 47-51] and a disablement allowance which would recognise the extra costs of disability [1987b, 29-30]. Meanwhile there is little doubt that disabled people stand in need of access to specialist welfare rights advice and the more so when the supplementary benefits system is abolished in 1988. Welfare rights is but one of the areas in which voluntary organisations, some poorly funded, have done sterling work, but as Becker and Macpherson [1986, 63] emphasise, it is local authority social service departments which are likely to face heavy demands from severely disabled clients who will 'lose out' when income support benefits and the cash-limited Social Fund replace supplementary benefit.

Increased poverty among severely disabled clients will impact upon their carers, mainly women, invalid care allowances notwithstanding. Though, as Luckhaus [1986b, 536] argues, the publicity surrounding the successful legal judgement on ICA has served to make 'carers' and 'the nature of the caring function' more visible. This has potential for opening up a much wider debate on the financial circumstances of carers and their dependants and the links between poverty and disability.

15

Frail Elderly People in Poverty:
A social work perspective
Olive Stevenson

THERE is now an extensive literature about elderly people in Britain, including discussion of demographic trends and of their financial circumstances. This chapter will not go over well trodden ground. Rather, it concentrates on matters of particular importance to social workers, which arise from the material and financial circumstances in which most elderly clients find themselves. We are not, therefore, here concerned with the large numbers of fit, active 'young' elderly people, nor with the growing number of old people with substantial occupational or private pensions. Furthermore, the focus is on the here and now, not on the well being of future generations of old people, who will, for example, be greatly affected by the policies which successive governments adopt on the State Earnings Related Pension Scheme.

Social service departments offer services of one kind or another to less than 20 per cent of the elderly population. For most of these elderly people, domiciliary care and support is the most important service which they receive [Audit Commission, 1985]. Most are over 70, many of these very old indeed; most receive supplementary benefit [income support] to top up their pensions. A relatively small proportion [about 2 per cent] are in local authority residential care, for which they are financially assessed. Numerous writers have pointed out that field social work with elderly people in social service departments has, for a variety of reasons, not been accorded high priority [Parsloe and Stevenson 1978; Rowlings,1980]. Much of the field work has been undertaken by social work assistants, many with skill and commitment, but without the status or the salary accorded to qualified social workers. We cannot here explore the extensive implications of that situation, except to point out that whatever the qualities of particular social work assistants, a policy by which elderly clients are allocated to those low in the social services hierarchy, plays a part in reinforcing the stigma associated with old age. However, it is not always noted that, the work of the large numbers of hospital social workers is mainly with old people, who form a majority of those entering hospital. Much of that work is focussed on the social and material circumstances of the old people on discharge. Furthermore, hospital social workers come into contact with substantial numbers of elderly people who are not usually in touch with social service departments or who are not receiving supplementary benefit. Included among these are the hidden poor, those who, for a variety of reasons, do not have sufficient disposable income to maintain themselves comfortably. They may, for example, have savings, just over the capital limit for supplementary benefit and be unwilling [or too frightened] to spend it. They may own houses, the cost of whose upkeep is disproportionate. Whatever the cause, there is no doubt that there are many more old people in financial hardship than the 2 million who, in 1983, were receiving supplementary benefit additional to their pension. A good social worker knows that for those who are not officially poor, there are no simple solutions. Advice like 'spend your capital', 'sell the house', 'take a lodger', ignores the social, emotional and practical complexities of peoples lives.

It is known that women bear the brunt of poverty in old age. The author has explored some of these issues elsewhere [Stevenson 1986; 1988 forthcoming], and the position both of large numbers of old women and of their middle aged carers has been thoroughly explored [Finch and Groves, 1983; Peace, 1986]. The large majority, therefore, of the old clients with whom social workers engage are women. Furthermore, in some parts of the country, a significant number of old clients will be from ethnic minorities, including those who are Asian, Afro-Caribbean, Chinese, Cypriot, European, Irish or Jewish. Their position in 'triple jeopardy' has been well discussed by Norman [1985]. Material and financial hardship may have different implications for men and women, and for people from ethnic minorities, which need to be understood by social workers.

From April 1988, the basic state pension will be £65.90 for a pensioner couple and £41.15 for a single pensioner. In 1981, the government broke the link with the rise in earnings in pension upratings and related increases solely to the rise in prices. Age Concern has shown how this has affected the level of pension. Between 1981 and 1987, the pensioner couple have 'lost' £12.50; that it is say, had the link with earnings been preserved, they would now be receiving £78.50; a single pensioner would be receiving £49.25 – £8.10 more than now. Age Concern have 'always argued for basic state pension to be half average earnings for a couple, and one third average earnings for a single pensioner. On the latest available figures [June 1987] average earnings were £200 per week which would give £100 for a couple and £66.65 for a single person' [Age Concern, 1987].

The proportion of earnings on which it is considered the pension should be based is, of course, a matter for debate. However, this comment draws attention to the gap between average earnings and the state pension. As the Social Security Advisory Committee [1985b] pointed out, 'this amounts to only about 19 per cent of average gross male earnings for a single person – little more than in 1948'. The Committee acknowledges that 'comparisons with net earnings over the same period provide a more favourable picture of its changing worth' [p.3]. Yet the continuing dependence of so many old people on supplementary benefit clearly indicates that present pension levels are simply not adequate for basic subsistence. Furthermore, the gap between pensioners and earners is steadily increasing and is a significant factor in the growing inequality between different groups of old people and between old people and the younger generation:

> If the prices-only rating is maintained, the value of the basic pension from 19 per cent of average male earnings at present, will fall to below 15 per cent by the year 2003 and to just over 10 per cent by 2025 [SSAC, 1985b, 6].

In the Green Paper [DHSS, 1985c] which preceeded the Social Security Act, 1986, the financial position of old people relative to others in the population, is shown to have significantly improved over the past 30 years. 'There are now fewer pensioners in the bottom quintile of the national income distribution' [Technical Annex p.11]. As Figure 15.1 shows, there has also been a marked shift in the proportion of different groups claiming supplementary benefit. Elderly people are no longer the largest group. They have been overtaken by the unemployed. However, the two million pensioners who received supplementary benefit in 1983 constitute a sizeable group in the claimant population. For field social workers, the fact that in general old people are better off now than yesterday, and that other groups increasingly claim income support, is of general rather than

Figure 15.1

Changes in the distribution of low incomes

Composition of bottom quintile by type of income unit, 1971 and 1982 [per cent]

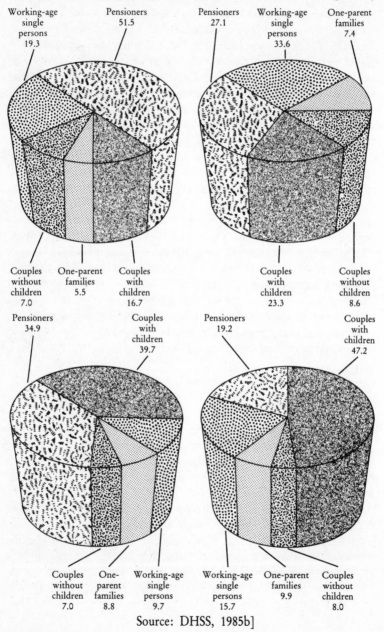

Source: DHSS, 1985b]

particular interests.

In April 1988, the new scheme will be in place and the basis of income support will have been fundamentally changed. On top of the basic scale rate, there will be premiums, paid to different groups at different rates. Those at age 60 will receive one premium, and a higher premium will be paid to the over 80s and to those who are receiving benefits related to disability or continuing incapacity. The rates of benefit from April 1988 have been announced. For income support [formerly supplementary benefit], the capital limit is now £6,000 of which £3,000 is disregarded. Basic pensioner premiums have been set at £10.65 for a single person and for couples £16.25. The higher rates are £13.05 and £18.50 respectively.

With the announcement comes an analysis of the impact of the new structure on different groups [DHSS, 1987d]. This is an analysis of 'losers and gainers'. There is, of course, transitional protection so that individuals will not lose benefit at the point of change. These government tables show clearly that the group most affected, both positively and negatively by the changes, are the pensioners between 60 and 79 who are **not** on income support. As Table 15.2 shows more will gain than will lose, although some will lose substantial amounts [see also Svenson and MacPherson, this volume].

It is too early yet to assess the impact of this redistribution within this group or, indeed, within the elderly population as a whole, not least because of the complications of housing benefits and the new requirement of a 20 per cent contribution to rates. The government calculations are acknowledged to be to an extent speculative.

For the frail elderly, the loss of the additional requirements provision, which enabled payments for such items as special diets, is the most likely to give rise to hardship. These were tailored to individual need and there is no provision for such payments in the new income support scheme.

Social Fund

Calculations of losers and gainers from the income support changes do not include the Social Fund factor; that is to say, the overall impact on claimants income of single payments has not been taken into account in making the comparison. Old people were never heavy users of that provision but it is unclear to what extent the provision of community care grants [as distinct from loans] to old people in their own homes will become widespread. Early statements on the Fund seem to suggest that grants were intended primarily for those, usually mentally ill or handicapped, being

Table 15.2

People not on income support: Changes in disposable income after meeting housing costs: By Client Group

(Thousands)

Cash position at point of change

Client Group	Increases						Total Increased	No Change	Total Decreased	Decreases					
	£5†	£4-5	£3-4	£2-3	£1-2	£1				£1	£1-2	£2-3	£3-4	£4-5	£5†
Pensioners	10	30	50	60	60	30	230	20	70	10	30	10	‡	‡	20
Pensioners age 60-79	50	50	160	410	590	170	1440	220	500	100	150	70	30	30	130
Sick or disabled	50	10	20	30	10	10	130	10	10	‡	‡	‡	‡	‡	10
Lone parents	70	10	10	10	‡	‡	100	20	90	10	20	10	20	20	20
Couples with children															
— In full-time work	170	20	20	40	20	10	290	20	70	10	10	10	‡	10	30
— Others	‡	‡	‡	‡	‡	‡	20	10	10	‡	‡	‡	‡	‡	10
Others															
— In full-time work	‡	‡	‡	‡	‡	‡	10	10	110	10	30	20	10	‡	30
— Others	‡	‡	‡	‡	10	10	20	30	90	10	20	‡	10	‡	50
Total	360	130	250	560	700	240	2240	340	950	160	270	130	70	50	270

discharged from hospital to the community. Recently, however, assurances have been given that they should be used to support those already in the community of whom, of course, a very large number are elderly people and that elderly people should be given high priority. Few elderly people will apply for loans; the attitudes of old people to credit, their fear of being in debt and the fact that their circumstances are unlikely to change for the better will all work against such applications.

The extent, therefore, to which Social Fund grants will be made to elderly people is as yet uncertain. It seems unlikely, however, that the present pattern, in which the majority of such payments are made to families with children, will change. The budgetary limits which are to be introduced into the Social Fund will ensure that there will be no unplanned increase in the sums paid out and the needs of children and families are likely to dominate calls on the Fund. It is sad to think that old people may continue to lack simple items, such as a new safe electric fire or a higher chair, to lessen the risks in daily living.

Many old people who exist in, or at the margins of, poverty live alone, especially the very old. For example, in 1980, 34 per cent of elderly people lived alone, and 53 per cent of women over the age of 85. The financial and social consequences of this bald statistic are extensive. There is no doubt that there are 'economies of scale' in daily living; it is not easy to shop for one on a limited income in a way which offers some choice and variation in diet, especially since many of today's very old people do not have freezers and are not in any case accustomed to using them. [Age Concern has for some years urged supermarkets to provide smaller portions of those staple commodities which do not keep well].

Heating

However, the cost of heating causes old people the greatest anxiety. The dramatic rise in the cost of fuel, following the oil crisis in the 1970s, has left many old people frightened and very worried about their heating costs. Even when they are not very hard up, some are unwilling to incur the expense involved in heating their dwelling adequately. Social workers, therefore, have to help their clients both with the reality of heating costs and with the anxiety, sometimes excessive, which they engender. The variations in heating costs are great, depending on the type of housing occupied. Particular problems can arise for owner occupiers who may have spent a lifetime in a family house not designed for their needs in later years, and for some of the 8 per cent of the elderly population who live in privately rented accommodation, some of it in poor repair in old housing stock in the inner cities.

For some years attempts have been made to provide some additional help with fuel costs when the weather is exceptionally cold. Old people, obviously, are the prime beneficiaries of such allowances. It has proved extraordinarily difficult to devise a system which is perceived to be just and is easy to operate. Were it not such a sad reflection on the need of so many old people in Britain today for basic warmth, it would be laughable to see successive ministers tripped up in the bureaucratic web which their officials have spun. There have been four main problems. First, temperatures vary across the country so mechanisms have to be devised which trigger payments in particular places. This is fraught with practical difficulties. Secondly, the period of time for which the very cold weather runs must be taken into account. Thirdly, earlier insistence on providing receipts for fuel was impractical and unfair. Fourthly, and most important, it has so far proved impossible to make such payments, which are now a basic entitlement, without a claim being submitted. This clearly restricts take-up. It has been particularly unfortunate in the case of old people, sometimes confused, living alone, who are most unlikely to make the claim unless helped to do so.

The original plans for the Social Fund made no reference to this provision. However, it has now been agreed that it will be added to the maternity and death grants within the Social Fund as a means-tested entitlement. That is, it will not be discretionary and will therefore operate in much the same way as heretofore. Given past history, its operation is unlikely to be smooth! Administratively it is a complex scheme which is disproportionately expensive for the benefit it offers. For as long as the incomes of so many old people are basically inadequate for their heating costs, it is the price governments have to pay when public concern and alarm mounts in periods of harsh weather. Many of us feel ashamed that it should be thus.

One of the emotive issues which comes to the fore as temperatures drop is that of hypothermia. This is a complex subject and arguments about the numbers of those who become hypothermic should not deflect us from the much bigger problem of the numbers living in uncomfortably cold conditions, well below the various recommended temperatures, ie below 65 or 60 fahrenheit, 16 centigrade.

Hypothermia means low body temperature. There are different ways of measuring it, but it is generally agreed that it is the inner body or core temperature that is critical. The diagnosis of hypothermia is usually made at 35 centigrade, or 95 fahrenheit. There is a relationship between endogenous [internal] and exogenous [external] causes. Some medical conditions are associated with lowering of the body temperature. It is also common for hypothermia to occur when an elderly person has fallen and lies where she falls. Her flat may be cold and she may have defective temperature control reflexes.

There has been one major research study in Britain on the social factors associated with hypothermia [Wicks, 1978]. The fieldwork was undertaken in the early 1970s and there is clearly a need for more up to date information. However, Wicks' study remains a useful contribution to the subject in which there is often a muddled and ineffective lobbying by a pressure group on government.

Wicks' findings, which cannot be reported in detail here, are a mine of information about the conditions in which old people live and the policy implications for different services. Some critical points, however, were as follows. First, in general many of the elderly in the survey lived in cold conditions and the majority had living room or bedroom temperatures below recommended levels. Fewer than one in four had central heating.

Secondly, nearly 10 per cent of the sample were at risk of developing hypothermia. Thirdly, a complex and fascinating finding, 'poverty was not directly related to low core temperature but the receipt of supplementary benefit was', [p. 164]. Wicks showed that the room temperatures of those receiving supplementary benefits were not on average lower than those with higher incomes. But a significantly higher proportion of these claimants had dangerously low body temperatures. Of these, the very aged were the most vulnerable. Wicks concludes:

> this is probably due to the effects of a declining physiology, perhaps exacerbated by illness, combined with the most deprived social conditions [p. 164].

This finding cries out for further investigation, concerning the long term effects of physical deprivation on the bodies of the aged and the impact of other contemporaneous factors such as clothing and nutrition.

Wicks found hypothermic risk to be substantially lessened where the old person had an electric blanket. This simple suggestion also carries a warning for such blankets need to be checked regularly. Many frail old people living alone will need help to arrange this.

The general implication of Wicks' research for social work practice are clear. Social work clients are at greater risk than others of hypothermia, but not for the obvious reasons. Therefore a room temperature check may not suffice. However, not all that many will fall victim to hypothermia. Rather they will live and they will die not warm enough. This is a social disgrace. Social workers will use a wide range of individual strategies and activities to improve the lot of individuals. Bearing in mind, however, the small numbers of old people with whom social workers, or even social service departments, are in touch, this grave social problem clearly needs to be tackled on a much wider front.

Housing

It is obvious that adequacy of heating is bound up with adequacy of housing. The housing conditions of many elderly people give rise to grave concern and cannot be fully explored here. Recently, however, more attention has been focussed on the difficulties of owner occupiers, more than half the pensioners in Britain. For those on supplementary benefit or, as earlier discussed, just above the official poverty line, there are major problems in maintaining their property in a good state of repair and decoration. Many who find their accommodation unsuited to their needs in old age cannot afford the necessary adaptations. Relatively few can move into sheltered accommodation even if they want to do so. Wheeler [1986] explores this in detail:

> Pensioner households in the private sector have ... increasingly become trapped in poorer and older housing, without the resources necessary to consider a move or to carry out repairs or improvements. Home improvement policy through the 1970s and early 1980s failed to recognise the particular difficulties low income owners have in maintaining or improving their homes [p. 223].

Wheeler points out that there has been a limited response to this neglect by both the private and voluntary bodies. Mortgages are now offered by some building societies for house improvements, with payment of interest only until the house is sold or inherited. In the voluntary sector housing associations 'grasped the opportunity for older people by setting up 'Staying Put', and 'Care and Repair' experiments which helped with elderly home owners with repairs, improvements and adaptations to their homes' [p. 224]. Wheeler points out that this involves not only financial assistance but technical and organisational help. Similar schemes have been started in some local authorities and a government Green Paper from the Department of the Environment in 1985 has produced 'some welcome assistance with home improvement for these households' [p. 224]. Wheeler rightly insists that all this is but a drop in the ocean and that major and urgent policy issues regarding the housing needs of old people and their relation to housing problems generally have not been tackled. Nevertheless, for social workers who properly seek to engage the needs of particular old people, awareness of the possibilities of obtaining advice, support and financial assistance may be critical to helping them stay in their own homes, where most of them want to be.

The importance of warm and safe housing for the physical and emotional well-being of frail elderly people can hardly be overestimated and must be a priority in any strategy for support in the community. This seems obvious; yet younger people may not adequately appreciate the impact of housing on so many dimensions of daily living. Old people stay indoors more; the contraction in living space which often accompanies old age is not necessarily welcome. Arguably, it is important to preserve space as opportunities for going out grow fewer. Old people usually have fewer roles and activities. Therefore, there are fewer distractions from domestic worry or irritation; dingy decorations, damp patches, dripping taps, all are the more likely to upset when they are confronted for hours in each day and there is little else to think about. The cost of even minor repairs is a shock to many elderly people especially to women whose partner was a 'handyman'. There are also acute feelings of powerlessness; the difficulty of getting someone to attend to small repairs may create a kind of angry dependence. 'My husband would have done it in five minutes.' Conversely, when these matters are attended to there is a real sense of relief and an obvious improvement in morale.

The issue of housing, therefore, illustrates the interaction of the financial and material factors with social and emotional ones. Sensitivity to those interactions is at the heart of good social work practice; effecting improvement in daily living conditions, even in relatively trivial matters, may be profoundly significant for the person concerned. Given that so many old clients live at or below the poverty level, to acquire the resources needed for some forms of home improvement and comfort is often difficult. It is part of the social work task to mobilise these resources.

As this chapter is being written, the Housing Bill has just been published. Described as 'the biggest housing shake up for 30 years' [*The Guardian*, 1987b], its ramifications and complexities are very great and its implications for old people as yet unexplored. However, the *The Guardian* suggested that the proposed changes to rules for housing associations which would give them a 'crucial role in the provision of social housing', may 'turn associations into providers of housing for the middle classes'. Housing associations will have to raise more cash through the private sector and rents will increase, while housing benefit changes which come into force in the spring have altered in various significant ways the eligibility of old people.

Housing associations have been an important and growing element of provision for elderly people. It remains to be seen, and no doubt pressure groups will play an important part in this, how far the provisions of the Act will safeguard the position of elderly people in this area.

The Observer [1987b], notes another potential problem. It suggests that 'thousands of people who care for such relatives will face eviction from their privately rented accommodation when their relatives die' because 'the Bill takes away the automatic right of succession for tenants in the private sector, which has been the law since 1915'. The proposed assured tenancies, will not, it is suggested, keep rents at a level which the successor will be able to afford. If this is the case, it will clearly affect many elderly people, such as sons or daughters in their 60s and 70s who have looked after parents.

It seems unlikely that the present government would press through changes which will bear very harshly on the old. The political cost would be too high. However, the potential for unforseen hardships is clearly considerable. Furthermore, in the next few years many old people on the margins of poverty will be anxious and frightened about their housing tenure, bewildered by conflicting rumours and reports, unless the government decides upon general exemptions to the provisions for certain categories. Social workers will need to keep abreast of the position.

Cash and care

The present situation, in which millions of old people live in or at the margins of poverty, is shameful. To improve their financial position should be a political priority. The costs of such improvements are, however, very great and it is unrealistic to expect governments, of whatever colour, to raise substantially for the forseeable future the standard of living for those elderly citizens who are dependent on state provision. Desirable as such improvements may be, it would be simplistic to assume that higher income alone would be sufficient to solve daily living for older people. Consumers of services such as chiropody or physiotherapy, for example, depend on there being a sufficient supply of qualified personnel in the area in which they live. This in turn depends on some coherent national strategy for the recruitment of paramedical staff. There are many examples of services which old people need which are not necessarily available even when there is money to buy them. Furthermore, some of the very frail who need them most may not always know what they need or how to get it – hence the attractions of the Kent scheme.

We still await the Green Paper on the personal social services, but it is likely to recommend greater use of the private sector in the provision of services. Indeed it is not impossible that some system of 'vouchers for service' might be introduced, by which old people on benefits could, for example, purchase domestic help. Midwinter [1986] has recently undertaken the first survey of domestic agencies in Britain. This is an expanding field in which those who need various forms of assistance pay agencies to provide them. Social workers and domiciliary care organisers will need to think out their position on this carefully. If old people can control the transaction and pay for it directly, is this not desirable? Midwinter suggests that a number of these agencies are more flexible in what they can offer than are social service departments. Is there anything more objectionable in this than in the large numbers of private arrangements made for domestic service which we take for granted. A great many old people with occupational and private pensions at present buy what they need. Why not extend that facility to those whose income will need supplementing?

Such questions challenge us all and must be addressed. In particular, social workers need to bear in mind the needs and problems of a client population which is not typical of old people in general, but includes a higher proportion of the isolated, those without kith or kin, the physically very frail and, most important of all, the mentally frail. If cash in hand brings more autonomy and more choice to an old person it must be welcome. If, however, the person concerned is unable to make informed choices [for whatever reasons, and they are various] or if he or she is unable to exercise personal control over the quality of the service received, the possibility of exploitation for commercial gain is obvious. Furthermore, the capacity or motivation of the private market to cope effectively with the more 'awkward customer' [for example, elderly people with mental illness], is as yet unproven.

The Kent experiment

It is for this reason, among others, that what is described as 'the Kent experiment' has such attractions [Challis and Davies, 1986]. The scheme was in essence very simple. Social workers were authorised to spend up to three quarters of the cost of a place in residential care for the purpose of supporting frail old people in the community. This money could be spent in any way thought necessary and could include specific items as well as payment for services given by specially recruited helpers. The implications of such schemes are extensive and not the focus of this chapter. For our purpose here, however, it draws attention to a critical element in any consideration of frail elderly people – the interface between cash and care.

We cannot here explore the ramifications of welfare pluralism and market forces in the area of the personal social services. Social workers, however, are in a unique position to identify and to assert the principles which should underly the arrangements which society makes to support old people in the community. They can distinguish between real and hypothetical choice, between persons who can exercise it and those who cannot. They can prick the bubble of rhetoric in which so much of this debate is contained and ask themselves and others, for example, 'how much would Mrs Jones or Mr Brown benefit from an arrangement in which they had cash vouchers for care? Above all, social workers should be examining the relationship of income maintenance to service provision and the impact of poverty on the physical, social and emotional aspects of their clients' well-being.

16

Poverty and Social Work Education

Roy Bailey

Recession, unemployment, poverty, urban decay, vandalism, alienation and inadequacy are everywhere evident in the advanced industrial countries. The role of welfare agencies in ameliorating the less pleasant symptoms of western society is widely recognised as crucial to its preservation. Social workers, the front line agents of the welfare state, may well find that paradoxically the justification of their profession lies in the maintenance of a social and economic system that is the case of the ills they are employed to confront [Bailey and Brake, 1975].

T HUS read the cover of *Radical Social Work*, published in 1975! That such a statement found a responsive audience then might appear now, in the late 1980s, to be incredulous. If a series of essays with such an outline, written at a time we have since come to see as the 'tail-end' of the period of consensus politics, could receive the welcome it did, what would we need to write today to catch the imagination of a reader?

The book contained eight original essays concerned to challenge the accepted stance of most, if not all, social work courses. A primary objective was to establish, as a legitimate part of social work education and training, consideration of both the structural and political issues that we argued, were essential elements in understanding the crises and difficulties facing social work 'clients'. We sought to legitimise cultural diversity as a context for social work theory and practice, rather than work on assumptions about normality. We argued the case to explore the development of social policy in terms of class struggle and interests:

> Radical work . . . is essentially understanding the position of the oppressed in the context of the social and economic structure they live in . . . Our aim is not, for example, to eliminate casework, but to eliminate casework that supports ruling-class hegemony [Bailey and Brake, 1975, 9].

In short, we sought to change the model of social work practice that professionals adopted in their daily work.

The book attracted a great deal of interest. It was subsequently published in the United States and translated and published in both Sweden and Norway. As one social work colleague put it, when introducing me to an audience of social work students and tutors, I was one of those ' . . . who had made radical social work respectable'[?]. A double-edged observation I remember commenting at the time! The volume did not invent radical social work, there were plenty of social workers who were seeking methods of intervention and practice that recognised the political nature of their profession. It was not long before other books emerged developing further this debate. As we observed in a subsequent reader, [Brake and Bailey, 1980] social work educators, professional and academic, were soon to have a substantial library of publications that could be identified within the broad category of Radical Social Work! During the 1970's this 'library' began appearing on most CQSW course bibliographies and there occasionally appeared a section of proposed syllabus headed: Radical Social Work. I recall doubting the appropriateness of such a section.

It may well be that the issues discussed in the extensive literature of radical social work are now part of most social work courses. To what extent does this literature affect practice? Have social work courses accommodated the perspective and perhaps neutralised it? The concerns pressing upon social workers tend to push consideration of policy and structure to the periphery of practice. The titles are included in the course bibliography, students no doubt write essays on the topics, but when it comes to practice in the agencies, either as students on placement or as employed workers, dealing with the ever present crisis of managing their time [a scarce resource], such considerations are often elevated to the realm of luxury. Pragmatism demands social workers deal with pressing issues and such pragmatism is presumed to render this wider perspective interesting but not immediate.

It would be arrogant of social work educators concerned with such a perspective, to accuse professional workers of ignoring their efforts. Those of us interested in such issues must be sure we have provided the basis to translate this perspective into effective practice. Unless there is available a 'taken-for-granted' response to client problems, radical social work will remain an interesting topic dealt with in social work education but with little direct impact on practice! I am not aware of any survey of this issue, but from extensive visiting of social work departments around the UK in Polytechnics, Colleges and Universities over the past ten or more years and talking with professional and academic tutors and with students, my impression is that the perspective we and others have sought to encourage, the conceptual frame of reference espoused, has indeed, become widely accepted and developed within professional courses. Invitations to talk with colleagues in other countries support my impression. I suspect that part of our diffficulty is that we claim too much for such an approach. There is a danger of the 'more radical than thou' accusation. The goal posts keep shifting. As education and training programmes accommodate the perspective, it is always possible to put the question: 'what's so radical about that?' Since our claim is not that social work can effect major social and political change, we are humbled and silenced by the rhetorical question. However, to the extent that the consideration of social problems and individual experience has been identified within a perspective that draws upon a variety of critical theoretical frameworks, then the [possibly too] limited objectives of the radical stance have been established. It is arguable at least, that such a teaching approach has affected the attitudes of many social workers. One important achievement I suggest, has been to make the consideration of the issues this literature espoused a legitimate part of most [if not all] social work courses. Since all social work practice is concerned with *purpose*, the way a professional worker perceives the problems of 'clients'; the recognition of inequality of opportunities; the lack of significant control over circumstances and the identification of such structures as being to some extent independent of particular 'clients', will affect practice. While social work methods may not dramatically alter, the objectives the social worker and the 'client' may seek to obtain will be significantly different from those borne of a perspective which comprehends a 'case' in terms of individual pathology or inability to deal with day-to-day stresses [see Becker this volume].

To claim that economic and social policy, the prevailing political ideology and a particular location within the social structure, conceptualised in class terms have a direct bearing upon day-to-day living, would hardly be contentious today. The experience of us all over recent years, whether as social workers, academics, professional tutors, practice teachers or students has made it almost inconceivable that a view that blames insecurity, unemployment and/or poverty on the insecure, the unemployed and/or the poor, could go unchallenged, at least within our own constituencies. Those of us in employment, wherever we are, may not be poor, but who among us can say we are not constantly looking over our shoulders, anxious about the latest discussions by management within our respective institutions that are to do with priorities and hence have implications for resources, staffing plans, academic development and organisational changes . . . 'Is my job secure?' Insecurity stalks us all! Within higher education, for example, are we not all aware of the 'need' to seek yet more funding for research? The ability to obtain income increasingly appears as the only criterion being used to assess our worth! Effective teaching of our courses, demand from students, publishing in appropriate journals and for the academic publishing houses, academic and professional achievement and student success in gaining employment, appear less and less relevant! The world about us has changed. What was once deemed appropriate is now less so!

The issues are no longer the legitimacy of the perspective, they are how do we incorporate it into our courses and hence into practice? Which aspect of our work, whether as educators or practitioners, enables us to develop the wider concerns that may then inform and influence our practice in immediate and utilisable ways?

British society has been and continues, manifesting profound changes in its social, economic and political organisation. We are witnessing a demographic shift, with a growing number of people living longer beyond the age of retirement, [and I mean beyond 60 and 65 years of age!]. There is a shift in attitudes, with wider communities [including women and ethnic groups] demanding greater opportunities for higher education and employment. Economically, we are having to adjust to the cumulative effects of increased international competition and the dramatic decline of once staple industries, Increasingly, people must be able to deal with periodic changes in their work, with the possibilities of several moves in a lifetime, a shorter working week and periods spent outside employment, either in retaining and updating or regrettably [and increasingly] in unemployment. The upheaval to our social life is considerable and has yet to be fully appreciated, researched and accommodated. The rediscovery of poverty as a widespread social condition is, arguably, one aspect of these changes. Whereas twenty years ago, Herbert Marcuse might have been able to convince many of us that society was 'delivering the goods', there can be few who remain convinced. It is increasingly evident that contemporary society in Britain is not 'delivering the goods' to an ever increasing number of people. The extent of the deprivation may not be fully recognised or acknowledged but poverty and deprivation are back on our agenda without a doubt! In recent months a number of reports have appeared indicating the growing divide between the rich and poor and the consequences for example, for health standards. In March 1987 the report *The Health Divide*, commissioned by the Health Education Council, was published [Whitehead, 1987]. Given the considerable difficulty of obtaining a copy of this report, perhaps 'escaped' is a better description of the event! The report revealed the marked differences in terms of health, between rich and poor in Britain. It is a difference, it argued, that is getting wider. The poor are now affected by the major killer diseases to a much greater extent than the rich. As one commentator put it:

Working class people are found to be shorter, more liable to obesity, more prone to disease, with higher blood pressure, lower survival rates for cancer and coronary heart disease, and worse teeth. The so-called 'diseases of affluence' have all but disappeared [*The Observer*, 1987a].

This present volume of essays indeed, is an example of the growing awareness and seriousness of poverty and its implications for personal social services.

Peter Townsend and others have for a number of years, been arguing that poverty never really left the agenda for a significant proportion of the population. The formulation of a theory of poverty as involving more than subsistence; more than what is 'needed' privately and provided for within the community; as making sense only in terms of people's social activities, in terms of what is culturally and socially expected of them generally, in particular societies at particular times, has revealed the problem of poverty as being far more wide-reaching than might otherwise be thought [Townsend, 1983]. Poverty has indeed been rediscovered! Grudgingly and slowly maybe in the late 1960s and 1970s, but with less resistance in the 1980s. To conceptualise poverty in terms of 'relative deprivation' is to locate it, necessarily, within a wider cultural and socio-economic structure. To fail to do so would render the concept meaningless. This is not the place to explore the concept. The point is that such an approach to problems of poverty provides a legitimate way to locate individual experience in the wider society, and hence a way to explore the implications for social work practice.

If social work education and social work practice have moved away from the over concentration on the social pathology model of 'client' behaviour, the persistent dilemma for all practice-oriented social work studies and the contributory social science disciplines, is how to connect structure to individual behaviour? A telling observation that is often made when arguing that increased deprivation, poverty and unemployment are responsible for the increase in many of our universally agreed social problems is: why is it that not everyone who is deprived, poor and unemployed commit the offences we identify, and/or become social work clients? In statistical terms the rise in crime, in various forms of delinquency, in disorder, in domestic violence and more, is an increase that cannot be denied. Social workers and probation officers, however, do not deal with 'statistical phenomena' they deal with individuals, families and groups. Until we can provide an explanation that enables social workers and others to act with the individual client who has either been referred or who has sought help, we will not avoid the charge laid by Stan Cohen in 1975: *It's alright for you to talk* [Cohen, 1975]. There are many social workers who would willingly practise in this way if only they had the 'equipment' to do so. It is to the theorists, the educators, the academics and the researchers that they turn for such 'equipment'. As I suggested earlier, in many ways the approach we advocated in the 1970s has been adopted by courses and no doubt influences practice. We should avoid claiming too much, but we should be claiming something. Within our professional courses we should explore and demonstrate the context for the many problems facing us all and how these can affect daily lives in ways that turn people into 'clients'. We must explore in some detail, the implications and consequences of material poverty for individuals and their families and communities.

Family networks are more fragile than perhaps we realise. An aging and dependent parent can create demands that can make family life intolerable. This in turn can lead to feelings of guilt and inadequacy by everyone involved. A partner 'hanging around the house' can place strains where none might have been expected. Frustration, boredom and apparent impotence to change anything, can play havoc with previously strong and secure relationships. I have elsewhere discussed the networks and conditions that contribute to a family's ability to 'manage intolerable dilemmas' [Bailey, 1973]. All families and individuals have to contend with, to manage, stress and strain. Such circumstances, I suggest are 'normal'. The problems we need to examine, the questions I raised in an earlier essay and which I believe, are relevant here, are:

[a] under what conditions do actors fail to cope or deal with 'normal' antagonisms, contradictions and conflicts of everyday family life, and: [b] what are the conditions that are enjoyed by others that do enable them to cope and deal with the same contradictions, etc? [Bailey, 1973, 74].

We need research into such questions to help social workers in their dealings with families. If we can provide some insight we will begin to understand the question why it is that not all people who experience considerable difficulties become either law breakers or social work 'clients'.

There are clearly many ways, developed at some length in this volume, in which poverty can effect and damage social relations for example, between parents, between parents and children, with the elderly and with those who suffer physical and mental disability.

The issue of poverty and its implications for many aspects of daily life, offers an important perspective in this respect. This is not to provide a justification for all behaviour. This approach does not 'make allowances' for domestic violence, for drunkeness, for racism, for sexism or whatever. This approach does not remove personal responsibility. We should not seek to deny responsibility for our actions. We do indeed make choices, but we do not choose the circumstances under which such choices are made or even which choices are realistically available to us. To reveal ways in which poverty can 'poison' family relations and parental care, is not to justify or 'forgive' abuse of children. I do believe, however, that as we comprehend the circumstances and difficulties of individuals and families, located within an increasingly hostile environment, we will approach both understanding and practice in different ways. A major objective for social workers, I suggest, should be to assist their 'clients' in retaining or regaining their self respect and integrity. To people who find themselves unemployed through no fault of their own and who as a consequence, lose the very conditions which provide them with their self respect, social workers should be experienced as supportive. 'There but for fortune . . .' is increasingly an appropriate sentiment. Professional tutors and those academic social scientists who collaborate in devising education and training programmes, have the theories and ease of access to the research. Professional social workers 'in the field' have day to day experience of the problems of practice. It is essential that more collaborative work from both sectors is undertaken, not solely to provide knowledge of the world in which social workers intervene, but on how to translate such knowledge into practical activities for daily use. The implications of poverty and deprivation for social work 'clients' must be explored and researched if our courses are properly to prepare students for practice. Collaborative research should increasingly be seeking not just to understand the social and individual conditions of 'clients', but also to assist the 'client' to change them! The research must be concerned with practice. To encourage joint research between the academic and the practice communities will serve this purpose.

If this present volume does nothing else, it should lay once and for all any .lingering view that the issue of poverty in our education and training programmes is mainly an issue of welfare rights, important though these are. The complexity of poverty as a social phenomenon, its distribution, its consequences and the overwhelming evidence that an increasing number of clients are facing difficulties related, sometimes directly, sometimes less obviously, to material deprivation and poverty, demands that our training courses explore the category far more extensively than perhaps we have previously. People who find themselves redundant and unemployed, at an age and in a place where new work is scarce, will experience immense difficulties in handling the conditions into which they have been plunged. The future changes from reasonable optimism to uncertainty and bewilderment. Suddenly, to find oneself unemployed and with few prospects, yet with responsibilities remaining, is possibly to face despair. To be confronted with a dramatic decline in income is to experience insecurity and poverty, whether or not the income received 'on the dole' is sufficient to provide bare subsistence for a family. A life-style does not simply dissolve without consequence.

As far as welfare rights are concerned, our students will need detailed knowledge concerning the rules and regulations governing welfare payments, or at least to know where to get the information. They will need advocacy skills to represent their clients in what is an increasingly hostile world for claimants. To assist people to claim what social security regulations identify as their 'right', is to run the risk of being publicly attacked as irresponsible by government agencies. Inability to live on limited welfare payments is too often presented as a problem of bad management of resources, rather than inadequacy of resources. In spite of such attacks our courses must not shy away from the issues. Responsible advocacy must remain part of a social worker's practice and a professional worker must retain the right to exercise that responsibility.

An increasingly important aspect of practice that workers will need is access to information. No general framework will suffice without the empirical detail to hand. As Geoff Fimister has argued [1987a], we must develop facilities available with new technology. Computer comprehension and/or skills do not figure very prominently in either our initial or post qualifying courses. Speed of access to information will greatly facilitate, among other things, the advisory role of social workers, a role that will become more important. Whether social services departments or voluntary agencies offer this service is immaterial for current purposes; professional workers must be able to exploit the technology for the benefit of the client and the service. As such technology becomes more widespread within social services, as I believe it will, our professional education and training programmes must provide social workers themselves with the ability to comprehend the systems. They must be able to retrieve and to update information. Failure to do so will leave the professional social worker in the hands of computer professionals, and with respect to the latter, I'd rather the social workers understood the technology.

'Social work and race'; 'social work and gender'; 'social work and disability'; 'social work and mental health'; '. . . . and class', these and others, are common enough categories within syllabuses. Poverty seems all-embracing and should inform all aspects of the programme. I will no doubt be reminded that not all problems and issues with which social workers and others have to deal, are to do with poverty. The middle class, the employed and the materially comfortable, have their problems too. I'm sure that's right [some no doubt have their therapists], but the evidence is that a very high proportion of social work clients are also claimants [Becker and MacPherson, 1986].

Even with the materially comfortable there are some concerns that relate to poverty. The poor emerge in what may seem the most unlikely of places. For example, if we measure family income as an index of familial poverty or well-being, we may well miss the important factor of distribution within the family. How many women and mothers, experience considerable financial difficulties as a result of the husband's control of the income? Changes in the tax system, the withdrawal of child dependancy allowance and the increase in child benefit to put money directly into the hands of the mother, was some recognition of a problem of income distribution within families. Recently published research by Julia Brannen and Gail Wilson provides a vivid indication of the extent of 'poverty' in families that in terms of total income might not appear to be problematic [Brannen and Wilson, 1987]. The distribution of income within the economy at large, as well as within the individual 'family economy', are clearly important for our understanding of problems. We often ignore the latter. We too often operate on a high level of generality and miss important processes. We were sceptical of the individual model in understanding personal circumstance and behaviour, we should also be sceptical of an over reliance on the holistic one.

Central Council for Education and Training in Social Work and the new training policy

CCETSW has embarked on an ambitious restructuring of basic education and training [CCETSW, 1987]. The scene is set for a radical reconstruction of the social work qualifying course. In this respect the issues I wish to discuss are: the proposed collaboration between employing agencies and education institutions to provide future courses and the implications for course content, and the development of post-qualifying courses.

The Qualifying Diploma in Social Work [QDSW] will be three years in length and will be developed jointly between education and employing institutions. Whereas within education the people involved in the development of professional programmes are the staff teaching the courses, who will be the staff in the employing agencies to contribute to the planning process? This is, I believe, an important question. The planning and management group for the new qualification must include practitioners. By this I mean practitioners 'in the field', workers who have first hand experience of clients. Chief officers and their deputies or assistants must not dominate the process. The development of a curriculum is I suggest, a political process. Not party political, but a process that is critically affected by the particular participants. Objectives for courses are not somehow 'there' to be achieved. They are argued for by participants in the development process. No amount of CCETSW guidelines can avoid the different emphases of interpretation, nor should they. In order to achieve the development of courses that genuinely reflect the needs of both education and training, the teachers and the social workers are the parties who should be collaborating. A professional course leading to the QDSW should be *practice led*. A professional course that is *employer led* will be a very different course. To achieve the kind of education and training that places theory and practice as a central concern will require the practitioners to work together from both education and the profession. A professional worker's concerns are not the same as a chief officer's concerns, an educator's interests are different again and none of them need be the 'client's' concerns. These issues may never be wholly resolved, but we should recognise that the different interests are legitimately part of the development of a professional qualifying course. Aren't they? Poor clients often need resources; social workers have to manage, among other things, these two realities. Academics draw our attention to the contradictions!

The task facing the development of the new qualifying programmes will be daunting. The evergrowing complexities associated with poverty and clients will make it impossible for an initial course to be adequate to cover all the implications. The chapters of this book alone reveal the extent of the issues associated with poverty that social work education will need to cover. The experiences of social workers themselves will need to be incorporated in the planning and the teaching process. The teachers of courses must listen to the practitioners and the practitioners must not presume there is nothing other than immediate practice to deal with. These constituencies will work together productively only as they learn to respect each other's skills and concerns. Collaborative research is likely to be a way forward in this. My experience is that professional tutors and employed social workers currently undertake less research than do their academic colleagues. There are often good reasons for this. Education institutions have not, on the whole, learned how to acknowledge the work professional tutors have to undertake over and above teaching. Within the workplace of a busy social services department there is often little or no time to undertake research. For education and training courses to improve and genuinely confront theory and practice issues, I suggest 'space' has to be found to encourage and enable social workers themselves and the professional tutors within education, to develop research projects. I recognise that such a demand will need resourcing. So be it, this is an important issue for successful social work education. This applies no less to research concerning practice with 'poor clients' as with any other clients.

In the process of developing the new QDSW there are many discussions taking place, many 'lobbies' emerging, to ensure that future courses deal more substantially than hitherto with such items as race and gender. Policies can be adopted to ensure that ethnic minority communities and women are involved in the teaching and the studying. This alone affects the treatment of such issues. Who will speak for the poor, however? There is no organised lobby of the poor. *To be poor is to be without power.* This present volume is obviously a focus for these issues, but whereas other areas such as race and gender have ethnic groups and women to urge inclusion in programmes, the poor will always be represented by the 'not-so-poor', by social workers, by academics, by the middle class. Those of us who are concerned to raise the issue of poverty and its far-reaching implications must seek a way to give a voice to the poor. We cannot presume to speak wholly on their behalf. Poverty is an issue. The poor are people. Who will listen to them? Social workers, probation officers, with sympathetic educators, should seek to develop collaborative strategies to provide those who suffer poverty with a means to influence the education, the training and the practice of professionals with whom they, as 'clients', have to deal.

One persistent weakness of the existing two year CQSW is, I believe, less to do with the length of time of the course or its generic objectives [serious though these are], than with the lack of serious in-service, post-qualifying development over the past 15 years. The complexity of the concerns of social work, illustrated time and again in this volume, cannot be handled within a single initial course. Indeed, the changing circumstances which both affect poverty as well as what is regarded as poverty, will require constant reworking and updating. The introduction of the CQSW in 1971/2 as a generic course was argued at the time, to represent only an initial qualification . . . 'a beginning level of competence'. There was every intention to develop a post-qualifying structure for social workers and probation officers. This did not materialise to any significant extent. Whereas within the teaching profession, for example, there exists a well-developed and resourced in-service programme for teachers, no such programme emerged for social work. Each Local Education Authority, for example, has an extensive teachers' advisory structure, with specialised staff in constant liaison with the schools and colleges, identifying areas of need and developing in-service courses. The social work advisory system has not developed in anything like the same way. Largely, I suspect, through a lack of resources but also because the service is aimed primarily at education and not as well at the employing and delivering institutions. It is less easy, if not impossible, for social work advisers to explore with employing agencies the continuing professional development needed. The agencies 'do it themselves', and I suggest, they don't do it very effectively!

The weakness of the generic CQSW is in large part the result of it too often being the first and the last education and training programme a social worker attends. I suggest the three year QDSW will suffer a similar fate if we fail to develop a substantial post-qualifying, in-service programme of studies. It is not so much the length of time, or the objective of an initial qualification that will prove the critical issue contributing to success or failure, it is when that initial qualification becomes the only qualification. Social work education must not now recommit the 'error' of presuming that because we are about to have a three year programme, we have resolved the problem of continuing professional training. Experience in the field, in the workplace, is a necessary but not sufficient basis for professional development.

It is often the case that employers express serious reservations about the adequacy of training provided for social work and probation. Employers who fail to provide the time and the resources that professional development requires, will continue to criticise the education and training programme. If they are serious about improved training and continuing staff development, they must add their voice to those expressing the need to develop a sophisticated in-service structure to support the work of the staff in their departments.

It will not be enough for CCETSW to encourage the development of post-qualifying courses by exhortation, the Council should create a new post-qualifying diploma. Employers and professional unions should explore the possibility of recognising, within the salary structure, those who achieve the award.

This is not the place to propose particular post-qualifying programmes. This Reader alone provides a range of possible in-service initiatives. Such courses will need to be worked out with educators and professional practitioners. In recent months there have appeared a number of reports and surveys that highlight among other things, the effects of poverty: *Faith in the City*; *Excluding the Poor*; *Health and Lifestyle Survey*; *Poverty and Labour in London*; *The Health Divide*. All these and more, have considerable implications for the problems with which social workers and other such workers will have to contend.

No initial qualification course can possibly incorporate the detail or the implications of issues, let alone the other essential aspects of professional practice. Post-qualifying programmes will become ever more critical. Additionally, we must encourage collaboration between practitioners and teachers, to ensure that research includes the concerns and difficulties that social workers, practising in pressing and often frustrating circumstances, are having to manage. Our course construction at all levels, must evolve from the participation of teachers and practitioners, including listening to 'clients'.

This chapter has necessarily discussed education and training for social work beyond the question of poverty. The need to explore in our professional courses the consequences of the 'growth' of poverty in one of the wealthiest countries of the world and of its impact on all aspects of economic, social and political life, the need to develop collaborative research to improve both theory and practice, together with the need to reconstruct social work education, offers us the opportunity to ensure that both future professional social workers and existing ones, have available a range of initial and in-service educational and training opportunities, more suited to the conditions in which they are practising.

17

Race and Poverty
Gary Vaux and David Divine

T HE most notable point when researching this chapter is the paucity of information that is available. This may reflect the approach to race and poverty of both the benefit provider [national and local government in the main] and the poverty lobby.

Until recently, most research was 'colour-blind' except on a very local level in a few instances. Even now, much of the data is patchy and incomplete, as it predominantly has been provided by small-scale independent or local survey methods.

There is no or little attention being paid to the issues of race and poverty by the main agencies of the state who are in a position both to collect the data and then to implement change.

As the Greater London Council [1983] pointed out:

The Family Expenditure Survey collects no data on the colour, country of orgin or ethnic group of respondents, and, although such data are collected by the General Household Survey, the sample sizes are too small to permit any useful analysis. There is unfortunately no other source which provides data on the household incomes of ethnic minorities.

In their evidence to the Royal Commission on the Distribution of Income and Wealth, the late Community Relations Commission suggested that because of the higher proportion of large families and one-parent families among the ethnic minorities they had a greater than average likelihood of having an income that was low in relation to their needs. However it is difficult to generalize as there is no conclusive statistical evidence that ethnic minority groups as a whole have a disproportionately high incidence of low income [*Low Incomes in London*, GLC, 1983].

Given this background, how can social services departments address this issue in their work?

Firstly, there will have to be acknowledgement of the extent of the problem facing Britain's black communities. This will only come about if the extent of financial poverty can be detailed and, in turn, linked to the poverty that arises from denial of access to other public services such as housing, health care, transport, personal social services etc. Financial poverty represents only one portion of that deprivation.

Secondly, there will then need to be strategies for addressing that deprivation both on a micro and macro level. If, as a social services department, we aim to make all our services accessible to all parts of the community, and to make those services relevant, then combating financial poverty must form part of that strategy. Some of that battle can be fought locally – access to information, advice and resources – so that the black community can achieve its own targets of economic independence. Other issues have to be considered outside a strictly local sphere – national employment trends and policy for example.

Finally, the extent of the problem and our responses to it must be continually monitored to ensure that changes in social conditions, legislation or department policy do not have adverse effects [or such effects can at least be acknowledged].

So what is the extent of the problem of poverty facing black people? What are its causes and what are the effects? The most obvious answer is in the relationship between employment and poverty. In a society where benefits are pitched at a bare subsistence level, the main way of avoiding poverty is by obtaining full-time adequately waged employment. A second way is by the inheritance of wealth.

Generally, black people in the UK have been denied access to either of those routes. In particular, in employment the discrimination against black people is reasonably well-documented. It is worth showing however that the pattern is being repeated into the next generation.

Evidence from the MSC's *YTS Leavers Survey* [April 85 – January 86] showed a reduced chance of finding a job after YTS for young black people. In addition, they are less likely to get a place on employer-led YTS schemes that offer a better chance of finding a job. Recently announced plans to make YTS compulsory on the threat of benefit withdrawal, will not improve the benefit or employment position of black youth.

The much-heralded British economic recovery has largely been achieved by an expansion of part-time working patterns. It is rare for part-time work to generate enough income to lift people out of poverty yet black people are again over-represented in this area.

Table 17.1
Proportion of workers who are part-time by age and sex

Age	16-19				20-24				25+			
	Men		Women		Men		Women		Men		Women	
	Black	White	Black	White	Black	White	Black	White	Black	White	Black	White
	%	%	%	%	%	%	%	%	%	%	%	%
1979	5.1	3.9	10.0	8.2	3.3	0.7	11.16	10.0	0.8	2.2	27.9	51.2
1981	11.9	12.5	13.2	20.0	3.7	1.2	12.8	10.2	2.1	2.8	25.5	51.9
1983	15.8	13.1	26.2	24.2	3.8	1.8	15.5	10.2	3.0	2.4	26.5	51.1
1985	22.6	19.3	35.3	30.1	10.7	2.6	17.5	13.7	4.0	2.5	30.6	53.1

Source: *Youthaid Information Papers*, 1986, mimeo.

Even when in full-time work, average earnings show major inequalities. In 1982 the average weekly earnings of white men were £129, compared to £109.20 for Afro-Caribbeans and £88 for Bangladeshi men [Walker and Walker, 1987].

Future employment prospects look no brighter. Abolition of wages councils and the privatisation of public services will all lead to a reduction in wage costs in those areas of employment where black people have been employed – transport, hospital services, catering and other public services.

The above employment points are emphasised to show that financial poverty amongst black people is not a consequence solely of the benefit system. [In many ways, such as access to occupational pensions, redundancy pay, etc., income out of work is often determined by income in work]. As such it is outside the direct control of social services departments. However, local authorities have begun to look at inter-departmental anti-poverty strategies and the stimulation of local economies. Social services departments should not be marginalised in those activities.

Provision of child care facilities to enable full-time employment opportunities, direct creation of jobs at adequate salary levels, domiciliary services for dependent adults, training and development packages etc., can all play a part, at least locally, in redressing some aspects of the poverty facing black people.

The extent of poverty can be measured fairly accurately. In London for example the 1981 census was used as a basis for a measurement of the index of deprivation. On a local government ward-by-ward basis, the indicators of deprivation included unemployment rates, numbers of single parents, single pensioner households and households headed by a person born in the New Commonwealth or Pakistan. This showed tremendous disparities between and within local authorities, as could be expected. Evidence suggests that such disparities have increased rather than decreased since 1981 [Walker and Walker, 1987].

Of interest to our own local authority, Brent, was that of London's 40 most deprived wards, six fell within Brent, including three out of the worst eight. However, these figures do not allow us to specifically consider the details of the deprivation.

This leads to a consideration of the role of state cash benefits. There is a school of thought within the black community, partly inherited from an American model, that 'welfarism' saps the strength and initiative of black people, individually and collectively:

> One must recognise that discrimination is an act designed to separate individuals or people for the purpose of allowing one group to receive preferential treatment and/or advantage: and second, that in a system characterised by racism and oppression, almost every element or process managed by the racist system is designed primarily to continue and secure the status of the 'advantaged' by guaranteeing in all arenas their preferential treatment [Nobles, 1981, 79].

In essence this means that the benefit system in terms of its structure and operation promotes the disservicing of black people. One of the major obstacles facing conscious black staff is that of convincing the consumer that he/she can gain control over his/her life when one knows how subject black people are to manipulation by an oppressive system apparently unaccountable to the group. The role of 'victim' is counterproductive in that it subverts the desire to 'get over' as Barbara Solomon would put it, [Professor of Social Work at the University of Southern California], and is self-reinforcing. The hallmark of the victim is hopelessness, helplessness and being expendable. The black professional has a key role in demonstrating that one can intervene in the system and manipulate it to the consumer's advantage. With advice and guidance the consumer can learn how to do it on his/her own, thereby reinforcing the fact that there are other roles which can lead to rewards in addition to that of 'victim'. Reliance on state benefits is therefore seen as a passive acceptance of inferior status and of dependency upon a racist state. This view manifests itself in practice in the behaviour of many young black people, who have been excluded from the job market and who do not wish to rely on state benefits. There has been little research into the extent of such alienation from the benefit system, but the anecdotal evidence is substantial. Such people cease to exist as far as both the employment and unemployment figures are concerned. The whole debate on race and poverty is therefore skewed because the views of key people are effectively discounted.

The welfare rights movement starts from an assumption that to claim all benefits, and to defend the rights of claimants, is a justifiable cause. The black community is not homogeneous and so such an approach may be largely valid. But we must not forget that encouraging the take-up of benefits will not in itself solve problems, not in the long-term enable the black community to escape from the poverty ghetto.

Having added that proviso, it is posssible to look at the question of benefit take-up. Certainly, if being in receipt of state benefits defines someone as poor, to be living below that level is scandalous. Social services departments may therefore have a role to play in encouraging benefit take-up. Elsewhere in this volume [Hannam; Fimister] there is discussion of the relationships between social work practice and welfare rights – the integrative vs. specialist approach. There is a case to be made for either but such a debate should not take place without consideration of the needs of the black population.

If the overall aim is to increase the take-up of benefits, we need to consider if and why black people do not claim. Again, research is poor. However, some useful evidence is provided by benefit take-up campaigns which, at the least, establish that non-claiming exists, even if it is hard to compare the extent against the population as a whole. Mary Rose Tarpey [1984, 3] states:

> it is not an easy process to claim full entitlement and negotiate the complicated DHSS system . . . limited literacy and limited use of English language serves to aggravate the process even more and results in a considerably lower take-up compared to other groups of claimants. For example, in our contact with the Bengali community it was apparent that people were not claiming child benefit in contrast to English speaking claimants where take-up of this benefit is high.

The author then goes on to look at factors other than language/literacy, which is a welcome change from what had been a traditional welfare rights approach – that the key reason for non-claiming is linked mainly to knowledge. Certainly benefit take-up campaigns which have been based solely on the idea that all you had to do was translate benefit leaflets, circulate the translations and wait for the claims, by and large failed. Knowledge is important of course, but not in isolation.

A more sophisticated model for explaining non-take up of benefits by black people is needed before we can begin to suggest how social services can help readdress the issue. The work of Kerr [1983] is useful here. Kerr's model of claiming behaviour attempts to link attitudes and behaviour to explain differential take-up. Kerr suggests that there are six dimensions in which people make decisions that determine whether or not they apply for a particular benefit:

Kerr's model for claiming behaviour:

basic knowledge	is the individual's awareness that the benefit exists
self-perceived need	is the individual's perception of the extent to which he/she is having difficulty paying for his/her requirements
perceived eligibility	is the individual's perception of the likelihood that he/she is eligible for that benefit.
perceived utility	is the individual's perception of the usefulness of the benefit in meeting his/her needs.
beliefs	is the sum total of all the positive and negative forces exerted by the individual's beliefs about the consequences of applying, and his/her feelings about such beliefs.
perceived stability of the situation	is the extent to which the individual believes that the situation is unlikely to change.

The suggestion is that a threshold has to be reached on all six dimensions for a claim to go ahead. Each on its own is not sufficient to initiate a claim, but a low threshold on any one dimension is sufficent to block the claiming process. Such blocks are the barriers to claiming – lack of knowledge, the ability to manage on present income, uncertainty about eligibility, a low estimate of the value of the benefit, any strong negative feeling about the consquences of applying, or the expectation that things are going to change.

This could well be a generally accepted model, even though it makes no specific reference to the experience of black people. Their experiences however can be intensified and illuminated using this model.

'Basic knowledge' is a prerequisite to claiming and the DHSS's own attempts to promote benefits amongst ethnic minorites show how little emphasis they place upon it. In the main, it has been local authorities who have attempted to publicise benefits.

'Perceived eligibility' is crucial to the black community. As Tarpey says:

> They [the Bengali community] were confused by the available information and wary of approaching local authority and DHSS services for advice. Fears were expressed of the consequences of claiming anything that might bring attention to them and cause trouble . . . there was fear that their right to stay could be affected by claiming [Tarpey, 1984].

This clearly links to the dimension of 'beliefs'. This is where Kerr's model may need amplification as it concentrates on the positive and negative forces exerted on the individual.

By and large, there is a common myth of the lazy black scrounger with x children living off the state. This racist stereotype is reinforced by all sections of the media, and the weight of it vastly counters the occasional pro-claimant exercises, few of which are effectively addressed to black claimants anyway. In addition, the treatment of black claimants by some staff at DHSS and Housing Benefits Offices, who over-zealously implement a system that is itself racist, will also deter claims.

Racism can be found in the benefit systems assumptions about family living arrangements, dietary and clothing needs, passport checks, funeral costs etc. For example, it was not until May 1987 that the DHSS accepted that sickle cell disease, which predominately affects black people, was a 'serious illness' for the purposes of getting extra benefit for heating, even though the medical knowledge about sickle cell crisis being caused by cold has been known for many years. It is ironic that from April 1988, all weekly extras for heating will be abolished, including those paid for sickle cell sufferers. Replacement 'premiums' have been defined in such a way that many people with sickle cell, especially children, will not get any compensatory help. Many black claimants are therefore back to square one. [For an analysis of how racism operates in the social security system see Gordon and Newnham, 1985.]

Bearing in mind the above, it is not suprising that black people don't claim – it is almost as surprising that some do! When these pressures are allied to internalised, possibly culturally derived, individual beliefs, one can see why Kerr's 'thresholds' are not reached. All claimants face discrimination by the DHSS – black claimants face what Leicester CPAG refers to, in their leaflet of the same name, as 'double discrimination' [Leicester CPAG, 1984].

So what can social services departments do?

Brent Social Services covers a population of a quarter of a million people in the London Borough of Brent, which is the most multi-racial geographical area in the country. During 1987 the social services department had been subject to a major review; an important report concerning the total restructuring of the department, in order to facilitate the development of more relevant and accessible services to the consumer, was presented to the Social Services Committee in December 1987. We believe that this restructuring which involves a radically different way of perceiving and of meeting need, is a prerequisite for effective service delivery. In this outer London borough which has inner-city characteristics of multiple deprivation [Table 17.2 and 17.3] any proposed service delivery which aims to be relevant must take note of the socio-economic and cultural context of Brent. Obviously some of the solutions are out of its control but in considering the provision of welfare rights advice, there are some quite clear policy decisions that can be taken.

Table 17.2
Deprivation and social need

Measures of urban deprivation can be obtained from the 1981 Census. Table 5 shows Brent's position relative to other English local authorities.

		%	Rank position
1	Ethnic origin	33.5	1
2	Overcrowding	8.7	3
3	One parent family	7.8	10
4	Lacking basic amenities	8.1	17
5	Population change	-9.8	19
6	Unemployment	10.1	95
7	Pensioners living alone	12.5	235
8	Mortality rate[2]	0.86	317

Notes 1 Rank position out of 365 English local authorities.
2 Mortality rate is only variable not from 1981 Census.

Source: *Census Information Note No 2 – Urban Deprivation*, Inner Cities Directorate, Department of the Environment.

Table 17.3

	Basic index	Housing index	Social index	Economic index
1	LB Hackney	LB Hackney	LB Hackney	LB Hackney
2	LB Newham	LB Newham	LB Lambeth	LB T Hamlets
3	LB T Hamlets	LB Lewisham	LB T Hamlets	LB Newham
4	LB Lambeth	LB Hammersmith	LB Newham	LB Lambeth
5	LB Hammersmith	LB T Hamlets	LB Hammersmith	Manchester
6	LB Haringey	LB Haringey	LB Islington	LB Kensington
7	LB Islington	**LB Brent**	LB Southwark	Liverpool
8	**LB Brent**	LB Islington	LB Haringey	LB Hammersmith
9	LB Wandsworth	LB Wandsworth	LB Wandsworth	Wolverhampton'LB
10	LB Southwark	LB Camden	Manchester	Haringey
11	Manchester	LB Southwark	**LB Brent**	LB Southwark
12	LB Camden	LB Lambeth	LB Camden	Knowsley
13	Leicester	Manchester	Leicester	Leicester
14	Wolverhampton	Wolverhampton	LB Lewisham	Corby
15	Liverpool	LB Westminster	Liverpool	**LB Brent**
16	Birmingham	LB W Forest	Nottingham	Birmingham
17	LB Lewisham	LB Lewisham	Birmingham	LB Wandsworth
18	LB Kensington	LB Ealing	Wolverhampton	Sandwell
19	Coventry	Liverpool	Blackburn	Coventry
20	LB W Forest	Birmingham	LB Kensington	Scunthorpe

Source DOE, 1981 census
NB This table only shows the 'worst' 20 of 365 English local authorities.

First welfare rights work must not be seen in isolation, either within the department or authority or within the black community, as the sole means of alleviating the proven economic hardship. The state benefit system is at best a poor safety net. It is essential that those entitled to benefit but not claiming are encouraged to claim. In addition, however, there must be work done on more widespread anti-poverty measures, to create the opportunities for black people to be independent of the benefit system.

The two approaches can work in tandem if the political will is there. It does not require an endorsement of prevailing government economic policy to support the development of the black community. It would in fact demand a directly interventionist approach, rather than a reliance on market forces which have in the past failed black people.

Second, local authorities are in a position to redress the paucity of information on poverty and race. When this information is collected it should be used as the catalyst for a thorough review of all policies and procedures to ensure that this poverty is not being contributed to by the local authority. This could involve, for example, the policy of charging for nursery placements or the level of financial support given to childminding.

In addition, the research and resulting policy considerations will have to be far-ranging and developed in conjunction with the black community. As an example, it may be necessary to ascertain the extent of financial hardship being caused to the black community if the local education system fails to meet the needs of the black population and, as a result, compensatory additional education is being purchased. The local authority would need to consider its educational policy and its voluntary sector funding as a result. If it does not, the black population, with low incomes from wages or benefits already, will be effectively paying twice for the education of its young, with a consequent adverse effect on their overall circumstances.

Third, where a local authority exercises discretionary financial powers, eg the use of Section One payments [Child Care Act 1980], it needs to ensure that such money is used creatively. The encouragement of credit unions and other community responses would seem to be a better response than short-term measures designed solely to plug gaps in DHSS provision. There needs to be an acknowledgement that for many black people, the official organisations of the state, either local or national, are seen as oppressive at worst and irrelevant at best. As a result, financial crises are met by reliance on friends, relatives or neighbours or by recourse to extortionate money lenders rather than using official agencies. If this fact is recognised, we can then, through our policies, begin to strengthen the support from the former and weaken the hold of the latter.

Fourth, local authority social services must be made responsive to the needs of the black population. This can be no better specified than by Tarpey [1984] who argues that:

> there be routine translation of all information and forms of local authority benefits and services; and that they are as freely available as English language leaflets.
>
> That local authorities accept responsibility to provide translators, based in all council departments and area based offices. This duty should not be tagged on to existing posts.
>
> That local authorities employ staff at all levels to represent the ethnic minority communities living in the boroughs.
>
> That funding is made available to independent welfare rights projects serving ethnic minority communities as the present independent advice sector is not equipped to deal with the specific needs of ethnic minorities.

That local authorities employ in their own services specialist ethnic
minority welfare rights workers that could back up the welfare rights
work being done by other local authority workers in the minority
communities. They should have a brief to train workers, provide
back-up resources and co-ordinate policy issues [pp13-14].

The obvious need is to have staff and services which are acceptable to
ethnic minority communities. Whether these staff are to be specialist
welfare rights workers, or generic staff with the ability to integrate welfare
rights into their work, is for local determination. However, all experience
shows that to increase the take-up of benefits among the black community
requires acceptance, patience, tact and a clear understanding of both a racist
benefit system and the reasons why black people don't claim. Benefit
take-up work done in Leicester, Nottingham, Greenwich and elsewhere all
indicate the need for such an approach.

Finally, any information produced on both the extent of poverty and the
methods of combatting it must be used to achieve improvements in the
structure and delivery of benefits. Poverty in the UK is being added to the
political agenda via discussions about the North-South divide and
'inner-city' policy. We must ensure that informed debate takes place that
incorporates the views, experiences and aspirations of black people.

The future of the welfare state is up for discussion now. Changes in the
benefit system in April 1988 will not assist the plight of many black
claimants, as the system moves increasingly onto a discretionary [and
therefore potentially discriminatory] basis. Introduction of a community
charge, which disproportionately affects large households, and changes in
employment rights, tax and wages, may all serve to damage the financial
position of black people.

Local authority responses to this may be little more than a drop in the
ocean, especially as local authorities are left with fewer powers and abilities
to provide. This does not mean, though, that black people's economic
position can be ignored or assumed to be no worse or better than that of the
population as a whole.

Services must be directed into this area, under the control of those very
communities wherever possible and social services management have a part
to play in setting the agenda for change.

In Nottingham, for instance, Parul Desai and Jeet Osaan decided that:
'the most effective work resulted from relying on a word of mouth
approach within the community network' when they surveyed the Asian
population in the city. They concluded:

There is a proven need for additional advice workers to provide
information, advice and assistance for Asian people and that workers

in statutory welfare agencies should be trained in issues affecting the black community [*Welfare Rights Bulletin*, 1986].

Brent social services is intending in 1988 to undertake its own research into poverty in the borough and a review of existing means at the social services department's disposal for potentially alleviating the above, will be carried out in order to realistically assess in the light of increasing central government constraints on local authority expenditure, what role Brent social services can play in this area.

18

Women, Poverty and Social Work

Becky Morley

A S poverty reaches epidemic proportions in Britain, we hear of unemployment's crushing effects on male self-respect, of poor families and their children; but women's poverty is virtually ignored. Women are invisible too in most poverty measurement and research which takes the family as the unit of analysis. Yet poverty is very much a women's issue. Women are more likely to be poor than men.

We know from official measures of income that women living without men are particularly at risk of poverty. Among recipients of supplementary benefit [SB], 75 per cent of pensioners and 95 per cent of heads of one parent families are women [DHSS, 1986b]. An analysis of the 1983 Family Expenditure Survey finds 61 per cent of female compared to 51 per cent of male lone pensioners, and 61 per cent of lone mothers compared to 43 per cent of lone fathers, in or on the margins of poverty [Millar and Glendinning, 1987]. [These percentages represent many more women than men, since women form a much higher proportion of elderly and lone parent populations].

Official measures do not investigate the family unit. But other evidence indicates that family poverty is especially relevant to women. 'One parent families', known to be among the poorest, is a euphemism for *female headed* families: 90 per cent are lone mothers [Haskey, 1986]. In two parent families the wife's earnings may be critical: without them, four times as many families would be in poverty [Land, 1983]. In poor families, women bear a disproportionate burden of sacrifice, deprivation and ill-health to enable their families to survive with as much dignity as possible. Thus the extent of women's poverty may be hidden inside the family. Studies aggregating income of all members implicitly assume resources to be distributed equally. However, not only do women 'voluntarily' sacrifice, but men often maintain control of income, sometimes leaving women and children in poverty when total household income is adequate.

The assumption that women are responsible for family functioning, hence naturally self-sacrificing [Land and Rose, 1986], obscures inequalities of resource control and distribution. However a socially just definition of poverty must include inequality of control of society's resources, and exploitation of the labours of some for the benefit of others. Using this definition, most women are poor in the sense that they have little independent access to resources; and much of the work they do is unvalued, unpaid, exploited. This situation applies to women world-wide. A frequently quoted UN report states that women constitute one third of the world's paid work force and do four fifths of its unpaid work, but receive only ten per cent of the world's income and own less than one per cent of the world's property [Leghorn and Parker, 1981].

Not all women are equally poor. Race and class contribute to the amount and type of work women do; the extent and configuration of their exploitation. But all women share a special vulnerability to poverty structured and rationalised by two assumptions: that they have responsibility for providing unpaid caring and domestic work in the family, and that their access to resources should be through the men they live with. These assumptions have been instrumental in limiting women's access to income from the labour market and from the state, and have contributed in many cases to their economic dependency on men while in no way guaranteeing that men will provide. Women's poverty trap consists in their precarious access to resources from the major sources of material survival: the labour market, the family, the state.

The 'poverty trap', women's style

The Labour Market. Paradoxically, women are essential contributors to the British economy and work largely out of economic necessity, but their work is deemed marginal and is so undervalued that most working women must depend on additional income sources for survival.

Women's formal labour market participation is higher than ever, restricted primarily by the presence of young children [Martin and Roberts, 1984; EOC, 1987]. Rates are highest for Afro-Caribbean women and lowest for Muslim Asian women [Brown, 1984], who are heavily represented in homework, the most exploited and invisible paid work. Part time work, central to employers' strategies for handling the recession, is done almost entirely by women. Women with dependent children, particularly white women, are most likely to work part-time.

Women predominate in sex-segregated, low paid, low status, low benefit, low security jobs. Like their unpaid work, most of these jobs involve servicing other people's needs. Most women work in non-manual jobs, but black women are more likely than white women to work in lower level and less desirable semi-skilled manual jobs, working longer and more unsociable hours. Median average weekly earnings of full-time women workers are two thirds of the male average. Part-time earnings are disproportionately less. Women's unemployment is rising faster than men's, and the rate for black women is twice that for white women. Women's occupational segregation and unemployment are expected to increase as new technology wipes out predominantly female office jobs, replacing them with 'skilled' jobs for which they are unlikely to get training. Recession in manufacturing makes substantial entry into traditionally male jobs unlikely.

Women's inferior labour market position is commonly viewed as the inevitable result of their domestic roles, especially childcare. And children do limit labour market activity. But women today spend most of their adult lives in paid work, taking increasingly less time out during child-rearing. From a different perspective, the problem stems from the structure of the labour market itself, where 'real' work is defined as full-time, continuous, 'skilled'/professional/managerial, and of course male.

This is not inevitable, but the historical result of struggles between workers and capitalists [and women and men] during the growth of industrial capitalism [Phillips and Taylor, 1980; Land, 1981]. In the process male workers crushed female competition, excluding them from 'skilled' work and relegating them to the 'home', while arguing for the necessity of a 'family wage' to support their 'dependants'. However not all women became economic dependants of men. Today many women do not live with men and many men do not earn an adequate family wage. This is particularly the case with black families where male unemployment is higher, wages lower and there are more dependants to support. Also, more Afro-Caribbean families are female headed [Mama, 1984]. Nevertheless, the resulting occupational segregation and ideological construction of women as men's dependants, reinforced by the refusal of men and the state to take serious responsibility for caring, continue to be primary causes of women's inferior labour market position and their poverty.

The Family. Women may be pushed into dependent relationships with men as much by poor labour market prospects as by socialisation into domesticity. Indeed, the marriage contract promises economic support in exchange for unpaid domestic servicing. But time-budget and household resource distribution studies [studies almost exclusively of white families] suggest that marriage remains an unequal relationship structured to male advantage.

Many married women go beyond the terms of their contract. Regardless of paid work commitments, women still do most of the housework and caring, and bear responsibility for getting it done. Piachaud [1984] found that mothers of children under five spent on average over six hours a day on childcare tasks; their husbands spent 47 minutes. When men 'help', they appear to specialise in less immediate tasks while women do routine, life-sustaining tasks [Coote and Campbell, 1987]. Nissel and Bonnerjea [1982] found similar demarcations of time and task in families looking after elderly disabled relatives. The vast majority of such carers are women, and they are less likely to get formal help with caring than male carers [Walker, 1983]. With state childcare provision limited to priority need, many of these on waiting lists, most working mothers must rely on [often unsatisfactory] informal arrangements. Black mothers, whose need is greatest, have even less access to adequate childcare than white mothers [Parmar, 1982].

Caring is not just a job, but a 'labour of love' involving commitments and personal relationships defining one's identity [Graham, 1983]. As long as they bear full responsibility without adequate resources, women will experience enormous contradictions around caring work. It can be a source of great joy, but cannot be discarded at whim or in exhaustion. Free time is conditional and cannot be set aside as fixed time available for leisure or paid work. Women who work full-time with full responsibility for caring are under constant pressure, risk being labelled unreliable workers and inadequate mothers, and may suffer considerable physical and mental strain.

Studies of money distribution within families [Pahl, 1983; Homer *et al* 1984; Wilson, 1987; Brannen and Moss, 1987] suggest that typically men control income while women are responsible to varying degrees for managing household expenditure. Men tend to retain money for personal spending. In contrast, both partners view the money women handle to be for household needs, even if this money is women's earned income. In low income families, the situation is most extreme. Wives often have complete management responsibility without being able to restrict their husbands' access to housekeeping money. In other cases husbands retain all the income, appropriating even child benefit. Gail Wilson [1987] found that nearly all the married women in her low income group would have been financially better off living without their husbands who spent enough money on themselves to counteract the increased SB rate for couples as compared to single parents. A considerable minority of women, even from higher income households, feel better off as lone parents on SB. Lone parenthood may mean a movement from a poverty they cannot control to one they can [Graham, 1987].

The law does not obligate wage earners to share income with dependants and, although husbands have a legal duty to support their wives and children, it has never been enforced while partners are living together [O'Donavan, 1985]. But the law steps in at separation and divorce, promising maintenance. In practice most ex-wives receive little, and the Matrimonial and Family Proceedings Act 1984 while emphasising the best interests of the child, reduces women's claims to maintenance on the grounds that they should become self-sufficient as soon as possible . While responding to male complaints of hardship in supporting two families and cries of 'alimony drones', the Act fails to recognise that the best interests of children are strongly linked to the welfare of their mothers, and that the problem of women's financial dependency after divorce is a consequence of their dependency in marriage [Smart, 1984]. Time lost from the labour market, continuing responsibilities for childcare, and bleak labour market prospects make self-sufficiency an optimistic goal.

Maintenance orders are made primarily for children, and are typically too low to provide the main source of income for one parent families [Eekelaar and MacLean, 1986]. Moreover, if the mother receives SB, the father's payments go to the DHSS, counting against entitlement, rather than to his children. For many women the only solution to grinding poverty and dependency on SB is dependency on another man through remarriage.

The State. Beveridge structured the social security system on the assumption that women would be economic dependants of men in marriage, without need of benefits in their own right and available for unpaid caring work. The system has changed somewhat towards equality of treatment, but persons living in couples are still not assessed independently as individuals and women are still assumed to be available for unpaid caring.

National Insurance remains linked to a model of male full-time uninterrupted employment. Benefits are earned according to wage levels and amount of time worked. Thus the scheme indirectly discriminates against women, given their characteristic patterns of part-time, interrupted, low-paid work, limiting their access to state pensions and to unemployment, sickness and maternity benefits [Jordan and Waine, 1986/7]. The Social Security Act 1986 tightens up eligibility criteria for these benefits, further disadvantaging women.

The majority of SB claimants are women. Married women were only recently able to claim in certain employment related conditions. But the couple's resources were still aggregated, and given eligibility requirements and cultural tradition, men usually claimed. Moreover these rules continued to apply to unmarried people who the DHSS deemed were 'living together as man and wife', resulting in countless lone mothers losing their only means of survival.

The new income support scheme does not abolish aggregation or the cohabitation rule. It makes most claimants worse off. Particularly offensive is the removal of special needs payments and their replacement by discretionary, recoverable loans from the social fund for 'financial crises' and 'budgeting problems'. Not only may the most financially deprived be tutored in budgeting skills, but 'claimants [may be] in effect borrowing from future inadequate benefits in order to survive on present levels of benefit which are inadequate' [Land and Ward, 1986]. Also, savage cuts in housing benefit erode women's already precarious access to state housing.

The European Court's ruling that Invalid Care Allowance must be extended to married women has made a small dent in the assumption that women are available for unpaid caring work. But the Social Security Act 1986 does nothing to help carers. It does mention 'community care', suggesting that state services may be cut still further and women required to shoulder even greater burdens of unpaid caring. Child Benefit remains women's only access to income as of right. Its revolutionary potential in providing women independent access to income in recognition of their caring role is in no danger of becoming reality. It has proved too popular to scrap, but its value is being run down and it may yet be taxed.

Black women's access to benefits is further limited by state racism. The ideology of motherhood and the family was central to the organisation of the Welfare State [Wilson, 1977], whose origins were bound up with ideals of white supremacy and imperialism [Jacobs, 1985]. *The Beveridge Report* captures this relationship: 'in the next 30 years housewives as mothers have vital work to do in ensuring the adequate continuance of the British race and of British ideals in the world' [Beveridge, 1942]. This concept of womanhood was not meant to apply to Afro-Caribbean women. Recruited as workers after the war, they bridged the contradictions between the ideology of women as natural homemakers and the post war economy's need for female workers [Carby, 1982]. Although Asian women arrived in Britain as dependants, they too fell outside the Welfare State's concern. Britain encouraged black immigration to acquire cheap, malleable, exploitable labour and 'never, conceivably, equal citizens' [Jacobs, 1985, 12].

Racist treatment of black women is justified in part by stereotypes of black families as pathological and undeserving. Afro-Caribbean female headed families are depicted as weak and unstable; 'black women [are] seen to fail precisely because of their position as workers' [Carby, 1982, 219]. Asian communities are viewed as close-knit and self-sufficient; their families oppressive to their totally passive women.

Black SB claimants get worse treatment than white. All black people risk the label 'welfare scrounger'; Afro-Caribbean single mothers especially risk the accusation that they breed in order to live off the state. Asian women have been denied benefits from the DHSS while their husbands are temporarily out of the country on the grounds that Asian families always have relatives to borrow from [Guru, 1986].

Today wives and children of many men may reside in Britain only if they have a sponsor who has pledged to maintain them 'without recourse to public funds' [Gordon and Newnham, 1985; WING, 1985]. Claiming SB is always considered recourse to public funds. The DHSS works closely with the Home Office as an arm of internal immigration control. Black claimants are routinely required to produce passports, especially if they do not speak fluent English. Black women have been starved out of the country by the DHSS's refusal to grant them SB or Child Benefit when they are separated from their husbands. In many cases the women involved are fleeing domestic violence. Fear of deportation may lock women in unsatisfactory, even dangerous, domestic relationships.

Women, poverty and social work

Social work largely presumes that women are responsible for the welfare of their families. Hence, however unwittingly, it has played a part in reinforcing women's unpaid caring role in the family and their vulnerability to poverty.

Since its origins in nineteenth century Poor Law work, a major task of British social work has been intervention into 'inadequate' working class families to improve women's domestic and mothering skills [Davis and Brook, 1985]. The profession grew up after World War II, charged with rebuilding working class family life on the Beveridge model: the [white] middle class nuclear family with its full-time male breadwinner and full-time female homemaker. When state provision for childcare virtually disappeared, mothers who worked outside the home risked being labelled neglectful. 'Maternal deprivation', 'latch-key children', and the rise of juvenile delinquency became linked to mothers' abandonment of the family through paid work and divorce.

Social workers are still much involved with women in their role as carers, a role which now includes responsibility for elderly and handicapped relatives. *The Barclay Report* [Barclay, 1982] reinforces this responsibility by advocating a 'community social work' deploying informal caring networks [read women's unpaid caring] to aid social work tasks. The Report shows little sensitivity to the effects of community care policies on women's vulnerability to poverty.

Social workers have frequent contact with 'dysfunctioning' families, many of whom are in or at risk of poverty. They may hold that family problems are linked to *family* poverty and [male] unemployment. But because women are deemed responsible for the family's well-being, especially for children, intervention often focuses on women's failures in domestic and caring roles: neglect of children due to immaturity, depression, working outside the home; failure to handle family conflict; failure to protect children from male brutality; poor housekeeping; etc. Thus women may be blamed when things go wrong and encouraged to get their domestic act together. Women who live outside conventional family structures, particularly black women, may be deemed beyond redemption. But women may fail not because of personal inadequacies, but because without adequate resources and power, their family responsibilities present intolerable burdens.

Many social workers are attracted to 'family therapy', which views the family as an autonomous and harmonious system with inherent tendencies towards stability. Since the system is made up of interdependent parts, malfunctioning of one member is said to put the whole system out of balance. The therapist's task is to restore balance by helping each member to re-adjust their role. But the nuclear family system is not neutral or harmonious. It is structured by inequalities of power and resource control leading to inevitable tensions and conflicts. Thus in the guise of value neutrality and support of the system, the therapist is likely to collude with its strongest member, and to locate the source of malfunctioning in the member on whom the system puts most strain.

Because the systems view fails to acknowledge that familial power, resources, and roles are necessarily structured by power derived from the wider society [the labour market, the state, etc.], family therapists may invert true relationships of power and dependency, further entrapping the least powerful into structures of exploitation and poverty. In treating father-daughter incest for example [Dale *et al*, 1986; Furniss, 1983], fathers are typically required to take full responsibility for the act of incest, but mothers and daughters are said to be actively involved in maintaining the system. Daughters are deemed to exert considerable power over fathers through threat of revelation and over mothers by winning their fathers' sexual attentions. Fathers are construed as demanding but weak, immature and emotionally dependent on their wives. Mothers bear the brunt of responsibility both for failing as wives by being sexually rejecting and for failing as mothers by not protecting their daughters. Their passive and withdrawn appearance is interpreted as strength. However, in the context of women's structural vulnerabilities, the assertion that 'withdrawal can be a very powerful position' [Dale *et al*, 1986, 6] must be questioned.

In working with families, social workers frequently meet violence to women and children. They often view wife abuse, in contrast to child abuse, as an inappropriate area for intervention, believing that relations between husband and wife are private, and that the wife must tolerate, even enjoy, the violence since she has not left. Yet studies of battered women who have escaped to refuges [Binney *et al*, 1981; Homer *et al*, 1984; Pahl, 1985] indicate that poverty often underlies their failure to extricate themselves. Before entering refuges, many women live in extreme poverty due in part to a very low total family income, but also to gross inequalities in resource distribution. Many have young children and are totally economically dependent on their husbands, who may allow them no access to money at all. Beatings often occur in the context of conflicts over money distribution and control. Thus severe poverty may underlie the more notable emotional dependence, isolation, depression and guilt which battered women experience. And women who gain some financial security in marriage may rightly fear that leaving home will plummet them into dependence on welfare. Few women have the resources necessary to allow meaningful choices between staying and leaving.

Moreover welfare agents such as DHSS and housing officials and social workers may be actively involved in enforcing women's poverty and constructing the battering syndrome, to the extent that they control but refuse access to resources. Some social workers give vital practical help, often by referring women to refuges, but many are more concerned with the sanctity of the family. A random sample survey of social work case files found evidence of wife abuse in one third of cases [Maynard, 1985]. But the main focus was almost always on the children's welfare and the wife's inadequacies. Social workers' comments included: 'Apart from domestic incompetence, she is also failing to meet his sexual demands'; 'It is most important that this couple stick together for the sake of the children and I think this could be achieved more safely by encouraging Mrs Blank to accept her husband's decisions'; 'And although he beats his wife frequently he rarely hits the children'. In most cases the social worker gave no immediate practical help. Black women may encounter particularly harsh responses. For example social workers who believe that oppression is part of Asian women's culture may severely pressurise them to stay in the family against their wishes [Jervis, 1986]. Afro-Caribbean women may find that requests for practical help are refused and their children taken into care because social workers view their culture as violent and volatile [Bryan *et al*, 1985].

Wife abuse may be linked to child abuse, although not through intergenerational transmission. The claim that abused children become abusing adults is based on faulty methodology. Most adults abused as children are not abusing adults, and most abusing adults are not from violent families [Stark and Flitcraft, 1985; Morley, forthcoming]. Work in the USA by Evan Stark and Anne Flitcraft [1985] indicates that first, while wife beating is far more common than child abuse, child abuse is six times more likely to occur in families where the mother is beaten and in the majority of these cases the father is also the child's abuser; second, more than half of physically abused children have mothers who are beaten; third, wife beating 'is the single most important context for child abuse'. These findings suggest that framing the problem of child abuse in terms of unemployment and **family** poverty or of maternal/parental inadequacies may be misplaced and dangerous to the extent that solutions offered leave women and children even more isolated within the family structure. As Stark and Flitcraft suggest, 'case-workers and clinicians would do well to look toward advocacy and protection of battered mothers as the best available means to prevent current child abuse as well as child abuse in the future' [p.168].

And this advocacy and protection would require dealing with issues of **women's** poverty.

Conclusion

With Britain's deteriorating employment situation, women are shouldering ever greater burdens in their roles as paid workers and unpaid carers. It is likely that they will increasingly find themselves social work clients. Social work's ideological and material legacy and its current structural position as agent of the state, mean that interventions into women's lives are bound to be laced with contradictions. In some cases statutory duties will virtually require responses which ultimately may be deleterious to the interests of women and their children.

However, there is room within the present structure for responses sensitive to women's vulnerability to poverty and the stresses it produces [Hale, 1983; Hudson, 1985]. Through sensitive work with individuals and especially through groupwork, women can be helped to understand that they need not shoulder total responsibility when things go wrong; that their situation stems in part from the pathology of their structural position in society which they share with other women. Most importantly social workers can act as advocates for women attempting to gain access to material resources essential to their well-being.

Ultimately, the solution to women's poverty requires that we fundamentally re-evaluate our conceptions of productive work, value, and social responsibility [Scott, 1984]. It requires that all individuals have independent access to and control over resources necessary for survival. This would have revolutionary implications for relationships between men and women, adults and children, individuals and the state. Ironically time may be ripe for re-thinking. Structural unemployment is likely to be a permanent feature of society; new models of socially useful work may be essential for men as well as women. In the meantime as long as the labour and commitment involved in caring are not shared by men and are not recognised as socially necessary and socially rewarded, women will continue to be exploited by the men they live with and by the wider society; and will remain poor.

19

One Parent Families and Poverty:
Strategies for hope and their implications for help agencies
Sue Slipman

T HERE are now one million one parent families in Britain. They exist in all classes and among all ethnic communities, but ninety per cent of them are headed by women. This pattern is consistent in all Western European countries and within the United States, and the numbers are on the increase. Despite the popular myth that the majority of lone parents are single women flouting society's conventions, 84 per cent of one parent families are created through the loss of death or divorce. In Britain the sharp rise in the numbers of one parent families occurred in the years immediately after the introduction of liberal divorce laws in 1969. In reality they are a product of the crisis in relationships between men and women. In the vast majority of cases, women are still left holding the baby.

Moralistic reformers may wail and governments quail, but the one parent family is now a permanent family form. Individual families may go in and out of this form when the lone parent takes on another spouse, but the form itself is here to stay. Exhortation or coercion will not force couples who want to separate to stay together. If they could not divorce, they would still live separately. It is high time that decision makers accepted the facts, and began to plan on the changed nature and structure of family life, for even where a lone parent remarries what is created is a stepfamily with its own special problems and tensions, not a remoulding of the nuclear family.

It is dangerous to make too many assumptions about one parent family life. The only common feature is one parent becoming both sole nurturer and sole breadwinner to their children. It is stunning how well the majority manage these tasks. Despite this there is a vast over-representation of one parent families in any indices of deprivation.

Poverty is the spectre that haunts the one parent family. Put simply it is women's poverty tied to children's poverty. Together they make a formidable trap from which it is difficult to escape; which cuts off all aspects of life opportunities. The real boundary line of the trap is that between professional reasonably paid work and the low status, low paid work which is all that is available to most women. The pit gets deeper at the further cut-off point between low pay and unemployment, mainly because it changes character to become long term dependency upon state benefits which increasingly removes its recipients from the labour market and the independent choices in life. The life of the professional, working lone mother is by no means easy and her income may be up to 42 per cent less than in marriage, but her lot is likely to be preferable to her poorer counterpart, and the life chances of her children considerably enhanced.

The acute problems are experienced by the many lone parents who drop into poverty with a shocking rapidity upon relationship breakdown. They experience a spiral of poverty that removes their own control over their lives and enforces a dependency upon state benefits and welfare system, that determines both their future life chances and those of their children. It is the poverty trap that creates the problems of one parent family life. In the popular imagination the problems emanating from poverty are often reconstituted cementing the belief that the form of the one parent family is a problem in itself. Many lone parents report that instead of having their problems recognised and dealt with, they are themselves treated as the problem, rather than the situation in which they have been placed. The human response to being viewed in this way at a time of great trauma is often depression and resignation. If people are also being made dependent by the operation of the system they may never find their way out. In this way one parent families are forced into the growing underclass in Britain from which the ladder of opportunity has been removed. The priority now is to build the steps in the ladder of opportunity to enable lone parents to climb out of the poverty trap and the underclass. These linked steps are adequate housing, training and employment opportunities, together with the childcare facilities at a level that allows parents to participate in the labour market.

Relationship breakdown often leads to problems in housing and homelessness. Even homeowners go downmarket when divorce settlements divide property. Women on low incomes are unlikely to become property owners in their own right unless the previous family home was a large enough property for an equity share out equivalent to the purchase of a new, smaller property. Those who were previously in the rented sector are likely to be forever excluded from the vision of a home owning democracy. Many will end up homeless, seeking emergency accommodation under the Homeless Persons' Act, allocated the least attractive or suitable accommodation that other families have already refused. At a time of great personal trauma desperate women take any accommodation they are offered and as a result of the chaos in housing allocation within local councils increasingly find themselves on poorly maintained, run-down estates with high numbers of one parent families, becoming more vulnerable to vandalism, crime and harassment than other families because they are women alone. The worst schools are found in these areas and hence the life opportunities of their children are often depressingly determined by the facts of the family's housing. In recent years the shortage of housing stock has seen the rise of the awful bed and breakfast accommodation, at too high a cost financially to the local authority and in every other way to the families forced into overcrowded accommodation, often without the bare minimum facilities to support childrearing. To families living in this accommodation, even the sink estate can look bearable.

Even if accommodation problems can be resolved, the living standard available will be determined by the availability and status of work. Women's wages at the lower end of the spectrum are hardly adequate. In the service sector the average female wage is only £2.20 per hour. It is not much better in manufacturing, and the bonus and overtime earnings that make up men's take-home pay are not available to women who's time is demanded by childcare. The major differentials in earnings between men and women are produced both by discriminatory differences in basic pay and in the accumulated pay accruing from different patterns of work. Women who are brought up to see marriage and motherhood as their real employment choice will lack the work skills and record to find decent work. They have only low paid work to fall back on which, because it is often part-time or below relevant tax thresholds, does not yield the benefits of tax breaks available to more highly paid workers. Many are trapped above an earnings level that would give them access to social security benefits and below the level of wages where they would benefit from tax benefits.

If they have high child care fees on top of low incomes, it may simply not be worthwhile financially for them to work. In the past many lone parents have worked part-time and government policies in the benefit field have enabled them to do so, but the most recent changes to social security have introduced a worrying disincentive to lone parents even to take up part-time work.

Previously working lone parents were allowed to claim a sum of half the value of earnings between £4.00 and £20.00 plus the real costs of their work expenses consisting largely of travel and childcare costs. The government have changed this to a standard disregard of £15.00.

The government conveniently misquoted a survey indicating that average childcare costs were £3.00 per week, but of the sample group used, some 77 per cent had no childcare costs to meet, indicating that 23 per cent had costs significantly above this minimal sum [Weale *et al*, 1984]. For these parents the new regulations will introduce a further disincentive to work, and if they do give up work the current balance between wages and benefits that make up the income of the one parent family and currently tip it in the direction of wages would tip the scale over to benefits. At present 40 per cent comes from wages, and 32 per cent from benefits.

The Earnings Disregard is an important issue. It indicates how easily an ill-thought-out policy can have a major, negative impact on the life chances of those living at the margins. It is vital that women who can, take the opportunity to maintain work records while on benefit with a view to working full-time when their children are older. Unless they are able to do this their poverty will become a permanent feature of their lives even when their children no longer dominate its shape. Clearly, work outside the home is of positive benefit in other than financial terms. It helps end the social isolation of lone parenthood and fosters a sense of self-determination and respect that comes from coping and a sense of purpose. It is perhaps for this reason rather than for the cash alone, however vital, that the majority of lone parents indicate that they would like to work.

The quality and status of the work available to women becomes an ever more urgent issue. In order to stand alone they must be able to break into the higher paid hitherto largely 'male' employment areas in both blue collar and professional work. Training in order to qualify for jobs is essential to women, and a government serious about tackling one parent family poverty would need extensive plans for positive action on training for women that enabled them to break out of sexual stereotyping on the job front. Prejudice still creates training schemes that push women and girls into secretarial and service-based options. This may still be compounded by women's choices made on the assumption that work is a temporary pastime until marriage, but decision makers should be wiser by now even if romantically inclined young women are not.

If it remains difficult to break into male bastions of blue collar work there is really no excuse in the better paid positions in the new technologies for so few women coming through. The patterns of unemployment within the new industries are not yet set hence there are opportunities for making progress here. It would be tragic if women missed out or became excluded from these jobs which by their nature are not sex specific and which require brain rather than brawn for success.

Positive strategies for training are not enough without adequate access to child support whether through providing facilities or by including childcare fees as part of training grants. Childcare facilities, while clearly a concern of all working parents, are even more crucial for the lone parent. At present there is no political will in Britain to provide adequate childcare resources, or even to recognise that the world of work needs changing to accommodate a dual role as parent and worker. Indeed the government's refusal to introduce the European Economic Community's directive on parental leave and leave for family reasons deliberately perpetuates the current problems.

Over the years since the Finer Commission there has been an uneasy consensus in the policies of all governments towards the one parent family. The 'choice' of women who work has been accepted, and they have been allowed to remain as long term recipients of social security. Some limited opportunity to work was created by the disregard, but many government ministers still adhered to the theory that women with children should not really work. Indeed some felt it was downright immoral for women to work and leave their children. So far that has left lone parents living passively in poverty, but apart from cohabitation checks, largely without harassment. The trends in government social security policies coupled with the general anxiety to push people towards taking training opportunities and the jobs available, indicate a sea change is on its way. Undoubtedly its path will be fraught with difficulties and paved with dangers for lone parents. Many of its contradictions will be located as they are at present in a wider debate about the nature of family life and whether or not deliberate social engineering can put the clock back. In government, as elsewhere, the moralists and the pragmatists will slog it out.

The family romantics stand on one side of the debate. They yearn for the golden age of family life located somewhere in Victorian England where women and men inhabited a cosy domestic sphere and were content, and where men ran the world and were content. The family for the romantics remains a moral structure upon which depends the survival of civilised society. The breakdown of traditional family forms is a seamless degeneration linking contraception and abortion, juvenile delinquency and crime, pornography and a lack of respect for humanity. Leading public figures decry the one parent family as the symbol of such degeneration, as the 'greatest evil of our times'. They fail to recognise that the separate spheres of male and female influence have gone forever; that women's aspirations have changed and that they now require a fairer distribution of both wealth and power between men and women. They further fail to recognise that men are highly resistant to such redistribution. For such moralists the only real solution is for women to become 'good mothers' again so that men will again take up their burden of being 'good husbands'. They will stop deserting their families and settle down to being the breadwinner.

Turning back the clock, despite the best endeavours of the romantics seems a remote possibility, but there is yet no sign of making real progress towards the more equal partnerships of tomorrow, which might be the one hope for greater family stability, or at least if and when families do break up, less bitterness between the spouses, and increased chances of security for the children.

The new pragmatists in government have yet to prove that despite their acceptance of the facts, they intend to make life better for one parent families to any significant degree. Our current government has shown so far only that is is inherently hostile to strategies designed to redistribute opportunities. They seem particularly hostile to creating better opportunities for women. In recent legislation on local government they have restricted the duties upon local authorities in such a way that its proponents fear that contract compliance will become illegal, thereby denying the use of purchasing power within public authorities from supporting equal opportunities in a positive way. Instead the government will fall back upon exhortation in the case of race, and one suspects little or nothing at all in the case of women.

The government's employment strategies within the May 1986 White Paper *Building Businesses . . . Not Barriers* continue their general line of removing what they see to be unfair burdens upon employers. The impact of these if implemented will take thousands of part-time women workers out of employment protection and limit maternity rights for working women. In addition there have been other hostile policies towards maternity rights and benefits. Tax breaks have been removed from employers providing workplace nurseries, which since 1984 have been judged as a perk in line with the company car rather than a vital resource for the working parent. There has been some movement on positive training opportunities but access remains inadequate. It all adds up to a climate of continued disadvantage for women.

However, the government's stated intention is to tackle the problems of the inner cities. It should be clear to Ministers that this cannot be done unless the problems of one parent families and the opportunities facing their children can be tackled. It is not yet clear how inner city decline is to be arrested. So far there is little sign of special consideration being given to one parent family needs. The recent benefit changes failed to recognise that the housing needs of one parent families are exactly the same as two parent families, at least on the assumption that spouses living together share a bedroom. The new Social Fund will be cash limited, subject to local discretion and carry no appeal rights. Further it will give loans that will have to be paid back. The prospects for lone parents struggling to survive on benefits are grim. A new army of debt counsellors will arise to advise them, but they will not have the cash or control over their own lives necessary for survival. Dependency upon state benefits is mirrored by an increasing dependency upon the professional to interpret and negotiate for vulnerable lone parents. This is bound to inhibit their ability to manage their own lives and to make the transfer to full, independent citizenship.

There are indications that the government will move closer to the American 'workfare' system of removing benefit from those who will not take whatever work is available. A start has already been made with the proposals that young claimants will lose benefit unless they take up places on YTS and other training courses. The government's argument is that the state should not pay people to remain idle when there are opportunities to work or train. Even if one accepts their central belief, the plan becomes straightforward coercion unless the schemes themselves are of proven quality and will benefit their participants. And even in this case there would have to be exceptions, particularly for young mothers or those whose confinement will occur during a course. For young mothers who have no access to childcare for their babies, resources must either be supplied on courses or exemption given. Without such provisions or exceptions there are clear dangers in a straightforwardly coercive policy in a democratic society that has accepted a welfare safety net regardless of work record. Whilst this may not have been the original intention of the Beveridge plan for state welfare, demographic, social and family changes have lead to this outcome.

The government's intentions seem riven with contradictions that go back to their ambivalence about the family and the new realities of its forms. Unless these contradictions can be engaged at the level of practical policies the outcome may be simply a confirmation that non professional and non working women on their own with children become permanently trapped into poverty within an underclass. The real battle is to win the government, however reluctantly, to an acceptance of the strategies for equal opportunities.

Many of the government's opponents and those who seek to speak on behalf of the client groups in poverty have had a defensive reaction to policies. They have found themselves grimly defending inadequate services, many of which far from meeting clients' needs have themselves become institutions creating dependency and treating client groups with contempt. They have, therefore, and however unwittingly, become supporters of the growing tendency to count out the vulnerable from full citizenship. The government remained intent on reforming these institutions, and their defenders became a conservative and uncreative force attempting to keep intact services and benefits that were no longer operating positively for their client group. It is of course true that the first reforming attempts of the Conservatives were to cut back expenditure and that it was then clear in what way, if at all, vulnerable groups could possibly benefit from reforms that cut some of their lifelines. Nevertheless there were possibilities even within this terrain that opposition forces failed to grasp. Often the reason for such failure was that any increasing choice for clients as consumers of services were in conflict with the immediately perceived interests of the trades union groups whose members supplied the services. Hence some of the opposition had self-interested and cynical roots mixed in with the idealism of the caring professional.

These strategies and the opposition viewpoints have now been tested in two further general elections and, whatever the fears of electors and their concerns for the growing divisions in the country and the growth of poverty, they have returned the Conservatives to follow through their radical and painful strategies. In these circumstances, even if opposition forces remain convinced of their own propaganda it should be clear that it has been rejected to such an extent that unless they are capable of engaging with the government's agenda they will be totally failing their client groups. They will in fact have sacrificed their client group to shore up their own ideological commitment. The challenge is to find a way of working with the grain of the government's intentions and objectives whilst protecting the interests of the client group. It may well be that government will not accept the policy proposals of opponents even where these are presented to positively enhance the government's direction, but it may mean that forceful alliances can be created in so doing that will force the government to concede ground even when most unwilling. There has only been one victory in recent years from which to generalise, and this was of a defensive kind. Nevertheless it was significant. It was the successful campaign to save the child benefit as a payment made direct to the mother and to ensure that the new replacement for Family Income Supplement, the Family Credit, be similarly retained. The government's argument for a transfer from purse to wallet was based upon the strike of public sector workers in 1979. Here Ministers had been shown wage slips indicating that a man could no longer earn enough to keep 'his' family. The government was responding to this in their Green Paper on benefit reform by attempting to give the control of the family income back to the man [DHSS, 1985c; 1985d]. The same Child Benefit campaign largely succeeded because the alliance of forces supporting it was broad and strong enough to be irresistible, particularly as it included the Conservative women's organisations, forcibly arguing to defend women's interests. It also picked out the contradictions in the government's position where the stated aim was to direct financial help to the area of most need and to the most efficient point of delivery. It totally contradicted this aim to wish to give control back to men in providing care for children and belied the new, practical realities of family life.

The alliance-building approach of this campaign now needs to be coupled with a positive policy approach. If the government is serious about tackling the housing deprivation of the inner city, interest groups representing lone parents must engage with the allocation policies post-renovation when one parent families, having been removed from estates for the renovation period may be moved even more down market as properties are sold off to yuppies. Now it may be necessary to sell off some properties to realise capital investment, but we must make sure that there are advantages to be gained from such renovations for lone parents and their children. Simply opposing the involvement of private finance in public housing is the high road to obsolescence, and will ensure there is no voice speaking up for one parent families and negotiating for and with them.

The positive approach is one that seeks to count back in to society those who have become increasingly marginalised within it. It also works with the grain of choices that lone parents have increasingly been making for themselves with self help projects in a variety of crucial fields. A lot of the self help activity was initially motivated and supported by Gingerbread. It is now emulated and developed by increasing numbers of diverse groups. Such activity offers personal growth for people who have emerged from the trauma of relationship breakdown and who do not wish to be trapped within the psychology of dependency.

Professionals working with lone parents in theory welcome self help activity. In practice the reality of their caseload and institutional priorities mean that they can take control away from people and exercise it during periods of trauma, but that letting go and encouraging independent growth is more difficult. There is rarely real liaison between self help groups and professionals, although in isolated cases there may be cross referrals. Links can be difficult to establish. Professionals work to the filofax and the office timetable. Activists in self help groups work from scrappy pieces of paper, public call boxes, their own homes and the timetables of childcare. Dealing with the routine of an office day is often anathema to them. As a result it is difficult to work in synch, let alone to work out shared objectives and strategies through a cooperation with other agencies designed to enable clients to gain knowledge of the opportunities open to them and the confidence necessary for grabbing them.

There are clearly serious professional concerns about the process of letting go. If a professional gets it wrong there can be a heavy price to pay and all letting go requires risk taking. There are the practical problems about the lack of information and advice to support client and professional alike. Agencies duplicate resources in an endless stream of hit and miss effort with either no awareness of the need for strategic thought and shared planning or without the practice, time or even perhaps training and skills to accomplish it. It is not easy. Nevertheless the professional goal has to be to enable people to lead independent lives wherever it is possible for them to do so and to protect those who for one reason or another cannot do so in either the short or the longer term.

It may be that the tasks for over worked, understaffed social services departments in local authorities will degenerate from their current levels of fire fighting to take on debt counselling as part of the growing problem of poverty. The strains are likely to increase even further if the descent into the underclass for one parent families is not halted. Social Services may become far more closely associated with policing services and their besieged staff pushed into increasingly ambivalent roles which deny a befriending function as they find themselves forced to play a control function over increasingly hopeless and depressed lives. If we cannot find positive strategies that enable lone parents to become independent there will be no alternative to an increasingly fraught and thankless management of their dependency.

The goal of independence is a difficult one to attain, and may for many prove impossible. It requires linked strategies for decent housing allocation, adequate training and employment opportunities and a level of childcare that can, at the very least, offer care to the children of working lone parents after school and in the school holidays. None of this will be enough to create ideal conditions, and it does not begin to tackle the sexual division of labour in blue collar jobs for those unable to undergo training for decently paid jobs. But it does offer a way forward that could be achieved and which could set patterns for future development. It would at least demand consistency in policy approaches to overcome the ambivalence in moral attitudes to family forms in bypassing ideological debate for practical projects of support. It would also utilise the self-help positivism of lone parents themselves and create positive channels for professional workers to advise and guide clients through. In many instances social services could play a role in providing support services. Where their function would remain with the more vulnerable lone parents and their children, they will have to develop better coordination with the self help and voluntary groups which could best develop the support role to such practical projects, and learn to work in partnership to maximise available resources.

20

Poverty Awareness
Saul Becker

The need for poverty awareness

SOCIAL workers are increasingly confronting and addressing complex and controversial issues relating to race and gender. Not least, they have become more aware and sensitive to how their assumptions, beliefs and prejudices in these areas affect their practice and service delivery. Cheetham [1987] for example has argued that 'colour blindness' among social workers can, and does, have many negative consequences for the welfare of black children and their families. Social workers' beliefs about clients 'clearly shape the help that will be offered' [p. 11]. But many social workers have been slow, and others reluctant, to respond to parallel issues concerned with poverty and deprivation. This is despite the fact that issues of race, gender and poverty very often overlap.

Negative images of welfare and hostile attitudes to the poor are informed and maintained by historic and economic processes and social and cultural traditions. As a profession social work has developed, operates within and contributes to dominant, and often contradictory, welfare belief systems. As individuals, social workers are affected by these. For centuries and across continents the poor, and especially those who have become dependent on welfare support have been labelled as lazy, criminal and responsible for their poverty. Controversy has also been attached to the systems of welfare that have supported, maintained and, often, controlled them. Distinctions between those who are 'deserving' of state or charitable assistance and those who are not have been paralleled by mechanisms to regulate and police the 'non-deserving' and to target both 'cash' and 'care' services to those in most need.

Fuller and Stevenson [1983] have argued that there is a need for 'substantial and detailed studies' to show how the wide range of factors influencing social workers and their practice with poor clients operate and interact. They stress that information is needed to evaluate the extent to which certain values inhibit or distort social work services. Similarly, in the United States, Grimm and Orten [1973] have also argued that 'social workers' attitudes are a crucial factor in the way they will deliver services to the poor and how clients, in turn, will react to the services they receive' [Grimm and Orten, 1973, 94; see also Silberman, 1977; Orten, 1979; Macarov, 1981; Becker, 1987a]. A number of studies of social workers' attitudes to poverty have been produced in the United States. In Britain, however, there is a serious lack of poverty awareness in its broadest sense: First, virtually nothing is known about British social workers' attitudes to poverty and the poor. Second, social workers themselves have little understanding of the complex processes that generate and maintain financial poverty. Third, few social workers have any developed insight into how their ideologies and perceptions of poverty affect their daily practice with poor people. Fourth, departments have often failed to place poverty directly on the agenda for social work activity; emphasis is directed at working with cases, rather than on issues.

A study of social workers' attitudes to poverty

The study reported here, and conducted by the author, is the first in Britain to examine social workers' attitudes to poverty [both their position and strength of feeling], to interpret and explain a number of associations with these attitudes, and to explore perceptions of appropriate social work roles with poor people. The findings have important implications both for the selection and training of social workers and for the organisation, operation and practice of social work. They also raise a number of fundamental issues about poverty awareness among social workers.

The study was conducted in the first instance by a mailed questionnaire to 451 social workers between June and August 1986, followed by detailed individual and group interviews with over 50 selected respondents between December 1986 and February 1987. The resulting quantitative data and interview material provides a detailed picture of the background and personal characteristics of social workers, their beliefs, values and attitudes towards a number of poverty related issues.

Eight out of ten of these social workers believe that people live in poverty because of 'injustice and inequality'. This is a far greater proportion than the public with the same view; in 1977 only 16 per cent of the UK public thought this, and by 1985 the proportion was still only 32 per cent [EEC, 1977; Mack and Lansley, 1985]. The public were more likely to stress laziness or the 'inevitable' nature of poverty. Again, in contrast with the public, social workers are also far more likely to have strong and supportive feelings towards supplementary benefit claimants. Seventy eight per cent of social workers [compared with only 25 per cent of the public in 1985] strongly agreed that most supplementary benefit claimants are in real need. Fifty three per cent of social workers [23 per cent of the public] feel strongly that 'a lot of people entitled to claim supplementary benefit don't claim it'. Nearly one in ten social workers, however, agree that many claimants are 'on the fiddle'. But this compares dramatically with 62 per cent of the public with the same belief. The public – in 1977 and 1985 – are far more likely to be hostile towards and blame the poor for their poverty.

Most social workers on the other hand view the poor as a powerless group, their poverty caused and maintained by structural inequalities or policy decisions beyond their control. Linked, however, is an enduring belief in the 'cycle of deprivation', that the poor have poor parents and come from places where there are few opportunities and life chances. While there are individual and important variations in perceptions and beliefs, most social workers define poverty in terms of restricted life opportunities and restricted access to resources – 'being trapped in poverty'. This lack of access, or opportunities for access to higher income and wealth, is a common component in the injustice/inequality notion.

Perceptions of the *cause* of poverty relate closely to *definitions* of poverty. As a group, social workers think of and define poverty in relative terms – relative to other countries, times – or relative to the needs and wants of the non-poor population. Poverty is seen very much as the lack of resources and opportunities to live an 'adequate' or 'reasonable' life, relative to others:

> Poverty is a relative concept . . . you may feel deprived relative to others. But poverty is about lack of resources, a lack of money. At the end of the day, because of their sparse incomes, their potential to do things and to be regarded as respectable members of society – whether rightly or wrongly – is reduced, and it boils down to money

at the end [group respondent, February 1987].

To live an 'adequate' type of lifestyle requires that the poor have incomes above subsistence level and which allow them to exert real and genuine choices in how this money is spent:

> Poverty is where, if you expand in one area like the use of a telephone, you have got to cut down on something else . . . this . . . is not a positive choice because you have to deprive yourself of food, or activities, or going out, so if its cold and you have to have extra heat, then you can't afford something else [group respondent, February 1987].

Social workers are concerned that people should have the opportunities and resources to make real choices and exert control over their lives. The poor lack access to opportunities, resources, adequate lifestyle and social participation because, to a degree, *they are victims*.

Social workers' definitions of poverty relate closely with their beliefs about the adequacy and purpose of supplementary benefit. And beliefs about adequacy rely very much upon opinions about purpose: if a social worker believes that supplementary benefit should only provide for basic subsistence needs, then supplementary benefit as currently structured is more likely to be thought of as adequate. As a group, there is considerable diversity among social workers in their attitudes towards the adequacy and purpose of supplementary benefit. The dominant view, however, is that supplementary benefit should provide for relative needs and allow for participation and real choice. But these opinions vary considerably depending on which claimant group is being considered.

Ninety three per cent of social workers for example feel that the supplementary benefit rate for a couple with two young children is too low; 6 per cent think it is about right. On average the amount social workers feel such a family needs each week is £104.35p, compared with the actual 1986 rate of £68.05p. Ninety four per cent of social workers feel that the weekly rate for a single parent and baby is too low; 91 per cent feel the rate is too low for pensioners, 78 per cent believe it to be too low for school leavers with parents on benefit and 63 per cent believe it is too low for school leavers with parents in work. For this last group, three per cent think the rate is too high.

These variations in perceptions of adequacy are linked to other considerations and beliefs about particular claimant groups and the poor in general. Not all of these beliefs are 'positive' ones; again, the vast majority of social workers believe that some of the poor waste their money on drinking and smoking or lack motivation and will-power. Many also believe that individual abilities, personal characteristics and family process often maintain people in poverty. These beliefs are especially prominent in attitudes towards poor clients. Nearly 60 per cent of social workers think that the poor who become clients [as opposed to the poor who do not] have personal problems, are unable to cope socially, have relationship problems or have suffered from some sickness or illness. While the 'visibility' of particular groups obviously affects the likelihood of them becoming social work users or cases, there is a belief that is widespread amongst social workers that those who use their services are generally unable to cope:

> We have a group of people who come to us because of their coping ability – which is not very strong or well developed – they have not had the experiences in life, training, whatever, to enable them to cope well with stress and adverse circumstances . . . the people who don't come to us are those who, because of their up-bringing and experience, may still be in poverty but have better coping abilities, more determination perhaps, the sort of personalities and networks that have enabled them to cope even though they are in poverty' [area director, early 40s].
>   ... an awful lot of clients we deal with do cope at a slightly less able level than others. For some reason they do not seem able to cope with complex bureaucracies. They don't seem able to, not that they don't manage their poverty any better – they are just slightly handicapped by possible different layers of handicapping factors . . . they just get overloaded . . . which in total swamp their ability to cope. But we also get just the families who are on a low income and perhaps Dad goes out for a drink on Friday night and he drinks most of the money away [social worker, early 30s].

These perceptions are important. Personal social services that are directed at 'non copers' may be quite different from those provided for people perceived to have other needs.

Factors associated with social workers' attitudes

The survey data also suggest that individual social worker's attitudes are associated with a number of different personal characteristics, experiences, backgrounds and ideologies. Social workers who are most likely to perceive poverty in structural terms and generally have positive attitudes and strong supportive feelings towards the poor are young [male or female, aged

25-40], are highly educated and professionally trained [especially with a combination of degree and CQSW], with some experience of claiming benefit, decided to become social workers earlier in their lives [before leaving school or as students], or while unemployed, lived in small cities during their childhood and now live in relatively deprived areas, with prior experience of social work related or voluntary work, who are relatively new to professional social work practice. Additionally they will support the Labour Party [and may well be a member of it], will be involved in pressure groups [either poverty related such as CPAG or non-poverty related such as CND]. Class origins, past financial circumstances, sex, housing tenure, marital status, number of dependants and religious practice do not appear to be associated with social workers' attitudes to poverty to any large extent.

Those with the most negative and hostile attitudes are social workers who, as children, lived in rural [village] areas, decided to become social workers while in some form of work [social services or other non related], are under 25 or over 40, have no or few educational or professional qualifications, spent time in non-social work employment before becoming social workers, never claimed benefit [or have claimed it some considerable time ago], live in relatively affluent areas, support the Conservative Party and are not members of a pressure group. Many of these will also have the least intense feelings towards the poor.

Discussion

The survey data show that social workers have a matrix of opinions, beliefs and values about poverty related issues. Their attitudes are inferred from a range of these responses. The position and intensity of their attitude towards each issue range along a continuum from 'positive' to 'negative', but there is not one overall continuum, rather a larger number that relate to each issue and dimension being examined. As a group, social workers have a number of clusters of opinions and beliefs, which in general appear to be associated with positive attitudes towards the poor. But on an individual level, attitudes are not always consistent, nor are they consistently supportive. Individual social workers are often positive or negative or feel more strongly about one issue but may be more negative or feel less strongly about other issues. Their attitudes are characterised by inconsistency, paradox and contradiction – which is inherent in the operation and practice of social work itself.

The important point here is not that there is a group of social workers with particularly hostile views [although the findings on associations suggest this may well be the case], but that *all* social workers have beliefs, opinions and values which are sometimes hostile towards some of the poor. As a group they appear supportive [especially in comparison with the general public]. But as individuals their poverty awareness has tendencies towards hostility and prejudice. Certain experiences, circumstances and ideologies appear to be associated in different ways with these attitudes and beliefs.

Perceptions of appropriate practice

Despite locating poverty in the context of structural inequalities, most social workers also believe that they can have little strategic impact upon the nature of the problem itself. They respond on the margins because it is at this level that change is most likely to occur.

These perceptions are associated with beliefs about the appropriate role, aims and methods of social work in general, and about possibilities for social change through social work in particular. Objectives are seen very much in individualising terms. Casework is not only the dominant method, but also the method that most social workers believe is the legitimate focus, and purpose of their work:

> we very much encourage people to live within their means, to be satisfied with their lot, survival mechanisms . . . we are a safety net to prevent great suffering and not necessarily to alter things largely, but only slightly, to stop the worst effects [group respondent, February, 1987].

Helping individuals in poverty through advice, the provision of services, money, toys or 'minor structural manipulation' [for example, helping clients move up a housing list] are seen as the natural limits to effective and appropriate social work with poor people:

> As a worker I have to accept the system that is around and the structures that people have to live within and I see my job as ensuring that they get all the resources that the structure makes available . . . beyond that there is nothing I can do about the structural side . . . I am looking at how that person or family deals with the poverty situation they are in [fieldwork supervisor, early 30s].
>
> There is little you can do about poverty. If anything comes my way – material possessions – I never refuse them because I have got somebody for it . . . I am doing nothing at all to alleviate the problem of poverty . . . I think I have a job which involves looking after individual families to the best of my ability. I don't see my job outside that brief [social worker, early 40s].

Additionally there is considerable ambivalence towards roles and tasks associated with money. There is reluctance to accept welfare rights as a legitimate social work activity. The use of social workers' direct financial powers also vary considerably between and within offices. Professionally, social workers are concerned not to enter even further into income maintenance work [Becker, 1987b]. What work that is conducted of this kind is not particularly well done, or done with any consistency or overall objective.

Social workers beliefs that they are most effective in helping poor people cope or adapt to their economic status and circumstances are also influenced by their perceptions of organisational priorities and barriers. Pressure of work, specialisation by cases rather than issues, and the overburdening demands of bureaucratic procedures and statutory duties encourage the development and maintenance of a reactive and individualising service, rather than one which is preventive or developmental:

> Sometimes you are under so much pressure that you can't do what you would want to do . . . we have to prioritise and we have to when we are allocating work – deal with those that look very pressing – and then the others just have to wait . . . we feel constantly under pressure . . . we would like to do more work in the community . . . we don't have the time and we don't have the resources [group respondent, February 1987].

Issues

Findings on social workers' attitudes to poverty, perceptions of appropriate social work roles in general, and with poor people in particular, raise a number of important issues about poverty awareness among social workers, their agencies and trainers.

First, how can professional social work training and practice confront negative attitudes and prejudices which appear to be held by all social workers? Likewise, how can they overcome the influence of certain past experiences, current circumstances and ideological orientations that appear to be associated with particularly negative images of the poor?

Second, how can social workers develop their poverty awareness on a number of fronts? Namely a clearer insight into their attitudes towards the poor and how these affect not only what they do *with* poor people but also *how* they do it. Do beliefs about why poor people become poor clients shape the form and tone of the service provided?

Third, how can social workers be better informed and made more aware of the processes at work in maintaining poverty and inequality? How can this education be placed in the context of a coherent body of knowledge on which to inform practice?

Fourth, How can social workers best respond to poverty at an organisational level? How can they overcome the boundaries and constraints perceived to be present within the operation of their agencies, which inhibit alternative methods of working both with and for poor people, and against poverty [see Dhooge and Becker, 1988].

Poverty is perceived by social workers as powerlessness, lack of real choice, lack of participation and restricted life chances. Effective social work, aimed at combating poverty or ameliorating some of its harsher consequences for poor people must contain within it objectives and methods which are designed to promote choice and participation and which enhance life chances. It must allow and encourage a transfer of power, skills, resources and knowledge, even in the confines of the casework relationship, and no matter how modest, between worker and client. Without a re-appraisal of current practice orthodoxy, social workers may continue to confirm poor clients in their dependency, ultimately managing the poor, not poverty.

21

The Social Construction of Unemployment
Defining out a social work role?
Yvonne Dhooge and Jennie Popay

I T is undeniable that in the 1980s any discussion about poverty and
social work needs to include unemployment. Despite the recent drop
in the number of people officially registered as unemployed,
unemployment and in particular long-term unemployment, are still
dominant features of our society. However, it should also be noted that
within the context of social work, unemployment is far from a recent
phenomenon. People in contact with social services have always held a
marginal position in the labour market, carrying with it job insecurity and a
high risk of unemployment.

As much research has shown, unemployment and poverty are closely
linked [Moylan *et al*, 1984; White, 1983]. The 1985 *Family Expenditure
Survey*, for example, shows that the gross income of a family whose head
was unemployed for less than one year was only half that of a family whose
head was in employment. And Berthoud argues in his study of the
adequacy of supplementary benefit:

> With the possible exception of the down-and-out homeless, direct
> measures of hardship show that there is no poorer group of people
> than unemployed couples with children [Berthoud, 1986].

Furthermore, an upturn in the economy does not mean less poverty.
There is evidence that part of the present economic growth is taking place in
the secondary labour market characterised by low pay, poor conditions and

[Byrne, 1987b].

...ent has had a profound impact on social services. Work
...wn as referrals for financial hardship and debts have
...families in contact with social services are experiencing more
...plex problems. Additionally, traditional social work responses are
becoming impossible to implement. The concept of rehabilitation, for
instance, is threatened as specific client groups such as physically and
mentally handicapped people and people with a criminal record become
excluded from the labour market. Similarly without access to employment
young people are finding the transition from residential care to independent
living very difficult [Balloch and Hume, 1985; Dhooge and Popay, 1986,
1987].

It is now a rare exception for social services to work with people who
have paid employment. This situation has led to a growing concern about
the increase in demand for and the effectiveness of social services. The
various studies on unemployment and social work and the inclusion of the
issue in conferences for directors and fieldworkers alike are a reflection of
these concerns. However, there is still a profound gap between the concern
expressed and practical action. For example, the AMA report *Caring for
Unemployed People* points out that:

> the generalised effect of economic recession and unemployment is
> often not perceived by social services staff, or where perceived is
> often not translated into their daily work . . . [Balloch and Hume,
> 1985].

More recently a report from BASW states:

> although nine out of ten people seeking social services help in cities
> are unemployed, professionals have not adapted the way they work
> when confronted with such consequences of unemployment as
> bitterness, ill-health and suicide [BASW, 1987].

And while BASW has called for ongoing training to equip social workers
better to work with people experiencing unemployment, they had to cancel
a conference on unemployment in May 1987 due to lack of interest. During
our own training initiative, part of which focussed on social services'
responses to unemployment, we experienced a similar disjunctive between
expressed concern and practical action.

In this chapter we offer some explanation as to why social services appear
to have failed to take on unemployment as an issue for practice. Whilst we
recognise that there are a number of organisational constraints on the
development of social work responses, the chapter focuses particularly on
the way social services professionals perceive unemployment and the
unemployed. We have chosen this as our focus for two reasons. Firstly, the

development of social service responses depends in the first instance on whether unemployment is seen as an issue relevant to practice. And if, as appears to be the case, social services professionals define out an acceptable social work role by constructing the problem in a particular way, it is not surprising that little progress is made in addressing other professional and organisational constraints on the development of responses. Secondly, the way the problem of unemployment is constructed and the way this influences practice have a more general relevance as they exemplify how social service workers 'deal' with structural factors affecting people's lives.

Most of the material presented in the chapter is drawn from a small scale, qualitative study, carried out in 1983 and 1984, and a subsequent two year training initiative [1]. While the scale of this study limits the extent to which the findings can be generalised, discussions with other people involved in social services research and training have confirmed that they provide an important insight into what is happening in social services generally.

'We could do more but . . . '

To many 'outsiders' social workers seem to be beset by a siege mentality. Considering the pressures under which they are presently operating this is perhaps understandable. While the demand for their services is growing, cuts in local authority resources are making it increasingly difficult to respond. The increase in reported child abuse cases and the conflicting messages social workers are presently receiving about their intervention in such cases are creating high levels of anxiety and stress. Changes in the Social Security system will have a similar effect. Then there is the tendency to constantly add 'new' problems or client groups to their responsibility. This book which at various places calls for a greater involvement in welfare rights and problems associated with unemployment is only one example. Over recent years social workers have already seen their statutory obligations extended under the Criminal Justice Act and the Mental Health Act.

All these pressures were very much evident among the social workers we interviewed. To our question of whether they thought they could provide more and better support for people experiencing unemployment, their answer was invariably 'maybe we could do more but . . . ' The **but** consisted of a whole series of organisational and professional constraints. The sheer lack of time and resources combined with the demands of statutory work were most frequently mentioned. They also pointed out that without any clear directive from management they could do no more than respond on an ad hoc basis:

> We have high case loads, there's a lack of staff, a high expectation of
> written work, case recording has a huge priority put on it, there's
> various fresh demands on the service in terms of the Criminal Justices
> Act . . . Everything is supposed to be a priority, nobody will say that
> you do this or that, but there's a sort of unwritten list of priorities,
> like child care which takes precedence . . . unemployment hasn't a
> high priority, it's just an accepted fact.

The development of responses to unemployment is further constrained
by a great uncertainty about how social services can respond. Social
workers feel that most of what they can do is ameliorative and within the
context of unemployment this appears to create not only severe dilemmas,
but also a resistance to becoming involved. As we will discuss in more detail
later, this is in part connected with seeing social issues and the related
individual needs as two totally separate things, and with the view that the
client-centred model on which most social work is based, is essentially a
model directed at helping people deal better with their 'private' problems
and therefore inappropriate to deal with structural factors affecting people's
lives. This reflects the influence of Radical Social Work of the early 70's
which rejected responses to individual needs and placed all the emphasis on
social-structural issues and political action [Pearson, forthcoming].

Many of these constraints, particularly the organisational ones, are real
and need to be more openly acknowledged in order to break through the
siege mentality among many social service professionals. At present social
workers appear to be so defensive that they are no longer willing to exercise
constructive self-criticism about the way they work and about their
personal beliefs, attitudes and assumptions which are influencing their
practice. Yet it is precisely these images of unemployment and the
unemployed which are a major barrier to the development of
responses.

The social construction of unemployment and the unemployed

Our research suggests that social services consider unemployment to be
qualitatively different from any other problem they are asked to deal with.
For them unemployment belongs basically to the arena of politics and
economic policy:

> Unemployment is different in that it involves a problem for which
> there is a solution and for which social workers and departments have
> no possibility of solving . . . it's political . . . we have to be realistic;

there are no jobs around, so what can we do?

While we certainly would not argue that the political and economic dimensions of unemployment should receive less attention, discussing unemployment solely in the above terms carries with it the danger that unemployment *as an individual experience* is given little or no attention at all. This is already happening among the public at large. As Sinfield has put it '"The unemployed" have become "unemployment" again, an aggregate which only attracts attention when it changes size' [Sinfield, 1987].

On the basis of our study this does not appear as yet to have happened within social services, though BASW's recent warning that Britain's social workers need educating on what it is like to be unemployed seems to suggest otherwise. The social workers and managers we spoke to were still sensitive to the health and welfare needs of people experiencing unemployment. For most of them unemployment was first of all a financial crisis, causing or exacerbating other problems. In contrast to the health professionals involved in our study, they attributed the poverty associated with unemployment to the inadequacy of the benefit system rather than to 'bad' money management. They were also very much aware of the psychological difficulties associated with and the stigma attached to unemployment.

Despite this awareness of the individual needs arising from unemployment, social workers tend to give priority to the political and economic dimensions of unemployment – unemployment as a social issue – and by doing so they in actual fact define out a social work role.

Though they do visualise a role in relation to the individual health and welfare needs, such a role is defined as trivial or at best ameliorative. Work on welfare rights for instance, and increased use of Section One monies are the most obvious responses to unemployment and many of the social workers we interviewed appeared to get more and more involved in such work. But as indicated elsewhere in this book there is considerable ambivalence about this, both at fieldwork and managerial level:

> You make all the arrangements you can for fuel direct, rent out cooking equipment etc . . . until the DHSS and the fuel boards sort it out . . . I think what's happening is, and I think it's a by-product of unemployment, is that we are becoming poor law relieving officers and I don't want to be a poor law relieving officer [senior social worker].
>
> So much of the work is becoming money work . . . I'm not sure social services are the right people to deal with this [district manager].

Providing support in relation to the emotional and psychological effects of unemployment on an individual, family or group basis meets with similar reservations. Counselling people tends to be regarded as not dealing with the real problem, ie not having a job. Furthermore, this kind of support tends to be seen as helping people cope and accept their unemployment and social workers would thereby become involved in legitimising the problem:

> We will be trying to help people accept unemployment. This is in complete contrast with what social work is about, prevention, intervention, and trying to cure the situation. Helping people accept their situation is something I don't like. It means helping people to fit the system instead of changing the system.

At one level then, it appears to be the interplay between the social construction of *unemployment* and the way the established social work model is being defined which inhibits the development of social services responses to problems associated with unemployment. However, the images social services professionals have of *unemployed clients* are also an important factor.

Though many of the social workers we spoke to pointed out that unemployment is not a new phenomenon among people in contact with social services, the relevance of labour market disadvantage and unemployment to their problems seems to have been largely ignored. The recession with its dramatic increase in the number of people experiencing unemployment has had some effect and some of the social workers in our sample were beginning to be more sensitive to labour market issues:

> It has only recently filtered through to me that unemployment can be an important factor in the lives of people I work with. Social workers generally are not aware enough of unemployment as a specific issue. Particularly when working in a long term team, clients have other serious problems and it is often difficult to sort out what is due to what. Unemployment is often not picked out as a major factor.

However, only a very small proportion of the social workers we interviewed explicitly stated that unemployment was the main cause of a client's problem and that a lot of people would not be in contact with social services if they were not unemployed.

Our data suggest that this situation is related to the distinction social service professionals tend to make between unemployed people who receive social service support and unemployed people not in contact with social services. Only the latter seem to be defined as the real unemployed.

'People made redundant, and still unemployed, the genuine unemployed, don't on the whole become social work cases . . . '

In the case of clients, employment problems are more often perceived as the result of personal problems rather than the cause of the difficulties they are experiencing. The following statements are the most extreme ones made to us, but even the more subtle statements suggest that many of the individuals and families who are experiencing unemployment and receiving long term support are seen as somehow 'personally inadequate':

> We are dealing with difficulties and with inadequate people . . . the unemployed aren't so we can't deal with them.
>
> Unemployment is not relevant to social work . . . Most clients who are unemployed always have been . . . unemployment then is the result of a person's life, not put on them . . . you need to look at why a person is unemployed, why a person can't keep a job, look at factors in the family.

These perceptions are operating at a very general level. When considering specific groups a more complex picture emerges and it seems that the employment problems of some groups are much more visible than those of other groups.

Young people are very visible. Their unemployment is regarded as totally unacceptable and consequently their unemployment related problems create a lot of concern both in terms of what it means for the young people themselves and what it implies for social work practice:

> Unemployment does make my work difficult. You are dealing with teenagers and if the person has no hope of work, how do you deal with them? How do you speak with them if they don't see a future.

So the social workers in our sample who indicated that they were spending more time helping people find paid employment were invariably referring to activities with young people. This contrasted quite sharply with their approach to employment problems of people with disabilities or with a history of mental illness. Here there appears to be an acceptance of labour market inequalities and the total marginalisation of these groups:

> In this area 'normal' people feel that there is no work available. So I have also changed my attitude. I am no longer pushing my clients [people with a history of mental illness] towards jobs. I am afraid that they will fail to get a job, which makes the situation worse.

The perceptions of women's experience of unemployment are the most complex. Women's family role and their earning capacity in the labour market tend to be the major factors in whether or not their unemployment is seen as important [McKee and Bell, 1985; Coyle, 1984]. Among our sample of social workers most women of economically active age on their caseload were single parents. There was a strong tendency not to include them when discussing the impact of unemployment on their practice. For example one social worker when asked whether there had been an increase in the number of unemployed among her clients, replied that she was not aware of any increase because most of the people she worked with, were single parents. Their problem was not unemployment but poverty. It was only among the very young single parents that unemployment was seen as relevant.

The overwhelming majority of case studies we collected of social workers' involvement with unemployed clients were family case studies and focussed on the experiences of men as individuals or in families. Though women were seen to be adversely affected by the unemployment of other family members, their own unemployment was far less visible. Social services appear to reflect the popular image that unemployment is essentially a man's experience.

Social issues and individual needs: the great divide

So far we have argued that social services have failed to develop a response to unemployment because, in relation to the problems people receiving social work support are experiencing, unemployment is either not seen as relevant or as no more than an aggravating factor. And even where unemployment is perceived as the cause of people's problems, responses are very limited because of the emphasis on unemployment as a *social issue*. As a result social services support in relation to *individual* health and welfare needs is considered trivial. It is important to recognise that this divide is not confined to the area of unemployment. It comes up when looking at poverty and social work or at any other structural factor which might affect the lives of social services clients [Barter, 1973; Becker and MacPherson, 1985a].

In terms of practice social service professionals appear to be unable to translate social issues like unemployment or poverty into individual needs and vice versa, and to deal with them in an integrated way. They seem to approach them as two distinctly separate areas and not as interactive areas. Social issues are not seen as a collective term for individual needs which have a structural basis, but solely as 'the system'. Within this framework responding to social issues means 'changing the system' and responding to individual needs is seen as in conflict with this, as it will adjust people to the system or in more radical terms 'prop up' the system [Bull, 1970; Holman, 1973].

Obviously, it is not that the structure of our society does not need changing. But in this process individual clients or client groups should be involved as *actors*. Responding to individual needs is an essential part of this because through addressing such needs social workers create the potential to address the social issue in partnership with people and work for structural changes.

There is another dimension. The views social workers expressed to us about their way of working indicate that there is confusion about *the method* and *content* of practice. An individually oriented approach tends to be seen as equivalent to working on 'individual' changes which in turn is regarded as synonymous with helping people adjust to their situation. Community oriented work, on the other hand, is seen as equivalent to working on 'social' changes which in turn is defined as changing the system.

The associations social workers appear to make between method and content of particular ways of practice seem to us to be unsound. Helping to bring about changes on an individual level does not have to mean making people accept their situation and does not necessarily exclude working on 'social' changes. It can in fact involve a process of empowering individual clients [Pearson, forthcoming]. Similarly, using a community oriented method of practice does not automatically imply working on 'social' changes. Unless critical attention is being paid to content, it might be no more than the application of the often criticised case work model at a group level instead of an individual level.

What can be done?

In terms of social work practice unemployment is a complex problem and the contribution social services can make is clearly limited. However, social services can no longer afford to ignore the relevance of unemployment to their practice. In this final section we want to indicate briefly some ways for social services to move forward and develop responses which recognise and address both the structural roots of individual and family problems and the personal pain involved.

Both fieldworkers and managers need to look critically at their perceptions of unemployment and the unemployed and at the way they conceptualise models for practice. At present the framework in which they are operating largely 'defines out' a social services role. It is only in this way that progress can be made in the development of responses.

Responses are possible at three related levels. First, systematic record-keeping of employment status and employment history, and monitoring the effects of unemployment on people receiving social work support and on social services are important. This will not only help to inform practice and contribute to the planning of more appropriate services, it is also essential for the development of a strong advocacy role. When dealing with a structural problem like unemployment taking on such a role is one of the most obvious ways of trying to bring about structural change. As Atlee pointed out 67 years ago:

> The social worker must have definite views and must have formed some clear conception of what society he [sic] wishes to see produced . . . I think it is a mistake for him to hold aloof from social reform movements . . . The social worker has as much right to make clear his views to anybody else . . . Every social worker is almost certain to be also an agitator. If he or she learns social facts and believes they are due to certain causes which are beyond the power of an individual to remove, it is impossible to rest contented with the limited amount of good that can be done by following old methods [Attlee, 1920].

Second, social services can contribute to extending people's rights and access to resources. As argued at various places in this book, providing a good welfare rights service is an important aspect of this. However, social services also have a role to play in facilitating people's access to other local resources. For instance, since 1979 unemployment initiatives have proliferated, particularly in the voluntary sector. They represent a potentially valuable resource for people experiencing unemployment. But if clients are to benefit from local initiatives, social services need to be actively involved in building up contacts with such projects, informing people about and referring them to these local resources. Third and finally, extending people's rights and access to resources is also about non-stigmatising services. When carrying out our research we identified examples of such services which were provided on a universal basis yet positively discriminated towards those experiencing unemployment, or were developed with active involvement of recipients and eventually run by them [Popay and Dhooge, 1986].

Perhaps most importantly, for responses to be developed at these three levels a concerted effort by managers as well as field workers is essential. We cannot ask field workers to take more account of unemployment in their practice if managers keep saying 'unemployment is not really a social services' issue'.

Notes

1. The research on which this article is based was funded by the Health Education Council. The study took place in three areas in Britain and involved both health and social services. Following the research a two year training initiative, *Responding to Unemployment*, was set up to encourage health and social services to consider the relevance of unemployment for their practice and explore how they can respond. This project was funded by the King Edward's Hospital Fund for London, the Baring Foundation, the Central Council for Education and Training in Social Work and the former Health Education Council.

22

Housing, Homelessness and Social Work

Alan Murie

1987 was the United Nations International Year of Shelter for the Homeless. During that year very much more attention has been given to homelessness. Britain is by no means alone in experiencing a rise in homelessness over recent years. However, it has been the dramatic increase in homelessness in Britain rather than the IYSH which has brought homelessness back on to the agenda. Figures for households accepted as homeless by local authorities have risen dramatically [Table 22.1]. And these figures by no means represent the scale of the problem. Hidden homelessness and especially homelessness among single persons and childless couples is not reflected among these figures. In many other countries, and in Britain in the past, homelessness was regarded as a problem associated with personal inadequacy and deviance. However, the post-war development of policy in Britain has been associated with an acceptance that homelessness was a problem arising from the supply and access to housing. As a housing problem homelessness became the primary responsibility of housing departments and responsibility was shifted away from social service departments. In the 1980s housing departments' capacity to deal with homelessness has been increasingly open to question. Increasing inequality and poverty, the impact of the recession, rising unemployment and demographic change have coincided with a decline in the supply of rented housing [including those rented from local authorities]. The need for rented accommodation has grown in a period when local housing authorities' capacity to meet it has declined. In order to cope with this situation and with the rising levels of homelessness which have resulted, local authorities have adopted policies which often exacerbate rather than relieve the circumstances of the homeless. The most striking example of this is the increasing use of bed and breakfast accommodation for the homeless. While this development raises questions about housing policy and practice it also raises questions about the role played by other social services and especially the extent to which these services have adjusted to the needs of a key group of disadvantaged people.

Table 22.1

Homelessness acceptances

	England	London
1979	52,700	16,600
1980	62,920	17,480
1981	70,010	18,470
1982	74,800	21,100
1983	78,240	24,050
1984	83,550	24,820
1985	93,780	27,390
1986	102,980	30,036

Source: *Shelter Fact Sheets* and Department of Environment

Legislation and practice

The Housing [Homeless Persons] Act 1977 completed the post-war process of shifting responsibility for homelessness to housing departments. The legislation was significantly amended during its parliamentary progress [Richards, 1981] and never reflected the aspirations of pressure groups, especially in relation to definitions of priority needs and to the inclusion of 'tests' of intentionality and a local connection. The Act imposed a duty on local authorities to provide housing for people 'unintentionally homeless' if they were in 'priority need' of accommodation and had a 'local connection'. The Act was primarily intended for those with dependent children and continued to marginalise the single homeless [Watson, 1986]. Since the legislation the numbers of people being accepted in the homelessness category have risen significantly and many local authorities in developing their housing service have redirected resources towards the homeless and others in the greatest housing need.

However, this is by no means an indication of even qualified success. Four initial observations on the operation of legislation are relevant:

1. Many of those currently housed as homeless would previously have been housed through another route [say the waiting list].
2. Many local authorities use the legislation to minimise the number of households accepted as priority homeless.
3. Many local authorities have continued to use 'deterrent' hostel and temporary accommodation for priority homeless households.
4. Homeless households commonly are given few offers and 'worse' offers for accommodation than others being allocated permanent council housing.

The development of homelessness legislation has not increased the supply of housing available to those in the most acute housing need and 'homelessness' has often been absorbed into council housing management. It provides an 'official' category which helps allocators and managers to categorise applicants and ensure that there are households desperate enough to accept and unable to refuse [if they refuse they may be seen as intentionally homeless and undeserving] those properties which other categories of applicants would not accept. This absorption of the homeless category so that it is of mixed benefit to those who are in it is not an inevitable consequence of legislation although the preoccupation with abuse and intentionality does make this more likely.

Experience in respect of homelessness since the passage of the Housing [Homeless Persons] Act 1977 has reinforced the view that those who become homeless are normal, local households affected by housing shortages. The vast majority of households accepted as homeless lived in the same borough, district or county as the borough of acceptance one month before acceptance and this applied to over 80 per cent of cases one year before acceptance.

Rather than the legislation, the homeless themselves or the policy implementers being 'at fault', the time *when* the legislation was introduced was not the most favourable. The housing market restructuring and decline of private renting, which are widely recognised as generating the demand for legislation, were not terminated by it. The decline has continued. Moreover, other factors have exacerbated the situation. Watson states:

> The most important point about the Act was the economic context in which it was passed. The Act was brought into force at a time

when Britain was suffering severe effects of economic recession. By 1977 in Britain the gross domestic product was below the 1973/74 level in real terms; there had been successive cutbacks in current spending on public housing since 1976, and capital expenditure [on new and renovated housing] in the public sector [including housing associations] had fallen in real terms every year since 1975. The crucial point, therefore, was that there was a wide gap between the intentions of the Act and the resources provided to meet its requirements. Inevitably the result of the situation was an increased hostility towards the homeless. They were seen to be 'jumping the queue' of those people 'in real housing need' on the waiting list, they were the new scroungers and rent evaders. The right-wing elements of the media had a hey-day [Watson, 1986, 67].

In the 1980s the decline of public renting has been added to the decline of private renting. Opportunities to rent at all have declined. This is a new situation in the 1980s. At the same time economic recession and the end of the period of full employment have generated new demands for lower price accommodation. There are a growing number of failed owners and poorer households are priced out of private renting in inner city areas. The increase in the size of the marginalised population has coincided with a decline in the supply of accommodation to them. Various evidence shows a trend for the marginalised poor to funnel towards social rented housing [eg Forrest and Murie, 1983]. However, in the 1980s the outlet from the funnel has been becoming more restricted.

It is this changing environment which involves some *new* elements in homelessness. There are important continuities in the class characteristics of households. However, in contrast to the 1960s, homelessness is less likely to result from landlord action and the households involved are less likely to be in employment.

There is a further perspective on this view of 'causes of homelessness'. It is to seek to distinguish between immediate and underlying causes and argues that, for example, family disputes result from tensions created by problems of obtaining employment – especially for younger people.

The new homeless are more obviously affected by economic change and restructuring rather than housing market changes alone. One consequence is that the homeless include those most vulnerable to economic change, those who have not yet negotiated access to council housing or home ownership, and those whose economic vulnerability threatens their continuing occupation of current housing. This involves younger households and those in vulnerable economic groups, those with recent or substantial mortgages or affected by marital breakdown. The prominence of black households reflects both their historic under-representation in council housing and their economic position. Women headed households form another group more heavily represented among the new homeless.

Bed and breakfast homelessness

There is another dimension to the new homelessness in Britain. The significant growth of homelessness in recent years has been accompanied by an increasing use of temporary accommodation in bed and breakfast hotels. In 1980/81 there were 32,000 homeless households in temporary accommodation in England and Wales. By 1985/86 this figure had risen to 41,000. In 1985/86 some 17 per cent of homeless households were initially housed in bed and breakfast accommodation and 20 per cent in hostels [compared with 12 per cent and 16 per cent respectively in 1979/80].

The experience of the new homeless is less likely to be of rapid permanent rehousing or of a short stay in temporary accommodation than was true in the past. Homelessness acceptances and the use of bed and breakfast accommodation in London is highest in some inner London boroughs where high prices in the owner occupied and privately rented market pose particularly severe problems for lower income households.

Table 22.2

Homeless households placed by London councils in bed and breakfast and other types of temporary accommodation

	Numbers in B & B	Numbers in other temporary accommodation
Jun 1981	890	3,760
Jun 1982	1,300	3,570
Jun 1983	1,807	3,280
Jun 1984	2,357	3,730
Jun 1985	3,251	4,140
Jun 1986	5,206	5,522
Sep 1986	6,142	5,901

* Includes hostels, short-life schemes etc.
Source: *Shelter Fact Sheet and Surveys*, 1986.

Perhaps the most effective way of illustrating the new position of the homeless is to refer to interview data for households in bed and breakfast accommodation [see Murie, 1987]. Interviews completed in London do not present identical histories. There is a variation in the nature of accommodation, in previous experience and in encounters with officialdom. However, the variation is within a low standard sector. For families, cramped space, lack of privacy and absence of playspace is severe. While lack of privacy is most likely to be expressed by adults, children's awareness of their housing situation is evident in expressions about their lack of a home. All of these factors contribute to behavioural and psychological problems and to increasing stress in the family. These problems are made worse the longer the time spent in such accommodation. Moreover, they are complicated by the impact of this form of housing on ability to maintain or obtain work, by the lack of social service, health care and other facilities targetted on a 'temporary' population and by the distancing from kinship and community networks. A wider range of health and safety issues are directly linked with conditions in the hotel. The inadequacy of cooking and toilet facilities, problems of sharing and overuse, and inadequate cleaning are directly linked to bouts of sickness, weight loss and faster development of latent health conditions. These are also linked to lack of fresh air and play space and dependence on takeaway food often with low nutritional value. The lack of kitchen, cooking and food storage facilities forces families to rely on what is an expensive as well as unhealthy coping strategy. Pressure on budgets also arises from lack of laundry and especially drying facilities for clothes. The facilities in hotels are not suitable for long stay residents in these and other ways. The status of the homeless has turned full circle – from households with individual and personal problems rather than housing problems, to households where the response to their housing needs generates health, work and other personal problems! Heating, electrical and other safety, the provision of hot water and facilities for visiting or telephoning all leave a lot to be desired. In late 1984 a fire in a hotel in Westminster resulted in the death of an Asian mother and two young children placed in the hotel by the London Borough of Camden. Other fires and incidents have not led to any response which has reduced the use of bed and breakfast accommodation.

Even though the costs of hotels are higher than almost any alternative form of provision [Greve *et al*, 1986; Walker, 1987], the pressure for policy change has had almost no impact. The antagonism of central government to increased spending on municipal housing has not been affected by evidence of wasted expenditure or low standards. The lack of political power of the homeless has been evident from evictions by Tower Hamlets and is apparent in the actual histories of individuals. One explanation for the quality of service being delivered lies in the very powerlessness of the homeless, their lack of economic and political bargaining power and the ease with which the category 'homeless' can be manipulated and associated with undeserving and undesirable categories. Hotels are expensive and although the accommodation is totally inadequate there is a confusion over how generous provision is. The families involved are aware that if they were able to use the same level of resources to obtain other accommodation they could establish more satisfactory homes for their families. They could also begin to increase their independence because it would be easier to find work. The benefit and 'credibility' problems associated with working [usually in low paid jobs] while living in a hotel are generally regarded as insurmountable. And, in some cases, becoming homeless had led to loss of employment. The response to this situation adds to depression and frustration. Some families retain a belief that they should wait patiently for rehousing – others make more vociferous demands. While a feeling of powerlessness pervades this should not be interpreted as resignation or apathy. The families involved develop active coping strategies to help children attend schools and to develop social contacts. Some adults [usually the men] can spend a lot of time away from the hotel and their family. Women, and usually those with younger children and those most at risk of harassment, are trapped all day long in hotels.

The disruption experienced by the bed and breakfast homeless has various dimensions. The location of hotels is in established hotelling areas – not the areas where families lived. Schooling and friendships have been disrupted and the neighbourhoods are more threatening. Distance from familiar neighbourhoods and communities involves a break in caring and friendship networks and less familiarity with available services and resources. General problems of poverty and low income are exacerbated by loss of possessions and loss of community support. The very fact of moving requires renegotiation with health and income maintenance services and 'temporary' status means that this negotiation is often difficult. The experience of homeless families [who have moved house regularly] in these negotiations is more difficult than that of poor families in general although some have found real support from health visitors, social workers or voluntary organisations. The most directly involved local authority department – the housing department – often maintains sporadic contact and homeless families have no real appreciation of how long they will be in hotels or of how best they can negotiate permanent housing. Some of this reflects the general pressures placed on local authority housing but there is variation in response which reflects policy.

Many of these problems are equally experienced by homeless single people although issues of crowding and privacy are less apparent. Among both families and single homeless people issues of racism and racial harassment are important, given the disproportionate number of families from ethnic minority groups among the homeless.

Most of this paper has referred to official homelessness and it has been argued that there are new elements in relation to this group. It is important to acknowledge [briefly] that these same new elements also affect other homeless households. The preceding discussion has referred to families in priority need and the groups of 'vulnerable' persons accepted in official policies. These do not represent the full extent of homelessness.

It is important to acknowledge that while in London in 1984/85 some 42,000 homeless households were placed in temporary accommodation and some 75,000 were accepted in official priority need homeless categories there were some 150,000 to 200,000 sharers, 80 per cent of whom would prefer to live separately. On another estimate there were some 300,000 potential households, many of which could be regarded as potentially homeless, given their modest incomes and savings and poor prospects of rehousing in the rented sector. Moreover, it is also important to distinguish between the flow of new homeless households and the number in homeless categories at any time. All of these issues are concerned both with numbers and with the characteristics of the homeless – for example, moving away from official definitions increases the importance of the single homeless.

Discussion

Legislative and public acknowledgement of homelessness as the extreme form of housing stress experienced by ordinary decent people has resulted in substantial rehousing of homeless people. In comparison with some countries and with the past this may imply increasing the bargaining power and access of the homeless. However, the change is not as dramatic as might be assumed. Flaws in the legislation, lack of resources to mobilise on behalf of the homeless and a changing economic, housing and political environment have been reflected both in the nature and scale of homelessness and in responses to it. The problems and dislocations associated with bed and breakfast accommodation in particular raise questions about how the housing service deals with its clients and how capable other services are of redeploying resources and directing advice, assistance and other provision towards people without 'permanent addresses' and who are 'temporary' residents. Social security, medical and social services procedures often involve special hurdles for such groups. The impression is that many of these services are inclined to see the bed and breakfast homeless as a transient group for which there is limited priority in organising provision. In reality this group – and others among the homeless – are likely to remain a substantial group requiring substantial support over long periods. The need for services other than housing to review how their resources are deployed in relation to homelessness is not removed by legislation which places primary responsibility on a service which is struggling – and failing – to meet need.

23

A Pocket of Small Change

David Townsend

MOST directors of social services agree broadly about poverty's two main ingredients: a lack of cash and of self-fulfilling opportunities. The two are like a game of Russian dolls. However that same majority of directors of social services believes it is not their prime responsibility to take on the problems of income support or cash provision. Ironically, perhaps, the Association of Directors of Social Services' newly adopted constitution refers in one of the articles to 'the relief of poverty' as a fundamental aim. In particular circumstances of financial poverty there is certainly a limited discretion to be exercised. But it is secondary to the creation of personal opportunities through what are intended to be custom built services. After that there is a directorial babel of voices. Views about how to relieve or eliminate poverty will prove as varied as the local authorities for which each director works, though probably not more diverse than the political views of those who employ them.

National and local political fashions play a part in defining poverty and, more importantly, shape the policies of how or sometimes *if*, to tackle it. Some are new or perhaps only exhumed but represent a break with tradition. Thus Mrs Thatcher's New York speech in 1975 entitled 'Let Our Children Grow Tall' in which she said: 'The fact about economic inequality [as opposed to the myth] is that the rich are getting poorer and the poor are getting richer', indicated unequivocally what direction her policies were likely to take.

There are enduring themes; none more so than sexual inequality. *Working Class Wives*, a study published by Pelican Books in 1939 recommended, long before the advent of the Personal Social Services:

> A considerable increase in the number of nursery schools and day nurseries and **highly desirable** that the educational system of this country should be developed in such a way that each child should have provided for him by the community the education best suited for his abilities and needs, instead of such a provision being, as at present, largely dependent on the income of his parents [Spring-Rice, 1939, 191].

This same book recommended the introduction of a scheme of family allowances **payable to the mother,** but commented that the wholehearted support of the Labour Party and the TUC was not behind such a scheme. This lack of support may also be said to be an enduring theme.

Then there may be selective or universalist arguments in the ascendant at any one time, though there is always rationing. The 1970s *cause célèbre* for disabled people of mobility allowance versus invalid trikes was a case in point. Legislation will circumscribe the extent to which any free choice will be allowed to a local authority to deal with aspects of poverty. There may be specially designed weaknesses and exclusions which prevent or deter help to certain groups: there may be requirements, for example, to inspect and regulate private residential homes. And in each local authority poverty will manifest itself differently and with subtle [and not so subtle] dimensional changes. For example, the added problem of racial discrimination and other forms of racism may overlay or worse, underpin a particular form of poverty whether unemployment, shortage of suitable accommodation, or access to holiday schemes for elderly people.

The arguments about how best to spread municipal services includes questions of means tests and charges. If a national climate, warm toward both, has been established, then the likelihood is at local level such impositions will be accepted with less argument. For those local politicians who secretly believe or publicly pronounce that the chief source of poverty is the level of the local rate, then a post-means test fall in demand for a service, say 'home helps', will prove to their satisfaction that a more basic provision has replaced unnecessary luxury.

A director's position in such arguments is likely, at times, to be equivocal. To take an extreme example, if the only likelihood of increased cash to expand a service to meet further identified needs is by means-test, then that director may weigh up the least-worst choice; the arguments reflecting that emphasis. Depending on the strength of council members' political opinions the arguments of the director may or may not be influential.

What is common too, at least in some Labour controlled authorities, is a minutely detailed election manifesto to which the director of social services must have regard. The director should also have a thick skin, because blame for the inability to fulfil the politician's millennialist aspirations in a year or two, will be shared about equally between the occupant of No. 10 Downing Street and the director of social services. The manifesto usually contains specific promises about the vaguer aims and vague promises about what could be quite specific. For example, 'we will create a better environment' and 'we will work towards more residential places for mentally handicapped people'. They are the necessary result of compromises and an uneasy coalition of interests within a controlling political group. Other directors who now work for 'hung' councils believe a qualification in psephological or astrological studies is an even greater advantage there. So one directorial attribute required is opportunism. A half chance to improve or increase a necessary service must be taken, regardless of any overall strategy which might exist; indeed in some local authorities, the half chance is the essence of the strategy.

There are also conflicts between policies. Various agreements made by councils with their own staffs for overtly political reasons result in restrictions on the ability of departments to develop policy. For example, as a result of agreements made by councils with their own architects and direct labour organisations, it may cost many hundreds of thousands of pounds more to provide day nurseries than it would using outside firms.

Not raising council rents will certainly help some people keep money in their pockets. It may keep votes in the right place too. But it will certainly cost a council dear. £1 million or more government subsidy may be lost for every time rents are not even raised in line with inflation. And that will make the task of trying to provide resources for children's day care or centres for elderly confused people all the harder. Such facilities do provide, if not in cash, then certainly in kind a great relief to the burdens of poverty of opportunity. Not just for the children who benefit in many ways – in social or multi-cultural contact and educational content – or elderly mentally inform people who are warm, cared for and stimulated, but those who otherwise would carry the day [and night long] responsibility of caring. The vast majority are women. It is perhaps here, overall, that any director, no matter what his or her own particular approach or personal views might be, could define a strategy to advocate allocation of resources and priorities. It would be a route out of 'care in the community' and into 'who cares in communities'? However, the director will not be surprised to find that in the swirling contradictions, limitations and bureaucracy of local government it is rarely a sellers' market.

So acknowledging all the restrictions and controls which surround the director as an employee of a local authority, and trying to avoid direct competition between one part of the service and another for resources, a director might start from the simple premise that what benefits women in the community is likely to make a major impact on counteracting poverty.

That could be by indirect financial means, through subsidised care services, but directly by opportunities offered to women as carers, mothers or income earners. A programme which looked at how to support, relieve or enhance the lives of carers would be of immense benefit. It could be specific; it would also offer job opportunities to those same people, and the question of employment chances in a selectively expanding social services department should not be overlooked as a limited counter to poverty. It would, in some parts of the country, catch a tide of political interest in what matters to women; usually, what always has. There are three obvious examples.

A director of social services will know roughly the total number of mentally handicapped people cared for by families in his or her authority. If he or she does not, then a priority must be to find the means to get to know. The number will be likely to range from a few hundred to perhaps four or five thousand. The facilities to help support their care will be almost uniformly limited. Over a four or five year period a relatively modest sum set aside each year [out of a real growth rate which usually varies from not more than one per cent to five per cent] could, with additional monies from other agencies, for example the Health Service or Inner Area Programmes, transform the position.

The same is true of day care for small children. Minimally, it is well within the bounds of possibility for fifty places in day care to be provided every year for five years in each local authority, at a cost, [free of restrictive, vested interest] which would not be substantially more than a fraction in the same years of money spent on Section One to keep children out of care, agency placements to put children in private and voluntary homes, community homes, enhanced payments to foster parents and the paraphernalia of child abuse registers. Indeed while it is speculation, it is not unreasonable to suggest that such an expanded programme might reduce the need for expenditure in all of those areas over a period of years.

Thirdly there are several hundred thousand elderly mentally infirm people in England and Wales, whose only care is predominantly from their daughters, or other women relatives or friends whose own possible fulfilment in their lives has come at a sacrificial end. At the very least there ought to be in each local authority the prospect of respite care, or part-week day care and domiciliary support to those women and their families. The costs, for the range of services described, would be less per week than the DHSS now pays for private residential care for those whose needs are frequently far from desperate. Each of these priorities is well within the reach of almost any social services department in England and Wales. Of course there are other allocations demanded, and other demands become priorities. There will always be differences between local authorities in what they define as a local priority.

And yet, while these may be the aims, hesitation, qualification and reservations begin before the concepts are even dry on the page. If a policy to help pre-school and their families is not to remain on the fancy promises shelf, it cannot be just more of the same. Incrementalism is not enough. But nor can plans be based on vague goodwill and a feeling that every family ought to have access to day care support as a right. If, to take an example from one end of the needs graph, a respite care scheme to help sustain families with handicapped children is established, then it must be respite. Such schemes are, per child, among the most expensive of social services activities. [Though not more expensive than a great many other schemes would be if they too were personalised and small scale as the Personal Social Services are intended to be.]

So, to allow by default or misguided good intention, a respite scheme to become a permanent prop is to undermine the will of families to look after their own. It would also deny to other families a necessary or desired support which is an inducement to continue caring and an easement of the difficulties in doing so. Social services are not in the business of forcing families to look after their dependants, as politicians as diverse as the Ancient Athenians and President [then Governor] Reagan have attempted. Social services departments, on behalf of their local authorities certainly do care full time and permanently for thousands of different individuals; but these are people for whom there was no other way at the time or perhaps in the future. The department's purpose is positively to encourage care by families and friends. Such encouragement must, inevitably, take different forms.

All this points up the fact that there are bound to be many dilemmas in a social services department looking at poverty but hedged in by over 20 Acts of Parliament, supported by very different local economies, elected councils and with essentially particular requests for help. Targetting of limited services and strictly applied criteria for access are the automatic consequences. So, for example, day nurseries by themselves are only a partial answer. There is a current fashion which at its extreme decrees they have no modern use, though the parents of users might well disagree, *nem con*. 'Family centres' in all their 57 varieties are the flavour of the decade, and very good some of them are. They represent greater parental, sibling, group or community involvement, sometimes control but always with an emphasis on maximum informality. Since one of poverty's faces is powerlessness, then the family centre could be an indirect counter to that.

To a similar extent lack of choice is both an indication of poverty, and certainly a result. Social services departments are in the business of encouraging choice so while day nurseries and family centres both have a significant place in providing different kinds of support to families, so too do subsidised or grant-aided self-help groups, childminders and day fostering arrangements.

These elements in a programme will founder in confusion, however, unless it is clear who are, and who are not, going to be the immediate, medium term and longer range beneficiaries. Talk of priorities does induce a sinking feeling among directors, chairpersons and social services committees. But priorities are the only way to dispose of the bargains-galore manifesto approach. And, for some of those members of councils not so readily disposed to spend public money, priorities provide a reasoned, and planned, way to help people over a measured period of time. Value for money ought to be built in to any service. Assuming there is agreement on priorities then the policy will not be in difficulties; disagreement means it will be in tatters. The more so if potential users have been a party to consultations about developments.

The most severe limitations on directors and committees in exercising a wide discretion apply across all user ages and conditions in the absence of bottomless purses, limitless human resources and elaborate accommodation programmes. For under-fives, social services directors have child protection at the top of the priorities; that means, shorn of any other arguments protecting them from neglect or physical and emotional abuse. In that, of course, sexual abuse has emerged from a special secrecy to being a blazing front page concern. Good ideas like helping parents to find jobs or 'socialising' children in day care have to take second place. So too do inclinations to help low paid social services staff by using an existing service to care for their own children, while they work. Each of those suggestions would undoutedly help, individually, to relieve hardship or even poverty, and at least alleviate some of the problems, but cannot be entertained at the expense of risk to children.

If, in discussing small children, the proposals begin to resemble policy by caveat, so they are in the case of another major dependent group of people; frail, confused elderly citizens. Most of them have probably already experienced a degree of personal poverty in their own lives, though gradually, ownership of property, occupational pensions and generally better health will reduce that number in future generations. Indeed, that process is already in train and only the very poorest, weakest and isolated are likely to come to rely on local authority services. That is, of course, because they have to. Choice is denied them because they are so often alone. Increasingly, as with other vulnerable groups and individuals in society, they could be sidelined, and quite deliberately become a residual problem: part of 'the poor we ever have with us', to use a favourite Victorian maxim.

In facing their poverty and the enforced hardship which their dependency sometimes spreads to those relations and friends who care for them, the social services department has to extend choice so far as possible. A department must concentrate services where they best create opportunities for relief. While many should and will benefit, even more will not. Those who can be supported or temporarily relieved of responsibility, must above all be reassured that the service offered whether directly or by another agency, is a kind, well-resourced and fair one. Many old people's homes in the public sector are poor: lack of proper investment neglect of facilities and self-serving staff are contributory factors. At their worst they are an outrage. They *increase* poverty and spice it with a degree of cruelty. At their best they are as good as human generosity can make them. Choice is there: stimulating companionship; even a sense of belonging. But is part III what is required? Is a well run economy class hotel the best way of providing opportunity into old age?

The answer is probably no, though since the discussion centres on human behaviour, a qualified 'no'. Assuming, and a little assumption is a dangerous thing, that proper medical services are available when required – less likely than ten years ago – then privacy is one of the choices which ought to be available. That is a privacy paid for by the public purse. It is increasingly more the standard in the bourgeoning private sector, financed by the public and inspected by public servants, than in local authority homes. It is a director's job to persuade council members that the enjoyment of old age ought to be indivisible between those in the Golden Acres Private Home and the Alderman Pennyfarthing Elderly Persons Home. Converting some of the latter type of homes from the economics of large scale, group living to individually supported care is very expensive. Nevertheless, it must be done, preferably by setting sights on the abandonment of part III homes and their replacement by sheltered accommodation, localised day centres and domiciliary services. Given the recent expansion of private homes there is clearly scope for a much bolder policy toward, and for, elderly people and their cares.

However differently priorities may be defined a solid core of poverty remains common to all. There has been an inexorable increase in measureable hardship, brought about by continuously high levels of unemployment spreading across the past decade. It is based on a government philosophy rooted in the expense of individual success at the cost of community goodwill and care. The sharp elbow against the comforting arm. The need for social services departments to create opportunities to counteract poverty's worst effects is therefore even more important. While social service departments have significant a role to play in welfare rights work the fact is that if the welfare rights themselves are simply non-existent or at best mean, then advocacy is a question of arguing with brick walls. The new Social Security Act is in itself a wall, dividing even more drastically the poor from the really poor, and both from the rest of society. But the new Act has an added dimension. With the inclusion of the 'new' though conceptually ancient, Social Fund in the Social Security Act, social services staff may find themselves on the wrong side of the wall. Far from simply arguing for entry for the poor as now, they will be auxiliary gatekeepers for a government policy to reduce expenditure on the poorest.

Setting up teams of welfare rights workers in social services offices has its advantages; it is clear where people can obtain advice and sometimes advocacy, and most people who use social services are poor. It is also clear what it will cost. The same is true of the establishment in some health centres of welfare rights work; there is a close link between ill health and poverty. But there is a limit to what any bureaucracy open from 9.00 am-5.00pm can provide. Welfare rights might more satisfactorily be available in a non-statutory way, available outside office hours, through a network system of informed users supported by paid staff, funded, though not necessarily employed directly by a local authority. It would be a way of assisting poor people to gain independence, achieve self-help and prevent them becoming even further dependent on another system of public support. That same principle applies to the extent to which a social services department can encourage, frequently more economically, and certainly to better effect, the development of services which will overcome the special disadvantages suffered by minority ethnic communities. Those disadvantages related to cultural, religious, race and language differences as well as by access difficulties to what is already provided by local authorities. There is a growing movement within minority ethnic communities to provide self-sufficient and self-managed services. It represents a real chance to plan *strategically* with minority ethnic consumers; it is a way, as with other consumers, of making choice available, of letting the users and would-be users define their own needs, the particular hardships they feel they experience, and then design services to counter them.

The director of social services looking to the 1990s could do worse than aim the services at carers, with some or all management devolved to consumers, free of monolithic and self-interested ideology and based on self-assessment, including private and voluntary provision. These could be the methods, without a reversion to local Poor Law Guardians and an inadequately administered local income support system, by which the Personal Social Services as they are already broadly established can be most effective in challenging poverty where it starts.

24

Getting By and Getting Through:
Living with poverty
Stewart MacPherson

This chapter is in three parts. The first discusses the nature of poverty, and concentrates on the reproduction of personal pain by a socially produced problem. The second looks at some features of family poverty and particularly at the ways in which families respond to external pressure. The chapter concludes with a brief case study. This family is not among the very worst off or the most severely affected. But they are poor and while definitions are discussed and policies are debated, they must live with poverty and do the best they can.

The nature of poverty.

FOR the most part, poverty in Britain is not like the relentless, decimating poverty which affects more than a third of the world's population [MacPherson and Midgley, 1987]. It is poverty relative to the comfortable life of the great majority of people in Britain. This does not make it less tragic or less miserable. A minority poor, surrounded and assaulted by relative affluence, can feel its deprivation as deeply as the majority poor in those places where material poverty is the norm. The pain may take different forms but it is just as real and just as damaging. As evidence of the widening of the gulf between the poor and the comfortable mounts we are forced to acknowledge that there is a prevalent philosophy which truly believes in the right of the wealthy and privileged to inflict injustice on the less fortunate. There is a callous disregard of those who have not succeeded in the unequal struggles for material gain and economic security. Latent social values have gained ground and shown their power; the successful are morally entitled to privileges, the poor should suffer accordingly.

The struggle against these views and their practical expression takes place in many ways, but the ground that is fought over is the lives of the poor themselves. If many of the poorest seem inactive in their own cause, could this be that for most, surviving is a full-time occupation? The poor are simultaneously excluded from the mainstream of a still affluent society and at the same time continously exhorted to pursue its material goals and endlessly spiralling wants. To a greater or lesser extent, all poor people live under what has been described as 'the cutting edge' [Harrison, 1983].

Poverty is a great source of pain, hurt, suffering and distress. Its effects can spread and can last for many years. The arrogance, complacency and blinkered neglect of so many of the comfortable compound the hurt. Despite the evidence, very many scarcely know of the present extent and nature of poverty. Many do not want to know. The conjunction of the material, the social and the psychological is basic to any understanding of poverty, not least in the context of the work of social service departments. Jeremy Seabrook, in a powerful and compelling exploration of the nature of poverty in contemporary Britain argues that:

> poverty in the rich world is an elaborate artefact created by a dynamic process between money on the one hand and its inextricable and living relationship with social and psychological structures on the other [Seabrook, 1984, 90].

It is in these structures that people live their lives.

One of the cruellest tricks played on poor people is that by which they are persuaded that they are personally responsible for their poverty. In an elaborate and wicked deceit, 'individuals can be persuaded to take personal responsibility for a pain that is socially produced' [Seabrook, 1984, 95]. When pain is socially produced it should be a social responsibility, with mutual effort by poor and non-poor alike. But for the most part this has not been so. The operation of the benefits systems, the labour market, the welfare state and the social, economic and psychological structures which maintain the poor in their poverty have compelled the poor to find their own individual answers to surviving socially imposed hardship. Other chapters in this book demonstrate the massive significance for social service and social work departments of contemporary poverty. They demonstrate also the complexity, the dilemmas and the contradictions of the action which those departments seek to take in response to poverty as a social problem and to poverty as a 'personal trouble'.

The pressures

Studies of employment and the family have traditionally been kept separate. The falseness of this divide is shown as unemployment affects employment patterns and creates changing family needs. There have been few attempts to relate employment and the family in a comprehensive way; to relate trends in employment and the labour market with analysis of effects on the family, and the family's use of and dependency on the state social security system. The major link between employment, the family and means-tested welfare benefits is through earnings; indeed much of the social security system is linked to employment status and earnings. Employment status is vital for benefits such as unemployment, maternity, sickness and retirement pensions which are all dependent on contribution records. In particular, eligibility for unemployment benefit is crucially affected by patterns of work. An increasing proportion of unemployed people are dependent on income support and hit by regulations which mean they are unable to qualify for any more benefit, however long they remain unemployed.

The family dimension of unemployment is too often overlooked. Like official measures, most studies, especially large-scale ones, treat the unemployed as individuals and pay relatively little attention to their domestic and family relationships. As Rimmer and Popay [1982] point out, however many workers are registered as unemployed perhaps two or three times as many people are in families directly experiencing unemployment. The family dimension needs development in the analysis of unemployment and its consequences [Fagin and Little, 1984]. For most people unemployment is a debilitating experience, but not an individual one; the vast majority of unemployed – men, women, young and old, – are living in families – where there may be more than one person experiencing unemployment. What little evidence there is suggests that 'multiple unemployment' may be more common than is realised [Hakim, 1982; White, 1983].

Pahl [1984] points to new social divisions emerging based on the number of income earners a household contains. The average family suffering unemployment is not cushioned by the earnings of secondary workers. There are an unknown number of workers currently 'discouraged' from seeking employment by the welfare benefits system and the rules are such that these will be mainly women. Only about half as many wives of unemployed men work as compared to the population as a whole. One crucial factor in this must be the way the state operates its welfare programmes. There are disincentives embodied in the welfare benefits system.

Few discussions of unemployment have included the family dimension; the consequences for families, as well as individuals. Increasingly, earnings within families bear no relation to family needs and responsibilities. Even with two parents in work, more working families are being forced to turn to state support, in the form of Family Credit, an explicit recognition in the state of the inadequacy of wages. But its predecessor [FIS] had one of the lowest take-up rates of the means-tested benefits, about fifty per cent, and there is little reason to expect much better of the new benefit, Family Credit. There are thus many working families with incomes lower than their benefit entitlement. The detailed regulations of entitlement to Family Credit and Income Support relate both to levels of income and hours of work. This sets in train a complex series of choices for families. Decisions as to whether or not to work, whether to work full time or part time, who in the family or household should work and for how long, will all be affected to a very great degree by the operation of the benefit rules as they are operated in practice. Behaviour will clearly also be affected by knowledge of the benefits system and perceptions of how it really operates. Many studies have shown how far these perceptions may be from the 'official view'. The interaction of these constraints with those imposed by the realities of the local economy produces domestic calculations of infinite subtlety and complexity. It may also lead to division, suspicion and emnity within the household [Cusack and Roll, 1985].

Recent changes in the law affecting young unemployed people will undoubtedly put more pressure on already strained households. Very young women are taking the decision to have children as a deliberate strategy which will enable them to leave the parental home when unemployment means that other possibilities are closed off to them. The lack of adequate accommodation for the young, compounded by the multitude of other pressures on them, and their families, is producing very serious problems in many parts of the country [Campbell, 1984].

There is a powerful purpose embodied in the rules and operational practices of the unemployed welfare benefits system – that claimants of welfare need a special stimulus to seek employment; poor people must be forced to work, and for poor wages if necessary. This is despite all the evidence to the contrary, that many poor families work without economic increases legitimises the dismantling of welfare programmes. Mingione sees a cyclical process developing: 'the informalisation process deepens the fiscal crisis of the State and the fiscal crisis accelerates the informalization processes' [1983,320]. The present situation benefits the limited proportion of the working classes with permanent steady jobs, but penalises large groups such as the poor, ethnic minorities, women, the young and the aged and other economically marginal groups who are dependent on their capacity to gain social assistance from the state.

Social and community networks are critical for the economic survival of many poor families. Some studies have found considerable investment by the poor in network members. This produces social obligation for reciprocal action. There is strong pressure for a sharing of economic and social resources; sharing is viewed as a right and proper method of ensuring survival [Stack, 1974; Massiah, 1983]. But it may be that unemployment turns a supportive network of friends and relations into a financial and social drain. A high unemployment rate across a whole community restricts the potential for informal activities and work. If neighbours, relations and friends are all unemployed, no-one has the money to pay for odd jobbing. Network support helps people to cope with job loss. Cheeseman [1975] found a great deal of informal help given by kin and neighbours in the community he studied. But a more recent study by Calleja [1984] found that in fact working class women failed to exploit all available social support networks. She argues that this is a product of the working class ideal of independence and automony. But it may also be a product of a changed economic climate, where unemployment creates new problems beyond the capacity of old responses.

The state, in its various guises, plays an important part in sustaining conventional forms of family life and limits choices open to couples. Various policies based on a set of assumptions about the nature of family life play a part in encouraging and maintaining a particular form of domestic organisation. Most state provision of income maintenance is based on the ideology of a 'normal' family therefore discouraging the development of any alternative forms of organisation; 'tacitly encouraging the standard form of gender and generational relations within families' [Allan, 1985, 169]

The complex of forces acting on the poor has many components. The benefits system and the labour market are the two most immediate. The changes which have taken place in social security provision in recent years have had many serious consequences for poor families. Beyond the effects of inadequate benefit payments there are the effects of the benefits security and for only as much or even less than welfare:

> Contrary to the widely held opinion, what the great majority of poor people need is not a stronger work ethic but added skills and more employment opportunities [Schiller, 1973, 22].

In fact, recipients of benefits often remain largely ignorant or confused about benefit regulations, not knowing whether or by how much employment will raise their incomes. The core of much welfare policy is the persistent distinction between the 'working' poor and the 'non-working' poor.

This is a perverted version of an ethic of self-help and self-reliance. It is combined with a benefits system which first gives families barely sufficient to keep them out of debt, and then subjects them to the most stringent and arbitrary limitations on earnings. These are the forces that encourage moves into the underground informal economy. They discourage formal employment, encourage dishonesty and drive self-help and self-reliance underground, to form a large and growing 'hidden economy' of welfare. Parker [1982] argues that welfare is a nightmare – the antithesis of the Beveridge dream. The regulations are virtually incomprehensible and constantly changing.

This has a two-fold effect; either families steer clear of the whole system, hence the low take-up of many benefits, or they ignore the law and maximise their income from all possible sources, including 'non-legal' ones. Employers take advantage of this and use 'hidden employees' for whom they pay no national insurance [Parker, 1982; Seabrook, 1984].

Britain's social security system is a relic of the past hammered almost beyond recognition by the economic and political forces of the present. It is based on assumptions which now seem outrageous; full employment, net wages of a single-wage married couple sufficient to maintain a family above social security, and contributory benefits well above social assistance levels. In the 1980s unskilled and semi-skilled jobs come and go without even predictable regularity. Women's wages are essential to keep families out of poverty and some of the lower paid are worse off than the unemployed.

Mingione [1983] demonstrated the remarkable flexibility of families facing increasing and persistent unemployment or under-employment. He agrees with Parker that unemployment causes considerable pressure for change. Chronic unemployment brings forth adaptation and survival tactics which absorb the workforce into unpaid work or illegal employment, and increases the need for permanent public subsidies to families. Further, the resistance of employers and workers in the productive formal sector to tax administration itself [MacPherson, 1987] and the rules which govern payments. Other chapters show how all of these act on poor claimants. The changes which will come into effect in 1988 will make things very much worse for many poor people. With inadequate levels of basic weekly benefit and only the possibility of loans from the Social Fund, the pressures will be even greater than now.

A complex series of choices is created for those dependent on state benefits. The divide between those forced to depend on income support, or on incomes close to these levels, and the relatively better-off majority is growing wider [Walker and Walker, 1987]. As pressure gets harder, so do the decisions. Decisions as to whether or not to work [when low wage work is the only work there is], whether to work full or part-time, who in the family or household should work, and for how long, are all affected by benefit rules. There are no margins for error here; the decisions are vital and must be made under strain and pressure.

One family: the Jays

This is Mrs Jay's second marriage; she is 33, her husband is 30. They have two children, a boy aged two and a half and a girl of six months. They feel very lucky to have the house – her house from her first marriage. It's a two-bedroom terrace and the mortgage is only £26 per month. Mr Jay has been out of work for three years – he was a dairy roundsman. Being on supplementary benefit, they get their rates paid and the interest on the mortgage. One way they thought they might be better off was to sell the house. They went into this and now think they would be worse off. The local council told them that the only way they would be rehoused would be if they sold the house, but stayed in it so that the new owner evicted them. Otherwise they would be considered 'intentionally homeless'. Even then they could be put into any accommodation the council had, even 'really bad housing', and would have to accept whatever they offered. The house insurance has just been increased by £25 as the house was undervalued. They asked the DHSS for help, but were told that because they get this allowed for already in their weekly benefit, no additional payment is available. For the first year Mr J got unemployment benefit; he's now on supplementary [income support after April 1988]. They just about manage – 'second hand clothes, either from the "flea market" every Tuesday morning or the Children's Charity Shop', and she 'runs a catalogue.'

Everything has to be worked out carefully:-

Only social life we can have is in these four walls. We've only been

out three times in the last year and one of those was a free evening at
County Hall.

If it wasn't for the second hand clothes market, we
couldn't manage.

We haven't got a dog. I know that's a luxury. We have
a few cigarettes a week, but I know we shouldn't smoke
on this money.

We have to monitor things very carefully, watch every
penny.

We buy second hand toys now. He was a good man that sold us
this though [a toy telephone]; he told us the winder
didn't work.

We get very worried when the bills are due especially
gas and electricity [gas fires, electric water heater].
[This quarter the electric was £72 and gas was £65. They
underestimated it last time.]

When working the budget out, if we've got anything left
we have to keep it for the next fortnight. We know we'll
be short.

At one time there were lump sum grants, which could be got sometimes
from the DHSS. They've had a carpet for the son's bedroom, a single bed
for him with bedding automatically; money to have a gas fire fitted that
they bought when they were both earning; high chair, pram, pushchair [£15
each]; £20 for redecoration. 'We don't claim for some things because we
feel we may need other things more at a later date'. They got a severe
weather payment last winter, but that came very late, didn't make them any
better off and the house was still very cold. When they asked about things
for the new baby they were told that whatever they claimed for the first
child, they can't claim for the second child; they are expected to use those
things again. 'Have to buy things you think are going to last.' They bought
a cheap buggy for the first child, but it kept breaking and cost a lot to repair
so they a bought better one out of the catalogue for the second baby – so
much each week. 'Its lucky that child benefit comes – it pays the catalogue
bill.' They claimed for nappies for the second baby because their older son
was still using his – but they only got half a dozen. 'Had to beg, steal and
borrow money for more.' They have just put in an application for repairs to
the bathroom window, which is rotten – they are waiting to hear.

A while ago, the DHSS forgot to put the milk tokens on their benefit. Mr
Jay rang the DHSS and they promised to send him some in the post – they
didn't arrive. He rang the DHSS again. They said the first person had told
him the wrong information, but that now they would send the order
through. He popped into his 'signing-on' office, they confirmed the order
had come through but told him the DHSS should have paid them arrears.

He doesn't know where he stands now. But in this fortnight they've had to buy four tins of baby milk, at a cost of £6.56. Luckily they've 'got a good milkman, who will take the tokens when/if they come' against their milk bill but they still have to pay out the money in advance and rely on the good will of their milkman. 'The DHSS get very indignant if you phone up.'

They have found out about benefits through different leaflets. At the 'Skill Centre' there are social workers. One took an hour one day sorting out his benefits, telling him what he was entitled to and telling him which forms to get. Husband took the time, a long time, to read through all the leaflets. 'You get much more with children. We couldn't get anything before we had the children. You have to be one in front of the DHSS all the time and know what to expect.' She reckons she could get a job easily – telephonist, clerk, receptionist. But she'd have to be away from the children which she doesn't want and they'd be no better off – probably worse off. He would look after the children, he enjoys it and can do it all. But he doesn't want her back at work. 'It's a man's perogative to be out at work.' He sends job application after job application. Hears nothing. Even when he includes a stamped addressed envelope there is no reply. He's got his name down with the post office, gas, electricity, traffic warden – just waiting for a post. 'The worst part is I see a job I'd like in the Job Centre and I'm too old at 30!' They have the local newspaper delivered six nights a week [this is a heavy expense]. He delivers the free newspaper – gets £3; takes him two hours. He declares this every week to be on the safe side; 'there are some very nosey people around'. If they deliver supplements it might take his wages up over the £4 he can earn. The DHSS take each penny from the benefit right away. They used to wait until it added up to £1 – now they take it off each week.

They both have relatives in the area. Mr Jay's mother is a pensioner and lives about eight miles away, but is housebound. But she gives them money when she can, buys them joints of meat, and does knitting for her son. Mr Jay has a half-fare bus pass, but his wife isn't entitled to one. They have to get two buses there and two back if they visit his mother – £5 both of them. So he goes once a week and Mrs Jay goes once a month. Mr Jay's mother is on supplementary benefit as well. She wouldn't ask for anything, but eventually 'had to put her pride in her pocket,' Mrs Jay's mother and father are both retired and live close by. They also give the family money and food when they can.

The Jays are concerned that there are always 'hidden expenses', however much they plan. They need new teats for the baby's bottle; she has thrush in her mouth and has trouble feeding. They fear that their son may have asthma – he's been given medicine by the doctor. They spend more than £4 a fortnight just on washing materials – there are nappies to be washed every day. The coming winter is a real worry with the new baby and the cost of heating. The gas fire needs to be serviced and they need money for playgroup costs [the health visitor thinks their son would benefit from it]. There doesn't seem to be anywhere to get money for these.

Still, at the end of the day we count our blessings.
You can always find some worse off.

PART FOUR

Anti-Poverty Action

25

Social Services Responses to Poverty

Susan Balloch and Brian Jones

Background to the AMA research

A research programme for assessing the impact of increasing poverty on local authority services was initiated by the Association of Metropolitan Authorities in January 1987 through its Social Services Committee. The AMA represents the thirty six metropolitan district councils, thirty one London boroughs, the City of London and ILEA with corporate membership also open to the joint authorities responsible for police, fire and civil defence and passenger transport. The aims of this research were twofold: to assess the growing burden of work affecting local authority departments as a direct result of increasing hardship among consumers and to describe and evaluate the range of local authority action developing in response to this. Such was the importance of the task and the uniqueness of the opportunity that a survey as wide-ranging as possible was judged to be necessary. All the Association's authorities rather than a small sample were therefore invited to participate in this research by completing a lengthy questionnaire. Out of a possible 67, 55 agreed to participate as well as ILEA and most of the passenger transport and fire authorities. Of the 55 original participants, three have since withdrawn and it seems unlikely that another five will respond.

At present full or partial responses to the questionnaire have been received from 40 authorities and it is on these that this chapter is based.

About another seven responses are anticipated shortly, bringing the response rate to an acceptable 85 per cent of participants or 70 per cent of all AMA members.

The research has been facilitated by a 'liaison officer' nominated by each authority, who has taken on the responsibility of distributing and explaining, chasing and collecting the completed departmental responses. Many of these liaison officers are themselves in research posts, generally in the chief executives' and social services departments and without their help and advice this research would not have been possible. One idea being currently discussed is the feasibility of creating a research and information network on social policy issues for the metropolitan authorities and other interested bodies such as the universities on the basis of the relationships developed through this research. Such is the growing range and volume of research within and about local authority departments, that such a network could be of considerable value to town and gown alike. Something along these lines is already emerging through the 'Social Security Research Consortium' and Social Services Research Officers Group/Benefits Research Unit projects for monitoring the effects of the government's Social Fund.

The impact of poverty

The 'impact of poverty' has two dimensions in this project. It encompasses both the effects which poverty may be having on local authority workloads and the responses being made by local authorities to such effects. Poverty itself, which is extensively discussed elsewhere in this volume, is seen as including both 'income poverty' and 'relative material and social deprivation' as well.

The questionnaire that, after two pilots in Southwark and Richmond, was ultimately sent to authorities in the summer of 1987 was in five parts. The first part, for chief executives' departments only, aimed to discover the extent to which discussions above poverty and the development of anti-poverty strategies had been taking place. The second part looked at area or geographical targeting of poverty, through questions to all departments and the use of different indices for assessing poverty and the development of specific programmes. The third asked about groups known to be at risk of poverty and the measures authorities were taking to counteract this. Interestingly only one authority has emerged so far with its anti-poverty strategy based on the targeting of such groups.

Fourthly a series of general questions was directed at all departments to find out what steps were being taken towards consumers' income maintenance and improvement, welfare rights, and access to services, and what measures were being supported for economic development either with or without direct reference to an anti-poverty strategy. The role of local government as an 'enabler' was very much in mind at this point. The fifth and largest part of the questionnaire was sub-divided again into five parts, with each sub-part directed at a particular department or unit, ie education, environmental health, housing, social services and welfare rights. Questions were asked about evidence of growing workloads resulting directly from consumer hardship and policies and practices that might be affecting this. Response to this part has been slower, as might be expected, than to the first four parts, but is nevertheless quite sufficient to reveal a depressing picture of both staff and consumer difficulties. This chapter is based on the responses received to date to parts of the social services departments [part five] questionnaire. Such responses must be set against the background of cuts in the personal social services budgets and consequent loss of social services personnel.

Evidence of hardship

Previous research has already established that most social services consumers are poor, unwaged, unemployed or low paid [Balloch *et al*, 1985; Becker and MacPherson, 1986; Popay, Dhooge and Shipman, 1986]. Such research has also demonstrated the difficulties facing those attempting research into social services departments that result from the lack of recorded and/or easily available information. Not surprisingly, therefore, our research has so far shown that evidence of financial and material hardship among social services users goes mainly undocumented and is largely anecdotal. Even where records are kept, on inspection these are found to be inadequate for both research and policy planning purposes; they are geared more towards internal administrative needs or central government returns.

Although lacking specific information, among the respondents to this survey only one was able to say that there had been no increase in referrals over the last five years. Most of the others reported a steady increase with figures of between 25 per cent and 30 per cent regularly mentioned. Some examples are shown in Table 25.1.

The rise in referrals demonstrated in Table 25.1 requires an explanation. While increasing candidates for community care may account for it in part, as may also decentralised and more efficient services, it seems likely that the most significant reason for increased referrals is the growth of material and

Table 25.1

Total referrals to social services department
in selected metropolitan districts

Authority Code	1982/3	1983/84	1984/85	1985/86	1986/87	Area Population
PQ11	14,277	14,332	15,141	16,502	15,360*	310,000
PQ13	18,502	19,808	20,326	22,480	25,692	301,000
PQ15	11,703	12,164	13,951	15,343	14,714*	207,300
PQ25	36,109	39,163	47,740	51,748	51,491	711,000
PQ39	23,309	26,022	27,782	29,811	24,397*	239,000
PQ48	19,402	19,676	19,768	20,210	20,330	215,000
PQ53	28,798	30,415	30,994	32,733	33,463	307,000

* Changes in local authorities recording procedures

financial hardship [Becker and MacPherson, 1986]. This is corroborated by one West Midlands authority whose liaison officer circulated our questionnaire to all the district social services teams. They reported an increase in the number of people contacting them for material help, particularly over the last year since the DHSS criteria for single payments were made more restrictive, a fact frequently mentioned by other authorities as well. Teenagers leaving home to move to independent accommodation were thought to have suffered particularly as a result. Problems have repercussed onto Section One budgets, used to prevent children coming into care. Other authorities complain about the very high incidence of houses visited by social workers which are 'grossly unfurnished'. A separate analysis of the effect of the Suppmentary Benefit [Single Payments] Amendment Regulations is currently being prepared for the local authority associations.

Authorities were questioned about increases in applications to charities for cases of hardship. While many could produce no evidence of this, others presented a disturbing picture. In one authority the development officer for the elderly stated that the three main charities being used were inundated with applications. Sixty to seventy per cent of these applications were for basic necessities refused by the DHSS [furniture, bedding, cookers]. Most applicants were said to be unemployed, or ex-servicemen or on disability pensions. Many authorities said that since the introduction of the DHSS single payment restrictions, items previously sought from the DHSS were being sought from charitable funds. Alarmingly, another authority reported that its charities were now refusing requests because resources were exhausted. This bears out a report from the Family Welfare Association that applications to charities had trebled since the changes in single payments came into effect [*Times*, 10th June, 1987]. Charities are anticipating a rising tide of applications from April 1988, much of which they will be unable to meet. Could there not be some systematic monitoring of this?

Responding to poverty

Local authorities' responses to poverty may be categorised under the broad headings of income maintenance, advice and advocacy [welfare rights], care and support, access to services and employment creation and protection. Throughout these categories may run a common theme, such as area targetting, or an equal opportunities policy or special concern for particular groups such as ethnic minorities, single parents or homeless people.

Within this chapter the focus will be on three of the five general categories, ie income maintenance, care and support and access to services.

A discussion of welfare rights, on which a separate questionnaire was prepared, will be available shortly. An inter-departmental assessment of employment creation and economic development policies and practices will also follow later this year.

Income maintenance

There are a number of ways in which social services departments may affect the income levels of their clients [Hill and Laing, 1979; Wainwright, 1985]. Among those we chose to look at were negotiations with fuel boards to ease the burdens on consumers of fuel debts, negotiations with the DHSS on benefit claims and single payments, payments made under Section One of the Child Care Act 1980, financial assistance for travelling for the parents of children in care and contributions demanded from these parents towards the cost of care.

Fuel debts

During the 1980s concern over fuel poverty has escalated [AMA, *et al*, 1982]. Departments were asked to what extent they were concerned with issues related to 'fuel poverty'. Responses were as follows:

Table 25.2
Time spent dealing with fuel problems

[1] Very extensively	10%
[2] Quite a lot	60%
[3] From time to time	25%
[4] Hardly at all	–
[5] Never	–
[6] No response	5%

In spite of the fact that 70 per cent of responses saw fuel debt as a time consuming problem, few authorities gave details of a coherent fuel poverty policy, either within their authority or their own department. Only one mentioned the appointment of fuel debts liaison officers, though doubtless these exist elsewhere. Some authorities make occasional use of Section One money to help in cases of hardship, while others will not do this to offset fuel debts but do provide a range of emergency heating equipment and support direct payments of supplementary benefit to maintain fuel supplies. Among a wide variety of other measures adopted were a hypothermia training project for home helps, publicity campaigns and the funding of local heating advice centres.

Authorities were asked to indicate which in their opinion were the main problem areas in this instance. They recorded the following [Table 25.3]

Table 25.3 Fuel problems

Main problem areas	Authorities mentioning these areas
[1] Gas	19
[2] Electricity	24
[3] Solid Fuel	2
[4] Estate Heating	3

Commonly, authorities report equal difficulties over gas and electricity. While half reported that the code of practice adopted by the fuel boards, DHSS local offices and local authorities was being used more extensively in negotiations with fuel boards, others reported serious difficulties. Some typical comments are recorded below:

> Between June and October one gas board will cut off clients regardless, for arrears, arguing this will stimulate people saving. The board seems to plead ignorance of children under five in a household after cut-off. The code of practice is being ignored, much to our dismay.
> The code of practice is invoked, but is ignored by public utilities during occasional purges.
> The code of practice I feel to be almost meaningless. The fuel board appears to be construing failure to keep to agreements as clients breaking the code of practice, this giving them 'carte blanche' to proceed with disconnection without reference to us or further leniency. The code of practice requires external policing.

Ironically, typical social services consumers, such as mothers at home with young children, elderly, handicapped or unemployed people, face higher fuel costs than those in work who enjoy the free warmth of offices, shops and factories. Social services departments find it very difficult to help alleviate their fuel poverty where fuel boards remain intransigent. Moreover our survey confirms other reports to the AMA that since the privatisation of British Gas, the situation in some areas may have deteriorated even further, with greater arrears accruing and a harder line on debtors being pursued.

Welfare rights officers and specialist welfare rights units as well as the CABx and other voluntary bodies provide support here, but social workers are still left with much of the work. Among our own respondents less than a third employed specialist welfare rights officers within SSDs and only a handful could call on welfare rights units [See Berthoud *et al*, 1986].

Negotiations with the DHSS

Liaison in Practice, a document whose purpose has been to develop good working relationships between local DHSS offices and social services departments, appears to be having less effect these days than when last revised in 1980 [DHSS, 1980c]. Our survey suggests that less than half the respondents follow *Liaison in Practice* and some are uncertain as to what it involves.

The responses received confirm relationships between social services staff and the DHSS have been difficult and stressful for some considerable time, with little in the way of improvements recorded. Relationships are very much of an *ad hoc* nature, relying heavily on personal contacts between social workers and DHSS officers and these are jeopardised by high staff turnovers especially in inner city areas. About half the respondents felt that contacts with the DHSS had increased in volume, but others, reporting no increase, commented that this was simply because contacts with the DHSS had been running at a maximum, saturation level for some time and could not possibly be any higher. Two authorities, however, reported a decrease in contacts, in each case said to be due to their own activities in welfare rights and in work with young homeless people. One even observed drily that any decrease might well be due to an increase in the number of 'long term' unemployed people whose benefits, presumably, had been sorted out.

Where an increase was felt to have occurred, a variety of reasons were suggested, including changes in the law, the complexity of benefits and of form filling, understaffing and industrial disputes at the DHSS, fuel debts and Gas Board inflexibility in relation to disconnections, an increase in the numbers of mentally handicapped and mentally ill people moving into the community from hospital, large numbers of older people using private residential facilities for respite care, household break-up, liable relative enquiries, unemployment and poverty. This seemingly endless list of problems indicates the pressures which have built up on social services staff and DHSS officers alike, making effective negotiations on behalf of consumers very difficult indeed.

Such difficulties, added to the restrictions placed by the DHSS on single payments, and the ultimate replacement of these in April 1988 by budgeting loans, crisis loans and some community care grants from the Social Fund, may be shifting the pressures for income maintenance increasingly away from the DHSS and towards the social services. We may indeed be witnessing a watershed in state provision of welfare funds. This situation is exemplified by the growing use of Section One payments, a usage which some object is turning the social services into a 'poor relief' agency [Jordan, 1974].

Payments made under Section One of the 1980 Child Care Act

Authorities were asked if they could give details for the last five years of payments made under Section One of the 1980 Child Care Act either as grants or as loans. It was thought that this might provide evidence of the extent to which hardship among social services consumers was increasing and would also demonstrate the sort of guidelines along which departments were reacting to requests for help.

Very few authorities have as yet been able to supply us with the complete set of figures requested. They were listed as either 'not available' or 'not separately recorded' by a majority although this seems scarcely credible. Where authorities were able to provide a full set of statistics, it became clear that there has been a steady rise in the total volume of Section One payments this decade [Table 25.4]. What is more, virtually all of these payments are listed as grants with only a tiny proportion given as loans. Although only three authorities stated categorically that they never gave loans, all the rest recorded a very relaxed attitude towards loans. Loans are only recovered where this can be easily achieved and without causing hardship. Most loans are converted into grants if not repaid, mainly on compassionate grounds, but also because their collection is not cost effective. Court action is rarely, if ever, considered.

Estimates for Section One payments for 1987/1988 vary widely among AMA members, from as little as £2,900 to as much as £559,000. Estimates may well be an indication of exceptional hardship in boroughs but are also an indication of a policy which may seek to relieve poverty through social services funds. As stated earlier, not all agree that this is an appropriate course of action.

Support for the parents of children in care and parental contributions

The majority of children coming into care are from social classes four and

Table 25.4

Section One grants, 1982-1988 1987-88 prices

Authority Code	1982-83	1984-84	1984-85**	1985-86	1986-87	1987-88	Area Populations
PQ16	11,150	12,275	14,280	23,052	31,895	28,770	218,000 [Lnd Brgh]
PQ20	11,893	15,706	13,947	27,682	–	20,590	195,000 [Lnd Brgh]
PQ25	14,107	16,553	67,252	24,693	28,478	23,940	711,000
PQ30	–	107,483	124,583	151,600	69,782	102,550	281,000
PQ32	13,369	27,842	210,954	28,270	50,661	115,000	192,000
PQ40	–	–	13,842	18,191	32,113	33,000	301,000
PQ49	7,368	6,536	6,499	6,654	5,228	6,912	216,000
PQ53	7,445	10,321	12,195	15,374	16,176	18,300	307,000
PQ55	8,030	7,918	8,583	29,133	–	53,940	252,000

[Payment 1987-88 Prices*]

* Adjusted to take account of the government's estimate of general price increase in the economy.

** [Some authorities payments rose dramatically during this period because of the miners' strike] five, with a disproportionate number from an ethnic minority background [House of Commons, 1984]. Most are therefore from poor families with parents who can ill afford the travelling and telephone costs that may be involved in keeping in contact with their children. Almost all respondents said that they provided financial assistance for travel costs to the families of children in care by a variety of methods; some said they had a special 'children in care,' fund or budget, others specifically referred to the use of Section One money. Only two authorities said they made no formal provision at all.

In spite of this recognition of need, the same authorities demonstrated a surprising determination to secure parental contributions towards the costs of keeping children in care. Under the 1980 Child Care Act local authorities are empowered to charge parents for keeping their children in care up to the amount of the weekly boarding-out rate. Among our respondents, only three say they do not charge parents at all. The others do not charge parents receiving supplementary benefit, but charge the rest according to a variety of means-tests and sliding scales.

Whereas some will charge no more than the weekly child benefit of £7.25, others go by the letter of the law and charge an amount equivalent to that paid to foster parents, eg £28.70-£57.33 per week according to the child's age. It is possible for some parents to be charged up to one third of their income.

To have your child taken away and then to be charged for his or her keep seems to demonstrate a punitive attitude towards parental 'failure' that has long been endemic in social policy. This is borne out by the reports received from respondents on recovery policies and practices for payments on which parents have defaulted. Most authorities cite court action as a likely step and have a standard set of procedures which build up to this. Whereas court action to recover Section One loans is never taken, court action to enforce parental contributions seems to be much more commonplace. Yet the parents of children in care are known to be generally poor and recognised as such [as the payment of travel costs suggests]. There is here an inconsistency in both policy and practice towards poor people encouraged by relevant pieces of legislation that so far only a handful of authorities have recognised.

Authorities were also asked to what extent they thought more children were coming into care because of the material and financial hardship experienced in their families. While quite a few felt they couldn't express an opinion on this, over half said that this was not the case. Only six perceived poverty as a source of stress leading to an inability to cope and potential child neglect. In the light of current literature this is surely an attitude that needs further questioning [Becker and MacPherson, 1986; Fagin 1984].

Conclusion

In the case of income maintenance social services departments operate in diverse ways, often exhibiting a deep concern for particular types of poverty without being able to do anything very effective about it. Difficult relationships with powerful bodies such as fuel boards and the DHSS compound frustrations. In other areas, such as that of children in care, individuals within social services departments seem much less aware of the implications of poverty although in a more powerful position themselves to offer relief. Such inconsistency possibly has its explanation in the historical origins of the legislation in question and, in particular, may be rooted in punitive attitudes to inadequate parenting which date from the 1950s and earlier.

Care and support

There are many ways in which social services departments offer care and support to their consumers and, in particular to elderly and mentally and physically handicapped people. Domiciliary services and day centres are the primary focus of this care, both of which can mitigate the effects of material and social deprivation.

In this survey we were concerned with the new demands being placed on social services departments by community care policies and the resultant increase in the numbers of people, particularly mentally handicapped children and frail, elderly people being cared for at home by relatives. A question was therefore asked about the services being developed to meet the needs of carers. It is well known that most such carers are women and many become seriously impoverished as a result of their caring role with its implications for their employment and pension prospects. Many also become stressed and exhausted to the point of mental and physical collapse. If community care policies are not to cut across a legislative commitment to equality between the sexes, a commitment strongly supported by many local authorities, then ways have to be found of sharing this burden more equally [Finch and Groves, 1980; 1983].

All authorities agreed that measures had been taken to support carers, measures which will be in line with Section 8 of the Disabled Persons [Services Consultation and Representation] Act 1987. The most common examples were of forms of respite care, including short term fostering and holidays, carers support groups, family placement schemes and family relief schemes such as 'Family Link' and support for voluntary groups assisting carers. Few mentioned expanding day care services to take the daily responsibility off relatives and to free carers for employment. Previous studies have already shown that day care centres are currently over subscribed and understaffed and ill placed to meet the extra demands that 'care in the community' imposes [Balloch, *el al*, 1985]. On a superficial appraisal it looks as if local authorities are supporting the concept of 'care by the community' more vigorously than the 'care *in* the community' that is more popular among the population at large.

A few authorities have been moving away from piecemeal schemes to developing a more coherent package for carers. Authorities such as Birmingham and Stockport, both DHSS demonstration districts, are examples of the new approach here. In Birmingham a major development project addressing the specific needs of carers is currently in progress and is likely to lead to considerable expansion in available support for carers.

Concern for carers would seem to be growing among respondents and this was one of the more encouraging aspects therefore at which this survey looked. Many mentioned future plans for expanding and for assessing and raising costs. One authority had recently appointed a specific social worker to look after the needs of carers. Others had mounted or were about to instigate their own surveys. Tameside, for example, mentioned its 'Carers' Survey' and its 'Black Workers' Report' on the needs of the ethnic elderly community as examples of surveys conducted to seek the views of service users. Both surveys are to be used to shape future policy.

Access to services – decentralisation

Both politically and administratively, decentralisation may be seen as a positive local authority response to poverty. A final aspect of this questionnaire was concerned with attempts to decentralise services. Several studies have indicated that decentralisation may increase take-up of services and improve their preventive element [see for example Hadley and Hatch, 1980; Hadley and McGrath, 1980]. Only five authorities had taken no steps towards decentralisation. The majority had moved towards patch-based systems of one sort or another, and had experienced an upsurge in demand. Three quarters of these were now extending their schemes either among their own consumers or along with other departments such as housing. Only one department said that localising services had in fact reduced demand, and this was seen as a result of improved efficiency. Among AMA members there seems as yet little sense of disenchantment or disappointment with decentralisation policies [Hoggett and Hambleton, 1987, 139-155]. It is not possible to tell from a general survey of this sort to what extent decentralisation has proceeded to challenge bureaucratic power structures or is an indication of a movement widespread throughout an authority. Only a case study, of the sort with which it has been proposed to follow up this survey, could resolve such questions.

General conclusions

In this discussion only part of the material from the social services questionnaire has been used, both time and space prohibiting an analysis of other issues included in the survey such as welfare rights, aids and adaptations for disabled people and links between poverty and violence. When complete a full account of the social services responses will also have to be placed within the context of the survey as a whole, in order to expose the complex forces created by the pressures of poverty on all local authority services.

Any survey of this kind, relying on written information from individuals within large bureaucracies, runs several risks. Firstly the information offered may not be accurate; secondly, available information may be omitted because the respondent does not know where or how to locate it; thirdly, questions may be misunderstood; fourthly, pressures of work may make it difficult to complete a lengthy questionnaire with any degree of detail.

In defence, it should be noted that many authorities have taken this survey very seriously. Many have scrutinised the completed responses carefully and liaison officers have worked hard to locate missing pieces of information. Some have begun to use their completed questionnaire as a discussion document and have been able to turn not only the information required but also the blank spaces to their advantage by reviewing recording procedures where they have seemed wanting. This has confirmed a belief that the research process itself can provide a valuable opportunity for participants to reappraise policies and practices otherwise taken for granted.

This is not, however, to belittle the preliminary findings of such research. Evidence of material and social hardship, or difficult negotiations with fuel boards, of pressures on social services relationships with DHSS local offices and of other dimensions of income maintenance involved in the care and protection of children all illustrate the present impact of poverty on the work of social services departments. Responses to these pressures are emerging in various ways, including extending budgets for Section One payments, developing community care packages and decentralisation; in addition the expansion of welfare rights work, to be documented in later reports, is of great importance. Further in-depth research is clearly required on all these changes.

These findings need to be viewed in the context of a service increasingly short of funds. The latest personal social services block grant was set at £3035 million, leaving a shortfall of £87 million on the PSS Expenditure Group's requirement of £3122 million. Capital expenditure has been especially restricted, although more is now urgently required in a number of areas – for more day care provision to support community care and for drug and alcohol misusers, for new residential accomodation and for improvement to existing residential accommodation to improve standards and cope with higher levels of dependency.

26

Social Services and Welfare Rights
John Hannam

WELFARE rights can be defined as increasing access to and use of welfare law. Local authorities are a major source of funding for advice work and the majority of advice given by advice agencies concerns welfare law. Some local authorities fund welfare rights through law centres, community advice agencies and Citizens Advice Bureaux. Other local authorities employ their own welfare rights workers but most use a mixture of internal provision and also fund voluntary provision. Most welfare rights work carried out directly by local authorities specialises in maximising the take-up of those cash benefits provided by DHSS.

Welfare rights workers are employed in a variety of local authority departments including trading standards, leisure and housing departments but most workers are employed within social services and chief executives departments. Most local authorities locate welfare rights within social services departments. The majority of welfare rights workers are also located in that department [Berthoud *et al* 1986].

Limitations

Direct welfare rights provision by local authorities has its limits. Independent community based voluntary advice agencies are as good at providing walk-in advice sessions, particularly where claimants have identified themselves as having a welfare law problem. It can be argued that properly funded community based independent advice agencies can provide a more effective advice centre than one provided directly by local authorities [National Consumer Council, 1985].

Welfare rights activity cannot obtain any more than the minimal income defined by the state. The supplementary benefit scales do not provide an income which allows people to take part in the day-to-day activities of most people in Britain in the late 1980s. For example supplementary benefit scale rates for children seriously underestimate the actual cost of bringing up a child [Piachaud, 1979].

Successful welfare rights activity does not alter the benefit system significantly. The 1986 cuts in supplementary benefit single payments occurred partly because welfare rights activity had ensured that many more people were claiming their full entitlement to benefit in law. A successful test case which changes case law to the advantage of the claimant can mean that the status quo is restored in a matter of days by urgent amending legislation [Prosser, 1983]. Welfare rights are not a significant method of altering the distribution of income between the rich and the poor. It is a reformist rather than a radical activity [Hannam, 1987].

History

Welfare rights have existed as an activity for longer than generic social work. The first welfare rights worker was employed by Oxfordshire Children's Department. The number of local authorities directly employing welfare rights works expanded from the early 1970s, largely with the appointment of one welfare rights officer for a local authority area. The 1980s saw a further growth of welfare rights appointments, but this time welfare rights teams were often established. There are now over 350 welfare rights workers directly employed by local authorities in Great Britain [Berthoud *et al*, 1986].

Roles

The usual target of welfare rights activity is the benefits administration part of the DHSS, which was created in 1966 by the merger of the National Assistance Board and the Ministry of Pensions and National Insurance. This merger was an attempt to emphasise the right to the minimum nationally defined income, but the basic structure remained as it had been when set up in 1948 following the *Beveridge Report* of 1942. Since 1980, the supplementary benefit scheme has been governed by statutory regulations rather than determined by largely discretionary rules.

Social services departments provide a range of services such as residential and domiciliary care, and employ social workers who offer support to families and individuals [DHSS, 1980c]. These workers were gatekeepers for access to scarce resources provided by their social services departments. The departments provide services based on an assessment of individual need often determined by a social worker. The services provided by social services are based on a model of individual treatment and not upon clearly defined individual rights.

Social workers are used to providing services for those who need them. These services would be overwhelmed if they were available to all those who fitted the current broadly defined categories of entitlement. For example if day care for the under fives was available on demand, social services would be swamped. Day care is therefore rationed according to both the legislation and a wide policy remit. This policy is interpreted by social workers according to supply and demand. The decision on the provision of resources can rarely be challenged by the client. The training and practice of social workers makes them uncomfortable in a system of rights, rather than discretion.

Social services are however heavily involved with people in poverty and are providing services largely for the poor [Becker and MacPherson, 1986]. Of all clients, 90 per cent are benefit claimants and most clients are at or on the margins of poverty. Recent surveys have shown that most clients and potential clients of social services hope for, and usually expect, guidance and assistance with money problems, particularly help with benefit.

It is rare for social work managers to share the claimants' perceptions of need. It is not unusual to hear that the demands of statutory work with childen and families dominate, overwhelm and preclude effective work with other client groups and with community involvement. Requests by clients for assistance with cash problems tend to be treated as a diversion from the real problem, and consequently as of low priority.

In spite of social workers' reluctance to engage on issues related to poverty, the clients do not go away. Half of all duty referrals in many city areas relate to benefit problems. These referrals often consume a great deal of social work time because of their intractable nature. They frequently relate to deficiencies in other agencies, such as DHSS money orders which do not arrive, the cutting off of fuel supplies, or debt. It is rare for social workers to be involved in any other form of welfare rights activity such as work with the claimants groups, maximising benefit take-up or campaigning on benefit issues. Yet even the most progressive local authorities are unlikely to employ more than one welfare rights officer for every 50 social services fieldworkers.

Clients and claimants do have certain minimal, but legally enforceable welfare rights. It is very difficult for them to enforce these rights. The 'welfare' client lives in a world of services which are increasingly designed only for the poor. The social security system is becoming even more heavily dependent upon means testing – at least one-eighth of the entire population are now dependent on supplementary benefit [Walker and Walker, 1987]. Supplementary benefit claimants are heavily dependent upon secondhand clothing and furniture for example. In many inner-city areas there is an economy based upon selling secondhand and sub-standard goods and services [Hannam, 1987].

Services designed exclusively for the poor are usually poor services; the error rate in high-street bank accounts is relatively low whereas approximately half of all supplementary benefit claimants are not receiving their correct weekly entitlement and three-quarters of claimants are not receiving their full entitlement [Berthoud, 1984]. Claimants and clients have a clear need for independent advice and assistance in fighting their way through the jungle of potential welfare benefit entitlements. There are currently over 1,000 different combinations of welfare benefits available to different claimants.

It is necessary for a welfare rights service to set itself clear priorities because of the inevitable limitations on its resources. For example, a welfare rights agency must choose which groups of claimants or aspects of welfare law it wishes to emphasise. If it chooses to offer a walk-in service, it specialises in work with ambulant people who are motivated to seek advice and assistance on welfare rights issues. If it chooses to specialise in work with physically handicapped people, then its style of work will obviously be different.

The introduction of welfare rights to a social services department will often produce healthy and challenging conflict, while workers re-determine their roles and responsibilties towards people in poverty. At worst it can produce muddle and misunderstanding of the roles of welfare rights and social workers.

Why are welfare rights important?

Welfare rights should be important to local authorities and particularly social services departments because:-

– It has a direct and positive impact. For example three welfare rights officers recently increased the payment of benefit to mentally handicapped people and their families by £500,000 by one year's persistent casework [Nottinghamshire Welfare Rights, 1986].

– It has a direct impact on people's quality of life. Welfare rights intervention will only bring people to the poverty line but a prolonged existence below the poverty line will encourage many of the symptoms social services departments exist to treat.

Welfare rights activity assists individuals who have very limited access to mechanisms for enforcing their individual rights, and often insufficient knowledge of the laws and regulations which govern entitlement to cash benefits.

Welfare rights attempts to enforce basic rights to food, shelter and warmth. This is in line with the other activities of social services departments and is particularly important at a time when legislation has reduced many provisions, for example DHSS reductions in the payment of board and lodging charges for young unemployed people and the coming cuts in housing benefit.

 Social services departments are a useful base for welfare rights provisions because these departments have a vast range of social and financial information which can be used to claimants' advantage. Departments are in touch with at least one-fifth of all supplementary benefit claimants in their areas through provision of services such as Home Help, Day Nurseries, registration of people with a handicap for Car Badges, Aids and Adaptations, or additional housing benefit [Becker and MacPherson, 1986]. A social services department is therefore uniquely able to provide advice, guidance and assistance on benefit problems to the substantial proportion of claimants who are clients. Work in Nottinghamshire has shown an estimated unclaimed benefit entitlement of £4m a year among home help clients and £½m a year amongst severely physically handicapped people under 65 [McGavin, 1985; Hyde, 1986].

Recent studies have clarified the link between both mental and physical health and poverty [Whitehead, 1986]. Welfare rights and community care are therefore clearly linked.

Welfare rights should be an integral part of the social services department. Social Services – more than any other local government departments – deal with people living in poverty. All plans and activities of the department should be measured against a policy which recognises this, and seeks to minimise it. Welfare rights must be the important part of this policy.

The absence of adequate income maintenance provision undermines any good that can come from casework [Herbert Laming, Director of Social Services, Hertfordshire].

A fifth of the population of this country has a lower standard of living than the average Moroccan [Ken Livingstone, ex-Leader of the GLC].

It is the difficult duty of the personal social services to see that people are encouraged to avail themselves of all relevant social provisions [Committee on Local Authority and Allied Personal Social Services, *Seebohm Report*, 1968].

27

The Organisation of Welfare Rights Work in Social Services

Geoff Fimister

I N the previous chapter, John Hannam considered the arguments surrounding the place of welfare rights work in social services departments [SSDs]. In doing so, he contributed to a continuing debate which assumes ever greater importance as poverty looms increasingly large in the lives of the clients of the social services [for a summary of the evidence, see Becker and MacPherson, 1986; for a summary of the debate, see Fimister, 1986, ch. 2].

It is not my purpose here to pursue this question of whether welfare rights work has a place in social work or in SSDs. I shall assume that we are agreed that it does. The question is, how should such work be organised? What are the implications in terms of policy, management, support systems and training? What difference might the Social Fund arrangements make to these considerations? I shall try to outline some of the main issues. issues.

One of the major policy decisions to be taken is whether the department is to be in the business of providing advice services direct to the public on welfare rights problems as such, or whether welfare rights questions are to be taken up only when they arise in conjunction with other difficulties which a client is experiencing. If the more ambitious course is adopted, and advice services are to be extended to 'benefit problem only' cases, there is still a major choice to be made as to whether such services are to be delivered mainly by social workers, by specialist advice workers, or by some combination of the two. One SSD may decide that the most productive use of resources is to ensure that the social services area offices are fully geared up to give advice to all comers [the approach pursued by, for example, Strathclyde Social Work Department]. Another may decide that welfare rights services as such are better provided via separate advice centres [which is the current approach in, for example, Newcastle]. Advice centres may be provided directly by the local authority, or via voluntary sector funding, or both.

Each of the above philosophies seems to me to be perfectly respectable, provided that social workers have adequate knowledge to handle the income aspects of their regular caseloads, *and* that the decision to pursue one approach or another is taken deliberately and in the light of a proper assessment of advice facilities available in the area. There is nothing to be gained by referring cases to advice centres which lack the necessary resources, or which might not even exist. Such mishaps *do* occur. For example, one SSD recently limited radically the advice role of its area offices without undertaking any kind of review of the capacity and geographical distribution of advice centres. This gave rise to *unintended* 'blank spots' in advice coverage in several parts of the borough.

It should be stressed that, regardless of whether the SSD intends to provide advice services through its social workers or via advice centres, there will still be a need for access, by social workers and other staff, to adequate back-up in terms of information, training and specialist advice [see below]. This is because the great majority of clients, whatever their other problems, will be on low incomes and may well require benefits advice. Even if the intention is to get somebody else to handle that *aspect* of the case [and I would regard this as unsatisfactory unless the income issue really is very specialised] a reasonable level of diagnostic skill is going to be required if problems are to be recognised in the first place.

When considering advice and advocacy in SSDs, one tends to think of advice workers, social workers or community workers, because the task seems highly relevant to their concerns *and* because their remits are sufficiently flexible to incorporate this role. However, when we go beyond individual advice and advocacy and consider wider questions of take-up of benefits, possibilities arise for other groups of staff to play a part. For example, substantial gains for day centre attenders, and for the clients of occupational therapists, have resulted from various action research projects in recent years. Useful illustrations of take-up work involving a range of social services and health service personnel are provided by, for example, Ruth Cohen [1983] and Ann Davis [1984], reporting on projects undertaken in Islington and Birmingham respectively.

Whichever particular pattern of welfare rights work exists in a given SSD, there is one element which should be common to all of them: the availability of a 'welfare rights resource' to provide the necessary support to the staff concerned.

Back-up: the role of the welfare rights resource

While there will be local variations, the essential elements of a welfare rights resource in this context will be the provision of information systems, training and advice to relevant SSD staff [for an extensive discussion of the issues, see Fimister, 1986, chapters 3, 5 and 6]. The welfare rights resource unit may or may not *also* provide advice direct to the public – but these two roles should not be confused – they require different forms of organisation and have different resource implications. Management should ensure that this distinction is fully identified at the earliest planning stage and kept in mind throughout. There is in many parts of the country an often massive unmet demand for welfare rights advice, and it is easy for a welfare rights unit which is not geared up to function as a public advice centre to be pressed into playing this role informally, while lacking adequate staffing, reception facilities, waiting areas etc.

The welfare rights resource need not be provided from within the SSD itself, or indeed from within the local authority structure at all. It may be that a local voluntary sector advice centre could perform this role, given a suitably detailed agreement as to what services were to be provided to SSD staff, how and on what terms. There are obviously potential problems of communication, but they are not insuperable, given careful planning and active efforts to sustain good liaison on a continuing basis. There are, after all, considerable problems of 'organisational distance', between different departments within individual authorities and between different sections of the same department, so this is not an issue peculiar to links with voluntary sector agencies.

Nevertheless, it is likely that most local authorities will wish to make 'in-house' provision here. The welfare rights unit may still be in a different department – perhaps Chief Executive's/Town Clerk's – and wherever it is, it may service staff other than those in the SSD, including perhaps workers with outside agencies [for a recent survey of local authority welfare rights services, see Berthoud, Benson and Williams, 1986]. However, for the sake of our present discussion, I shall assume that we are talking about a unit within the SSD which is mainly concerned with supporting social services staff.

Training

Training is a key area. Concern has been expressed that welfare rights training on qualifying courses is frequently quite inadequate to prepare staff for the problems which they will face in the field. This conclusion emerged from McGrail's valuable study [1983] and is confirmed by more recent work produced for the Central Council for Education and Training in Social Work [Davis, Grimwood and Stewart, 1987]. SSDs can help by putting pressure on course planners to match such provision more closely to the demands of practice. However, it is in the realm of **in-service** training that SSDs have an opportunity to make immediate progress. Part of the role of the welfare rights unit should be to collaborate closely with the department's training section to provide the necessary initial and 'refresher' sessions and courses.

The *continuing* nature of the need for in-service training is of crucial importance: welfare rights is a subject which is not only complex but which is also constantly changing. Infrequent – and especially 'once only' – training is but empty tokenism. There should, therefore, be a reasonably substantial welfare rights element in induction courses for new staff and, at the very least, a thorough annual refresher session thereafter. This point is all the more important during a period such as the last eight years, when change has been taking place at every level, from the detail of ever-amended regulations to major upheavals such as housing benefits, large-scale single payment cuts and, of course, the changes of April 1988. [The particular challenge, both to training and to information systems, which the April 1988 changes represent, is discussed further below.]

The **content** of the necessary training will require careful consideration. There will be certain core elements, such as the most frequently-encountered areas of income support and housing benefits. There should also be a local flavour, taking account of the particular practices and approach of local benefit-administering agencies. Different groups of staff will also require training packages tailored to their own circumstances, especially where a specialised working context [such as a hospital] or specific client group [such as elderly people] is concerned.

It is also important that training should not confine itself to a purely passive treatment of the details of benefit provision. If staff are to liaise and negotiate effectively with bodies such as DHSS offices and fuel boards, then advocacy skills will also be required – especially if representation at social security appeal tribunals or housing benefit review boards is envisaged. The use of teaching techniques such as role-playing exercises and videos will be relevant here.

There are also simple practicalities which, nevertheless, are of great importance to claimants as they seek a solution to their income problems. Take as a notable example the question of referral procedures. In-service training [and information systems] should be sensitive both to agency policy as to when and in what circumstances it is appropriate to refer a case to another body; and to the location, procedures and opening hours of organisations to which claimants might be referred. This may seem obvious, but I receive with depressing regularity accounts of claimants who have been caused inconvenience, financial loss and general aggravation in being referred to the wrong building in the wrong part of town, or the right building when it is shut. 'Pot luck' referrals often originate, unhappily, from social services offices, confirming that training for good practice must sometimes concern itself with the most mundane of procedures, as well as with fine legal argument.

Training is, though, only part of the picture. Effective welfare rights work on a day-to-day basis will also require adequate, well-maintained information systems.

Information

An information system must be easily accessible to the worker who needs to use it at the appropriate time. If it is difficult to find, the temptation will be to try to do without it. This means that, for example, where an area team has a separate sub-office, then an information system must be maintained on **each** site. Similarly, if a hospital social work team is split between several locations, separated by long corridors, then each office must have its own set of information. It is physical location, and not the bureaucratic organisation chart, which matters here.

I do not have space to describe in any detail the **contents** of a suitable information package [see Fimister, 1986, chapter six for a detailed discussion]. As in the case of training, there will be core material relevant to most settings, with specialised variations as required. Effective and inexpensive packages can be constructed from the range of welfare rights handbooks produced by agencies such as the Child Poverty Action Group, Disability Alliance, SHAC and the Institute of Housing. Such handbooks are much to be preferred to boxes full of old journals and leaflets [although these can be useful **supplementary** sources, if properly indexed and updated] and there is a case for certain items – such as CPAG's *National*

Welfare Benefits Handbook – being issued individually to all staff.

New technology will undoubtedly have an increasing role in the years to come. Discussion of the application of computerised approaches to welfare rights work is often over-simplified, and quite different processes are referred to interchangeably. For example, the computerised administration of benefits; the use of a programme by an adviser to assess a claimant's across-the-board entitlements; the use of such a programme by the claimant directly; the computerised retrieval of information by an adviser: while these functions can overlap [for example, benefit administration can have a wider information role built in] they are essentially different processes, raise different issues and vary a good deal in their current state of development.

However, for our present purposes – that is, as regards information retrieval – it is likely that new technology will become much more widely used in the near future. The need to refer to highly detailed information, which is so frequently updated that is is difficult – indeed probably unwise – to commit too much to memory; the need for rapid access where advice may be required urgently, or where a queue may be building up in the waiting room; the need efficiently to update information in possibly several different locations simultaneously – all attest to the case for computerisation.

It is true that the Social Fund, with its absence of firm entitlements and bizarre 'maybe/maybe not' guidance manual, tends in the opposite direction: but with this exception, the case for new technology in information retrieval is strong.

Whatever the specific content of the information systems used, their efficient maintenance is crucial. New material must be ordered and distributed; old material deleted; the relevance of the current content of the system to practical requirements must be regularly monitored. In my view, the best approach to this task is for a welfare rights resource unit, such as that described above, to handle the distribution of information packages and updating material, with a **named contact** in each office taking responsibility for receiving this material and maintaining the system on each site.

Feedback from the individual sites to the welfare rights unit is also essential if the continuing relevance of the particular contents of the packages is to be assessed effectively, and any problems identified and ironed out. Regular meetings should therefore be held between welfare rights staff and 'on-site' representatives.

Ideally, a telephone advice line should also be made available, so that more complex cases can be discussed in detail – although care should be taken that this is not 'jammed' by queries which could easily be looked up in the office information system. [How to use information resources appropriately should, in fact, form part of the content of in-service training].

The implications of the April 1988 changes

The April 1988 changes in the benefit system will usher in many new difficulties in the relations between DHSS, SSDs and claimants/clients. The organisation of welfare rights work within SSDs will not be exempt from these upheavals. The main factors here will be the restructuring of supplementary benefit into 'income support', the abolition of single payments and the introduction of the social fund.

In the average SSD area office, while a variety of benefit problems may arise, the greater part of this area of work centres around supplementary benefit. The broad welfare rights strategy most commonly pursued pre-April 1988 [apart from simply chasing up unpaid basic benefit] is likely to be to seek to identify additional requirements [eg for heating, special diet, extra laundry needs] and also to acquire lump-sum single payments for essential items [such as essential furniture and household equipment]. The cutbacks in the latter since August 1986 have given a taste of things to come when single payments are abolished in April 1988. Additional requirements payments will also disappear, both they and the long-term rate of benefit being replaced by the new 'premiums'. The premiums will not be tailored closely to individual need and it therefore seems unlikely that there will be much scope to argue for an increase in a claimant's weekly benefit [in this, they resemble more the long-term rate than they do additional requirements].

There are considerable implications here for welfare rights work in social services which I and others shall explore elsewhere [eg Fimister, 1987b]. However, we are concerned in this chapter with implications for the organisation of such work. To appreciate the significance of these developments in this respect, we must recognise that much of what has been, hitherto, welfare rights work as such, will now split into three. Firstly, there will still be much welfare rights work to be done, for example around basic income support entitlements, and in housing benefit and benefits for disabled people. Secondly, there will be a lot more chasing of grants outside of the benefit system. Thirdly, there will almost certainly be a great deal more debt management work. Neither the second nor the third of these is welfare rights work as such [if we define welfare rights in terms of maximising entitlements within the benefit system]; but what implications do they have, to put it more broadly, for the organisation of work within the social services around income problems? I shall look separately at each of these two areas of work.

The pursuit of grants outside of the benefit system will embrace several elements, one of which will be 'community care grants' from the social fund itself – which, given its lack of legal entitlements and of a right of appeal, cannot properly be regarded as part of the benefit structure as such [see Fimister, 1987b]. Training and information systems will need to incorporate the nature, scope and provisions of the Social Fund. But, being cash-limited and dealing mainly in loans, the Social Fund will not go very far towards filling the gap left by single payments. Another potential source of grants will be SSDs themselves, mainly via section one of the Child Care Act 1980 – which may be amended to widen its scope [DHSS, 1987a, para 18] – and analogous legislation elsewhere in the United Kingdom. This will of course create a potential conflict of interest for social workers acting as advocates, and for those advice centres which are closely linked to the SSD. Training is therefore needed for management as well as for fieldwork staff in the procedures to be followed and dilemmas to be recognised in this context. Staff will also need to be trained, and good information provided, on local criteria for the making of Section One and analogous payments; and this would be assisted if such criteria were to be made more explicit then they generally are at present [a process which will doubtless take place anyway, if only to try to protect budgets]. The third source of non-social security grants will be local charities, and SSD staff will need to know what is available. Again, there is likely to be a tightening-up.

A further organisational issue which arguably arises from the inevitably greater pressure on SSDs to make payments is whether it is any longer appropriate for SSD staff to play an advocacy role, given a conflict of interests. This is certainly a problem, but it should not be exaggerated when one considers the likely tight rationing, and consequent small scale, of this area of grant provision.

I should add, perhaps, that I do not **advocate** a state of affairs in which claimants need to look to SSDs and charities for basic necessities: on the contrary, like all welfare rights advisers, I deplore it. However, given that the Government has brought such a state of affairs about, the implications for work within SSDs relating to income problems have to be thought through.

Let us turn now to the area of debt management. If a claimant cannot get a grant from anywhere, the next move may be to try to get a loan. Even a Social Fund loan [which is not interest-bearing] may give rise to unmanageable debts. At the other end of the spectrum of respectability in the money-lending business waits the loan shark and indeed, downright criminal element. It should be remembered also that abolition of single payments and introduction of the Social Fund will take place at the same time as the introduction of the requirement for all claimants to find the 20 per cent of their rates which will not be met by housing benefit. The penalties for non-payment of rates can be severe, leading to imprisonment.

It seems inevitable, then, that many more clients and claimants will be in debt in future, and to a greater extent. New liaison procedures, and consequent training and information, will be required as regards dealings with rating authorities. But most problematically, there will be a demand for greater involvement of SSDs in debt management work. This will create major dilemmas, for if SSDs simply throw up their hands and say, 'this is not our job', all other forms of social services intervention will run the risk of being undermined by the corrosive influence of multiple debt. To try to meet such demand, though, raises problems of training, information and staffing. Debt management is not a field in which to dabble: mistakes can be damaging and there are serious questions concerning liability. But adequate training, whether of social workers or of advice workers, must entail the acquisition of no less than a considerable skill, with all that that means in terms of time spent in training, in updating, and not least in subsequent financial casework. Of all the consequences, for SSDs and their clients, of recent social security legislation, the problem of multiple debt may prove to be the most damaging and the most intractable.

Last but certainly not least, SSDs should be keen to play their part, in conjunction with local authority associations and academic institutions, in monitoring and evaluating current changes, in publicising findings and in pressing for constructive alternatives.

Now more than ever, it is of course necessary to try to maximise claimants' receipt of their entitlements, so as to minimise the damage which will be wrought by setbacks such as the abolition of single payments and cuts in housing benefits. I hope that the above, as well as making for sometimes depressing reading, has given some indication of the type of welfare rights organisation which will be required to gear up the SSD for action in this area. Individual circumstances will vary, but the broad pattern should be generally relevant. Even in these financially difficult times, I believe that such an investment is appropriate – indeed, necessary – if the social services are to face up to the challenge posed by the social conditions of the 1980s and 1990s.

28

Community Work and Poverty

Fiona Robertson with Amanda Woods

I N this chapter, some ideas about the ways in which community work attempts to alleviate poverty will be discussed. First, though, it is necessary to have at least some idea of what we mean by community work, and poverty.

Definitions of community work abound. The debate on what community work is [and what its relationship to social work is] began in the 1920s and intensified with the growing interest in community work as an anti-poverty strategy in the 1960s and 1970s. There are three major approaches to community work, although variations and combinations of these are plentiful. Firstly, the 'social planning' approach, which is basically a way of introducing reforms from above; professionals deliver a service which is deemed to be appropriate to the needs of the people receiving it, who may be involved in the planning and delivery of the service only if their involvement is thought useful. Workers may also be involved in raising policy and planning issues, both within their own agencies and with other service-providing agencies 'on behalf' of the community.

Secondly, there is the 'neighbourhood development' approach, where the worker is based in a locality with the aim of building structures [for example, tenants' groups] which enable the community to overcome problems by expressing its needs and negotiating with the various bureaucracies which affect people's lives. In this approach, the boundaries of the community work project are geographical rather than categorical, although the needs of certain groups [eg women, young people] may be considered. Local people are encouraged to participate in and comment on the work that is carried out.

Thirdly, there is the 'social action' approach, the basic strategy of which is to struggle against [and hopefully overcome] the forces which oppress people by engaging in organised conflict. The worker, in this approach, assumes the role of activist and/or advocate. This approach was described by Saul Alinsky in 1946:

> A people's organisation is a conflict group. This must be openly and fully recognised. A people's organisation is a banding together of a multitude of men and women to fight for those rights which ensure a decent way of life ... a war is not an intellectual debate, and in a war against social evils there are no rules of fair play.

So much for the theories; in practice, the approaches community workers take are, of course, determined by a number of factors – who they are employed by and for what reasons, what their political viewpoints are, where they work, what resources are available to them, and so on. In recent years, the debates about community work have continued against a background of government cuts and increasing pressure on SSDs to prioritise statutory case work [see Parker and Dillon, this volume]. Community work is being increasingly marginalised – a minority of SSDs employ only small numbers of workers. The eighteen community workers employed by Nottinghamshire SSD are currently working on a policy for community work, which will include a combination of elements from the 'neighbourhood development' and 'social action' approaches.

Various definitions of poverty have been discussed at length elsewhere in this book. Generally, community workers take a broad view of poverty which is not just about lack of money:

> The poor are those who are excluded ... sudden job redundancy, low wages and arbitrary allocation to substandard housing are outward and visible signs of the lack of effective participation which particular groups of the population enjoy in the formal and informal decision making processes of industry, government, trade unions and even the social welfare agencies which are intended to relieve their poverty [Dennet *et al*, 1982].

Poverty should be seen, therefore, as an inevitable consequence of the political situation in which we live, rather than as a characteristic of the individuals or communities concerned. Predictable stereotypes of the poor persist; stories of scroungers appear regularly in the media; the only people in receipt of benefit who are regarded with some sympathy are the elderly and the disabled. The myth that everyone can pull themselves up by the boot straps and make good persists. Meanwhile, supplementary benefit levels continue to fall in real terms and other benefits are being scrapped. Public spending in other areas, such as housing, is falling and local authorities are being prevented from spending on housing and community facilities, etc, particularly if their priorities are not in line with government thinking.

How, then, does community work address poverty? A minority of SSDs in England and Wales employ community workers, and the numbers employed are small; community work occupies a marginal position. Current debates about the relevance of a community work element in social work training reflect, among other issues, the lack of job opportunities in this field. The SSDs that view community work as a necessary part of their function have varying views on what kind of work should be undertaken, and in what way. Where community workers are based – either as part of an area team, in an area office, in a community work team or in community group premises – can often be an indication of how their work is viewed. Community workers in Nottinghamshire are based in a community work team and/or in community group premises, and are part of the SSD's Community Division. This was set up to:

> improve the quality of life of individuals and communities [whether geographical or of interest] through diminishing inequality in access to opportunities for personal development, and in access to essential social provision, eg income, shelter, play, community facilities, and increasing the ability of the individual to influence decisions which affect them, whether as individuals or communities.

Community workers are employed as part of a strategy to 'enable communities [either geographical or of interest] to increase their ability to influence their environment and tackle their own problems'.

The possible reasons why some local authorities choose to employ community workers have been discussed at length; suffice to say here, however, that it seems obvious that any view of community work and its uses is determined mainly by political belief. Thus Conservative politicians may support community work for reasons quite at odds with the aims of community groups and workers, as this quote from a Conservative councillor from the Royal Borough of Kensington and Chelsea illustrates:

it is our policy to co-operate with groups ... where voluntary
bodies are willing to do things and can do things as well as a local
authority, the only difference being that the ratepayers are saved
money, then I'm all for it.

As the Gulbenkian study group found during research into community
work vacancies in the early 1970s:

Statutory and voluntary organisations which employ community
workers do so as a means of carrying out the organisation's
purposes ... the purpose of the employing organisation sets limits
to the kind of community work and has a strong influence on the
direction it will take.

Thus community workers may find themselves expected to fulfil a variety
of roles; as co-ordinators for other services, finding out the consumer view;
as deliverers of a variety of services; and as the workers who can 'sort out' a
variety of community issues.

It is obvious that the attention of community work is focussed on
deprived areas and communities, but how do we decide where we work?
Such studies as the *Nottinghamshire Disadvantaged Areas Report* can be
useful, using a range of indices to rank areas of the county in order of
disadvantage. However, at present we do not have sufficient resources to
work in every disadvantaged area; in fact, we can do little more than
respond to requests for help from the communities and groups living in
some of those areas.

In recent years, a change has started to take place in the way that
community work is viewed. No longer is it enough to work solely on issues
such as bad housing and traffic problems, pursuing solutions without really
considering how those solutions are being reached. Community workers
are realising that if we work without reference to challenging attitudes –
racist and sexist ones in particular – we will never achieve much change. It is
clear, for instance, that poverty is becoming more and more a women's
problem; women are supplementing men's wages in two-earner families
while becoming the sole earner in the increasing number of one parent
families. A minority of women earn enough to support a family
comfortably. Meanwhile, the majority of women carry out a huge amount
of unpaid work which is indispensable to the state. Therefore, it is clear that
in order to attack poverty we need to understand the importance of sex,
race and class. To this end anti-racist and anti-sexist ways of working are
high on the agenda, and are being written into policy documents, so that
these values should become integral to the way community work
operates:

> Just when standards of living are no longer rising, when poverty is still common, when the plight of the over-taxed wealthy is higher on political agendas than of those who are unemployed or low paid, and at a time when the twin evils of racism and fascism are becoming strident in their appeal, it does seem important to define a mode of community work which avoids either that utopianism in which true consciousness is cultivated for the day when bourgeois society is smashed, or that pragmatism which goes along in not too much discomfort with the world as it is. The focus for attention is not some alternative value-system hard to imagine in real terms, but those commonly held values which bourgeois society fails to attain – greater equality, lessening poverty, a clean, humane environment, a cultivation of creative abilities, a fostering of political knowledge and of active participation [Community Work Group, 1973].

What, then, do community workers do? Obviously, different circumstances and people produce different styles of work. In Nottingham, there are six workers, who work with a range of groups in different areas of the city. Our work includes working with a drug dependency group to develop a project in inner city premises; working with a Pakistani group who are setting up a neighbourhood centre; working with a tenants' group campaigning about the problems in their system-built homes; and working with an advice and resource centre, which handles around ninety welfare rights enquiries a week and houses reprographic equipment, computers and a dark room, for the use of local people and groups. A large part of the work is to secure resources – particularly grants, premises and equipment – to enable the groups to function effectively. We undertake a variety of other tasks, according to the group's needs; obtaining information, negotiating with officers, advising on campaign strategies, working on the development of the group, and so on. Often, we spend a lot of time with individual group members – although we are employed by the SSD, we are rarely viewed in the same way as social workers are popularly seen.

To understand how we work, it is worth looking in detail at the history of community work intervention with one particular group. Caunton Avenue Flats, situated about a mile and a half from the centre of Nottingham, were built by the council in the late 1960s and comprise a mixture of flats, bungalows and maisonettes. The estate is largely deck access and stands on an exposed hillside location. The problems there can be found on similar estates throughout the country; inefficient, expensive heating, damp, infestation, poor lighting and access and a lack of community facilities. A tenants' group, [Caunton Avenue Flats Tenants' Association, or CAFTA], supported by a SSD community worker, was active in the late 1970s and produced a report on conditions in the flats.

Improvements were carried out; £467,000 was spent on the complex. However, the problems persist. At the beginning of 1985, a member of our team began working with the group; CAFTA members were concentrating on providing a range of social activities for residents, and the social club was flourishing.

Campaigning around conditions on the estate continued; a second survey was carried out and a report entitled *Caunton Avenue – the lost civilisation* was produced and circulated to all residents, relevant officers, members and the media. The report included CAFTA's eleven demands, which covered issues such as the inadequacy and cost of the heating, the inappropriate allocation of families, the elderly, and people 'at risk' into the flats, safe removal of all asbestos, an end to pest and rat infestation, and an evaluation of the problems with condensation and damp. Press coverage of the report was considerable, and undoubtedly put pressure on the housing department to respond. Housing officers carried out their own survey; although a number of CAFTA's figures were disputed, the report which went to the housing committee acknowledged that complaints about the heating system were justified, and that a new system should be installed. Work on the system has recently been completed.

Meanwhile, the group had obtained a flat on the estate, at a peppercorn rent, to be used as a base for its activities and as a focal point for community activity. With the support of the community worker and a series of students on placement from CQSW courses, a welfare rights and repairs advice surgery has been established. Other resources – including the only pay phone on the estate – are available at the flat. A newsletter for all tenants has been produced on a regular basis.

Membership of the committee has fluctuated, not least because the turnover of tenancies is extremely high. In the past, the behaviour of one or two members has alienated a large number of tenants and resulted in the loss of credibility with officers, members and other organisations. These problems have been overcome by the commitment and hard work of several members, and the support of the community worker.

During the past year, the group has continued to campaign around a range of issues, and has carefully monitored the installation of the new heating system, to ensure that the work is carried out safely, and to the satisfaction of the tenants. Members have continued to organise social activities as well; bingo sessions, an after-school club and a youth group.

Obviously, major changes in living conditions do not come about easily, not least because they involve the council in considerable expenditure.

There are, however, other benefits in collective action. There are now well established support networks on the estate, ensuring that housebound and elderly people, in particular, are not so isolated. People who have served on the committee have developed an understanding of the way in which the various bureaucracies operate, and how to get things done where possible. Tenants know that there are other people on the estate that they can turn to for advice and support on a range of issues.

The involvement of the community worker is reviewed regularly to ensure that the work being undertaken is progressing effectively. All parties involved – the group, the worker and the SSD – have a say as to whether the work should continue or not. There are, undoubtedly, successes – when permanent funding is obtained, or a demand for new heating is won – and we aim to cease working with a group when they feel self sufficient. Much of the work, however, is long term; it may take one or two years, for example, to set up an advice centre. Groups face considerable limitations, at times, on what they can achieve. Often, the inaccessibility of local authority departments 'are not merely technical problems of communication but are also symptoms of the success of more advantaged groups in manipulating these services' [Dennet *et al*, 1982].

It has been known for people living in damp housing to be told by housing officials that they are causing damp and mould growth themselves, and the poor condition of some estates is regularly blamed on the tenants. When improvements are brought about, it is unusual for the people affected by the changes to be consulted in the planning stages. Local authority departments have a number of delaying tactics at their disposal; simply refusing to negotiate with groups, sometimes saying that they are not representative; not answering letters, missing committee deadlines, and not funding groups. The support of local councillors is almost essential to groups:

> community work efforts are a matter of politics, as the decisions about resources, priorities and recognition with which community work is concerned are, quite simply, political decisions [Curno, 1978].

Groups involved in activities which are seen by some officers and councillors as controversial [this may include nearly all black groups, women's groups and gay rights groups, as the fate of a number of equal opportunities initiatives shows] are treated with extreme caution, and/or fobbed off.

Many community groups find themselves moving away from the aims for which they were initially set up, either because of the pressures of providing services or facilities, or because their funding is dependent on carrying out certain tasks. Groups involved in MSC schemes, such as the Community Programme and the Voluntary Projects Programme, often find that administering the scheme and supervising the workers take up a lot of time which they would rather spend on other tasks.

When councillors and officers support community work, and are prepared to accept that it may result in some conflict with or criticism of their organisation, then useful change can come about. Both communities and individuals can benefit from involvement with community action; problems can be resolved, badly-needed facilities can be provided, and individuals can increase their knowledge, experience and ability to handle the bureaucratic systems which shape our lives. Community work is not an alternative to social work; it should be seen as fulfilling a completely different, but complementary role. Community work has a preventive, developmental role and, as such, should be an integral part of the services offered by SSDs. It can bring about changes in an individual's support network, changes in practices and policies in local and national government, and increase public awareness of social conditions:

> We are unlikely to return to an exclusively communal neighbourhood basis for our economic and social lives. At the same time, there is a need to bring economic and social service structures closer to the people, not just by decentralising large organisations, but by enabling people to participate directly in those structures which govern their lives. This would go some way to relieving the powerlessness of the poor. However, given that major decisions on the economy, the welfare system, and so on, will continue to be taken at city, national and international levels, there will always be a place for actions to ensure that the interests of the poor are taken into account, if necessary by making life uncomfortable for the rest of us.

29

Faith, Hope and Charity?

Malcolm Dillon and Jeff Parker

HOW far can a social work team have any impact on the poverty in the area it covers? Should this even be part of its responsibility? Some might say it is a political area of work which is outside the responsibility of fieldwork teams or that it is such a structural element that it is beyond the influence of social workers. We assume that most local authority middle-managers and practitioners would answer a cautious 'yes' to both of the questions. In many local authorities the responsibility of tackling poverty is undertaken in a manner which relates to the assessment of individual needs for cash benefits available through the DHSS. Although this is often a role a social worker undertakes, the plethora of legislation, statutory regulations etc., has developed to such a degree of complexity, many social workers themselves have to turn to welfare rights specialists for advice and guidance. The local authority we work for employs a specialist welfare rights team based centrally but in addition funds a relatively large number of diverse voluntary agencies such as law centres, community advice agencies and welfare rights groups. All of these services and organisations play a very important and difficult part in trying to achieve the goals of an effective take-up of the established benefits and rights due to local people. Yet it could be argued that this in itself is still an essentially conservative response to poverty which can make significant improvements to the lot of individuals and families. Alone it will not affect the more fundamental elements of poverty, which require organisation, pressure and influence if the distribution of resources and opportunities is to be altered in favour of areas experiencing extreme poverty.

The authors have been managing fieldwork services for an area of Nottingham City for approximately six years and while acknowledging the important role the 'specialist services' can play in the alleviation of poverty we have also been committed to trying to achieve some impact on poverty both structurally and for individuals.

The context of our work

Like many similar social work teams, in the early 1980s the team which we managed had become initially interested and then committed to providing a social work service which, while not totally 'going local', was certainly moving in that direction. Many of the workers felt that the area structure and service post-Seebohm had become more remote, traditional and bureaucratic. The overall style was defensive and reactive rather than preventive and responsive. Inevitably, given the nature of the communities which made up our patch, we were becoming overloaded with statutory child care work and crises particularly in relation to one large council estate. This estate, situated on the boundaries of the City of Nottingham, experienced multiple social deprivations and manifested many of those problems more commonly associated with the inner-city.

The estate was built during the 1930s and, like many of that era, lacked many basic amenities. There were no communal facilities, little public open space, few shops and poor standard housing. In addition, in a report entitled *Disadvantage in Nottinghamshire* [Nottinghamshire County Council, 1983] which was a study of deprived areas in the county, this estate figured prominently in most of the fourteen indices used to denote deprivation. These included the number of children on free school meals, numbers unemployed, overcrowded large families, houses lacking basic amenities and in particular, statistics which had a close correlation to financial poverty. Among these were the very high percentage of people entirely dependent on state benefit, be it supplementary benefit, long term unemployment benefit or invalidity benefit.

Residents of this estate suffered widespread financial poverty, but also poverty in the sense of severe relative disadvantage of resources and opportunity. Though many residents were fiercely loyal to their estate, they were also aware of the stigma associated by outsiders with living there and knew they were neglected in resource terms. Many residents felt cynical, distrustful and powerless in their relation to people with any degree of power.

Referrals to social services were very often to do with financial problems. In their case work, social workers often felt immersed in a whirlpool of linked deprivations, and clung to mottoes such as 'aiming to make things less worse'. Many clients were known over generations and ever-extending family networks formed patterns across the team's caseload. Referrals for disconnections, delinquency, relatively low growth in children, child abuse, low educational attainment were frequent. Financial poverty could not just be seen on its own but as part of the fabric of residents' disadvantaged existence.

Planning for change

Given such clusters of disadvantage how could one social work team respond? If the assumption is that social services departments have a role to play in combatting poverty over and above welfare rights advice and advocacy, what are the implications for policy formulation, structure and service delivery? We became involved in many debates around this issue involving value and socio-political judgements. We felt that 'traditional' casework models underpinned by views of the inability of individuals to deal with their life experiences were inadequate and at times insulting. Financial advocacy and assistance were often much more appropriate and effective forms of help to families and accepting this leads to perceptions of departmental ironies, eg the comparison between levels of foster parent payments and available 'extras' from these budgets for the benefit of children once they had come into care contrasted with the much stricter limits of Section One allocations, for families who could be judged on their ability to cope with much less money. But, given that this estate scored very high on a number of indices of poverty, the team were as likely in the long term to become overwhelmed by the deluge of individual 'welfare rights' referrals as it was becoming by statutory demands. The view of the social work team and local managers was that we had to try and have some impact on some of the factors creating the underpinning poverty of the estate, eg unemployment, education and day care facilities etc. At the time we were relatively newly-appointed managers, managing mainly recently recruited workers and optimism and enthusiasm was unlimited.

Greater flexibility and autonomy challenges the bureaucracy of a large department. The effective authority of a local team is often circumscribed by factors such as control of finance, shortage of resources, legislation, centrally-defined priorities and traditional attitudes of defensive tight control developed over many years within local government. We were fortunate in having the relative freedom of a policy devolving budgetary resources to the area, designed to enable workers to provide finance for a preventive approach. It was initially more difficult to change attitudes and thinking from using resources only to enable individuals or families to survive the current crisis, to exploring ways of using those resources alongside local initiative and energy in providing more long term, neighbourhood based preventative schemes.

Equally important, we were fortunate in being part of a local authority where responsibility for management of services and direction of services at a local level were in the main delegated to local managers. In addition it was recognised that this particular estate had been providing an increasingly unmanageable number of referrals over the past years and that these referrals were more and more requiring statutory solutions, ie removal of children, mental health sections and custodial sentences for young offenders. The senior manager of the department specifically responsible for the social work service within Nottingham was supportive of the attempt of the local team to have some impact on this spiral.

Thus encouraged, the team's approach to this estate developed on a number of strategic levels. Organisationally a sub-team was created to work within this estate alone. This entailed lengthy negotiation with other social workers and managers within the area over issues of allocation of resources, support for the philosophy and a willingness to share responsibility. Where opportunities arose, staff were recruited whose interests and experience lay in providing a more localised flexible service and whose values and socio-political views coincided with the area/team philosophy. Through advertising and 'word of mouth' the approach of the team became known and there was no shortage of applicants wishing to become part of this approach.

Managers encouraged workers to take a broad range of responsibilities, to become known on the estate and to use their initiatives to identify needs and resources within the community. Becoming more of a 'community social worker' necessitated the addition of different pace, outlook and skills for the workers involved. Becoming known on the estate in a way which would generate the trust of residents and a willingness to share their experience, frustrations and aspirations needed patience and humility and skills in formal and informal settings. Establishing effective links with residents required the ability to participate in meetings which were not controlled by the paid workers involved and where criticism of the practice and attitudes of agencies could be given and received without undue defensiveness – both experiences to which social workers are sadly often not accustomed.

Stereotypes of social workers that were strongly held by some residents did change through repeated informal contact with individual social workers, especially with the social workers spending time away from their base, and not just making brief excursions to fixed events. Social workers who would allow themselves to be known for their personal qualities as well as their role became more trusted and respected by many residents and consequently became much more directly aware of the needs and life of the estate. For some residents, establishing that social workers are 'only human' and usually haven't got the answers was an effective spur to their own self confidence and ability to ask for support when needed. An additional consequence for the social workers was an increase in 'referrals' from residents, but also a greater awareness of the networks of support on the estate that could be used.

Seebohm's vision of the breadth of a neighbourhood office and the *Barclay Report* further helped shape the frequent discussions about the philosophy and purpose of the team. Time was needed for the team to identify objectives together and allocate tasks. To enable the development of alternative approaches space had to be created within workloads. At that time limited additional staff resources were available, as ever, and this meant that we as managers had to develop strategies to create this space. The need for effective workload management became acute but in addition we had to accept responsibility for the risks involved in tackling some high priority work. This entailed negotiation and support from senior managers within the department. It also entailed the team's reaching agreement on its own priorities and learning through experience the consequences of saying 'no' to many other demands. These demands came not only from individuals but also arose from expectations of other agencies and so the priorities and role of the social services department had to be renegotiated and at many levels.

The team worked on trust and openess in its own relationships; it was recognised that not everybody in the team had the commitment or skills to involve themselves in new developments and approaches but the giving of time in different ways was validated and the taking of risks needed to be acknowledged and shared. Time needed to be given for the team's philosophical discussions as well as on the detailed and practical, to try to give both shape and progress, but some members of the team were liable to 'switch off' when more abstract issues were addressed! In the early days, much of the focus was on obvious social work agenda items, such as facilities for under fives and welfare rights advice.

Joint action

The evolution of a community-oriented team with objectives of sharing authority with local people and of impacting some of the structural issues of poverty and inadequate facilities coincided with other agencies' developments along similar lines. The local probation service, housing authority and leisure services were among prime movers towards a localised approach. In addition a county-council community work project had for some time been working with local residents to enable them to articulate their own views, needs and demands. With a recent change of administration at both city and county level, a number of politicians were sympathetic not only to the needs of such estates but also to looking at alternative ways of providing services and of involving local people.

Locally a forum of residents and local workers developed with the aim of identifying needs, developing services and acting as a pressure group. Although welcome, all these developments lengthened the team's agendas and created greater demand for participation in meetings, etc.

Following on from this, with tangible support and commitment of several county and city council departments, the community work project, the health authority and police, a working group of middle-managers was convened which was charged with three specific tasks:

a) to draw up a short term image boosting programme consisting mainly of environmental work
b) to examine ways of consulting and involving residents and
c) to examine the dimensions of the problem of producing a co-ordinated 'development plan' for the estate.

The process by which these tasks were achieved was by the formation of a number of topic groups consisting of various local workers and residents, each convened by a middle-manager. The groups eventually produced a report which was collated into a development plan. Scattered throughout the report is ample evidence of poverty and means of tackling such both short term and long term. These were recommendations ranging from welfare rights facilities, to vocational guidance to youth employment schemes. Other recommendations centred around day care facilities for under fives to enable single-parents to work, greater information and access to local authority benefits such as school meals and uniform grants etc. Perhaps with hindsight some of the most effective and realistic recommendations related to the setting up of a nearly-new shop for local residents and increased health provision.

Beneath this umbrella, the team's strategies developed in several different directions, now usually collaboratively. New organisations were formed and nurtured, eg a welfare rights advice service partially operated by tenants. Existing organisations in difficulty were supported, eg helping to strengthen the committee of the adventure playground. The policies of agencies were publicly examined leading for example to the housing department adjusting its repairs and modernisation programme and establishing a neighbourhood office. Skills and altruism within the neighbourhood were supported, eg in the development of a care group. Perhaps most importantly in the long run, time was given to helping residents articulate their needs and achieve greater influence in the process of shaping their lives. Thus, for example, the philosophy and management structure of a family centre that developed reflected the desires and opinions of residents as well as those of the funding agencies.

There were many dilemmas and tensions within these processes. For social workers, various roles did not always sit easily together, eg having to carry out a child abuse investigation in the family of a fellow committee member. A vacancy in the team led to partial withdrawal which residents saw as abandonment and a breach of trust. Timescales for bids for resources were often shorter than those which would allow full resident participation, and such dilemmas exemplified the degree to which power and resources were still held away from residents and distributed according to the goodwill and patronage of the holder.

Limits to achievement and some consequences

Now, some years on, what has been achieved? On the surface the estate has areas of improvement but it still suffers from structural poverty epitomised by the inexorable rise in the numbers existing on state benefits. Community resources have developed, public amenities have been built, and on a small scale, various local residents' self-help groups exist. The welfare rights service continues. There is a nearly-new shop and drop-in centre, localised leisure amenities managed by tenants, a resource centre, modernised housing and equally important, a number of residents willing and able to tackle issues with their local councils. The reverse of the coin has seen a major rise in referrals to the local area team both in terms of material need and in serious child care issues. For the workers who started out full of hope and enthusiasm, their time has increasingly become, like their predecessors, taken up in keeping pace with statutory child care demands, increasing expectations imposed by the local authority guidelines and procedures in areas such as non-accidental injury referrals, access rights of parents and 'the permanency philosophy'.

Few if any of the workers can afford more than a few hours per month on developing links with local people, in looking at long term solutions to the underpinning poverty of their clients. Fresh developments are around methods of providing better services to children in care or in danger of entering care, based almost exclusively upon the casework model. True, the flexible use of budget continues to flourish but again normally as a means of propping up inadequate incomes to enable social work with families and individuals to continue.

The development plan also unwittingly began to involve workers in a process of 'bureacratisation' of local groups and individuals. This with hindsight in many ways resulted in the local authority widening its influence and control rather than the decentralisation or sharing of its power with local people. Because this process had not been forseen, the machinery for discussion and decision-making became problematic and cumbersome. Workers and managers alike became increasingly involved in 'advising' or supervising both meetings and projects thereby becoming the dominant partner and creating the dependency it had hoped to move away from.

The structure of the development plan itself has had to change and with time feels more of a consultative process rather than a sharing of power. Two major issues emerged at local level which allied to the diminishment of support both financial and political, from the centre, have proved insurmountable. The local issues were firstly the dissatisfaction with the bureaucratic nature of the process which left local people unsupported and experiencing difficulty in fully participating in meetings with 'professionals'. Secondly, local council workers could not properly participate in pressure groups especially when campaigns were aimed at their own council or department. Furthermore, doors which some agencies had gingerly opened to allow scrutiny and criticism of their practice have quietly been pushed closed again.

Although a different approach had been adopted its major role now seems to have been a consultative exercise around issues which, while not cosmetic, rarely touched upon the fundamental issues of the estate such as unemployment, poor educational attainment etc.

Conclusions

Nationally and locally the growth in expectations around areas such as child abuse and the greater involvement of courts and local authority committees in child care decision-making has led to a plethora of often bureaucratic self-protective procedures and regulations which for this area at least has sounded the death knell of our community social work approach. This demise has been aided by a perceived diminishment in interest, enthusiasm and resources on the part of the local councils who themselves are fighting an economic rear guard action to maintain services in the face of central government policy.

Local people themselves are increasingly struggling to manage on their often inadequate incomes and many have returned to their cynicism about central and local government's ability or wish to improve their standards and are therefore less able or willing to seek out long term solutions alongside us. Despite all the efforts by both local residents and agencies, for most people the fundamental long term restrictiveness and oppression of poverty hasn't changed.

We feel that this situation, while depressing, is a realistic and far from unique view of a social work team's attempts to have a significant impact on the poverty that pervades much of its work. The community approach demands a major shift not only in resource allocation but in the acquisition of skills different from those of a caseworker, and most of all in attitudinal changes which reflect a broader, more pro-active role for social services departments.

Ironically it is at this time of economic depression when areas such as the one identified in this article most need support to combat the undermining effects of poverty that departments are most ill-equipped to meet that challenge. Resources have become scarce in the face of mounting demand; attitudes and priorities shift, but to accommodate a more traditional, defensive role; the casework model concerned with the traditional individual and family clientele re-emerges as the solitary approach of the statutory social work agency. Depressing, and in our view, doomed to be an inadequate solution.

Even with these not insignificant changes described, we wonder just how effective any local authority can be in having an impact on poverty in the face of a central government onslaught on poor people and their opportunities to gain a reasonable standard of living. Our fear, based upon a preliminary look at the Social Fund, its ethos, cash limits etc., is that for estate and this social work team, there are hard times ahead; ensuring take-up of benefits was described above as a relatively conservative response to poverty, but if social workers are to be gatekeepers and assessors for the Social Fund, the past will seem radical indeed in comparison.

30

Poverty, Social Work and the State
Bill Jordan

S OCIAL policy failures are often more instructive than apparent successes. The Thatcher government's record on poverty and the personal social services has much to teach us about the state's role in income maintenance and social work. It is also a case study in how the state can use social division as a means of rule and a source of power.

In 1979, the Conservative party presented to the electorate a radical programme for change in British society. Its social policy aims were fairly clear and explicit:

1. To reduce state spending on social services, including income maintenance and personal social services [Conservative Party, 1979 in Keesings, 1979, 29635].

2. To eliminate or reduce discretion in the social security system [DHSS, 1978].

3. To abolish the Manpower Services Commission's Special Employment Measures, and reduce unemployment by creating 'real' jobs, through market forces.

Significantly, its objectives did *not* include the prevention of poverty or the achievement of greater equality. But part of its ideological system was the claim that the standards of living of the poorest would improve as a direct result of allowing the rich to create more wealth, and grow richer [Conservative party, 1976].

In all its declared aims, the Thatcher government has been spectacularly unsuccessful. Public spending on health, personal social services and social security increased by 23 per cent in real terms between 1980-1 and 1986-7 [Central Statistical Office, 1987a, fig 6.21, 114]. The heralded reform of the Social Security system contains a major return to discretionary payments, in the form of the Social Fund. The MSC Special Employment Measures in mid-1987 provided places for about 700,000 unemployed people [and will be further expanded with the creation of the Job Training Scheme over the next year]; in 1979 there were only about 150,000 people in MSC schemes [Central Statistical Office, 1987a, 83]. Registered unemployment has increased from around 1.3 million in 1979 to 3 million in June 1987 [Central Statistical Office, 1987a, Fig 4.21, 79].

In this chapter I shall analyse the significance of these departures from declared policy aims, and show the government's faith in markets led paradoxically to a major expansion in its role in relation to the poorest sector of the population. But I shall also show how this same expansion of state activity required new ways of monitoring and regulating the poor, and how social work has adapted to the changing situation of its clients within the social structure.

Economic policy and poverty

The Thatcher government of 1979 regarded itself as having a mandate to carry out a social experiment in Britain, consisting of opening up the ailing economy to global market forces [Deakin, 1987, 91]. In no other advanced capitalist country were the precepts of free market economies so vigorously applied to the tasks of government, or the props of Keynesian and corporatist institutions so gleefully knocked away. Only in a few Third World countries [like Sri Lanka] were governments similarly persuaded, by a combination of speculative theory and international financial pressure, to conduct such radical experiments, with similarly divisive results [Rupesinghe, 1986].

The British experiment proved what history should by now have conclusively demonstrated, that there is no logical linkage between the market for labour and a subsistence level of income. Britain's economy was already the most open and the most vulnerable in the advanced world, and the new international division of labour had already made a substantial proportion of our industrial workforce redundant. What the government's policies showed was that for unskilled workers in low-tech industries, the floor on wages levels was effectively set by the pay of those in the newly industrialising countries in the Far East. As for workers in services, the huge pool of industrial unemployment, and the reserve army of female labour, meant that there was virtually no floor on their wages, as part-time, casual and self-employed people competed for often menial tasks.

If market forces could not save a large proportion of our population from starving, nor could that other Tory talisman, the family. Thatcherite ideology created the fantasy that, for every person with a disability or disadvantage, physical, psychological or economic, there was somebody somewhere who could be held responsible, and who would provide both subsidisation and practical support. In reality Britain – like every other West European country – had a rapidly rising proportion of elderly people, of single-person households, and of single parents. Although there is ample evidence of the enduring strength of family bonds and the sense of obligation to care [especially among women; Oliver and Briggs, 1985], and although the proportion of the population in residential care of all kinds has scarcely altered since the beginning of the century [in spite of the enormous increase in the elderly proportion of the population; Moroney, 1976, 42], the scope for further state enforcement of kinship duties on informal carers was strictly limited.

So the poverty that was the inevitable consequence of government economic policies rebounded onto the Thatcher administration, in the form of increased claims for benefits of all kind, increased need for health care, and increased demand for personal social services. This rise in dependence on the state consisted mainly of an increase in the numbers of those *wholly* reliant on state aid – for income as well as services – through unemployment; but it also included a large number of low wage earners, who needed subsidisation to reach subsistence level. The expression 'New Poverty' is used in France to denote working-age people who have become dependent on social assistance. This phenomenon had been common in Britain through the 1970s; what was new was that families with children had become the biggest component of Britain's poorest citizens [DHSS, 1985c, 9].

Regulating the poor

In these circumstances, the obvious way for the government to limit spending on the relief of poverty was to cut back the universal National Insurance elements in social security provision, and extend the use of selective means-testing. Supplementary benefits already constituted proportionally the largest social assistance scheme in Western Europe, before the Conservatives took office [DHSS, 1978], and family income supplements, rate and rent rebates had established the principle of means-tested assistance to low-wage households. Hence it was simply a matter of shifting the relative shares of selectivism and universalism within the system, a process which was begun early in the first Thatcher administration, with cutbacks in the rates of National Insurance benefits. The value of supplementary benefits was at first maintained [Howell, 1981, 10].

However, there are many notorious features of means-tested systems which critics, both inside and outside the Conservative party, were quick to point out. Where the global labour market provided no floor on wage levels, the benefits system did; people with a family to support would not be prepared to work for less than their basic entitlement, and only married women with a husband in employment had an incentive to take part-time work. Once in employment, workers encountered income taxation as they lost means-tested benefits, so that their effective marginal tax rates were very high – across a band of earnings, higher than 100 per cent – so they had little or no incentive to try to escape from poverty. Above all, the same American ideology which gave the government monetarism, market mindedness and tax-cutting also insisted that social assistance benefits fostered a culture of dependence [Piven, 1987], apathy and ultimately idleness – the very antithesis of the spirit of enterprise, and a threat of ever-increasing burdens on all forms of state services.

The Conservative government has set about trying to remedy these problems in three ways. First, in order to make idleness less possible, it has greatly expanded the MSC's 'training' and 'employment' schemes, and is well on the way to 'abolishing' long term unemployment. Already there are plans to cut off benefits of young people who refuse YTS places, and it seems certain that the same rule will eventually follow for adults who refuse JTS and CP. In this way 'workfare' – compulsory work for the state as a condition for receiving benefits – will have been established, the same principle as applies in the USA, but by a different route. The benefit authorities are getting machinery for this in place, through Restart interviews and more rigorous availability testing [Jordan and Greenwood, 1987]. It is ironical that the principles that inform such a system – compulsory poverty-wage employment in low-productivity, overstaffed make-work state schemes – represent an exact replica of the Soviet command economy that the Thatcher government purports to despise.

The second remedy is reform of the social security system itself. The first Thatcher administration was notable for its lack of any radical restructuring of the social services; the Fowler reform plan was the first attempt to apply new principles to the welfare state. Yet in spite of the rhetorical claim of Beveridgian scope, the results have been puny – more pruning of National Insurance benefits, a smoothing out of the worst anomalies of the poverty trap, and a return to the discretionary approach that had been so decisively abandoned in 1980.

This last retreat from its original stance follows the logic of selectivism. If the aim of poverty relief is to cut back provision to the bare minimum, and confine it to those with least resources, then there will always be a wide margin of those eligible for benefits who find themselves in debt or destitution, or who cannot afford occasional large outlays. The principle of entitlement to single payments, which was itself an attempt to limit these extra payments for exceptional needs, actually encourages the kind of calculative dependence that the government fears. So instead, and more consistent with its philosophy, it has created a quasi-social-work agency in the Social Fund to assess each need individually as a more reliable way of limiting single payments, especially when it is tied to a local budget, and there is no right of appeal [DHSS, 1986a].

The third remedy has been to try to shift part of the burden of poverty onto the local authorities and voluntary agencies, while at the same time strictly limiting their resources. The more services can be given in kind by these other agencies, the less claims can be made on central government services. This is most obvious in relation to the care of people who have hitherto been regarded as long-term hospital patients, but it is more subtly true of other large groups of poor people who are presenting their needs to social services departments. In this way, social work becomes involved in the management of poverty, both directly, as in the case of assessments for the Social Fund, payments during civil service strikes, and Section One payments; and indirectly, as in the implications of poverty for child care policy and practice.

Social work's reaction

Social work has always been reactive rather than proactive in issues of poverty. Because it deals mainly in individual and family distress, it is only through these phenomena that trends and policies in income maintenance are experienced by social workers or their managers. Hence social work responds to the symptoms of change, but seldom initiates it.

Social workers and their agencies embraced the tasks of emergency destitution relief and assistance for exceptional needs between 1963 and the mid-1970s, when resources were expanding [Jordan, 1974]. These tasks were largely thrust upon them by an increasingly overloaded supplementary benefits system, which could not do justice to its responsibilities for meeting short-term emergencies and rapidly-changing needs. With resource constraints came a new emphasis on stringency, and more commitment to advocacy on behalf of distressed claimants. But by then social services departments were already seen as involved in the relief of urgent poverty, so that as government policy has increased the number of claimants, and worsened their lot, social workers have reluctantly been dragged further and further into this field. Recent research has shown how much social work is now a service to the poor; over 50 per cent of all referrals are from claimants of supplementary benefit [Becker and MacPherson, 1986].

In an increasingly divided society, and with a more impoverished and dependent clientele, we would expect that social work would become a more adversarial activity. Unfortunately, most of the evidence points to a greater antagonism, and more use of compulsory measures, by social workers against their clients. This is particularly clear in the field of child care, where the trend has all been in the direction of statutory powers and orders, at the expense of voluntarism and negotiated solutions [Packman *et al*, 1986]. Obviously, as clients' plights become more desperate, and as they identify social workers more with the state agencies which do not meet their needs, the chances of co-operation are reduced; but the evidence points also to more punitive ideologies among social workers, more social distance between them and their clientele, and a greater emphasis on decisiveness, which often works against partnership and sharing [Satyamurti, 1981; Packman *et al*, 1986].

It is to social workers' credit that the change has not all been in this direction. In certain fields – notably divorce conciliation [Parkinson, 1983], and the community care of mentally ill and mentally handicapped people [Rush, 1980; Exeter Health Authority, 1984] – there have been real attempts to use negotiation as a means of achieving agreements, or establishing partnerships, or sharing care with previously neglected carers. Patch social work is an attempt to establish more informal and reliable communications between social workers and the communities they serve, and in many instances has reversed the trend towards heavy-handed interventions [Cooper, 1983].

The real difficulty of social workers' structural position, in a society which is divided along the lines of Britain under the Thatcher government, is revealed by the recent White Paper on *Child Care and Family Law* [DHSS, 1987a]. The DHSS seems to have been genuinely disquieted by the evidence of antagonism, misunderstanding an unmet need that was revealed by the research it sponsored on child care policy and practice [Fruin and Vernon, 1983; Millham *et al*, 1986; Packman *et al*, 1986]. The research showed that the attempt to use care as a last resort, rather than as a negotiated constructive option, led to increased compulsory admissions, which in turn led to longer stays in care, and an increase in the numbers of children who lost touch with their families. The White Paper proposed a restructuring of admission to care, which would enable parents to request short-term voluntary admissions for respite, and promote sharing of care between departments and parents. It also proposed enhanced powers for social workers to give financial support to families.

In one sense, these suggestions are entirely laudable and positive, and should catch a wave of revulsion against excessive use of statutory powers, and exclusion of parents from their children's lives. But they do nothing to help social workers recognise the small minority of cases where negotiated solutions are impossible, and where the situation demands statutory protection; or to resist pressure from other professionals, when they believe such situations exist. The Cleveland scandal over sexual abuse raises just these issues in an acute form, and has led to the postponement of legislation planned to enact the White Paper's proposals.

But perhaps even more difficult is the issue of the balance between local authority services in kind and central government income maintenance provision in relief of poverty [Jordan, 1987b, 31]. Conservative measures have led to huge numbers of people on bare-bones income support, in appalling houses, neglected communities, poor education, and with no hope of a decent job. People come to local authority services from this situation with so many unmet needs that social workers are being expected to solve total life problems, rather than to meet specific needs. This applies to all client groups, but perhaps most acutely to children.

For parents trying to bring up children in circumstances of extreme deprivation, it makes sense – in the absence of other forms of provision – to ask for care, simply as a way of improving children's life chances. In other words, if central government cuts back provision for income maintenance, and if local authorities lack the resources to provide decent housing, it is rational for poor people to try to improve their children's prospects of a better life by asking that they should be placed with someone in a less disadvantaged situation.

This is just a more exaggerated example of one of the major dilemmas facing social workers in deprived areas, and which is never acknowledged in the child abuse scandal enquiries [Jordan, 1985]. Every day social workers encounter people living in poverty, whose material needs could easily absorb the department's whole budget. Also every day, they make decisions about whether a child should be admitted to care, in order to place him or her in a social environment in which material standards, and hence life chances, could be better. Yet social workers operate as if this were not the dilemma, as if it was always *something else* – usually the parents' standards of emotional and physical care, or their health – that determined the decision. In fact, of course, these standards, and parental attitudes, are very much affected by their economic situation, and especially by their prospects, and how they see those of their children.

The ingenious thing [from the government's point of view] about using social work criteria for rationing poor relief payments [as in the Social Fund or in Section One, or in the White Paper proposal] or for allocating services in lieu of such payments, is that it makes the *criteria* for managing poverty *personal* [emotional, familial or relationship-based] rather than financial. In other word, decisions about relieving poverty are disguised as something else – as professional judgements about whether the person or family is 'helpable' by the provision of cash or services. This applies to community care grants from the Social Fund as well as to child care payments. Research shows that this form of decision-making is a very effective way of rationing financial assistance, because social workers often decide that their poorest clients will not be able to improve their lot with extra financial assistance, and so withhold it [Haywood and Allen, 1971]. Decisions about services in turn become a disguised way of dealing with economic deprivation, without acknowledging that this is one of the main issues, or addressing it directly.

Clients are not unware of this – indeed they often face the issue more squarely than social workers do. But if they are driven to channel all their material and financial needs, employment, housing, educational and health deprivations, into dealings with social workers, then they are inevitably going to feel frustration and anger. They know that their needs are not personal, but ones they have in common with most others in the neighbourhood, yet they are required to express these in personal, emotional terms to qualify for help. In asking for help in this way, they know they make themselves vulnerable to interventions that they do not want, and that the information they give social workers may be used against them, to take powers that will add to their disadvantages [Jordan, 1976]. I recently did a role-play exercise with a group of social workers on a training day in which I invited them as groups of disadvantaged people, first to identify their needs from *all* the welfare state services, and then to express these needs to the social services department only, as no other agency had the necessary resources. The participants [who did the exercise with a convincing mixture of menace and pathos] said the switch made them express their needs both more angrily and more manipulatively. The use of social work in this way is not conducive to good faith and honest, open negotiation. I fear, therefore, that the DHSS's good intentions in promoting a more sharing, partnership style of work with poor parents may be defeated by putting too many issues of poverty and need on the same agenda as the child care decisions.

The most worrying thing for social workers is when recognition of the hypocrisy of this system becomes part of the culture of the neighbourhood – as it already has in many black communities. When clients already have a cynical attitude – that they have to present themselves as in an emotional mess to get material help, then they naturally see social work as a very insidious part of an oppressive system. Above all, if black people see the power of white social workers as exercised in this way, they cannot be expected to regard it with anything but hostility and resistance.

Conclusion

I have argued that the logic of the Thatcher government's dual system of rule – global liberalism, market choice and prosperity for one sector of the population; neo-Hobbesian control, monitoring, enforced work for the state and social work rationing of public assistance for the other – uses local authority services as a means of sustaining social division. Yet the relative generosity and open-handedness of the White Paper proposals serves another purpose. It allows the flexibility of response, the kinder face of the state, which is equally essential if the harsh and unjust conditions promoted by the government are to be sustained without the outbreak of open rebellion. Local authorities, through their resources will be cash limited, will be allowed the powers to deal with clients in a spirit of partnership and caring, and will be required to manage the poor with sensitivity and sympathy, but without the power to relieve their poverty. This leaves social workers at a potentially explosive interface, negotiating all the most fundamental dilemmas of social injustice, racial discrimination, alienation and deviance.

It is of the nature of social work that it is open to being used in this way by an ingenious government like our present one, and that there are no easy answers to the dilemmas this creates. In dealings with clients, negotiation and partnership is still the right aim – it is just made much more difficult to achieve. Poverty and wider economic problems need to be acknowledged in this process, not swept aside, even if social work can only play a limited role in helping people organise to combat them. Above all, social workers, their managers and agencies should not try to disguise issues of poverty as issues of professional power and resources, and collude with attempts to redefine economic deprivation as personal and emotional inadequacy. In this, changes which bring departments closer to clients' lives, though painful in confronting us with reality, will enable a more realistic approach to the management of poverty.

Public issues, private pain

Notes on Contributors

SUE BALLOCH is a senior lecturer in Social Administration at Goldsmith College, London. Among her previous work was the AMA study concerned with caring for unemployed people. She has been recently working with the AMA on their major poverty study.

SAUL BECKER is Senior Welfare Rights Officer responsible for social security training with Nottinghamshire Social Services. He qualified and practised as a social worker. Between 1985 and 1987 he worked in the Benefits Research Unit at Nottingham University on the ESRC funded doctorate study of social workers' attitudes to poverty and the poor. He has researched and published widely on poverty and social work.

ROY BAILEY is currently head of the Department of Applied Social Studies at Sheffield City Polytechnic. Originally a graduate in Social Science from the University of Leicester, he has spent more than twenty years concerned with the application of Sociology and the Social Sciences to the development of social work education. He has contributed to and edited a number of books including *Contemporary Social Problems in Britain* with Jock Young (1973), *Radical Social Work* with Mike Brake (1975), *Radical Social Work and Practice* with Mike Brake (1978), and *Theory and Practice in Social Work* with Phil Lee (1982).

YVONNE DHOOGE, is an applied sociologist/anthropologist, since 1983 involved in research, and policy and training development, work on unemployment and health and social services. Currently member of a European research programme concerned with how neighbourhoods cope with economic and social change, and based at the Community Projects Foundation.

MALCOLM DILLON is assistant area director of a social services area in the City of Nottingham.

DAVID DIVINE is director of social services for the London Borough of Brent. He was previously a senior social worker and then principal manager in the social services Department of the London Borough of Hackney. Prior to that he was a senior practitioner in the London Borough of Tower Hamlets. He is primarily interested in how to manage social service provision in a multicultural society in order to create accessible and relevant service provision.

GEOFF FIMISTER: During the early 1970s, he was engaged in research on various social policy issues at Loughborough and Glasgow Universities, moving to Newcastle upon Tyne in 1974 to establish Newcastle Welfare Rights Service. He has been responsible for the development of that service since that time; a members of the National Executive Committee of the Child Poverty Action Group since 1979, and has for a number of years been an advisor on welfare rights to the Association of Metropolitan Authorities [and on various occasions also to the Association of Directors of Social Services and the European Economic and Social Committee]. He is the author of Welfare Rights Work in Social Services and of various reports and articles in the welfare rights field.

ISOBEL FREEMAN is senior research officer in the social work department of Strathclyde Regional Council. Previously she worked at Stirling University where she obtained a PhD on public attitudes towards social security.

DULCIE GROVES, a Nottingham graduate in social administration, has a Master of Social Service degree from Bryn Mawr College, USA and obtained her doctorate for research on women and occupational pensions. She teaches social policy at Lancaster University and has published various papers on informal care and on pension topics.

JOHN HANNAM is team leader of the Nottinghamshire Welfare Rights Service.

PAULINE HARDIKER is senior lecturer, School of Social Work, University of Leicester. She and Mary Barker are currently engaged in a DHSS-commissioned research project, examining policies and practices in preventive child care.

ROB IRVINE teaches at the University of Western Australia. He was previously research officer with the Scottish Society for the Prevention of Cruelty to Children based in Edinburgh.

BRIAN JONES is assistant secretary, social services, Association of Metropolitan Authorities. He was co-author, with Sue Balloch, of the report produced by the AMA on caring for unemployed people and presently co-ordinates and manages the AMA poverty project. The results of that project are to be published in a series of articles and reports during 1988.

BILL JORDAN read politics, philosophy and economics at Oxford University. He worked in the Probation Service from 1965 to 1974, the last five years part-time, and as a part-time social worker from 1975 to 1985. He was joint chairman of the Basic Income Research Group in 1985-6, and is currently chairman of the Board of the European Claimants Association. He is Reader in Social Studies at Exeter University.

BOB LEAPER is emeritus professor of Exeter University and is now teaching at the Roehampton Institute in London. He is engaged on a long term consumer survey of people over 65 in Devon. He has taught and researched on social provisions in other European countries for many years and was recently awarded an honorary doctorate from the University of Rennes for his work on comparative social policy and provision in France and Britain.

STEWART MACPHERSON currently teaches social administration at the University of Nottingham, where he is also a director of the Benefits Research Unit. Since 1980 the Unit has been involved in research on poverty and social security benefits, with particular emphasis on the implications of national policies for local authorities. From July 1988 he will be Professor, Department of Anthropology, Sociology and Social

Work, University of Papua New Guinea. He has published extensively on social welfare and social policy in the third world as well as on poverty and social security in the UK.

FRASER MCCLUSKEY is a research officer in the social work department of Strathclyde Regional Council. His specialist interests include poverty and welfare benefits issues.

BECKY MORLEY is a lecturer in the School of Social Studies at the University of Nottingham, where she teaches women's issues to social administration students and psychology to social work students. She is currently completing a book on male violence against women.

ALAN MURIE is a senior lecturer at the School for Advanced Urban Studies, University of Bristol. His background and interests lie broadly within urban studies and social policy and he has focussed largely on housing issues in recent years and has been involved in a range of housing research including a study of London's homeless carried out in 1986.

JAQI NIXON is senior lecturer in social administration at Brighton Polytechnic. Her publications and research interests cover social security, race relations policy, the parliamentary select committee system, and PSS policies and practice concerning families in financial need. She is currently engaged in a CNAA-funded project on the role of non-professional student placements in social administration degree courses.

JEFF PARKER is area director of a social services area in the City of Nottingham.

JOE PIDGEON has been a social worker in the Nottingham Rehabilitation and Community Care Services for the past three years. This service provides a variety of residential, day care and long-term after-care support for people who have enduring mental health problems. Prior to working in the mental health field he spent four years working in long term and intake teams in an inner city area office in Derby.

JENNIE POPAY is a senior research officer at the Thomas Coram Research Unit at the University of London. She is presently undertaking research on the health of men and women with dependent children.

Between 1983 and 1985 she was involved in research into the impact of unemployment for health and social services providers and has been an assistant director of a follow-up training programme since 1985.

FIONA ROBERTSON and AMANDA WOODS are community workers based in Nottingham who have previously worked with a range of voluntary organisations. The chapter was researched by Amanda Woods and Fiona Robertson and written by Fiona Robertson.

GILL SHEPPERSON was a social worker in the Nottingham Rehabilitation and Community Care Services for three years. Since 1987 she has been employed as team leader of the Community Support Team, Chesterfield. This project is part of the DHSS-sponsored 'Care in the Community' programme and will offer a support service to individuals with enduring disabilities arising from long term mental health difficulties.

RICHARD SILBURN is senior lecturer in social administration at the University of Nottingham. He has developed his interest in poverty and social policy for over twenty years. In 1970 (in collaboration with Ken Coates) he published *Poverty : the Forgotten Englishmen* (Penguin), now in its fourth edition. More recently he has been a co-founder of the Benefits Research Unit, which specialises in applied research in the area of social security, social policy and social work. For the next two years, he will direct a major research study of the Social Fund (in collaboration with more than 25 local authorities).

SUE SLIPMAN is director of the National Council for One Parent Families. She was the first woman president of the National Union of Students and before joining the NCOPF was an area officer for the National Union of Public Employees. She has extensive broadcasting experience and has written numerous magazine and newspaper articles. Among her publications is *Helping ourselves to power: a training manual for women* (1986).

OLIVE STEVENSON is professor of Social Work Studies at Nottingham University. She is a member of the Social Security Advisory Committee and past chair of Age Concern England. Her research interests include the personal social services and the social care of frail elderly people. *Age and Vulnerability: a guide to better practice* is to be published shortly by Age

Concern and Hodder and Stoughton.

GILL STEWART and JOHN STEWART work as lecturers in Lancaster University's Department of Social Administration. They research and write about social security policy issues that affect claimant clients, and about the implications of these for welfare rights work and for social work practice. Examples include an analysis of the origins of the Social Fund [*Boundary Changes*, published by CPAG]; and a survey on the effects of the amended single payment regulations, conducted for the Welfare Rights Officers Group. Gill and John are currently helping to organise national monitoring of the Social Fund's impact for the local authority associations.

ROGER SUMPTON is a research psychologist who has specialised in evaluating services for mentally handicapped people. He has a PhD in social psychology as well as a social work qualification and experience as a social worker in a community mental handicap team. His publications include *Homes for Mentally Handicapped People* (1987, Tavistock Publications), written with Norma Raynes and Margaret Flynn. He is currently working at Sheffield City Polytechnic on a CCETSW and ENB study of joint training for staff working in the community with mentally handicapped people.

MARK SVENSON worked in a community home for children in Hull social services department for 18 months until 1983. In 1986 he graduated in social administration from Nottingham University. At present he is employed as a research officer in the Benefits Research Unit at Nottingham University.

DAVID THORPE is senior lecturer in social work at the University of Lancaster.

MIKE TITTERTON was formerly with the Social Work Research Centre at Stirling University. He has worked in the Scottish Health Service and the Social Work Services Group. He is currently finishing his doctoral thesis on urban public services and urban politics in the Department of Sociology, Edinburgh University.

DAVID TOWNSEND: director of Social Services, Croydon; director of Social Services, Haringey, 1983 87; deputy director of social services, Camden, 1978-88; special adviser to the Secretary of State for Social

Services, 1976-78; Lewisham councillor, 1978-81; member of Lambeth, Southwark and Lewisham District Health Authority, 1978-82.

JO TUNNARD has been director of Family Rights Group since 1979. She is the author of *In Care: a money guide for families*. Previously she worked at CPAG where she gave advice on welfare benefits, co-ordinated the activities of the National Welfare Rights Officers' Group, and wrote guides and pamphlets about tax, benefits and mortgage problems.

GARY VAUX has been the welfare rights officer for Brent Social Services Department since January 1985. Previous to that he was employed by Ealing and Coventry councils and has also worked in the voluntary sector. A qualified social worker, he has been involved in the welfare rights field for over 10 years.

Bibliography:
Social Work and Poverty

This Bibliography contains the references cited in the text. It also includes others that will be of relevance to those requiring a more extensive selection of sources on social work and poverty.

Abel-Smith, B. and Townsend, P., 1965, *The Poor and the Poorest*, Occasional Papers in Social Administration, No.17, G. Bell and Sons Ltd.

Abrams, M., 1985, *A Survey of the Elderly Shopper'*, London, Age Concern

Abrams, P., 1980, 'Social change, social networks and neighbourhood care', *Social Work Service*, February.

ADSS., 1985, *Personal Social Services: Expenditure, Staffing and Activities, Report of Survey*, London, ADSS.

Age Concern., 1987, Information Circular, November, Age Concern.

Ahmed, S., Cheetham J. and Small, J., 1986, *Social Work with Black Children and their Families*, London, Batsford.

Alcock, P., 1987, *Poverty and State Support*, London, Longman.

Alinsky, S., 1946, *Reveille For Radicals*, New York.

Allan, G., 1985, *Family Life: Domestic Roles and Social Organisation*, Oxford, Basil Blackwell.

Altenmeir, W.A., O'Connor, S., Vietze, P., Sandler, H. and Sherrod, D.K., 1984, 'Prediction of child abuse, a prospective study of feasibility', *International Journal of Child Abuse and Neglect*, 8, pp. 393—400.

AMA, *et al*, 1982, *Fuel Hardship: Towards a Social Policy*.

Arangio, A.J., 1970, *Individual Change or Institutional Change? A Survey of Prevailing Attitudes of Professional Social Workers Toward Change Targets, Goals and Tactics*, PhD, Tulane University, unpublished.

Archbishop of Canterbury's Commission on Urban Priority Areas, 1985, *Faith in the City*, London, Church House Publishing.

Arrêté Royal, 1987, April 8.

Armstrong, L., 1978, *Kiss Daddy Goodnight — A Speak Out on Incest*, New York, Pocket Books.

Ashley, P., 1983, *The Money Problems of the Poor*, London, Heinemann.

Attlee, C., 1920, *The Social Worker*, London, Bell.
Audit Commission., 1985, *Managing Services for the Elderly*, London, HMSO.
Audit Commission., 1986, *Making a Reality of Community Care*, London, HMSO.
Bailey, J., 1980, *Ideas and Intervention: Social Theory for Practice*, London, Routledge & Kegan Paul.
Bailey, R., 1973, 'The family and the social management of intolerable dilemmas', in **Bailey, R.** and **Young, J.**, (eds), *Contemporary Social Problems in Britain*, London, Saxon House.
Bailey, R. and Brake, M., 1975, *Radical Social Work*, London, Edward Arnold.
Baker, R., 1976, The multi-role practitioner in the generic orientation to social work practice, *British Journal of Social work*, 6, 3, pp. 327—352.
Balloch, S. and Hume, C., 1985, *Caring for Unemployed People*, London, NISW/Bedford Square Press.
Bamford, T., 1983, 'A need to fight for change', *Social Work Today*, 15/12/83, pp11—12.
Barclay, P., 1982, *Social Workers: Their Roles and Tasks*, London, NISW/Bedford. Square Press.
Barrett, M. and McIntosh, M., 1982, *The Anti-Social Family*, London, Verso.
Barter, J., 1973, 'Comment on welfare rights', *Social Work Today*, 29/9/73.
BASW., 1985, *Report by Molly Meacher*, 3 September, mimeo.
BASW., 1987, *Unemployment and the Personal Social Services*, Birmingham, BASW.
Bayley, M. *et al*, 1985, *Practising Community Care: an Approach to Developing Locally Based, Integrated Participatory Practice*, Dinnington Project Paper 11, University of Sheffield.
Bebbington, A.C. and Davies, B., 1983, 'Equity and efficiency in the allocation of the personal social services', *Journal of Social Policy*, 12, pp. 309—330.
Becker, S., 1987a, *Social Workers' Attitudes to Poverty and the Poor*, PhD, University of Nottingham, unpublished.
Becker, S., 1987b, 'How much collaboration?', *Community Care*, 26/3/87, pp. 17—19.
Becker, S. and MacPherson, S., 1985a, 'Scroungerphobia — where do we stand?', *Social Work Today*, 18/2/85, pp. 15—17.
Becker, S. and MacPherson, S., 1985b, 'Cash counsel, the art of the possible', *Social Work Today*, 25/2/85, pp. 16—18.
Becker, S. and MacPherson, S., 1986, *Poor Clients: The Extent and Nature of Financial Poverty amongst Consumers of Social Work Services*, Nottingham University, Benefits Research Unit.
Becker, S., MacPherson, S. and Falkingham, F., 1987, 'Some Local Authority responses to poverty', *Local Government Studies*, May, pp. 35—47.
Becker, S., MacPherson, S. Silburn, R.L., 1983, *Saints, Ferrets and Philosophers*, Nottingham University, Benefits Research Unit.
Belson, W.A., 1975, *Juvenile Theft: The Causal Factors*, London, Harper Row.
Beltram, G., 1984, *Testing the Safety Net*, London, Bedford Square Press.
Beresford, P. and Croft, S., 1986, *Whose Welfare – Private Care or Public Services?* Brighton, Lewis Cohen Urban Studies.
Beresford, P., Kemmis, J., Tunstill, J., 1987, *In Care in North Battersea*, London, North Battersea Research Group.
Berger, J.M. and Bataille, L.M., 1985, *Aide mémoire des CPAS*, Union des Villes et Communes Belges.
Bernard, D., 1967, *The Impact of the First Year of Professional Education in Social Work on Student Value Positions*, PhD, Bryn Mawr College, Graduate School of Social Work and Social Research, unpublished.
Berthoud, R., 1984, *Reform of Supplementary Benefit*, Policy Studies Institute, Working papers, vols 1, 2, London, PSI.
Berthoud, R., 1986, *Selective Social Security – An analysis of the Government Plan*, London, PSI.
Berthoud, R., 1987, 'The Social Fund, will it work?' *Policy Studies*, vol. 8, pt. 1.
Berthoud, R., Benson, S. and Williams, S., 1986, *Standing Up for Claimants*, London, PSI.

Berthoud, R. and Brown, J., 1981, *Poverty and the Development of Anti Poverty Policy in the UK*, London, PSI/Heinemann.

Bertrand, D., 1987, *La Protection Sociale*, PUF.

Beveridge, W., 1942, *Social Insurance and Allied Services*, Cmmd. 6404, London, HMSO.

Bilson, A., 1986, 'A counter productive strategy', *Community Care*, No.623 pp. 16—17.

Binney, V., Harkell, G. and Nixon, J., 1981, *Leaving Violent Men: A Study of Refuges and Housing for Battered Women*, Leeds, Women's Aid Federation.

Birch, A., 1983, *What Chance Have we Got? Occupation and Employment after Mental Illness — Patients' Views*, Manchester, MIND.

Bishop, F., 1975, 'Meaning, perception and pathological identification of precipitating factors in parental attacks on children', *Medical Journal in Australia*, August.

Blagg, P., 1987, *Corporate Strategies and Social Space*, University of Lancaster, unpublished Paper.

Blau, P., 1984, *On the Nature of Organization*, New York, John Wiley and Sons.

Blaxter, M., 1974, 'Health "on the welfare" — a case study', *Journal of Social Policy*, 3, p. 39—51.

Blaxter, M., 1981, *The Health of the Children: A Review of Research on the Place of Health in Cycles of Disadvantage*, London, Heinemann.

Booth, A. and Smith, R., 1985, 'The irony of the iron fist: social security and the coal dispute 1984—1985', *Journal of Law and Society*, 12, 3.

Bosanquet, N., 1984, 'Social policy and the welfare state', in Jowell, R. and Airey, C. (eds), *British Social Attitudes: the 1984 Report*, London, Gower.

Bosanqet, N., 1986, 'Public spending and the welfare state', in Jowell, R., Witherspoon, S. and Brook, L., (eds) *British Social Attitudes: the 1986 Report*, London, Gower.

Bourne, R. and Newberger, E., [eds] 1979, *Critical Perspectives On Child Abuse*, Lexington, Mass, Lexington Books.

Box, S., 1983, *Power, Crime and Mystification*, London, Tavistock.

Bradshaw, J. and Morgan, J., 1987, *Budgeting on Benefit: The Consumption of Families on Social Security*, London, FPSC.

Bradshaw, M. and Davis, A., 1986, *Not a Penny to Call my Own — Poverty amongst Individuals in Mental Illness and Mental Handicap Hospitals*, London, Kings Fund and Disability Alliance.

Brake, M. and Bailey, R., (eds), 1980, *Radical Social Work and Practice*, London, Edward Arnold.

Brannen, J. and Moss, P., 1987, 'Dual earner households: women's financial contributions after the birth of the first child' in Brannen, J. and Wilson, G., (eds) *Give and Take in Families: Studies in Resource Distribution*, London, Allen and Unwin.

Brannen, J. and Wilson, G., (eds), 1987, *Give and Take in Families: Studies in Resource Distribution*, London, Allen and Unwin.

Brown, C., 1984, *Black and White Britain*, London, Policy Studies Institute and Heinemann.

Brown, G.W. and Harris, T., 1978, *The Social Origins of Depression: a Study of Psychiatric Disorder in Women*, London, Tavistock.

Brown, N. and Madge, M., 1982, *Despite the Welfare State*, London, Heinemann.

Bryan, B., Dadzie, S. and Scafe, S., 1985, *The Heart of the Race: Black Women's Lives in Britain*, London, Virago.

Buckle, J.R., 1971, *Work and Housing of Impaired Persons in Great Britain*, OCPS Social Survey Division, London, HMSO.

Bull, D., 1970, *Action for Welfare Rights*, Fabian Research Series 286, London, Fabian.

Bull, D., 1982, *Welfare Advocacy: Whose Means to What Ends?*, Sheila Kay Memorial Lecture, Birmingham, BASW.

Burghes, L., 1980, *Living from Hand to Mouth*, London, FSU/CPAG.

Burney, E., 1986, *What Went Wrong with the Criminial Justice Act 1982*, Aldershot, Gower.

Byrne, D., 1987a, *The Underpaid Millions*, London, Low Pay Unit.

Byrne, D., 1987b, 'Rich and poor: the growing divide', in Walker, A., and Walker C., (eds), *The Growing Divide: A Social Audit*, London, CPAG.

Calleja, J.M., 1984, *Network Interaction among Female Single Parents: the Effects of Economic Class World Views*, Wayne State University.

Campbell, B., 1984, *Wigan Pier Revisited*, London, Virago.
Carby, H., 1982, 'White women listen! Black feminism and the boundaries of sisterhood', in *Centre for Contemporary Cultural Studies*, 1982, *The Empire Strikes Back: Race and Racism in 70s Britain*, London, Hutchinson.
CCETSW., 1987, *The Qualifying Diploma in Social Work — a Policy Statement*.
Central Statistical Office., 1987a, *Social Trends 17*, London, HMSO.
Central Statistical Office., 1987b, 'The effects of taxes and benefits on household income 1985', *Economic Trends*, July.
Challis, D. and Davies, B., 1986, *Case Management in Community Care*, Aldershot, Gower.
Chartered Institute of Public Finance and Accountancy., 1987, *Personal Social Services Statistics 1985—86 Actuals*, London, CIPFA.
Cheeseman, D. A., 1975, *Kinship, Neighbours and Voluntary Work in a Midlands Town*, M. Phil, University of Nottingham, unpublished.
Cheetham, J., 1987, 'Colour blindness', *New Society*, 26/6/87, pp.10–12.
Chubb, B., 1983, Source Book of Irish Government, Dublin, IPA.
Cigno, K., 1985, 'The other Italian experiment', *British Journal of Social Work*, 15, pp. 173—86.
Clinard, M.B., 1970, 'The role of motivation and self image in social change in slum areas', in Allen, V., (ed), *Psychological Factors in Poverty*, Chicago, Markham.
Coetze, S., 1983, *Flat Broke*, Birmingham Welfare Group; version in Ward, S., (ed), 1985, *DHSS in Crisis*, London, CPAG.
Coffield, F., Robinson, P. and Sarsby, J., 1980, *A Cycle of Deprivation? A Study of Four Families*, London, Heinemann.
Cohen, S., 1975, 'It's all right for you to talk: political and sociological manifestos for social action', in Bailey, R. and Brake, M., (eds), *Radical Social Work*, London, Edward Arnold.
Cohen, R., 1983, *Able to Claim?*, London, Islington People's Rights.
Commission on Social Welfare., 1986, *Report*, Dublin, Stationery Office.
Community Care, 1987a, 13 August.
Community Care, 1987b, 3 September.
Community Work Group., 1973, *Current Issues in Community Work*, London, Gulbenkian Foundation.
Conservative Party., 1976, *The Right Approach*, London, Conservative Central Office.
Cooke, K.R. and Baldwin, S.M., 1984, *How Much is Enough? A Review of Supplementary Benefit Scale Rates*, Occasional Paper no.1, FPSC.
Cooper, M., 1983, 'Community social work', in Jordan, B. and Parton, N, (eds), *The Political Dimensions of Social Work*, Oxford, Blackwell.
Coote, A. and Campbell, B., 1987, Sweet Freedom, 2nd. ed., Oxford, Basil Blackwell.
Coser, L.A., 1965, 'The sociology of poverty', *Social Problems*, 13, pp. 140—148.
Coughlin, R., 1980, *Ideology, Public Opinion and Welfare Policy*, Berkeley, University of California Press.
Coyle, A., 1984, *Redundant Women*, London, Women's Press.
CPAG/Low Pay Unit., 1986, *The Rising Tide of Poverty*, London, CPAG/Low Pay Unit.
Creighton, S., 1976, *Child Victims of Physical Abuse 1976: The Third Report of the Findings of the NSPCC*, London, NSPCC.
Creighton, S., 1984, *Trends in Child Abuse*, London, NSPCC.
Creighton, S. and Outram, P.J., 1980, *Child Victims of Physical Abuse, A Report of Findings of NSPCC Special Units Registers*, London, NSPCC.
Cullingforth, D. and Openshaw, S., 1979, *Deprived Places or Deprived People: a Study of the Aggregation Effects Inherent in Area—based Policies*, Discussion Paper No. 28, University of Newcastle.
Curno, P., 1978, *Political Issues and Community Work*, London, Routledge and Kegan Paul.
Curnock, K. and Hardiker, P., 1979, *Towards Practice Theory: Skills and Methods in Social Assessments*, London, Routledge & Kegan Paul.
Curry, J., 1980, *The Irish Social Services*, Dublin, IPA.
Cusack, S. and Roll, J., 1985, *Families Rent Apart*, London, CPAG.

DHSS., 1986d, *Supplementary Benefit Statistics Annual Enquiry 1984*, Newcastle, DHSS.
DHSS., 1987a, *The Law on Child Care and Family Services*, (White Paper), London, HMSO.
DHSS., 1987b, *Study of Special Case Officers: Report Back to Postal Survey Participants*, Mimeo.
DHSS., 1987c, *The Social Fund Manual: Draft Guidance and Directions for DHSS Social Fund Officers*, London, DHSS.
DHSS., 1987d, *Impact of the Reformed Structure of Income Related Benefits*, London, HMSO.
DHSS., 1987e, *Supplementary Benefit Statistics Annual Enquiry 1986*, Newcastle, DHSS.
DHSS., 1987f, *The Social Fund Manual*, London, HMSO.
Department of Social Welfare., 1987, *Guide to Social Welfare Services*, Dublin.
Desai, M., 1986, 'Drawing the line: on defining the poverty threshold', in Golding, P., (ed), *Excluding the Poor*, London, CPAG
Dhooge, Y. and Becker, S., (1988 forthcoming), *Working with People Experiencing Unemployment and Poverty: A Training Pack for Social Workers*.
Dhooge, Y. and Popay, J., 1987, 'Social services and unemployment: impact and responses', in Fineman, S., (ed), *Unemployment: Personal and Social Consequences*, London, Tavistock.
Dingwall, R., Eekelaar, J. and Murray, T., 1983, *The Protection of Children: State Intervention in Family Life*, Oxford, Blackwell.
Disability Alliance, 1987a, *Disability Rights Handbook*, London, Disability Alliance.
Disability Alliance, 1987b, *Poverty and Disability: Breaking the Link; the Case for a Comprehensive Disability Income Scheme*, London, Disability Alliance.
Ditton, J., 1977, *Part-time Crime*, London, Macmillan.
Donovan, D. and Wong. P., 1965, 'The maltreatment syndrone in children', *New England Medical Journal*, 269, pp. 9—74.
Dunleavy, P., 1980, *Urban Political Analysis*, London, Macmillan.
Dupeyroux, J.T., 1985, *Droit de la Sécurité Sociale*, Dalloz.
EEC., 1977, *The Perception of Poverty in Europe*, Document V/17/77—E, Brussels, Commission of the European Communities.
Edinburgh District Council., 1987, *Poverty in Edinburgh: the Other Side of the Festival City*.
Eekelaar, J. and MacLean, M., 1986, *Maintenance after Divorce*, Oxford, Clarendon Press.
Egeland, B., 1979, 'Preliminary results of a prospective study of the antecedents of child abuse', *International Journal of Child Abuse and Neglect*, 3, pp. 269—278.
Epstein, I., 1968, 'Social workers and social action: attitudes towards social action strategies', *Social Work*, 13, 2, pp. 101—108.
Epstein, I., 1981, 'Advocates on advocacy: an exploratory study', *Social Work Research and Abstracts*, 17, pp. 5—12.
Equal Opportunities Commission., 1987, *Women and Men in Britain: A Statistical Profile*, London, HMSO.
Equality for Children., 1983, *Keeping Kids Out of Care, London: A Review of the Evidence given to the House of Commons Social Services Select Committee on Children in Care*.
Exeter Health Authority., 1984, *New Services for Old — Decentralising Care in Devon and Cornwall*.
Fagin, L. and Little, M., 1984, *The Forsaken Families*, Harmondsworth, Penguin Books Ltd.
Falkingham, F. 1985, *Take-Up of Benefits – A Literature Review*, University of Nottingham, Benefits Research Unit.
Falkingham, F. and MacPherson, S., 1986, *Local Authority Approaches to Take-up*, University of Nottingham, Benefits Research Unit.
Family Rights Group., 1985, *The Link Between Prevention and Care*, London, FRG.
Family Rights Group., 1986, *Promoting Links: Keeping Children and Families in Touch*, London, FRG.
Farmer, E. and Parker, R., 1985, *A Study of the Discharge of Care Orders*, University of Bristol, Department of Social Administration.

Dale, P., Waters, J., Davies, M., Roberts, W. and Morrison, T., 1986, 'The towers of silence :
  creative and destructive issues for therapeutic teams dealing with sexual abuse', *Journal of
  Family Therapy*, 8, pp. 1—25.
Daniel, J.H., Newberger, E., Reed, R.B. and Kotelchuck, M., 1978, 'Child abuse screening:
  implications of the limited predictive power of abuse discriminations from a controlled
  family study of paediatric social illness', *International Journal of Child Abuse and Neglect*, 2,
  pp. 247—259.
Davies, B. and Challis, D., 1986, *Matching Resources to Needs in Community Care*, Aldershot,
  Gower.
Davies, S., 1986, *Beveridge Revisited: New foundations for Tomorrow's Welfare*, London,
  Centre for Policy Studies.
Davis, A., 1984, 'Help on the hill', *Social Work Today*, 15, 40,
  18 June.
Davis, A. and Brook, E., 1985, 'Women and Social work', in Brook, E. and Davis, A., (eds),
  Women, the Family and Social work, London, Tavistock.
Davis, A., Grimwood, C. and Stewart, G., 1987, 'The benefits of benefits training', *Community
  Care*, 12 March.
Deacon, A. and Bradshaw, J., 1983, *Reserved for the Poor*, Oxford, Blackwell.
Deakin, N., 1987, *The Politics of Welfare*, London, Methuen.
Dennett, J., James, E., Room, G. and Watson, P., 1982, *Europe against Poverty: the European
  Poverty Programme 1975—1980*, London, Routledge and Kegan Paul.
Department of the Environment., 1985, *Home Improvement — A New Approach*, Cmnd.
  9513, London, HMSO.
DHSS., 1971, *Better Services for the Mentally Handicapped*, London, HMSO.
DHSS., 1977, *Records in Social Services Departments*, London, HMSO.
DHSS., 1978, *Social Assistance: A Review of the Supplementary Benefits Scheme in Great
  Britain*, London, HMSO.
DHSS., 1979a, *Relations with Social Services*, London, HMSO.
DHSS., 1979b, *Report to the Committee of Enquiry into Mental Handicap Nursing and Care*,
  London, HMSO.
DHSS., 1980a, *Child Abuse, Central Register System*, DHSS Circular.
DHSS., 1980b, *Progress, Problems and Priorities: A Review of Mental Handicap Services in
  England and Wales since the 1971 White Paper*, London, HMSO.
DHSS., 1980c, *Liaison in Practice*, London, HMSO.
DHSS., 1980d, *Social Security Statistics 1980*, London, HMSO.
DHSS., 1981a, *Care in the Community*, London, HMSO.
DHSS., 1981b, *Social Security Statistics 1981*, London, HMSO.
DHSS., 1982, *Social Security Statistics 1982*, London, HMSO.
DHSS., 1984a, *Report to the Secretary of State, year ending March 1984*, London,
  HMSO.
DHSS., 1984b, *Social Security Statistics 1984*, London, HMSO.
DHSS., 1984c, *DHSS Personal Social Services Local Authority Statistics*, London,
  HMSO.
DHSS., 1984d, *Supplementary Benefit Statistics Annual Enquiry 1983*, Newcastle, DHSS.
DHSS., 1985a, *Social Work Decisions in Child Care Cases*, London, HMSO.
DHSS., 1985b, *Reform of Supplementary Benefit — Background Papers Vol.3*, Cmnd. 9519,
  London, HMSO.
DHSS., 1985c, *Reform of Social Security: Programme for Change*, Cmnd. 9518, (Green Paper),
  London, HMSO.
DHSS., 1985d, *Reform of Social Security: Programme for Action*, Cmnd. 9691, (White Paper),
  London, HMSO.
DHSS., 1985e, *Review of Child Care Law*, London, HMSO.
DHSS., 1985f, *Social Work Decisions in Child Care: Recent Research Findings and their
  Implications*, London, HMSO
DHSS., 1985g, *Social Security Statistics 1985*, London, HMSO.
DHSS., 1985h, *Government Response to the Second Report from the Social Services Committee,
  1984—85 Session*, Cmnd. 9694, London, HMSO.
DHSS., 1986a, *Social Security Act*, London, HMSO.
DHSS., 1986b, *Social Security Statistics 1986*, London, HMSO.
DHSS., 1986c, *Low Income Families—1983*, London, HMSO.

Farrington, D., Gallagher, B., Morley, L., St. Ledger, R. and West, D., 1986, 'Employment, school leaving and crime', *British Journal of Criminology*, 26, 4.
Federated Workers Union of Ireland., 1984 *A New Law for a New Poor*, Report of a seminar in November 1984, Dublin, FWUI.
Fife Regional Council., 1986, *The Effects of Unemployment on Families Referred to the Regional Reporter to the Children's Panel in Fife*.
Fimister, G., 1986, *Welfare Rights Work in Social Services*, London, BASW/Macmillan.
Fimister, G., 1987a, 'Lend us your ears', *Social Services Insight*, 26 June.
Fimister, G., 1987b, 'Striking a delicate balance', *Social Services Insight*, 25 September, p. 14.
Finch, J. and Groves, D., 1980, 'Community care and the family: a case for equal opportunities?' *Journal of Social Policy*, 9, 4, pp. 487—511.
Finch, J. and Groves, D., (eds), 1983, *A Labour of Love: Women, Work and Caring*, London, Routledge and Kegan Paul.
Fisher, M., Marsh, P., Phillips, D. and Sainsbury, E., 1986, *In and Out of Care*, London, Batsford.
Flynn, M.C., 1986, *A Study of Prediction in the Community Placements of Adults who are Mentally Handicapped*, Hester Adrian Research Centre, University of Manchester, ESRC Final Report.
Forrest, R. and Murie, A., 1983, 'Residualization and council housing: aspects of the changing social relations of housing tenure', *Journal of Social Policy*, 12, 4, pp. 453—468.
Fox, L.M., 1982, 'Two value positions in recent child care law and practice', *British Journal of Social Work*, 16, 2, pp. 161—180.
Francis, V., 1963, *Child Abuse: Review of a Nationwide Survey*, Children's Division, Washington, American Humane Society.
Freeman, M.D.A., 1983, *The Rights and Wrongs of Children*, London, Francis Pinter.
Fruin, D. and Vernon, J., 1983, *Social Work Decision-Making and its Effect on the Length of Time Which Children Spend in Care*, London, National Children's Bureau.
Fuller, R. 1987, *Researching Prevention: a Research Note*, Social Work Research Centre Working Paper, University of Stirling.
Fuller, R. and Stevenson, O., 1983, *Policies, Programmes and Disadvantage: A Review of the Literature*, London, Heinemann.
Furnham, A. 1982,'Why are the poor always with us. Explanation for poverty in Britain', *British Journal of Social Psychology*, 21, pp. 311—322.
Furnham, A. and Gunter, B., 1984, 'Just world beliefs and attitudes towards the poor', *British Journal of Social Psychology*, 23, 3, pp. 265—269.
Furniss, T., 1983, 'Family process in the treatment of intrafamilial child sexual abuse', *Journal of Family Therapy*, 5, pp. 263—278.
Gale, F., 1985, *Aboriginal Youth and the Law: Problems of Equity and Justice for Black Minorities*, University of London, Australian Studies Centre.
Garbarino, J., 1981, *Children and Families in the Social Environment*, New York, Aldine.
Gelles, R., 1973, 'Child abuse and psychopathology: a sociological critique and reformulation', *American Journal of Orthopsychochiatry*, 43, pp. 611—621.
Gil, D., 1969, 'Physical abuse of children – findings and implications of a nationwide survey', *Paediatrics*, 44, pp. 857—867.
Gil, D., 1970, *Violence against Children: Physical Child Abuse in the United States*, Cambridge, Mass, Harvard University Press.
Gil, D., 1971, 'Violence against children', *Journal of Marriage and the Family*, 33, pp. 635—657
Gladstone, D.E., 1985, 'Disabled people and employment', *Social Policy and Administration*, 19, 2, pp. 101—9.
Glastonbury, B., 1985, *Computers in Social Work*, London, BASW/Macmillan.
Glendenning, C., 1980, *After Working all These Years: A Response to the Report of the National Insurance Advisory Committee on the 'Household Duties' Test for Non-Contributory Invalidity Pension for Married Women*, London, Disability Alliance.
Glendenning, C., 1983, *Unshared Care: Parents and their Disabled Children*, London, Routledge and Kegan Paul.
Glendenning, C. and Millar, J., (eds), 1987, *Women and Poverty in Britain*, Brighton, Wheatsheaf.

Goldberg, E.M. and Connelly, N., (eds), 1981, *Evaluative Research in Social Care*, London, Heinemann.

Goldberg, E.M. and Connelly, N., 1982, *The Effectiveness of Social Care for the Elderly*, London, Heinemann.

Goldberg, E.M., Cook, T., De'ath, E., Hatch, S., Richman, N. and Sinclair, I., 1987, *Support for Families: Practice, Policy and Research*, London, Joseph Rowntree Memorial Trust.

Goldberg, E.M. and Sinclair, I., 1986, *Family Support Exercise*, London, NISW.

Goldberg, E.M. and Warburton, R.W., 1979, *Ends and Means in Social Work*, London, NISW.

Golding, P., (ed), 1986, *Excluding the Poor*, London, CPAG.

Golding, P. and Middleton, S., 1982, *Images of Welfare: Press and Public Attitudes to Poverty*, Oxford, Martin Robertson.

Gordon, P. and Newnham, A., 1985, *Passport to Benefits? Racism in Social Security*, London, Child Poverty Action Group and The Runnymede Trust.

Graham, H., 1983, 'Caring, a labour of love', in Finch, J. and Groves, D., (eds), *A Labour of Love: Women, Work and Caring*, London, Routledge and Kegan Paul.

Graham, H., 1987, 'Being poor: perceptions and coping strategies of lone mothers', in Brannen, J. and Wilson, G., (eds), *Give and Take in Families: Studies in Resource Distribution*, London, Allen and Unwin.

Greater Glasgow Health Board., 1984, *Ten Year Report, 1974—1983*.

Greater London Citizens' Advice Bureau., 1986, *Out of Service, DHSS Local Offices in London: A Survey*, London, GLCABX.

Greater London Council., 1983, *Low Incomes in London*, London, GLC.

Greve, J., *et al*, 1986, *Homelessness in London*, University of Bristol, School for Advanced Urban Studies.

Grimm, W. and Orten, D., 1973, 'Student attitudes towards the poor', *Social Work*, January, pp. 94—107.

Groves, D. and Finch, J., 1983, 'Natural selection: perspectives on entitlement to the invalid care allowance', in Finch, J. and Groves, D., (eds), *A Labour of Love: Women, Work and Caring*, London, Routledge and Kegan Paul.

Guardian., 1987a, 'Mortgage rule traps jobless in poverty', 4 February.

Guardian., 1987b, 21 November.

Guru, S., 1986, 'An Asian women's refuge', in Ahmed, S., Cheetham, J. and Small, J., (eds), *Social Work with Black Children and their Families*, London, Batsford and British Agencies for Adoption and Fostering.

Hadley, R., *et al*, 1987, *A Community Social Worker's Handbook*, London, Tavistock.

Hadley, R. and Dale, P., 1987, 'Community work revisited', *Social Services Insight*, 18 September, pp. 13—15.

Hadley, R. and Hatch, S., 1980, *Social Welfare and the Failure of the State*, London, Allen and Unwin.

Hadley, R. and McGrath, M., 1980, *Going Local: Neighbourhood Social Services*, London, Bedford Square Press.

Hakim, C., 1982, 'The social consequences of high unemployment', *Journal of Social Policy*, 11, pp. 433—67.

Hale, J., 1983, 'Feminism and social work practice', in Jordan, B. and Parton, N., (eds), *The Political Dimensions of Social Work*, Oxford, Basil Blackwell.

Halsey, A.H., 1987, 'Social trends since World War II', *Social Trends 17*, London, HMSO.

Handler, J., 1973, *The Coercive Social Worker*, Chicago, Rand McNally.

Hannam, J., 1987, 'Using rights to get above the breadline', *Social Services Insight*, 1 May, pp. 18—19.

Hardiker, P. and Barker, M., (eds), 1981, *Theories of Practice in Social Work*, London, Academic Press.

Hardiker, P. and Barker, M., 1986, *A Window on Child Care Practices in the 1980s*, University of Leicester, School of Social Work Research Report.

Harris, A.I., Cox, E. and Smith, C.R.W., 1971, *Handicapped and Impaired in Great Britain*, OPCS, Social Survey Division, London, HMSO.

Haskey, J., 1986, 'One-Parent Families in Great Britain', *Population Trends*, 25, pp. 5—13.

Hawkins, K., 1987, *Unemployment: Facts, Figures and Possible Solutions for Britain,* Harmondsworth, Penguin.
Harrison, P., 1983, *Inside the Inner City: Life under the Cutting Edge,* Harmondsworth, Penguin.
Health Promotion Research Trust., 1987, *Health and Life Style Survey,* London, HPRT.
Hennessy, P., 1987, 'Public opinion about the social security system in the United Kingdom', *International Social Security Review,* 3.
Heywood, J.S. and **Allen, B.F.,** 1971, *Financial Help in Social Work,* Manchester, Manchester University Press.
Higgins, J., 1981, *States of Welfare,* Oxford, Blackwell.
Hill, M. and **Laing, P.,** 1978, *Money Payments, Social Work and Supplementary Benefits,* University of Bristol, School for Advanced Urban Studies.
Hill, M. and **Laing, P.,** 1979, *Social Work and Money,* London, George Allen and Unwin.
Hill, M., Tolan, F. and **Smith, R.,** 1985, *The Relationship between Local Authority Social Services and Supplementary Benefits After the 1980 Supplementary Benefits Changes,* mimeo.
Hock, S., 1987, 'Inequalities and the new Health Education Authority', *British Medical Journal,* 294, 4 April.
Hoggett, P. and **Hambleton, R.,** (eds), 1987, *Decentralisation and Democracy: Localising Public Services,* University of Bristol, School for Advanced Urban Studies.
Hollis, F., 1972, *Casework — A Psychosocial Therapy,* New York, Random House.
Holman, R., 1973, 'Poverty, welfare rights and social work', *Social Work Today,* 6/10/73.
Holman, R., 1980, *Inequality in Child Care,* Poverty Pamphlet 26, London, CPAG/FRG.
Holman, R., (forthcoming), *Prevention and Child Care.*
Homer, M., Leonard, A. and **Taylor, P.,** 1984, *Private Violence: Public Shame. A Report on the Circumstances of Women leaving Domestic Violence in Cleveland,* Middlesbrough, Cleveland Refuge and Aid for Women and Children.
Hooper, F., 1987, 'An advocate or a collaborator?' *Social Work Today,* 5 January, p. 9.
House of Commons, 1974, *Social Security Provision for Chronically Sick and Disabled People,* H of C. Paper 275, London, HMSO.
House of Commons, (Social Services Committee), 1984, *Children in Care,* Vol. 1, (Short Report)., London, HMSO.
House of Commons Debates, 1985a, 25 June, col.52.
House of Commons Debates, 1985b, 20 November, col. 379
House of Commons Debates, 1985c, 8 May, written answers, col. 451
House of Commons Debates, 1985d, 16 July., written answers, cols. 118—9.
House of Commons Debates, 1986a, 29 October, written answers, cols. 185—6.
House of Commons Debates, 1986b, 23 July, cols. 443—55, debate on 'supplementary benefit'.
House of Commons Debates, 1986c, 21 July, cols. 19—29, debate on 'single payments'.
House of Commons Debates, 1987, 5 May, col. 577, debate on 'civil service pay dispute'.
Howell, R., 1981, *Why Work? A Radical Solution,* London, Conservative Political Centre.
Hudson, A., 1985, 'Feminism and social work: resistance or dialogue?' *British Journal of Social Work,* 15, pp. 635—655.
Hudson, B., 1987, 'Steering a course through the myths of community care', *Health Service Journal,* 28 May.
Hume, D., 1984, 'Anti-poverty strategies: a role for local authorities?' *Poverty,* April.
Hunt, S.M., (forthcoming), *Housing as a Hazard to Health,* Proceedings from the International Housing Conference, Glasgow.
Huet, M., 1975, 'Le minimum social garanti', *Bulletin de l'UNBASF.,* No. 159, Touresing.
Hyde, S., 1986, *Income Maintenance — an Issue for the Physically Handicapped,* Nottinghamshire Welfare Rights Service.

Irvine, R., Becker, S. and MacPherson, S., 1987, 'Poor kids', *Social Services Insight*, March, pp. 19—22.

Isades, S., 1972, 'Neglect, cruelty and battering', *British Medical Journal III*, pp. 224—226.

Iwaniec, D., Herbert, M. and McNeish, A.S., 1985a, 'Social work with failure to thrive children and their families: Part 1: psychological factors', *British Journal of Social Work*, 15,3, pp. 243—259.

Iwaniec, D., Herbert, M. and McNeish, A. S., 1985b, 'Social work with failure to thrive children and their families: Part 2: behavioural social work intervention', *British Journal of Social Work*, 15, 4, pp. 375—389.

Jackson, M.P. and Valencia, B.M., 1979, *Financial Aid through Social Work*, London, Routledge and Kegan Paul.

Jacobs, S., 1985, 'Race, empire and the welfare state; council housing and racism', *Critical Social Policy*, 13, pp. 6—28.

Jacoby, R., 1975, *Social Amnesia: A Critique of Conformist Psychology from Adler to Laing*, Sussex, Harvester Press Ltd.

Jervis, M., 1986, 'Domestic violence: why asian women need a helping hand', *Social Work Today*, 18 August, pp. 7-8.

Jones, C., 1985, *Patterns of Social Policy*, London, Tavistock.

Jordan, B., 1973, *Paupers: The Making of the New Claiming Class*, London, Routledge and Kegan Paul.

Jordan, B., 1974, *Poor Parents: Social Policy and the Cycle of Deprivation*, London, Routledge and Kegan Paul.

Jordan, B., 1976, *Freedom and the Welfare State*, London, Routledge and Kegan Paul.

Jordan, B., 1985, 'Children and care', *New Society*, 74, 1198, p. 460.

Jordan, B., 1987a, *Rethinking Welfare*, Oxford, Blackwell.

Jordan, B., 1987b, 'Prevention and family work', in McHugh, J., (ed), *Creative Social work with Families*, Birmingham BASW.

Jordan, B. and Greenwood, J., 1987, 'The dole quiz', *New Society*, 79, 1255, pp. 16—17.

Jordan, L. and Waine, B., 1986, 'Women's income in and out of employment', *Critical Social Policy*, 18, pp. 63—78.

Keesings, 1979, *Keesings Contemporary Archives*, London, Longman.

Kempe, C.H., 1962, 'The battered baby syndrome', *Journal of the American Medical Association*, 181, pp. 17—24.

Kennedy, S., 1981, *Who Should Care?* Turoe Press.

Kerbo, H.R., 1976, 'The stigma of welfare and a passive poor', *Sociology and Social Research*, 60, 2, pp. 173—187.

Kerr, S., 1983, *Making Ends Meet*, London, Bedford Square Press/NCVO.

King, R.D., Raynes, N.V. and Tizard, J., 1971, *Patterns of Residential Care*, London, Routledge and Kegan Paul.

Kinnibrugh, A. D., 1984, *Social Work Case Recording and the Clients' Right to Privacy*, Bristol School for Advanced Urban Studies.

Krugman, R.D., Lenharr, M., Betz, L. and Fryer, G., 1986, 'The relationship between unemployment and physical abuse of children', *International Journal of Child Abuse and Neglect*, 10, 3, pp. 415—418.

Lakhari B. and Read, J., 1987, *National Welfare Benefits Handbook*, London, Child Poverty Action Group.

Lammertyn, F., 1987, *Les Ayauts Droit Au Minimex*, Dept. de Sociologie, Leuven.

Land, H., 1978, 'Who cares for the family?' *Journal of Social Policy*, 8, pp. 257—84.

Land, H., 1980, 'The family wage', *Feminist Review*, 6, pp. 55—77.

Land, H., 1983, 'Poverty and gender: The distribution of resources within families', in Brown, M., (ed). 1983, *The Structure of Disadvantage*, London, Heinemann.

Land, H. and Rose, H., 1985, 'Compulsory altruism for all or an altruistic society for some?' in Bean, P., Ferris, J. and Whynes, D., (eds), 1985, *In Defence of Welfare*, London, Tavistock.

Land, H. and Ward, S., 1986, *Women Won't Benefit: The Impact of the Social Security Bill on Women's Rights*, London, National Council for Civil Liberties.

Laurance, J., 1987, 'Benefits boost for handicapped', *New Society*, 12 June.

Le Grand, J., 1982, *The Strategy of Equality: Redistribution and the Social Services*, London, Allen and Unwin.

Leaper, R.A.B., 1975, 'Subsidiarity and the Welfare State', *Social Policy and Administration*, 9, 2.

Leaper, R.A.B., 1980, *Health, Wealth and Housing*, Oxford, Blackwell.

Leaper, R.A.B., 1986, *Cash and Caring*, University of Exeter, mimeo.

Leese, J., 1987, 'Helping people with disabilities into employment', *Employment Gazette*, 95, 7, pp. 320-4.

Leghorn, L. and Parker, K., 1981, *Women's Worth: Sexual Economics and the World of Women*, Boston, Routledge and Kegan Paul.

Leicester Child Poverty Action Group, 1984, *Double Discrimination*, Leicester, CPAG.

Lejeune, F.C., 1987, Editorial, *Bulletin des CCAS*, No. 225, p.5 (translation R.A.B. Leaper).

Lestor, J., 1986, *An Interim Report on Child Abuse*, London, Trade Unions' Child Care Project.

Light, R.J., 1973, 'Abused and neglected children in America: a study of alternative policies', *Harvard Educational Review*, 43, pp. 556—598.

Lishman, J., 1978, 'A clash in perspective?', *British Journal of Social Work*, 8, 33, pp. 301—311.

Lishman, J., (ed), 1984, *Research Highlights 8: Evaluation*, Aberdeen, Aberdeen University Press.

Lister, R. and Emmett, T., 1976, *Under the Safety Net*, London, CPAG.

Lister, R. and Lakhani, B., 1987, *A Great Retreat in Fairness*, London, CPAG.

Lister, R. and Walsh, A., 1985, *Mothers Lifeline*, London, CPAG.

Liverpool Health Authority, 1987, *Health Inequalities in Liverpool*.

Locker, D., 1983, *Disability and Disadvantage: The Consequences of Chronic Illness*, London, Tavistock

Loney, M., 1983, *Community against Government: The British Community Development Project 1968—78*, London, Heinemann.

Lonsdale, S., 1985, *Work and Inequality*, London, Longman.

Lonsdale, S. and Walker, A., 1984, *A Right to Work: Disability and Employment*, London, Disability Alliance and Low Pay Unit.

Luba, J. and Rowland, M., 1987, *Rights Guide to Non-Means-Tested Social Security Benefits*, London, Child Poverty Action Group.

Luckhaus, L., 1980, *Towards an Explanation of the Welfare Scrounger*, MA dissertation, Socio-legal studies, Sheffield University, unpublished.

Luckhaus, L., 1986a, 'Severe disablement allowance: the old dressed up as new?', *Journal of Social Welfare Law*, pp. 153—69.

Luckhaus, L., 1986b, 'Payment for caring: a European solution', *Public Law*, pp. 526—35.

Macarov, D., 1981, 'Social work students' attitudes towards poverty: a tri-national study', *Contemporary Social Work Education*, 4, 2, pp. 150—160.

MacGregor, S., 1981, *The Politics of Poverty*, London, Longman.

Mack, J. and Lansley, S., 1985, *Poor Britain*, London, George Allen and Unwin.

MacPherson, S. and Midgley, J., 1987, *Comparative Social Policy and the Third World*, Brighton, Wheatsheaf.

Maisch, H., 1973, *Incest*, London, Andre Deutsch.

Mama, A., 1984, 'Black women, the economic crisis and the British state', *Feminist Review*, 17, pp. 21—35.

Mandla, D., 1987, 'War on the dole', *New Society*, 26 June, pp. 13—15.

Manpower Services Commission., 1986, *YTS Leavers Survey, April 85 to January 86*.

Martin, C.J., Platt, S.D. and Hunt, S.M., 1987, 'Housing conditions and ill health', *British Medical Journal*, 2 May, pp. 1125—1127.

Martin, J. and Roberts, C., 1984, *Women and Employment: a Lifetime Perspective*, DOE/OPCS, London, HMSO.

Massiah, J., 1983, *Women as Heads of Households in the Caribbean: Family Structure and Feminine Status*, UNESCO.

Matza, D., 1964, *Delinquency and Drift*, New York, Wiley.
Maynard, M., 1985, 'The response of social workers to domestic violence', in **Pahl, J.**, (ed), *Private Violence and Public Policy: The Needs of Battered Women and the Response of the Public Services*, London, Routledge and Kegan Paul.
McGavin, P., 1985, *Unmet Need among the Clients of the Home Help Service*, Nottinghamshire Welfare Rights Service.
McGrail, S., 1983, 'We shouldn't really be teaching this sort of thing', *Community Care*, 15 December.
McIntosh, M., 1973, 'Crime', in **Hurd, G.**, (ed), *Human Societies: An Introduction to Sociology*, London, Routledge and Kegan Paul.
McKee, L. and **Bell, C.**, 1985, 'Marital and family relations in times of male unemployment', in **Roberts, B.**, *et al*, *New Approaches to Economic Life*, Manchester, Manchester University Press.
Meacher, M., 1974, *Scrounging on the Welfare*, London, Arrow Books.
Midwinter, E., 1985, *The Wage of Retirement*, Centre for Policy on Aging.
Midwinter, E., 1986, *Caring for Cash*, Centre for Policy on Aging.
Midwinter, E., 1987, *Redefining Old Age*, Centre for Policy on Aging.
Millar, J. and **Glendenning, C.**, 1987, 'Invisible women, invisible poverty', in **Glendenning, C.** and **Millar, J.**, (eds), *Women and Poverty in Britain*, Brighton, Wheatsheaf.
Millham, S., Bullock, R., Hosie, K. and **Haak, M.**, 1986. *Lost in Care*, Aldershot, Gower.
Millichamp, D. and **Thomas, H.**, 1982, *General Observations Related to Whatton Discharges January to December 1981*, Nottinghamshire Probation and After Care Service.
Mills, C. Wright., 1959, *The Sociological Imagination*, Oxford University Press.
Mingione, E., 1983, 'Informalisation, restructuring and the survival strategies of the working class', *International Journal of Urban and Regional Research*. 7, 3, pp. 311—339.
Moniteur Belge., 1987, 15 April.
Moore, K. and **Freeman, I.**, 1986, 'Poverty and planning — how technology can help', *Social Services Insight*, 5 December, pp. 12—15.
Morley, B., (forthcoming), *Violence against Women*, Brighton, Wheatsheaf.
Moroney, J.M., 1976, *The Family and the State: Considerations for Social Policy*, London, Longman.
Mortimore, J. and **Blackstone, T.**, 1982, *Disadvantage and Education*, London, Heinemann.
Mouvement Communal, 1987, Nos. 3-5, Union des Villes et Communes Belges, Bruxelles.
Moylan, S., Miller, J. and **Davies, R.**, 1984, *For Richer, For Poorer?*, DHSS Cohort Study of Unemployed Men, Social Research Report No. 11, London, HMSO.
Murie, A., 1983, *Housing Inequality and Deprivation*, London, Heinemann.
Murie, A., (ed), 1987, *Living in Bed and Breakfast: the Experience of Homelessness in London*, University of Bristol, School for Advanced Urban Studies.

National Children's Home, 1986, *Families Affected by Unemployment*, London, NCH.
National Consumer Council, 1985, *The Fourth Right of Citizenship*. London, NSPC.
National Schizophrenia Fellowship, 1974, *Living with Schizophrenia, By the Relatives*, London, NSF.
NSPCC, 1976, *At Risk: An Account of the Work of the Battered Child Research Department*, London, NSPCC.
Nelson, B., 1984, *Making an Issue of Child Abuse: Political Agenda Setting for Social Problems*, Chicago, University of Chicago Press.
Newnham, A., 1986, *Employment, Unemployment and Black People*, London, Runnymede Trust.
Newton, T., 1986, *The Times Parliamentary Report*, 22 July.
Nirje, B., 1970, 'The normalisation principle', *Bristol Journal of Mental Subnormality*, 16.
Nissel, M. and **Bonnerjea, L.**, 1982, *Family Care of the Handicapped Elderly: Who Pays?*, London, Policy Studies Institute.
Nixon, J., Pearn, J., Wilkey, I. and **Petrie, G.**, 1981, 'Social class and violent child death: an analysis of fatal non-accidental injury, murder and fatal child neglect', *International Journal of Child Abuse and Neglect*, 5 pp. 111—116.

Nobles, W.W., 1981, 'African-American family life: an instrument of culture', in McAdoo, H.P., (ed), *Black Families*, New York, Sage.

Norman, A., 1985, *Triple Jeopardy*, Centre for Policy on Aging.

Nottinghamshire County Council, 1983, *Disadvantage in Nottinghamshire: County Deprived Area Study*.

Nottinghamshire Welfare Rights Service, 1986, *Benefits for Mentally Handicapped People in Nottinghamshire*.

Observer., 1987a, Editorial, 29 March.

Observer., 1987b, 22 November.

O'Cinneide, S., 1970, *A Law for the Poor*, Dublin, Institute of Public Administration.

O'Donovan, K., 1985, *Sexual Divisions in Law*, London, Weidenfield and Nicholson.

O'Higgins, M., 1985, 'Inequality, redistribution and recession: the British experience, 1976-1982', *Journal of Social Policy*, 14, pp. 279-307.

O'Toole, R., Turbett, P. and Nalepha, C., 1983, 'Professional knowledge and diagnosis of child abuse', in Finklehorn, D., Geddes, R.J., Hotalung, G. and Strauss, M.A., (eds), *The Dark Side of Families: Current Family Violence*, Beverley Hills, Calif., Sage Publications.

Oliver, J. and Briggs, A., (eds), 1985, *Caring: Experiences of Looking After Disabled Relatives*, London, Routledge and Kegan Paul.

Oliver, M., 1983, *Social Work with Disabled People*, Macmillan, London.

Orten, J.D., 1981, 'Influencing attitudes: a study of social work students', *Social Work Research and Abstracts*, 17, 3, pp. 11—16.

Orten, J.D., 1981, 'Influencing attitudes: a study of social work students', *Social Work Research and Abstracts* 17, 3, pp. 11—16.

Packman, J., Randall, J. and Jacques, N., 1986, *Who Needs Care? Social Work Decisions about Children*, Oxford, Blackwell.

Pahl, J., 1980, 'Patterns of money management within marriage', *Journal of Social Policy*, 9, pp. 313—35.

Pahl, J., 1983, 'The allocation of money and the structuring of inequality within marriage', *Sociological Review*, 31, 2, pp. 237—262.

Pahl, J., 1985, 'Violent husbands and abused wives: a longitudinal study', in Pahl, J., (ed), *Private Violence and Public Policy: The Needs of Battered Women and the Response of the Public Services*, London, Routledge and Kegan Paul.

Pahl, R., 1984, *Divisions of Labour*, Oxford, Basil Blackwell.

Parker, H., 1982, 'Social security foments the black economy', *Journal of Economic Affairs*, 3, 1, pp. 32—35.

Parker, J. and Dillon, M., 1987, 'Against the odds', *Social Services Insight*, 29 May, pp. 17—19.

Parkinson, L., 1983, 'Conciliation: a new approach to family conflict resolution', *British Journal of Social Work*, 13, 1, pp. 19—38.

Parmar, P., 1982, 'Gender, race and class: Asian women in resistance', in *Centre for Contemporary Cultural Studies, The Empire Strikes Back: Race and Racism in 70s Britain*, London, Hutchinson.

Parsloe, P. and Stevenson, O., (eds), 1978, *Social Service Teams — the Practitioners View*, London, HMSO.

Parton, N., 1985, *The Politics of Child Abuse*, London, Macmillan.

Peace, S., 1986, 'The forgotten female: social policy and older women', in Philipson, C. and Walker, A., *Aging and Social Policy*, London, Gower.

Pearson, G., (forthcoming), 'Social work and unemployment', in Langen, M. and Lee, P., (eds), *Social Work in Recession: a Radical Contribution*, London, Hutchinson.

Pelton, L.H., 1978, 'Child abuse and neglect: the myth of classlessness', *American Journal of Orthopsychiatry*, 48, pp. 608—617.

Peters, G., 1987, 'Prevention – better than a cure', *Social Services Insight*, 2, 33, pp. 6—7.

Phillips, A. and Taylor, B., 1980, 'Sex and skill: notes towards a feminist economics', *Feminist Review*, 6, pp. 79—88.

Phillipson, C. and Walker, A., (eds), 1986, *Aging and Social Policy*, Aldershot, Gower.

Philp, M., 1979, 'Notes on the form of knowledge in social work', *Sociological Review*, 27, 1, pp. 83—111.

Piachaud, D., 1979, *The Cost of a Child*, London, CPAG.

Piachaud, D., 1984, *Round about Fifty Hours a Week: The Time Costs of Children*, Poverty Pamphlet No. 64, London, Child Poverty Action Group.

Piachaud, D., 1987a, 'The growth of poverty' in **Walker, A.**, and **Walker, C.**, (eds), *The Growing Divide: A Social Audit 1979-1987*, London, CPAG.

Piachaud, D., 1987b, 'Problems in the definition and measurement of poverty', *Journal of Social Policy*, 16, pp. 147—164.

Pinker, R., 1982, 'An alternative view', in **Barclay, P.**, 1982, *Social Workers: Their Roles and Tasks*, London, Bedford Square Press.

Piven, F.F., 1987, *Reaction to Reaction — the Limits of the New Left's Defence*, Address to the Social Administration Association's Conference, Edinburgh, July.

Piven, F.F. and **Cloward, R.A.**, 1972, *Regulating the Poor*, London, Tavistock.

Popay, J., 1977, *Fiddlers on the Hoof: Moral Panics and Social Security Scroungers*, M.A. thesis, Essex University, unpublished.

Popay, J., **Dhooge, Y.** and **Shipman, C.**, 1986, *Unemployment and Health: What Role for Health and Social Services?*, London, HEC.

Portsmouth, Social Services Research and Intelligence Unit, 1975, *Children in Care*, Portsmouth, Social Services Department.

Prosser, T., 1981, 'The politics of discretion: aspects of discretionary power in the supplementary benefit scheme', in **Adler, M.** and **Asquith, S.**, (eds), *Discretion and Welfare*, London, Heinemann.

Prosser, T., 1983, *Test Cases for the Poor*, London, CPAG.

Rainbow, H., 1985, *No Money? Who Cares. . .*, London, Finsbury CAB.

Raynes, N.V., **Sumpton, R.C.** and **Flynn, M.C.**, 1987, *Homes for Mentally Handicapped People*, London, Tavistock.

Rees, S., 1978, *Social Work Face to Face*, London, Edward Arnold.

Rein, M., 1970, 'The crossroads for social work', *Social Work*, 27, 4.

Reporters Department Fife Regional Council, 1986, *The Effects of Unemployment on Families Referred to the Regional Reporter and the Children's Panel in Fife*, Glenrothes, Fife Regional Council.

Republic of Ireland, 1937, *Bunreacht na h Eireann*, Dublin, Government Publications Office.

Revue Belge de la Securité Sociale, 1986, Nos. 4-5, Annexe, Ministere de la Riévoyance Sociale, Bruxelles.

Richards, J., 1981, *The Making of the Housing (Homeless Persons) Act. 1977*, University of Bristol, SAUS.

Rimmer, L. and **Popay, J.**, 1982, *Employment Trends and the Family*, London, Study Commission on the Family.

Robinson, L., 1987, 'Diary of a dispute',*Community Care*, 9 July, pp. 26—7.

Rowlings, C., 1980, *Social Work with Elderly People*, London, Allen and Unwin.

Rowntree, B.S. and **Lavers, G.R.**, 1951, *Poverty and the Welfare State*, London, Longman.

Rupesinghe, K., 1986, 'The welfare state in Sri Lanka', in **Oyen, E.**, (ed) *Comparing Welfare States and their Futures*, London, Gower.

Rush, J., 1980, *An Ordinary Life*, Kings Fund Project Paper, No. 24, London, Kings Fund.

Rutter, M. and **Madge, N.**, **1976**, *Cycles of Disadvantage*, London, Heinemann.

Ryan, W., 1971, *Blaming the Victim*, New York, Pantheon.

Sainsbury, E., 1975, *Social Work with Families*, London, Routledge and Kegan Paul.

Sainsbury, S., 1970, *Registered as Disabled*, London, Bell.

Satyamurti, C., 1981, *Occupational Survival, The Case of the Local Authority Social Worker*, Oxford, Blackwell.

Savina, M. and **Gruel, L.**, 1985, *Récarité et Logiques des Prestations Sociales Facultatives*, Université de Rennes.

Savina, M. and **Gaultier, G.**, 1987, *Revenu Minimum Social*, Université de Rennes.

Schiller, B.R., 1973, 'Empirical studies of welfare dependency: a survey', *The Journal of Human Resources*, viii, Supplement, pp. 19—32.

School of Social Work, 1981, *The Roles and Tasks of Social Workers in Social Services Departments*, University of Leicester, Paper submitted as Evidence to the Barclay Committee.

Schorr, A.L., 1975, *Children and Decent People*, London, George Allen and Unwin.
Scott, H., 1984, *Working your Way to the Bottom: the Feminization of Poverty*, London, Pandora Press.
Scott, P.D., 1975, 'The tragedy of Maria Colwell', *British Journal of Criminology*, 15, 1, pp. 88—90.
Seabrook, J., 1984, *Landscapes of Poverty*, Oxford, Blackwell.
Seebohm, F., 1968, *Report of the Committee on Local Authority and Allied Personal Social Services*, Cmnd. 3707, London, HMSO.
Sheffield Health Authority., 1986, *Health Care and Disease: A Profile of Sheffield*.
Sheffield Social Security Campaign., 1986, *To Each According*, Sheffield Alternatives Working Group.
Sheldon, B., 1986, 'Social work effectiveness experiments: review and implications', *British Journal of Social Work*, 16, pp. 223—242.
Shepard, M., 1982, *Perceptions of Child Abuse: A Critique of Individualism*, Social Work Monographs, Birmingham, BASW.
Silberman, G., 1977, *A Study of the Relationship between Education, Dogmatism and Concern for the Poor in a Public Welfare Agency*, PhD, New York University, unpublished.
Silburn, R., MacPherson. S. and Becker, S., 1984, 'Social workers and supplementary benefits', *Social Work Today*, 12/11/85, pp. 19—25.
Sinfield A., 1969, *Which Way For Social Work?*, Tract 393, London, Fabian Society.
Sinfield, A., 1987, 'foreword', in Fineman, S., (ed), *Unemployment: Personal and Social Consequences*, London, Tavistock.
Skimmer, R.A. and Castle, R.L., 1969, *78 Battered Children: A Retrospective Study*, London, NSPCC.
Smail, R., 1986, *Breadline Scotland: Low Pay and Inequality North of the Border*, London, Low Pay Unit.
Smail, R., Green F. and Hadjimatheou, G., 1984, *Unequal Fringes*, Low Pay Report 15, London, Low Pay Unit.
Smart, C., 1984, *The Ties that Bind: Law, Marriage and the Reproduction of Patriarchal Relations*, London, Routledge and Kegan Paul.
Smith, C., 1980, *Community Participation in Social Planning*, MA thesis, University of Exeter, unpublished.
Smith, L. and Jones, D., 1981, *Deprivation, Participation and Community Action*, London, Routledge and Kegan Paul.
Smith, S.M., Hanson, R. and Noble, S., 1973, 'Parents of battered babies: a controlled study', *British Medical Journal*, 4, pp. 388—391.
Social Services Insight., 1987, 10 April.
Sociale Dienst., 1986, *Analyse Van de Requistratie*, OCMW, Brugge.
Social Security Policy Inspectorate., 1984, *Special Case Officers*, London DHSS.
Spring-Rice, M., 1939, *Working Class Wives*, (1981 edn), London, Virago.
SSAC., 1985a, *The Supplementary Benefit (Single Payments), Amendment Regulations 1983 (SI 1983 no. 1630)*, Cmnd. 9468, London, HMSO.
SSAC., 1985b, *The Annual Report*, London, HMSO.
SSAC., 1987, *The Draft Social Fund Manual*, London, HMSO.
Stack, C., 1974, *All our Kin: Strategies for Survival in the Black Community*, New York, Harper and Row.
Stark, E. and Flitcraft, A., 1985, 'Woman-battering, child abuse and social heredity: what is the relationship?', in Johnson, N., (ed), *Marital Violence*, London, Routledge and Kegan Paul.
Steele, B. and Pollock, C., 1974,' A psychiatric study of parents who abuse infants and small children', in Helfer, R. and Kempe, C., (eds), *The Battered Child*, Chicago, University of Chicago Press.
Steinberg, L., Catalano, R. and Dooley, D., 1981, 'Economic antecdents of child abuse and neglect', *Child Development*, 52, pp. 975—986.
Steinmetz, S.K. and Spears, M.A., 1974, *Violence in the Family*, New York, Harper and Row.
Stewart, G. and Stewart, J., 1986, *Boundary Changes: Social Work and Social Security*, London, BASW/CPAG.
Stewart, G. and Stewart, J., 1987, *Impact of Social Security Policy on Social Work Practice: the Experience of the Board and Lodging Regulations*, Department of Social Administration, University of Lancaster, mimeo.

Stewart. G. and Stewart, J., 1988, *The Beginning of the End: Welfare Rights Workers' Experience of the Amended Single Payment Regulations*, Cleveland, Cleveland County Welfare Rights Service.

Stewart, G. and Stewart, J., (1989 forthcoming), *Social Work and Housing*, London, Macmillan.

Stewart, G., *et al*, 1986, 'The right approach to social security: the case of the board and lodging regulations', *Journal of Law and Society*, 13, 3, pp. 371—99.

Stevenson, O., 1973, *Claimant or Client?*, London, Allen and Unwin.

Stevenson, O., 1986, *Women in Old Age*, Nottingham University, Social Work Department.

Stevenson, O., (1988 forthcoming), *Age and Vulnerability: a Guide to Better Care*, London, Hodder and Stoughton/Age Concern.

Stone, D., 1984, *A Disabled State*, London, Macmillan.

Strathclyde Regional Council., 1982, *Facts about Child Abuse in Strathclyde*, Social Work Research Team.

Strathclyde Regional Council., 1984, *Social Strategy for the Eighties*.

Strathclyde Regional Council., 1986, *Social Needs and Social Work Resources*.

Strathclyde Regional Council., 1987, *Social Needs and Social Resources in Strathclyde 1986*, Overview Report.

Strauss, M.A., Gelles, R.J. and Heinmetz, S.E., 1979, *Behind Closed Doors: Violence in the American Family*, New York, Anchor Doubleday.

Struening, E.L., 1974, 'Approaches to evaluation: social area analysis', *International Journal of Health Services*, 4, 3, pp. 503—514.

Suchman, L., 1967, *Evaluation Research*, London, Allen and Unwin.

Sullivan, M., 1987, *Sociology and Social Welfare*, London, Allen and Unwin.

Sumpton, R.C., 1985, 'Welfare benefits for people with a mental handicap: the professional's role', *British Journal of Mental Subnormality*, 31, pp. 3—8.

Sumpton, R.C., Raynes, N.V. and Thorp, D., 1987, 'The residential careers of a group of mentally handicapped people', *British Journal of Mental Subnormality*, 33, pp. 3—9.

Sutcliffe, L. and Hill, B., 1985, *Let Them Eat Coal: The Political Use of Social Security during the Miners' Strike*, London, Canary Press.

St. Vincent de Paul Society, 1984, 1986, *Annual Reports*, supplemented by personal communications from Michael Dowling, Officer of the Dublin SVP Society in 1986.

Tarpey, M.R., 1984, *English Speakers Only*, London, Islington People's Rights.

Taylor, S., Walton, P. and Young, J., 1973, *The New Criminology*, London, Routledge and Kegan Paul.

Tester, S., 1985, *Cash and Care: The Relations Between Supplementary Benefit and Other Agencies*, Occasional Papers, 79, London, Bedford Square Press.

Thévenet, A., 1986, *L'Aide Sociale en France*, PUF.

Thévenet, A. and Désigaux, J., 1985, *Les Travailleus Sociaux*, PUF.

Thoburn, J., 1980, *Captive Clients*, London, Routledge and Kegan Paul.

Thoburn, J., Murdoch, A. and O'Brien, A., 1986, *Permanence in Child Care*, Oxford, Blackwell.

Thorpe, D., Smith D., Green, C. and Saley, J., 1980, *Out of Care: The Community Support of Juvenile Offenders*, London, Allen and Unwin.

Times, 1987, Family Welfare Association, 10 June.

Titterton, M., 1986a, *Conceptual and Methodological Issues in the Evaluation of Social Work Intervention*, Social Work Research Centre Working Paper, University of Stirling.

Titterton, M., 1986b, *Social Explanation, Causal Mechanisms and the Epidemiology of Personal and Social Problems*, Social Work Research Centre, University of Stirling.

Topliss, E., 1982, *Social Responses to Handicap*, London, Longman.

Townsend, D., 1987b, 'Civil disorder', *Social Services Insight*, 22 May, pp. 8—9.

Townsend, P., 1979, *Poverty in the U.K.*, Harmondsworth, Penguin.

Townsend, P., 1981, 'Employment and disability', in Walker, A. with Townsend, P., (eds), *Disability in Britain: a Manifesto of Rights* ,Oxford, Martin Roberts

Townsend. P., 1982, 'Worsening poverty among people with disabilities', in Disability Alliance, *Disability Rights Handbook for 1983*, London, Disability Alliance.

Townsend, P., 1983, 'A theory of poverty and the role of social policy', in Loney, M., Boswell, D. and Clarke, H., (eds), *Social Policy and Social Welfare*, Milton Keynes, Open University Press.

Townsend, P., 1985, 'Review of Poor Britain' (by Mack and Lansley), *Poverty*, vol. 61.
Townsend, P., 1986, *A Matter of Class and Internationalism*, BASW lecture, Birmingham, BASW.
Townsend, P., 1987a,'Poor health', in **Walker A.** and **Walker, C.**, (eds), *The Growing Divide: A Social Audit*, London, CPAG.
Townsend, P., 1987c, 'Deprivation', *Journal of Social Policy*, vol 16, pp. 125—146.
Townsend, P., 1987d, 'Conceptualising poverty', in **Ferge, Z.** and **Miller, S.M.**, (eds), *Dynamics of Deprivation*, Aldershot, Gower.
Townsend, P. with **Corrigan, P.** and **Kowarzik, U.**, 1987, *Poverty and Labour in London*, London, Low Pay Unit.
Treasury, 1987, *The Government's Expenditure Plans 1987-88 to 1989-90*, vol. II, London, HMSO.
Tunstill. J., 1985, 'Laying the poor law to rest?', *Community Care*, 20 June pp. 16—18.
UCVB., 1987, *CPAS et Travail Social*, Report of Wepion Conference (1986), Bruxelles.
UNCCASF, 1987, *Bulletin des Centres Communaux d'Action Sociale*, Touresing No 224.
Unemployment and Health Study Group *et al*, 1986, *Unemployment: A Challenge to Public Health*, Occasional Paper No. 10, Centre of Professional Development, Department of Community Medicine, University of Manchester.
Valencia, B.M. and Jackson, M.P., 1979, *Financial Aid Through Social Work*, London, Routledge and Kegan Paul.
Veit-Wilson, J., 1986, 'Paradigms of poverty: a rehabilitation of B.S. Rowntree', *Journal of Social Policy*, 15, 1.
Wainwright, S., 1985, *Local Authorities and Income Maintenance*. University of Birmingham, Social Administration Department.
Walker, A., 1981, 'Disability and income', in **Walker, A.** with **Townsend, P.**, (eds)., *Disability in Britain: a Manifesto of Rights*, Oxford, Martin Robertson.
Walker, A., 1983, 'Care for elderly people: a conflict between women and the State', in **Finch, J.** and **Groves, D.**, (eds), *A Labour of Love: Women, Work and Caring*, London, Routledge and Kegan Paul.
Walker, A. and Townsend, P., (eds), 1981, *Disability in Britain: a Manifesto of Rights*, Oxford, Martin Robertson.
Walker, A. and Walker, C., (eds), 1987, *The Growing Divide: A Social Audit*, London, CPAG.
Walker, B., 1987, 'Public sector costs of board and lodging accommodation for homeless households in London', *Housing Studies*, 2, 4.
Walker, C. and Dant, T., 1984, *The Reform of the Supplementary Benefits Scheme*, University of Leeds.
Watson, S. and Austerberry, H., 1986, *Housing and Homelessness*, London, Routledge and Kegan Paul.
Weale, A., *et al*, 1984, *Lone Mothers, Paid Work and Social Security*, York Social Policy Research Unit.
Webb, A. and Wistow, G., 1986, *Planning, Need and Security: Essays on the Personal Social Services*, London, Allen and Unwin.
Webb, A. and Wistow, G., 1987, *Social Work, Social Care and Social Planning: the Personal Social Services since Seebohm*, Harlow, Longman.
Webb, D., 1981, 'Themes and continuities in radical and traditional social work', *British Journal of Social Work*, II, 2, pp. 143—158.
Welfare Rights Bulletin, 1986, June, London, CPAG.
Westergaard, J. and Resler, H., 1975, *Class in A Capitalist Society: A Study of Contemporary Britain*, London, Heinemann.
Wheeler, R., 1986, 'Housing and elderly people', in **Phillipson, C.** and **Walker, A.**, (eds), *Aging and Social Policy*, London, Gower.
White, M., 1983, *Long-Term Unemployment and Labour Markets*, London, Policy Studies Institute.
Whitehead, M., 1987, *The Health Divide: Inequalities in Health in the 1980s*, London, HEC.

Wicks, M., 1978, *Old and Cold*, London, Heinemann.
Willis, P., 1978, *Learning to Labour*, Aldershot, Gower.
Wilson, E., 1977, *Women and the Welfare State*, London, Tavistock.
Wilson, G., 1987, 'Money: patterns of responsibility and irresponsibility in marriage', in
  Brannen, J. and **Wilson, G.**, (eds) *Give and Take in Families: Studies in Resource
  Distribution*, London, Allen and Unwin.
Wilson, H. and **Herbert, G.**, 1978, *Parents and Children in the Inner City*, London, Routledge
  and Kegan Paul.
WING, (Women, Immigration and Nationality Group), 1985, *Worlds Apart: Women under
  Immigration and Nationality Law*, London, Pluto Press.
Wresinski, J., 1987, *La Grande Pauvreté et la Précarité Économique et Social*, Paris, Conseil
  Economique et Social.
Wray, K. and **Wistow, G.**, 1987, 'Welfare initiative netted an extra £500,000', *Social Work Today*,
  7 September.
Yoder, J.A. and **Leaper, R.A.B.**, 1985, *Support Networks in a Caring Community*, The Hague,
  Martinus Nijhoff
Youthaid, 1986, Information Paper, Mimeo.

Index